The Archaeology of Inequality

Social Archaeology

General Editor
Ian Hodder, University of Cambridge

Advisory Editors
Margaret Conkey, University of California at Berkeley
Mark Leone, University of Maryland
Alain Schnapp, U.E.R. d'Art et d'Archéologie, Paris
Stephen Shennan, University of Southampton
Bruce Trigger, McGill University, Montreal

Published
ENGENDERING ARCHAEOLOGY
Women and Prehistory
Edited by Joan M. Gero and Margaret W. Conkey

EXPLANATION IN ARCHAEOLOGY
Guy Gibbon

THE DOMESTICATION OF EUROPE
Structure and Contingency in Neolithic Societies
Ian Hodder

THE ARCHAEOLOGY OF INEQUALITY
Edited by Randall H. McGuire and Robert Paynter

MATERIAL CULTURE AND MASS CONSUMPTION
Daniel Miller

READING MATERIAL CULTURE
Structuralism, Hermeneutics and Post-Structuralism
Edited by Christopher Tilley

In preparation
IRON AGE SOCIETIES
From Tribe to State in Northern Europe
Lotte Hedeager

THE ARCHAEOLOGY OF DEMOCRACY
Ian Morris

The Archaeology of Inequality

Edited by Randall H. McGuire
and Robert Paynter

BLACKWELL
Oxford UK & Cambridge USA

Copyright © Basil Blackwell 1991

First published 1991

Basil Blackwell Ltd
108 Cowley Road, Oxford, OX4 1JF, UK

Basil Blackwell Inc.
3 Cambridge Center
Cambridge, Massachusetts 02142, USA

British Library Cataloguing in Publication Data

A CIP catalogue record for this book is available from the British Library

Library of Congress Cataloging in Publication Data

The Archaeology of inequality / edited by Randall H. McGuire and
Robert Paynter.
p.   cm. – (Social archaeology)
ISBN 0–631–16043–4 – ISBN 0–631–17959–3
1. United States – Antiquities.   2. Social archaeology – United States.
3. Equality – United States – History.
4. Social classes – United States – History.
5. Material cultural – United States.
I. McGuire, Randall H.   II. Paynter, Robert.   III. Series.
E.159.5.A7   1991   973–dc20   90–1298   CIP

Typeset in 10.5 on 12pt Stemple Garamond
by Hope Services (Abingdon) Ltd.
Printed In Great Britain by
T. J. Press Ltd, Padstow, Cornwall

For Deborah McGuire and Linda Morley

Contents

Contributors

Mary C. Beaudry, Department of Archaeology, Boston University, Massachusetts, USA

Beth Anne Bower, Bechtel/Parsons Brinckerhoff Central Artery Project, Boston, Massachusetts 02110, USA

Lauren J. Cook, Department of Archaeology, Boston University, Massachusetts, USA

Leland Ferguson, Department of Anthropology, University of South Carolina, USA

A. L. McDonald, Dull Knife Memorial College, Box 98, Lame Deer, Montana 59403, USA

J. Douglas McDonald, Archaeology Laboratory, University of South Dakota, Vermillion, South Dakota 57069, USA

Randall H. McGuire, Department of Anthropology, State University of New York, Binghamton, New York 13901, USA

Stephen A. Mrozowski, Department of Anthropology, University of Massachusetts, Boston, Massachusetts, USA

Charles E. Orser, Jr, Department of Anthropology and Director, Midwestern Archaeological Research Center, Illinois State University, Normal, Illinois 61761, USA

Robert Paynter, Department of Anthropology, University of Massachusetts at Amherst, Amherst, Massachusetts 01003, USA

Ted Rising Sun, Dull Knife Memorial College, Box 98, Lame Deer, Montana 59403, USA

Suzanne Spencer-Wood, Information Dynamics, André Ruedi Associates, 81 Highland Ave., Arlington, Massachusetts 02174, USA

William Tall Bull, Dull Knife Memorial College, Box 98, Lame Deer, Montana 59403, USA

LouAnn Wurst, Department of Anthropology, State University of New York, Binghamton, New York 13901, USA

Anne Yentsch, Historic Annapolis, Inc., Annapolis, Maryland, USA

Larry J. Zimmerman, Archaeology Laboratory, University of South Dakota, Vermillion, South Dakota 57069, USA

1

The Archaeology of Inequality: Material Culture, Domination, and Resistance

Robert Paynter and Randall H. McGuire

Anthropological archaeologists generally draw on two dominant themes to construct and account for the past. Cultural historians stress the weight of tradition; cultural ecologists seek to understand change in the relationship between society and nature. Recently a small group of researchers have advanced a third position, a political economic approach, that emphasizes the struggles among members of society over the exercise of social power. This latter strategy is applied to a variety of issues including the origins of agricultural production, megalithic constructions, the siting of urban capitals, and regional settlement dynamics. The studies in this volume consider US culture and history from the perspective of power relationships. They do so through a refinement of power analysis that stresses the interplay between those who use structural asymmetries of resources in exercising power, known as domination, and those who develop social and cultural opposition to this exercise, known as resistance.

Power and Perspectives on the Past

Archaeologists generally pay little attention to how people exercised social power. Both cultural historians and cultural ecologists define their problems and construct their explanations in ways that marginalize or ignore the role of social power. When considered at all, the exercise of social power is treated as epiphenomenal to presumably larger issues, such as adaptation, complexity, or efficiency.

The most familiar research agenda in cultural history describes cultural traditions, objects and assemblages exhibiting little variation over reasonably large areas for reasonably long periods of time (Deetz 1977:40–1; Clark 1978), and enquires into the replacement and persistence of the various elements of the tradition. Archaeologists construct a culture history by describing the march of traditions through an area. The social processes of independent invention, diffusion, and migration are invoked to explain the culture histories.

Cultural historians identify an ever-present process of socialization which maintains traditions in all societies regardless of type. The material similarities of a tradition arise when numerous people make and use similar objects for several generations. Cultural historians believe these similarities result from shared cultural norms and values that include mental templates for behavior and material objects (Deetz 1967:45–9; Rouse 1939). This process of socialization is assumed to be a conservative one in which templates and objects are replicated with only minor modification (referred to as drift), unless powerful stimuli for innovation exist. They rarely consider the power relations implicit in the sharing of cultural norms and values. In fact, social power is relegated solely to the discussion of rapid and wholesale replacement of one tradition by another, through appeals to invasion, displacement, and/or conquest.

Research on contemporary society does find traditions and the replication of values, but these conditions are constantly created and recreated in power-laden situations. The appararent uniformity of tradition in the contemporary world results from experiences in highly structured institutions, such as schools, that only incompletely instill the next generation with the values of their elders (e.g., Henry 1963; Bowles and Gintis 1976; Graebner 1986). The academic disciplines charged with safeguarding the transmission of values result from the complex struggles within the wider society for control over the construction of meaning (e.g., Eagleton 1983:15–53; Foucault 1972, 1979, 1980). The essays in Hobsbawm and Ranger's (1983) *The Invention of Tradition* discuss how the powerful create and cast off traditions.

In contrast, in more "egalitarian" societies socialization is known to be less harsh (e.g., Leacock 1980; Draper 1976) and these traditions in fact lack the coherence and uniformity that the cultural historians are wont to give them. For instance, Heider (1979:30) notes

> the Dani have one word for "sweet potato," but then have dozens of names for sweet potato varieties . . . around seventy, which seemed like a lot for any one person to remember. . . . [D]ifferent people would call the same tuber by different names. Then I looked at names for axe and adze stones and found the same thing: a huge vocabulary inconsistently used. . . . [I]t is surprising to find these words being used inconsistently. . . . But it seems to me that it makes sense in the context of a general pattern of casualness . . . it

is not surprising that [the words] are not structured into a single, elegant system.

These observations suggest that cultural uniformity should be considered a phenomenon to be explained, rather than given, in cultural history. Indeed, periods of cultural uniformity, as well as culture change, should suggest the existence of powerful integrative relations and ideologies.

Cultural ecological theories also minimize the investigation of social power. Their basic explanatory scheme for cultural change posits that changes in the environment, or in the technology for obtaining and/or consuming energy, will result in changes in the way of life. These changes directly affect the lives of most or all members of the society; they include the use of novel foods, new procedures for construction, and the relocation of large numbers of people to form new settlements. Cultural ecologists rarely ask why so many people accept such major changes in their everyday lives. Instead, these archaeologists assume that the environmental and technical change occur so slowly that the people do not notice the responses, or that the stress is so extreme that the group can only choose one solution to avoid extinction. Recent archaeological research suggests that these assumptions about change need closer attention. Archaeologically observed cultural change can occur rapidly, on a scale well within human consciousness (e.g. Renfrew 1979; Sanders et al. 1979). In addition significant changes, such as the emergence of early states, do not always happen in the context of ecological stress so extreme that it threatens the existence of societies (e.g., Brumfiel 1976; Wright and Johnson 1975).

A consideration of exogenous change is never adequate to explain why large numbers of people adopt radically different lifeways. We must also consider how some people manage to convince/coerce others to adopt these new practices. Studies of the contemporary world show that power relations shape the direction of cultural response to environmental shifts. For instance, the Green Revolution, proposed by many scientists as a response to the degradation of overpopulation, rapidly affected rural life in the tropics but did not meet with universal acceptance. The greatest resistance to the new technologies, crops, and practices often came from the more materially deprived portion of the population, the lower peasants. The non-uniform and even counter-intuitive adoption pattern was because the elements of the Green Revolution enterd the local, village scene through pre-existing power networks. Those with power, the upper peasants, adopted the crops and technologies as means to enhance their economic position, precisely because those productive practices undercut traditional power bases of their work-force, the lower peasants (Scott 1985; Harris 1985:361–5). Innovation need not always reinforce existing power relations, as in the case of the Green Revolution. However, this case makes clear that power relations play a significant role in determining the responses to changed environmental conditions.

Recent archaeological studies have broken the silence of the dominant paradigms of archaeology by considering social power. Archaeologists have added power to their discussions of the evolution of social ranking and the state (e.g., Flannery 1972; Blanton et al. 1981; Kus 1982; Friedman and Rowlands 1978; Wright and Johnson 1975; Haas 1982), the use of the material world to construct legitimacy (e.g., Leone 1984; Miller and Tilley 1984; Shanks and Tilley 1982; Miller 1986), and of the origins of food production (Bender 1981; Gilman 1981; Kristiansen 1984).

As diverse and useful as these studies are, only a few of them explicitly observe and contemplate resistance (e.g., Bender 1985a, 1985b; Miller 1986). They mainly provide us with insights into the concerns and understandings of the elite. Sometimes this is by design, as in Kus's (1982) discussion of Imerina ideologies of legitimation and Leone's (1984) consideration of eighteenth-century white merchant capitalists. Sometimes it is less clear whose position is being elaborated, as in Flannery's (1972) analyses of systemic managerial crises or Pearson's (1982) study of changes in mortuary imagery and the sanitation of death. In such cases we wonder if there might not have been some people who failed to be impressed by these ideologies of legitimation or considered the systemic crises to be desirable chaos. And, upon posing such a possibility, we wonder what, if anything Imerina serfs, African-American slaves, working-class immigrants to Britain, and Oaxacan peasants might have done.

How prevalent was resistance and domination? How did agents manipulate material culture in this interplay? How might we observe the material traces of these interplays in the archaeological record? The remainder of this introduction considers these issues at an abstract level. The following papers provide more detailed analyses of how both the dominant and the subordinate manipulated the material world to bring about, and resist, orders of social inequality.

Power as Domination and Resistance

We, and our contributors, are intrigued by the means people use to exercise power over one another and concomitantly resist and succumb to these entreaties and pressures. These topics have attracted the concern of a large number of social theorists, in and outside of anthropology

THE ARCHAEOLOGY OF INEQUALITY 5

(Bowles and Gintis 1986; Mills 1956; R. N. Adams 1975; Skocpol 1979; Wolf 1982, 1990; Patterson and Gailey 1987; Gutman 1973; Braverman 1974; Genovese 1972; Wrong 1979; Fried 1967; Foucault 1979; Gramsci 1971). Many of these develop concepts that we find useful and we draw on them most freely in the delineation of these ideas. Few of these theories have commented on how people manipulate material objects in power relations.

Notions of power: the dyadic problematique

Most discussions of power pose the dyadic problematique: How does A manage to get B to do something? To the extent that A can accomplish this, A is said to have power over B. Social power is said to exist (1) when A and B take the form of individuals or groups, and (2) when the outcome, B complies with A's wishes, happens fairly regularly. Much clever analysis has gone into dissecting this situation (e.g., Wrong 1979 for a thoroughgoing overview). Some of the key contributions involve distinguishing the bases for exercising power and considering the interplay between coercion and legitimation. Most of these considerations result in an understanding of the formal, socially sanctioned institutions that exercise power, institutions concerned with government and politics.

Critics of this traditional approach to power offer elaborations on the dyadic problematique as well as radical reconceptualizations of the exercise of power. One line of critique stems from considerations of contemporary Western political movements. It extends the question of power beyond the realms of state and citizen, lord and serf, to also consider parent–child, teacher–student, husband–wife, and owner–worker dyads, emphasizing the heterogeneous nature of power. A second critique investigates the creation of the subjectivities in the dyad by means of social disciplining. A third notes that B's compliance is always at question, making power exercise the result of the interplay of domination and resistance. In the following we develop each of these themes: the heterogeneity of power, the creation of subjectivities through discipline, and the dialectic of domination and resistance.

The heterogeneity of power

Power is most often studied in formal, political institutions. This approach finds its foremost theoretical underpinning in the work of Weber (e.g., Weber 1978:926–40; Giddens and Held 1982:60–86). For Weber "power is the probability that one actor within a social relationship will be in a position to carry out his own will despite resistance, regardless of the basis on which the probability rests" (Weber 1964:152). In this conceptualization, power is ultimately an ability to thwart another, an ability to engage in a negative action. Persons and social groups thwart others by capturing the culturally constituted, formal institutions of power. As a result, the state and other forms of government have been studied as the sources and arenas for struggle over power (e.g., Service 1975:11–15; Jessop 1982; Corrigan and Sayer 1985). This focus on formal institutions leads to a notion of power as something set apart from society as a whole, something found in some institutions and not others, hence something possessed by some but not by others.

A less socially restricted siting of power is the starting point for alternative investigations. As Giddens (1987:7; or Giddens 1984:14–16) puts it, " 'Power' in this highly generalized sense means 'transformative capacity', the capability to intervene in a given set of events so as in some way to alter them." At a fundamental level all individuals possess the ability to intervene, and social action happens only through the action of these individuals. Thus, power permeates social life, acting "to power" relations in a constructive sense, as well as in the negative sense of thwart.

Miller and Tilley (1984:5–8) quite usefully relate these two notions of power through the ideas of "power to" and "power over." The former refers to power as a transformative capacity, present in any social relation; the latter refers to a relationship of domination, one in which the "power to" involves a "power over." This broader notion of power encompasses Weber's notion of thwart as but one strategy among many by which the "power to" involves a "power over."

Power as the "power to" is found in the traditional institutions of power, and in facets of life not usually analyzed as being power-laden. Bowles and Gintis (1986:23) capture this movement of power with the notion of the heterogeneity of power. "In opposition to the unitary conception of power we propose what we term the heterogeneity of power. Power is multifaceted and not reducible to a single source or structure . . . " If power is heterogeneous in nature then it is not limited to a single area of society. It is not simply a quantity that an elite dole out to or exercise over an acquiescent subservient.

Agents exercise heterogeneous power from a multiplicity of bases. For instance, Bowles and Gintis (1986:92) add to the traditional institutions of power "the tools with which we produce our livelihood" and "the words that give our lives and loyalties their meanings." Control of biological reproduction and sexual pleasure are particularly important bases that structure gender relations (e.g., Snitow et al. 1983; Caplan 1987; Coontz and Henderson 1986; Foucault 1978; Ortner and Whitehead 1981). The exercise of power through the reproduction of the material world, the construction of meaning, the giving pleasure, and the socialization of people enormously expands the social relations that are power-laden; they must now include husband–wife, parent–child, doctor–patient, owner–worker, all embedded in such institutional forms as "hospitals, prisons, schools . . . factories, state apparatuses, families, [and] interest groups" (Miller and Tilley 1984:6).

The analytical division of the bases of power into the state, family, workplace, etc. describe structures, not actions. People rarely, if ever, experience these structures separately. Further, these different domains of power are rarely integrated into a single functioning total society. The clash of the separate domains of power is most evident in colonial situations. In these cases, European forms of symbolic and material domination encounter indigenous power structures, creating complex fields with multiple bases for the exercise of power. These clashes result in highly contested redefinitions of race and gender, as well as new forms of production. For instance, Taussig (1980) investigates how Amazonian peoples reconceptualized the world to make sense of the arrival of market capitalism and the politics of racial terror. Silverblatt (1987) examines the changing gender line by studying the fate of Andean women, under the imperialism first of the Incas and then of the Spanish. Gailey (1987) studies how dramatic changes in the economic lives of Tongans transformed ideologies of kinship legitimation into ideologies of royal power.

The heterogeneity of power challenges archaeologists to extend their field of vision for interpreting power. Archaeologists have generally discussed power within the framework of the traditional, formal, Weberian model; as a result, we see power behind architectural splendors and material riches, mute testaments to the strength of centralized, formal leaders – chiefs, priests, and lords. Acquiring these accoutrements of power is tantamount to having power (e.g., Renfrew and Cherry 1986). Accepting the heterogeneity of power requires us to investigate the relations structuring a wide range of activity: for instance, we need to study the organization of work on rural farms as well as in palace work houses, to look for similarities in power exercise between kings and queens as well as peasant husbands and wives, and to consider how people in villages, nomadic camps, and isolated farms have, at times, consolidated their power to unseat the residents of urban palaces and temples. In short, the heterogeneity of power raises the issue of how A intersects with B throughout the regional settlement system, and not simply in the temples, palaces and sumptuous graves of the elite.

Creating subjectivities through discipline

The ideal situation for the As in the dyadic relationship of power is for the Bs to be inclined to follow the As' requests, nay, even anticipate the needs of A and provide without request. One way for this to happen is when the Bs consider the As' requests as legitimate. As Kus (1982) points out, no stratified system can operate long without being perceived as legitimate; it is simply too costly to continually run a stratified society with negative sanctions. The iron fist in the velvet glove, the veiled threat, the carrot rather than the stick are images about the exercise of power that point to the desirability of avoiding a regime run solely on force. The optimal order, from the point of view of the As, is one in which the Bs participate in their own oppression.

How is it that the Bs come to readily participate in their own oppression? The prevailing approach to this issue by archaeologists is to see the elites imposing a dominant ideology on the minds of the non-elites. We are all too familiar with this strong reading of the dominant ideology thesis in interpretations of pyramids, exotic goods, and fancy rituals as means to create an awestruck peasantry (Rathje 1971; Fletcher 1977). Recent analyses (e.g., Tilley 1984; Shanks and Tilley 1982, 1987; Root 1984) point out that effective messages sent by the elites to the non-elites can also deny the existence of power differences, despite their reality.

These arguments stress the explicit messages sent from elites to non-elites. Foucault (1979; 1980) investigates other means to create consciousness, particularly submissive consciousnesses, through the use of disciplinary technologies on a population. Disciplining a population begins with an elite notion of correct social behavior, proceeds to develop physical means to bring about this behavior in others, and ends with the original ideal being grounded into action. If this reciprocal relationship between an elite ideal and the population's behavior happens often enough, the ideal may make an empirical sense to the population, and the people adopt the ideal as common sense. This process of forging common sense may create people willing to act on their own accord in ways equivalent to the compliance which elites seek to create. Discipline uses the "power over" to inject in the minds of individuals a sense of how they can experience their "power to" (Rabinow 1984:17).

Elites often manipulate material culture to create common sense through discipline. For instance, Foucault (1965; 1979) discusses the arrival on the landscape of Western Europe of new buildings associated with the disciplinary tactics of capitalism – the asylum, prison and school. The buildings themselves are based on a paradigmatic form, Bentham's panopticon.

The panopticon consists of a large courtyard, with a tower in the center, surrounded by a series of buildings divided into levels and cells. In each cell there are two windows: one brings in light and the other faces the tower, where large observatory windows allow for the surveillance of the cells. . . . The surveillant could as easily be observing a criminal, a schoolboy, or a wife. (Rabinow 1984:19, see also Foucault 1979:200–28)

The point of the panopticon is not that its pure form is widespread throughout Western Europe, for it is not. Rather, it is that the principle of discipline through control of people by surveillance, influences and reshapes city plans, factory architecture, and domestic structures (e.g. Handsman 1987), thereby exerting considerable influence on people's everyday experiences.

Associating architecture with discipline may occur in the construction as well as the use of buildings. Johnson (ms) notes that early states have a proclivity for piling things up – stone, mud and/or rubble. Archaeologists often see the use of these monumental edifices as a means of inspiring awe, or of setting the elite off from the populace. Mendelssohn (1971; 1974), noting the relatively short time span during which such piling behavior occurred in Egypt, suggests that it was the construction, rather than the use, of such large edifices that was crucial: in the case of Egypt, Mendelssohn suggests that pyramid construction was a way to keep an as yet non-compliant population busy and out of "trouble" during the flood season. Johnson (ms), going beyond the notion of thwarting by diversion, argues that patterned large-scale construction has a disciplinary potential as a means of familiarizing a population with a given order of rule. Thus, the routine of work gave a common sense legitimacy to the new communal order of the state.

The structuring of domination into everyday activities, through architecture, town planning, and work rules, serves to mystify power relationships. The general populace complies because compliance does not differ from common sense. Analysts, measuring the tempo of everyday life, fail to see the dyadic confrontations of A seeking to exert power over B, and consider power to be absent from a particular setting. However, because power is exercised outside of the domains traditionally associated with it, the dyadic confrontations are often themselves highly structured and controlled encounters. Does this mean that everyday life for most people who have lived since 3000 BC has been wrapped in mystified compliance? Do the bases of power give the elite unlimited reach throughout society? If so, why do these social structures of domination require continual maintenance, and not infrequently break down in paroxysms of social violence? In short, is there a place for resistance in understanding the exercise of power?

Elites commonly express dominant ideologies in a material culture that is grand and lasting, and more likely to be found by archaeologists. We should be hesitant, however, to assume that Bs readily accepted such dominant ideologies (McGuire 1988). The thesis of a dominant ideology created by elites has been roundly criticized. Abercrombie et al. (1980) reviewed this literature and noted that non-elites often do not share the dominant ideology of the elites, and in fact have ideologies of resistance. This suggests that the dominant ideologies, in which royal burials, pyramids, megaliths, and so on, participate, were better suited to securing the coherence of the dominant class than the submission of subordinates.

Abercrombie et al. (1980) effectively dismiss a strong reading of the dominant ideology thesis but their essay does not necessarily deny a weaker version of this thesis (Bottomore 1980:x). Dominant ideologies often inhibit and confuse the construction of ideologies of resistance. The efficacy of dominant ideologies to unify an elite and subvert their subordinates will vary from time to time and place to place.

What is there of the material world that created subjectivities of resistance? This undoubtedly involves looking at different objects and looking at old objects in new ways. Most importantly, it requires that we study domination and resistance as outcomes of human action and not as separable things.

The dialectic of domination and resistance

Domination is the exercise of power through control of resources. For Giddens (1981:50), "domination refers to structural asymmetries of resources drawn upon and reconstituted in such power relations." In other words, if the rules of the game are such that some agents start with more strategic resources than others, specific power encounters are likely to favor those with the superior resources. In the long term these individual encounters create and reproduce structural domination.

A fair amount of social theory addresses the structures of domination in stratified societies. Sometimes researchers recognize that this perspective views the social world from the top (e.g., Kus 1982; Leone 1984; Patterson 1985; Wittfogel 1957), but more commonly they confuse this perspective with the totality of social life (e.g., Flannery 1972; Giddens 1984; Service 1975; Hindess and Hirst 1975; Althusser and Balibar 1970). The result is that social science usually assesses the control problems of those able to dominate others.

One point that emerges from most considerations of structures of domination, especially those of the formal institutions of power, is the heterogeneity of domination. Various authors propose to study the heterogeneity of power with such concepts as: intermediate, contadictory, subsumed or fractionated classes (e.g., Poulantzas 1975; Walker 1979; Wright 1978; Resnick and Wolf 1987); racial hierarchies and racial capitalism (e.g., Marable 1983; Reich 1981; Robinson 1983); gender hierarchies (e.g., Eisenstein 1979; Mies 1986; Moore 1988); or the mosaic of domination (Bowles and Gintis 1986). Empirical analyses are replete with individuals and groups seeking to consolidate incomplete power bases by subverting other power holders' control (e.g., Gledhill 1986; Patterson 1985; Renfrew and Cherry 1986).

These studies of the fractioning of power, particularly those emphasizing the competition between elite power blocs, rarely investigate the limits to domination imposed by non-elite groups and individuals. Yet abstract and concrete indications of such resistance exists. Most abstractly, if all individuals have a "power to", then the non-elite obviously have a power to fail to comply. When A strives to get B to do something A usually grants B access to strategic resources in order to accomplish the action of interest, albeit a constrained access: for instance, owners grant tools to workers, generals grant weapons to soldiers, ideologues tell stories to followers, and people sexually pleasure one another. Once the Bs possess these resources, the possibility exists that they will not do what is desired with them – e.g., they will not promptly turn out a product, not fight a battle, not believe an ideal, or not derive pleasure. They may even use these resources to socially resist the demands of A.

With the wider definition of "power to", a much broader range of actions can be seen as responses to and attempts to circumvent the multifaceted bases by which elites exert domination. Malingering, sabotage, and strikes are resistances to domination that controls the means of livelihood; desertion, "draft dodging," banditry, and guerrilla wars are forms of resisting force; ridicule, deceit, linguistic codes, and fully developed cultures of resistance suggest and validate resistance by beclouding and sometimes contradicting hegemonic power.

Studies that are sensitive to the potential for resistance confirm these theoretical possibilities for resistance. Rather than docile acquiescence, observers of slave quarters (e.g., Genovese 1972; Gutman 1976; Aptheker 1983), urban ghettos (e.g., Valentine 1978; Stack 1974), domestic spheres (e.g., Etienne and Leacock 1980; Rowbotham 1974; Tax 1980), peasant villages (e.g., Friedrich 1977; Scott 1985), and the "tribal world" (e.g., Fried 1975; Paynter and Cole 1980) report a social life that results from a subtle interplay between domination and resistance. Subordinates act in a compliant manner in those social spaces where they encounter dominators, but quickly become more defiant and critical when in their own social arena (i.e. homes, neighborhoods, barrios, clubs, etc.).

Since social scientists are most frequently associated with the dominators, they are implicated in the interweaving of domination and resistance, an implication that creates problems for the investigation of resistance. These problems result both from how elites structure access to data and from the social spaces we choose to search for power. Scott (1985:284–9) calls one such problem that of "the partial transcript." Elites structure the social processes that provide the data for analyses – the documents, surveys, interviews. Resistance, often of a covert nature, is not likely to emerge in the presence of elites, and hence not become apparent in their documents. These documents, surveys, and interviews represent only a partial transcript of social life: absent from the data, resistance is absent in the social scientist's study. A fuller transcript, one that presents domination and resistance, emerges only after researchers situate themselves in the backstage of the social theater.

An additional problem involves our traditional theoretical focus on formal institutions of power, especially the state. Researchers tend to recognize resistance only when it attacks the formal institutions of power and creates political revolutions. Empirical studies of such overt resistance, of revolutions (e.g., Moore 1966; Wolf 1969; Skocpol 1979; Friedrich 1977) and strikes (e.g., Gordon et al. 1982; Gutman 1973) provide important but incomplete insights into the realm of resistance. If power percolates throughout society, then resistance includes a wider range of actions than massive, confrontational, political resistance.

Studies that have seen power in all aspects of society have discovered a heterogeneity of resistance, just as there is a heterogeneity of domination. The heterogeneity of resistance emerges in such diverse practices as the malingering found in high-tech sweat shops (e.g., Juravich 1985; Bookman and Morgen 1988), the thievery and extortion of social bandits (e.g., Hobsbawm 1981; Blok 1974; Schneider and Schneider 1976), the alternative meaning systems articulated in pop music (Firth 1988), and the fully realized cultures of resistance described in studies of utopian experiments (e.g., Hayden 1981; Leone 1973) and ethnic and racial minorities (e.g., Genovese 1972; DuBois 1939). The Weberian perspective on power analyzes all of these forms as token or misguided resistance, but they exemplify the heterogeneity of resistance implicit in the notion of power as a transformative capacity.

Scott (1985:29) provides a useful distinction that alerts us to the heterogeneity of resistance and the problem of the partial transcript. He distinguishes between everyday resistance and open defiance. Everyday resistance involves "the ordinary weapons of relatively powerless groups: foot dragging, dissimulation, false compliance, pilfering, feigned ignorance, slander, arson, sabotage, and so forth. . . . They require little or no coordination or planning; they often represent a form of individual self-help; and they typically avoid any direct symbolic confrontation with authority or with elite norms" (Scott 1985:29). When subordinates add group organization and symbolic confrontations, everyday resistance becomes open defiance, most immediately visible in revolutions, strikes, and enclaves of cultures of resistance. Open defiance is what we traditionally study as resistance. Everyday resistance describes the field of social actions implicit in the recognition of the heterogeneity of power, actions in need of systematic discovery and analysis.

Further analysis of the heterogeneity of resistance is a difficult task, precisely because everyday resistance "covers its tracks" (Scott 1985:278–284). Archaeology, however, may have a special access to the resistance of day-to-day life. Wobst (1978) offers an interesting challenge to archaeologists, who, unlike ethnographers and historians, are not constrained by past elites in their walk across the theater of social power. We have access to the sanctuaries of the weak, the barrios and isolated villages. We, however, rarely enter these sanctuaries, preferring instead to dig in the temples, palaces, and tombs of the powerful. The challenge is to see the abodes of urban commoners, settlements distant from architectural splendors, and regions identified as cultural backwaters as quite possibly the realm of resistance.

In sum, traditional notions of power have been questioned. The Weberian notion of power as the ability to thwart by controlling public and formal institutions is but one way in which people exert power. More broadly, power exists in all human relations, as the capacity to alter events. This capacity rests on a number of bases, including the control of force, consciousness, tools, and the ability to create pleasure and a positive social sense of self. The structural orders of power are reproduced in their subtle interplays in daily life. However, this is not a perfect reproduction, because the power to resist is always a possibility, if not a completely realized one.

These explanations of the nature of power make the dyadic problematique, of how A exerts power over B, much more complex. The existence of structures and social orders of domination necessarily entails structures and social orders of resistance. Resistance is most clear to ethnographers and historians when it takes place in the public space, rather than backstage. Scholars have often missed everyday resistance and, as a result, ignored this resistance in theories of social change. Archaeology provides access to the full theater of domination and resistance, and is beginning to develop the interpretive methods to understand the working of power at individual sites and in regional settlement patterns.

The Material Manifestations of Domination and Resistance

Elites have used numerous tactics to exercise power, ranging from persuasion to nuclear warheads. It is hard to imagine how even the most ethereal of these tactics could lack a material expression. Our study of the archaeological record may find some of these expressions more easily than others, but this record results as much from domination and resistance as from the material expressions of tradition and adaptation. In short, the failure of archaeologists to consider domination and resistance results from a lack of trying and is not a logical necessity.

A number of recent archaeological studies have examined ideologies of domination. Some of the most provocative analyses in the archaeological literature have studied landscape and legitimacy. Leone (1984) interpreted William Paca's Annapolis garden as exemplifying how a crisis in the legitimacy of the colonial Maryland social order resulted in the construction of an ideology of precedence, and its associated spatial exhibition through perspective. Paca's garden, replete with the visual tricks of perspective, conveyed a sense of time that solidified a notion of precedence and thereby letgitimized the specialness of Paca's own unprecedented behavior, signing the Declaration of Independence. Kus's (1982) work on the Imerina Kingdom of Madagascar demonstrates how the ideologically sanctioned placement of cities and the particulars of urban design lent legitimacy to the social innovation of state formation. Marcus (1973) has shown us how the Mayan landscape made a sense, and had a legitimacy, in terms of the Mayan ideology of the sacred and the powerful. McGuire (1988) has discussed how cemeteries in upstate New York were constructed to create a landscape of death that sought to make eternal the social relations of power, family and gender that existed in life. Tilley (1984), Shanks and Tilley (1982), and Pearson (1982) investigate how the powerful rationalize, reify, or mask social inequality by manipulating landscapes and mortuary practices.

Other studies relate the manipulation of the resources of force and tools for production to the exercise of power. The pre-Columbian military of the Aztecs and the Incas have received recent study (e.g., Hassig 1985). Wittfogel's (1957) hypothesis about the control potential of irrigation systems, though not of universal value (Price 1973), does account for some imperial tactics (e.g., Adams 1981). Gilman (1981) argued that control over intensively prepared agricultural land was a key factor in the development of late Neolithic hierarchies in Western Europe. Root (1984) discusses how the decentralized distribution of key fixed resources in egalitarian societies contributes to limiting the development of social hierarchies.

Studies of resistance often focus on the conditions for success or failure in large-scale, violent confrontations such as revolutions. One of the most comprehensive of these studies is Wolf's (1969) consideration of six peasant revolts. An important characteristic shared by all successful revolutions was the ability of the rebels to physically isolate themselves from the central power: thus Mao went on a Long March, Castro gathered strength in the Plano Central, and the Atlases were a stronghold of the Algerian revolution. A geography of resistance, one stressing the construction of isolation and then strategic advances, may prove useful in addressing some of the cycles of civilization found in Mesoamerica, China, and Southwest Asia. For instance, Hamblin and Pitcher (1980), supporting Thompson's hypothesis (1966), make a case for peasant revolutions as the cause of the lowland Maya collapse. The physical act of stopping the practice of stelae construction, along with evidence of stelae defacement, provide data for a study of the timing and prevalence of deposed Classic lords. The aggregate pattern fits models developed from contemporary peasant revolutions. Their study calls attention to the relationship between monument construction/destruction and the social conditions of hegemony and revolution.

The technology and sociology of monumental architecture involves processes of domination; less well understood are acts of defilement and destruction. The dismantling and destruction of monumental constructions poses formidable technological problems. The pyramids were intractable to Caliph Malek al Aziz Othman's attempts to dismantle them (Mendelssohn 1974:85). The defacement of Olmec heads at La Venta and San Lorenzo (Drucker et al. 1959; Coe and Diehl 1980; Haas 1982:112) challenged even skilled stone knappers and masons (Cross, personal communication).

The material world of the capitalist world-system includes landscapes and objects used in domination and resistance. Discipline has a material dimension in the creation of the modern industrial working class. Industrial capitalists sought to habituate a populace, used to daily and seasonal rhythms of agricultural production, to the brutally regular 18–hour days of industrial work; they elaborated technologies involving clocks, bells, and belfries to create this time (Thompson 1967). Foucault (1979) considered the physical aspects of discipline associated with panoptic architecture, also a feature of Early Modern Europe. New England factory architecture complies with the principles of panopticism, as the owners of these structures sought to control their work-force through surveillance (Handsman 1987).

Instances of everyday resistance rarely figure in the analysis of material culture; and yet theoretical and empirical studies demonstrate how the battle between managers and workers over the pace of work stimulates material innovations (Slater 1980; Juravich 1985; Gutman 1973; Gordon et al. 1982; Braverman 1974; Paynter 1988). The evidence of these workaday acts of resistance may appear in the waste piles of pre-industrial (Tosi 1984) as well as industrial production sites (Nassaney and Abel 1988). For example, variation in form at specific points in the production process may be evidence of an inability to control sabotage, rather than of technical incompetence; variation in production rates may be evidence of malingering, as well as of variation in demand.

The archaeology of domestic sites also yields information about resistance. This is most obvious in cases where open defiance is exhibited in the realm of social reproduction. For instance, utopian communities such as the Shakers (Savulis 1989), the slave cabins of Southern plantations (Ferguson, this volume), or Native American villages (Rubertone et al. 1985) all were settings of social boundaries and material differences which involved the construction of cultures of resistance that enabled continual existence in settings of extreme oppression and cultural change. Equally intriguing, but more obscure, is how the material world figures in less socially cohesive acts of resistance, those of bandits, misfits, and eccentrics (Hobsbawm 1981; Scott 1985).

The papers in this volume add cases from the capitalist world-system in which the material world is used in the construction of domination and resistance. In particular, they examine a variety of cases in the history of North America; these range in time from the colonial period to the twentieth century. They look at inequalities in terms of race, class, ethnicity, and gender. All seek to use a refined notion of power to understand domination and resistance.

The contributions on racial inequalities highlight the variation in the form of the color line, across time and throughout the USA, and the associated variation in the material strategies used by whites to dominate and by people of color to resist. Leland Ferguson considers a ubiquitous source of archaeological data, pottery. He examines how slaves in colonial South Carolina used foodways in creating a culture of their own, and argues that this creation of a separate slave culture was the basis for overt and covert resistance by African-Americans to the domination of slavery. The ceramics and foodways, by clearly drawing on West African culture, represent an autonomy even within the repressive relation of North American slavery.

Charles Orser also looks at race relations in the Southern United States. He argues that the resistance of slave to master that Ferguson saw in the colonial period did not end with emancipation and the North's victory in the Civil War; rather, the terrain shifted from slave-based agriculture to a variety of tenancy arrangements. By reading documents and the spatial relations and material culture of the period 1865 to 1935,

Orser identifies new strategies by which plantation landlords sought to restore their domain over African-American tenants, and just as clearly how new forms of African-American resistance made use of the material world to ward off the effects of racially oppressive "Jim Crow" legislation and capitalist agriculture.

As these papers indicate, considerable attention has been given to the under-documented lifeways of Southern African-Americans. The nineteenth-century presence of African-Americans in the Northern USA has also received the attention of archaeologists. However, still largely invisible in archaeological and historical studies are the African-Americans in seventeenth- and eighteenth-century Northern colonies. Beth Ann Bower takes initial steps toward correcting this impaired vision by surveying the Black experience in colonial and early federal Boston. Her remarkable observation of free seventeenth-century African-Americans purchasing enslaved African-Americans to set them, in turn, free represents an act of resistance through the market place, an act that should give pause for thought to archaeologists who analyze their material assemblages with universal theories of consumer choice. What (or who) is on the market, who wants it (or them), and for what ends, can have no single answer in a race, gender, ethnic and class divided society.

The contribution by McDonald and others discusses how material culture, in the hands of archaeologists, plays an ongoing role in relations of domination and resistance in the contemporary world. Their study evaluates differing accounts of the escape route of Dull Knife's band during the Cheyenne Outbreak of 1879. A rather dangerous and stupid escape route is posited by establishment histories, whereas an alternative route likely to be taken by people skilled at moving around the landscape to resist capture and confinement has been championed by Cheyenne descendants of the escape. The use of archaeology in resolving this dispute points more broadly to how the questions we ask, and the objects we pursue, figure in the discipline's participation in orders of domination and resistance.

Change on the North American continent after the permanent arrival of Europeans has to reckon with the changes in these Europeans' class relations, relations by which wealth was increasingly accumulated from wage labor in the production of increasing numbers and forms of commodities. Stephen Mrozowski examines the growth and change in urban society in New England during the eighteenth and nineteenth centuries. He argues that the urban landscapes of these periods were direct expressions of the spatial requirements of economic regimes and the inequalities inherent in those regimes. As the economy shifted from mercantile to industrial capitalism, new urban forms appeared on the

New England landscape. The differing and changing mix of mercantile and industrial strategies required different kinds of urban infrastructure, differences explored by Mrozowski in comparisons of Boston, Lowell, Newport, and Providence.

Randall McGuire examines how industrialists in central New York state tried to build power through their manipulation of the cultural landscape. Each tried to create a landscape that would give physical reality to his ideology of class and society, thereby using the landscape as a tool in the negotiation of a new ideology of class and society. The working class of Broome County, New York, however, did not simply accept the reality and ideology they were given. The spatial divisions created by the landscape facilitated class-conscious resistance in the late nineteenth century. Workers in the early twentieth century read the elite ideology from their own perspective, gave it their own meaning, and used it to resist management actions.

Objects frequently figure in struggles between elites for the domination of subordinate classes. Returning to central New York state, LouAnn Wurst explores a conflict between rural and urban elite ideological, economic and resultant power structures. Urban and rural elites were vying for economic control of central New York in the mid-nineteenth century, and using markedly different strategies of labor control. The religious movement of the Second Great Awakening played a significant role in the strategies, lives, and objects of rural elites and workers, and is insignificant in the labor relations of urban classes. These different strategies of class control are most notable today in the landscapes of death of Broome County, in the different symbolic systems carried on the gravestones in rural and urban cemeteries. These stones provide Wurst with her point of entry into the shifting class relations of the mid-nineteenth century.

Ideological class struggles were conducted with material objects in the planned industrial towns of New England as well as New York state. Beaudry and others situate the objects recovered from working-class houselots in Lowell, Massachusets within the debates concerning the interpretation of the symbolic realm with material culture. They advocate an approach that makes use of etic and emic categories to interpret the meaning of things, mindful of the active role objects play in structuring social relations, and mindful also that this structuring results from a discourse about power, and not simply the imposition of the dominant ideology. Their analyses of the everyday objects of working-class lives – pipes, bottles, ceramics, and domestic landscapes – call attention to the diversity of these discourses within the working class, differences that not infrequently have to do with the social structures of race, ethnicity, and gender.

The shifting characteristics of the gender line in the seventeenth and eighteenth centuries and its relation to the distinctions between the domain of men and women, between public and private space, and between the objects that adorned and marked these space is the subject of Anne Yentsch's article. She studies the changes in seventeenth- and eighteenth-century foodways and ceramic assemblages, paying particular attention to the symbolic role of household objects in defining positions within the social structure. New activities associated with the ritual of dining, new physical spaces, and new ceramic forms all signaled and thereby helped create the emergence of the public man and private woman in colonial America.

Suzanne Spencer-Wood selected the domestic reform movement of the nineteenth and early twentieth centuries for archaeological research because these movements advocated material culture innovation as a primary means of culture change. Domestic reformers raised the status of women by raising aspects of housekeeping to the status of professional occupations; by doing so, they resisted male dominance and created female dominance in the public as well as in the domestic sphere. Spencer-Wood's paper supplies historical background, possible research problems, methods for identifying sites, and hypotheses about what archaeologists can expect to learn from different types of materialistic domestic reform sites.

Conclusions

Our studies are drawn from the historic United States, a society with documents, and in particular, those documents associated with the expansion and development of European capitalism. This should not be surprising. We wish to suggest that an analysis, heretofore lacking in many archaeological studies, may prove useful for probing material assemblages. Elaborating this point solely with prehistoric assemblages does run the danger of a circular argument, that is, of assuming that some material culture participated in resistance and then using that material culture to interpret and verify the existence of resistance in the case. The ready availability of documents in our studies somewhat alleviate the danger of such circularity. Thus our collection follows a time-honored tradition in historical archaeology, a proving ground for methodological developments.

The reader may also presume that since we draw the bulk of our examples from stratified societies, and capitalist societies to boot, the dialectic of domination and resistance applies only to this subset of societies. We are not convinced of this. Archaeologists have completed investigations of how individuals and groups extracted surplus and resisted this extraction in the pre-capitalist world (e.g., Childe 1936; Bender 1985a, 1985b; Saitta 1987; McGuire 1987, 1989; Hamblin and Pitcher 1980; Dincauze and Hasenstab 1986; Haas 1982). Continuing these lines of research seems useful, for capitalist and pre-capitalist societies.

In urging the application of the dialectic of domination and resistance to a wide range of settings we are not attempting to establish a new key to the past. We admit the utility of studying tradition, meaning, the human–nature dialectic, and the competition between power wielders for understanding the past. We simply argue for additionally considering how humans create misery in the course of domination, and remember that these actions spur others to resist domination in the hopes of alleviating their social conditions.

ACKNOWLEDGEMENTS

This book had its inception in the session "The Archaeology of Domination and Resistance" at the 1985 Annual Meeting of the Society for Historical Archaeology. Our thanks to Byron Rushing, Patricia Rubertone, Ellen Savulis, Russell Handsman, Mark Leone, and the meeting organizers for their comments and encouragement. We would also like to thank Martin Wobst, Art Keene, Jim Moore, Dean Saitta, Bill Fawcett, Tom Patterson, Dolores Root, Lynn Clark, Jane Collins, Mark Cassel, Lon Bulgrin, Tom Dublin, Immanuel Wallerstein, and the participants in the Wenner Gren Conference on "Critical Approaches in Archaeology." Thanks to Jan Chamier, John Davey, Margaret Hardwidge, and Ian Hodder.

REFERENCES

Abercrombie, N., S. Hill, and B. S. Turner (1980) *The Dominant Ideology Thesis*. Allen and Unwin, London.
Adams, R. McC. (1981) *Heartland of Cities*. University of Chicago Press, Chicago.
Adams, R. N. (1975) *Energy and Structure*. University of Texas Press, Austin.
Althusser, L. and E. Balibar (1970) *Reading Capital*. New Left Books, London.
Aptheker, H. (1983) *American Negro Slave Revolts*. International Publishers, New York.
Bender, B. (1981) "Gatherer-Hunter Intensification." In *Economic Archaeology*, eds A. Sheridan and B. Bailey, pp. 149–57 (British Archaeological Reports, International Series, No. 96). Oxford.
——(1985a) "Emergent Tribal Formations in the American Midcontinent." *American Antiquity* 50, 52–62.

——(1985b) "Prehistoric Developments in the American Midcontinent and in Brittany, Northwest France." In *Prehistoric Hunter-Gatherers*, eds T. D. Price and J. A. Brown, pp. 21–57. Academic Press, Orlando.

Blanton, R. E., S. A. Kowalewski, G. Feinman, and J. Appel (1981) *Ancient Mesoamerica*. Cambridge University Press, Cambridge.

Blok, A. (1974) *The Mafia of a Sicilian Village, 1860–1960: A Study of Violent Peasant Entrepreneurs*. Basil Blackwell, Oxford.

Bookman, A. and S. Morgen (eds) (1988) *Women and the Politics of Empowerment*. Temple University Press, Philadelphia.

Bottomore, T. (1980) "Foreword." In *The Dominant Ideology Thesis*, by N. Abercrombie, S. Hill, and B. S. Turner. Allen and Unwin, London.

Bowles, S. and H. Gintis (1976) *Schooling in Capitalist America: Educational Reform and the Contradictions of Economic Life*. Basic Books, New York.

——(1986) *Democracy and Capitalism: Property, Community, and the Contradictions of Modern Social Thought*. Basic Books, New York.

Braverman, H. (1974) *Labor and Monopoly Capital: The Degradation of Work in the Twentieth Century*. Monthly Review Press, New York.

Brumfiel, E. M. (1976) "Regional Growth in the Eastern Valley of Mexico: A Test of the 'Population Pressure' Hypothesis." In *The Early Mesoamerican Village*, ed. K. V. Flannery, pp. 234–48. Academic Press, New York.

Caplan, P. (ed.) (1987) *The Cultural Construction of Sexuality*. Tavistock, London.

Childe, V. G. (1936) *Man Makes Himself*. Pitman Books, London.

Clark, D. (1978) *Analytical Archaeology*, 2nd edn. Columbia University Press, New York.

Coe, M. and R. Diehl (1980) *In the Land of the Olmec* Vol. 1: *The Archaeology of San Lorenzo Tenochtitlan*; Vol. 2: *The People of the River*. University of Texas Press, Austin.

Coontz, S. and P. Henderson (eds) (1986) *Women's Work, Men's Property: The Origins of Gender and Class*. Verso, London.

Corrigan, P. and D. Sayer (1985) *The Great Arch: English State Formation as Cultural Revolution*. Basil Blackwell, Oxford.

Deetz, J. F. (1967) *Invitation to Archaeology*. Natural History Press, Garden City, New York.

——(1977) *In Small Things Forgotten*. Anchor, New York.

Dincauze, D. F. and R. J. Hasenstab (1986) "Explaining the Iroquois: Tribalization on a Prehistoric Periphery." In *Comparative Studies in the Development of Complex Societies*, ed. World Archeological Congress. Allen and Unwin, London.

Draper, P. (1976) "Social and Economic Constraints on Child Life among the !Kung." In *Kalahari Hunter-Gatherers: Studies of the !Kung San and their Neighbors*, eds R. B. Lee and I. DeVore, pp. 199–245. Harvard University Press, Cambridge, MA.

Drucker, P., R. F. Heizer, and J. J. Squier (1959) *Excavations at La Venta, Tobasco 1955*. Bureau of American Ethnology Bulletin 170, Washington, D.C.

DuBois, W. E. B. (1939) *Black Folk, Then and Now: An Essay in the History and Sociology of the Negro Race.* Henry Holt, New York.

Eagleton, T. (1983) *Literary Theory.* University of Minnesota Press, Minneapolis.

Eisenstein, Z. R. (ed.) (1979) *Capitalist Patriarchy and the Case for Socialist Feminism.* Monthly Review Press, New York.

Etienne, M. and E. Leacock (eds) (1980) *Women and Colonization.* Praeger, New York.

Firth, S. (1988) "Art Ideology and Pop Practice." In *Marxism and the Interpretation of Culture,* eds C. Nelson and L. Grossberg, pp. 461–75. University of Illinois Press, Chicago.

Flannery, K. V. (1972) "The Cultural Evolution of Civilizations." *Annual Review of Ecology and Systematics* 3, 339–426.

Fletcher, R. (1977) "Settlement Studies: Micro and Semi-Micro." In *Spatial Archaeology* ed. D. Clark, pp. 47–162. Academic Press, New York.

Foucault, M. (1965) *Madness and Civilization.* Vintage Books, New York.

——(1972) *The Archaeology of Knowledge.* Pantheon, New York.

——(1978) *The History of Sexuality,* Vol. 1. Random House, New York.

——(1979) *Discipline and Punish.* Vintage Books, New York.

——(1980) *Power and Knowledge.* Pantheon, New York.

Fried, M. (1967) *The Evolution of Political Society.* Random House, New York.

——(1975) *The Notion of Tribe.* Cummings, Menlo Park, CA.

Friedman, J. and M. J. Rowlands (1978) "Notes Towards an Epigenetic Model of the Evolution of 'Civilization'." In *The Evolution of Social Systems,* eds J. Friedman and M. J. Rowlands, pp. 201–76. University of Pittsburgh Press, Pittsburgh.

Friedrich, P. (1977) *Agrarian Revolt in a Mexican Village: With a Preface, 1977.* University of Chicago Press, Chicago.

Gailey, C. W. (1987) *Kinship to Kingship: Gender Hierarchy and State Formation in the Tongan Islands.* University of Texas Press, Austin.

Genovese, E. D. (1972) *Roll, Jordan, Roll: The World the Slaves Made.* Vintage Books, New York.

Giddens, A. (1981) *A Contemporary Critique of Historical Materialism.* Macmillan, London.

——(1984) *The Constitution of Society: Outline of a Theory of Structuration.* Polity Press, Cambridge.

——(1987) *The Nation-State and Violence;* Vol. II of *A Contemporary Critique of Historical Materialism.* University of California Press, Berkeley.

Giddens, A. and D. Held (eds) (1982) *Classes, Power, and Conflict.* University of California Press, Berkeley.

Gilman, A. (1981) "The Development of Social Stratification in Bronze Age Europe." *Current Anthropology* 22, 1–23.

Gledhill, J. (1986) "The Imperial Form and Universal History: Some Reflections on Relativism and Generalisation." In *Comparative Studies in the Development of Complex Society,* ed. World Archeological Congress. Allen and Unwin, London.

Gordon, D. M., R. Edwards, and M. Reich (1982) *Segmented Work, Divided*

Workers: The Historical Transformation of Labor in the United States. Cambridge University Press, Cambridge.

Graebner, W. (1986) "Coming of Age in Buffalo: The Ideology of Maturity in Postwar America." *Radical History Review* 34, 55–77.

Gramsci, A. (1971) *Selections From the Prison Notebooks.* International Publishers, New York.

Gutman, H. (ed.) (1973) *Work, Culture and Society in Industrializing America: Essays in Working-Class and Social History.* Alfred A. Knopf, New York.

——(1976) *The Black Family in Slavery and Freedom, 1750–1925.* Vintage Books, New York.

Haas, J. (1982) *The Evolution of the Prehistoric State.* Columbia University Press, New York.

Hamblin, R. L. and B. L. Pitcher (1980) "The Classic Maya Collapse: Testing Class Conflict Hypotheses." *American Antiquity* 45, 246–67.

Handsman, R. G. (1987) "Class Histories, Self Doubt, and the Archaeology of Preserved Landscapes." Paper presented at the Annual Meeting of the Society for Historical Archaeology, Savannah.

Harris, M. (1985) *Culture, People, Nature (Fourth Edition).* Harper and Row, New York.

Hassig, R. (1985) *Trade, Tribute, and Transportation.* University of Oklahoma Press, Norman.

Hayden, D. (1981) *The Grand Domestic Revolution.* MIT Press, Cambridge, MA.

Heider, K. (1979) *Grand Valley Dani: Peaceful Warriors.* Holt, Rinehart and Winston, New York.

Henry, J. (1963) *Culture Against Man.* Random House, New York.

Hindess, B. and P. Q. Hirst (1975) *Pre-Capitalist Modes of Production.* Routledge and Kegan Paul, London.

Hobsbawm, E. J. (1981) *Bandits.* Pantheon, New York.

Hobsbawm, E. J. and T. Ranger (eds) (1983) *The Invention of Tradition.* Cambridge University Press, New York.

Jessop, B. (1982) *The Capitalist State.* New York University Press, New York.

Johnson, G. (ms) *Dynamics of Southwestern Pehistory: Far Outside-Looking In.* Manuscript on file, Department of Anthropology, Hunter College, City University of New York.

Juravich, T. (1985) *Chaos on the Shop Floor.* Temple University Press, Philadelphia, PA.

Kristiansen, K. K. (1984) "Ideology and Material Culture: an Archeological Perspective." In *Marxist Perspectives in Archeology,* ed. M. Spriggs, pp. 72–100. Cambridge University Press, Cambridge.

Kus, S. S. (1982) "Matters Material and Ideal." In *Symbolic and Structural Archeology,* ed. I. Hodder, pp. 47–62. Cambridge University Press, Cambridge.

Leacock, E. (1980) "Montagnais Women and the Jesuit Program for Colonization." In *Women and Colonization,* eds M. Etienne and E. Leacock, pp. 25–42. Praeger, New York.

Leone, M. P. (1973) "Archeology as the Science of Technology: Mormon Town

Plans and Fences." In *Research and Theory in Current Archeology*, ed.
C. Redman, pp. 125–50. Wiley, New York.
——(1984) "Interpreting Ideology in Historical Archeology: The William Paca
Garden in Annapolis, Maryland." In *Ideology, Power and Prehistory*,
eds D. Miller and C. Tilley, pp. 25–35. Cambridge University Press,
Cambridge.
Marable, M. (1983) *How Capitalism Underdeveloped Black America*. South End
Press, Boston.
Marcus, J. (1973) "Territorial Organization of the Lowland Classic Maya."
Science 180, 911–16.
McGuire, R. H. (1987) "The Papaguerian Periphery: Uneven Development in
the Prehistoric Southwest" (Arizona State University Anthropological Research
Papers 37). In *Polities and Partitions: Human Boundaries and the Growth of
Complex Societies*, ed. K. Trinkhaus, pp. 123–39. Tempe, Arizona.
——(1988) "Dialogues with the Dead: Ideology and the Cemetery." In *The
Recovery of Meaning: Historical Archeology in the Eastern United States*, eds
M. P. Leone and P. B. Potter, Jr, pp 435–80. Smithsonian Institution Press,
Washington, D.C.
——(1989) "The Greater Southwest as a Periphery of Mesoamerica." In *Centre
and Periphery*, T. C. Champion, pp. 40–66. Allen and Unwin, London.
Mendelssohn, K. (1971) "A Scientist Looks at the Pyramids." *American Scientist*
59, 210–20.
——(1974) *The Riddle of the Pyramids*. Praeger. New York.
Mies, M. (1986) *Patriarchy and Accumulation on a World Scale*. Zed Books,
London.
Miller, D. (1986) "The Limits of Dominance." In *Comparative Studies in the
Development of Complex Societies*, ed. World Archeological Congress. Allen
and Unwin, London.
Miller, D. and C. Tilley (eds) (1984) *Ideology, Power and Prehistory*. Cambridge
University Press, Cambridge.
Mills, C. W. (1956) *The Power Elite*. Oxford University Press, New York.
Moore, B. (1966) *Social Origins of Dictatorship and Democracy*. Beacon Press,
Boston.
Moore, H. L. (1988) *Feminism and Anthropology*. University of Minnesota
Press, Minneapolis.
Nassaney, M. S. and M. Abel (1988) "'Up the Green River': Historical and
Archeological Investigations of the Russell Cutlery, Turners Falls, Massa-
chusetts." Paper on file in the Department of Anthropology, University of
Massachusetts, Amherst.
Ortner, S. and H. Whitehead (eds) (1981) *Sexual Meanings: The Cultural
Construction of Gender and Sexuality*. Cambridge University Press, Cambridge.
Patterson, T. C. (1985) "Exploitation and Class Formation in the Inca State."
Culture 5, 35–42.
Patterson, T. C. and C. Gailey (eds) (1987) *Power Relations and State
Formation*. American Anthropological Association, Washington, D.C.
Paynter, R. (1988) "Steps to an Archeology of Capitalism." In *The Recovery of
Meaning: Historical Archeology in the Eastern United States*. eds M. P. Leone

and P. B. Potter, Jr, pp. 407–33. Smithsonian Institution Press, Washington, D.C.

Paynter, R. and J. W. Cole (1980) "Ethnographic Overproduction, Tribal Political Economy and the Kapauku of Irian Jaya." In *Beyond the Myths of Culture*, ed. E. Ross, pp. 61–99. Academic Press, New York.

Pearson, M. P. (1982) "Mortuary Practices, Society and Ideology: an Ethno-archeological Study." In *Symbolic and Structural Archeology*, ed. I. Hodder, pp. 99–114. Cambridge University Press, Cambridge.

Poulantzas, N. (1975) *Classes in Contemporary Capitalism*. Verso, London.

Price, B. (1973) "Prehispanic Irrigation Agriculture in Nuclear America." In *Explorations in Anthropology*, ed. M. Fried, pp. 211–46. Thomas Crowell, New York.

Rabinow, P. (1984) *The Foucault Reader*. Pantheon, New York.

Rathje, W. L. (1971) "The Origins and Development of Lowland Classic Maya Civilization." *American Antiquity* 36, 275–85.

Reich, M. (1981) *Racial Inequality*. Princeton University Press, Princeton, NJ.

Renfrew, A. C. (1979) "Systems Collapse as Social Transformation: Catastrophe and Anastrophe in Early State Societies." In *Transformations: Mathematical Approaches to Culture Change*, eds A. C. Renfrew and K. L. Cooke, pp. 481–506. Academic Press, New York.

Renfrew, A. C. and J. Cherry (eds) (1986) *Peer Polity Interaction and Socio-Political Change*. Cambridge University Press, Cambridge.

Resnick, S. A. and R. D. Wolf (1987) *Knowledge and Class. A Marxian Critique of Political Economy*. University of Chicago Press, Chicago.

Robinson, C. J. (1983) *Black Marxism*. Zed Books, London.

Root, D. (1984) *Material Dimensions of Social Inequality in Non-Stratified Societies*. Ph.D. Dissertation, Department of Anthropology, University of Massachusetts, Amherst.

Rouse, I. (1939) *Prehistory of Haiti: A Study in Method and Theory*. Yale University Publications in Anthropology 21.

Rowbotham, S. (1974) *Women, Resistance and Revolution*. Vintage Books, New York.

Rubertone, P., P. Robinson, and M. Kelley (1985) "Preliminary Biocultural Interpretations from a Seventeenth Century Narragansett Indian Cemetery in Rhode Island." In *Cultures in Contact: The Impact of European Contacts on Native American Cultural Institutions, A.D.1000–1800*, ed. W. Fitzhugh, pp. 107–30. Smithsonian Institution Press, Washington, D.C.

Saitta, D. (1987) *Economic Integration and Social Development in Zuni Prehistory*. Ph.D. Dissertation, Department of Anthropology, University of Massachusetts, Amherst.

Sanders, W. T., J. Parsons, and R. Santley (1979) *The Basin of Mexico*. Academic Press, New York.

Savulis, E. (1989) "Alternative Visions: Shaker Gender Ideology and the Built Environment." Paper presented at the Annual Meeting of the Society for Historical Archaeology, Baltimore, MD.

Schneider, J. and P. Schneider (1976) *Culture and Political Economy in Western Sicily*. Academic Press, New York.

Scott, J. C. (1985) *Weapons of the Weak: Everyday Forms of Peasant Resistance.* Yale University Press, New Haven, CT.

Service, E. (1975) *Origins of the State and Civilization.* Norton, New York.

Shanks, M. ıand C. Tilley (1982) "Ideology, Symbolic Power and Ritual Communication: A Reinterpretation of Neolithic Mortuary Practices." In *Symbolic and Structural Archeology*, ed. I. Hodder, pp. 129–54. Cambridge University Press, Cambridge.

——(1987) *Re-Constructing Archeology.* Cambridge University Press, Cambridge.

Silverblatt, I. (1987) *Moon, Sun, and Witches: Gender Ideologies and Class in Inca and Colonial Peru.* Princeton University Press, Princeton, NJ.

Skocpol, T. (1979) *States and Social Revolutions.* Cambridge University Press, Cambridge.

Slater, P. (ed.) (1980) *Outlines of a Critique of Technology.* Humanities Press, Atlantic Highlands.

Snitow, A., C. Stansell, and S. Thompson (eds) (1983) *Powers of Desire: The Politics of Sexuality.* Monthly Review Press, New York.

Stack, C. (1974) *All Our Kin: Strategies for Survival in a Black Community.* Harper and Row, New York.

Taussig, M. (1980) *The Devil and Commodity Fetishism in South America.* University of North Carolina Press, Chapel Hill.

Tax, M. (1980) *The Rising of the Women.* Monthly Review Press, New York.

Thompson, E. P. (1967) "Time, Work-Discipline and Industrial Capitalism." *Past and Present* 38 56–96.

Thompson, J. Eric (1966) *The Rise and Fall of Mayan Civilization.* University of Oklahoma Press, Norman.

Tilley, C. (1984) "Ideology and the Legitimation of Power in the Middle Neolithic of Southern Sweden." In *Ideology, Power and Prehistory*, eds D. Miller and C. Tilley, pp. 111–46. Cambridge University Press, Cambridge.

Tosi, M. (1984) "The Notion of Craft Specialization and its Representation in the Archeological Record of Early States in the Turanian Basin." In *Marxist Perspectives in Archeology*, ed. M. Spriggs, pp. 22–52. Cambridge University Press, Cambridge.

Valentine, B. (1978) *Hustling and Other Hard Work: Life Styles in the Ghetto.* Free Press, New York.

Walker, P. (1979) *Between Labor and Capital.* South End Press, Boston.

Weber, M. (1964) *The Theory of Social and Economic Organization.* Free Press, New York.

——(1978) *Economy and Society* (2 vols). University of California Press, Berkeley.

Wittfogel, K. (1957) *Oriental Despotism.* Yale University Press, New Haven, CT.

Wobst, H. M. (1978) "The Archaeo-ethnology of Hunter-Gatherers, or the Tyranny of the Ethnographic Record in Archaeology." *American Antiquity* 43, 303–9.

Wolf, E. (1969) *Peasant Revolutions of the Twentieth Century.* Harper and Row, New York.

——(1982) *Europe and the People Without History.* University of California Press, Berkeley.

——(1990) "Distinguished Lecture: Facing Power – Old Insights, New Questions." *American Anthropologist* 92, 586–96.
Wright, E. O. (1978) *Class, Crisis and the State.* Verso, London.
Wright, H. and G. Johnson (1975) "Population, Exchange, and Early State Formation in Southwestern Iran." *American Anthropologist* 77, 267–89.
Wrong, D. (1979) *Power: Its Forms, Bases, and Uses.* Harper and Row, New York.

2

Struggling with Pots
in Colonial South Carolina

Leland Ferguson

In this paper I use the folk pottery of colonial South Carolina in presenting a fundamental aspect of the resistance of slaves to the European-American ideology that justified slavery. My goal is not only to report on the "archaeology of resistance," that is illustrating the material remains of past people we know to have overtly resisted the conditions of slavery, but also to use pottery and foodways to demonstrate how parts of the material culture of slaves were actively creating resistance. My general thesis is that the cultural differences between slaves and elite in colonial South Carolina were so great that they can be seen as an ever-present impediment to the plantation system; and I am looking for evidence of these differences in the foodways of the two groups.

Most writers (e.g. Aptheker 1974; Genovese 1974:585–660; Wood 1974:285–326) have dealt with resistance as conscious, covert or overt acts of defiance such as slowing down work, feigning ignorance, stealing, burning barns, murdering, running away, and openly rebelling. I propose that another, *unconscious* resistance must have been manifest in the content and structure of daily activities, such as foodways, that were controlled by slaves. That is, by striving to build and live their own subculture (see Stuckey 1987), different in kind as well as material quality from that of their white owners, African-Americans unconsciously distanced themselves from the kinds of rationalizations that would have helped make slavery work. They resisted slavery by being themselves.

The slave population of colonial Carolina was so large and rice plantations so remote that many slaves lived and died in a world apart from their masters and, in some cases, even from white overseers. In 1737 a Swiss visitor commented that Carolina was "more like a negro country than a country settled by white people" (Wood 1974:132). In this "negro country" a few enslaved Native Americans and a very large

28

number of enslaved Africans were struggling to build lives for themselves and their families within the harsh constraints of plantation slavery. They were building what would become African-American culture. Economic, social, demographic, and environmental factors resulted in the slaves of colonial South Carolina having significant control over their domestic lives, including foodways and the use of pottery.[1]

Following the notion of Ian Hodder (1982:10) that "the daily use of material items within different contexts recreates from moment to moment the framework of meaning within which people act," I think that the separate patterns of foodways including the different ceramic wares in planters' houses and slave villages were part of a larger, dual symbolic system that established contrasting and conflicting meaning on Southern plantations. Moreover, I believe that differences in the symbolic systems of the two groups, including the material symbols, created a schism between white and black understanding which countered, or more probably doomed from the beginning, the development of a consistent ideology for both owner and slave. Due to the dramatic cultural differences there could be no ideology allowing slavery to operate as efficiently as the planters envisioned. Aspects of this "resistance of incongruity" may have been unconscious on the part of the enslaved practitioners and apparently benign to the domineering elite. Yet where the system of meaning and posture of attitude of slaves were at odds with the ideology of the planters, there was an endemic, cultural resistance.

In his review of "Some Opinions About Recovering Mind," Mark Leone (1982) has restated Karl Marx's view of ideology as that class of "givens" and "taken-for-granteds" held unawares by society and functioning to mask contradictions and conflicts and to suppress resistance. According to Marx, in a class-structured society with a well integrated ideology, production without parity of profit would proceed without the necessity of physical coercion by the elite. "Common understanding" would provide an acceptable rationale for the differences. For slaves such a common understanding would have meant that they accepted the planter's view of their place in plantation society and believed that anything benefiting and pleasing to their masters was ultimately best for them. On the other hand, without this common understanding slaves would not have worked because it was their accepted role; they would have worked only to avoid punishment.

In the British empire of the eighteenth century, including colonial South Carolina, an elite ideology was established that effectively separated heaven and earth, souls and bodies, religion and science, and man and nature. White men, knowledgeable in science, were taken to occupy the pinnacle of a well ordered, earthly hierarchy – a position represented symbolically by the Georgian style (Deetz 1977), wherein material things were structured such that the hierarchy and the position of the elite was "obvious" (Leone 1984; Isaac 1982). In general, part of the power of such an elite resides in their access to material things that are valued by, and inaccessible to, the non-elite. These items serve as evidence of elite superiority, and their arrangement may be used to reinforce the relative status of elite and non-elite – to create and recreate the "obvious" hierarchy (Gero 1983). Moreover, with a consistent ideology the elite are in a position to manipulate subordinates through rewards consistent with the style and following the ideology. Carried to the absurd, the Georgian style and the ideology it represented had the aim of maintaining the British empire, and the component institution of slavery, without violence. If slaves recognized and accepted their place in the obvious order, they would serve without resistance, with some saying they would receive a more equitable reward in another realm – heaven.

Through exposition by Deetz and explanation by Leone we know the archaeological features of Georgian style and the relationship of this style to eighteenth-century ideology. Another important consideration of this style and underlying ideology concerns the social relations of production it was designed to rationalize, direct, and drive. Was the symbolic system successful in transmitting the ideology and thus effecting a more efficient agrarian capitalism based on slave labor? We know that the answer to this question is negative. Major aspects of the ideology disappeared, Georgian style became antiquated, and the institution of slavery was abolished. "Obvious" as the Georgian symbols may have been to the crafters, such distinctions, which were not fully accepted by British society, must have been of little import to slaves who suffered the violence required to maintain slavery.[2] I suppose that when most slaves looked upon Georgian mansions, elegant gardens and imported finery, they may have been impressed with the power of their oppressors to secure such items. Slaves, however, were from a different culture with a significantly different history from that of western Europeans and European-Americans. Despite the demands on their labor, in colonial Carolina they created a domestic environment based on their history and experience. Perhaps if they contemplated Georgian structures with separate kitchens and bedrooms, individualized place settings, and rigid, formal gardens, they reacted as runaway slave Charles Ball described in 1854 (Lester 1968:87) when he wrote that "the native Africans . . . generally place little, or even no value upon the fine houses and superb furniture of their masters . . . They are universally of the opinion . . . that after death they shall return to their own country." I believe Carolina slaves must have thought their oppressors had some fine things and some peculiar ways. The obvious question is: As European-Americans were building mansions and formal gardens, what symbolic world were slaves creating? A look at foodways gives us a start in answering this question.

Slave foodways were significantly different from those of European-Americans. The Georgian foodways of European-Americans drew from urban centers, used anonymously manufactured European utensils, and promoted individualism and hierarchy through differences in the quality and design of the items. Slave foodways, like the rest of slave culture, were concentrated and strongest in rural areas, primarily used locally made folk ceramics and displayed little evidence of individualism, group segmentation or hierarchy.

Archaeologists working on slave quarters in South Carolina have recovered various material effects of slave foodways including folk-produced ceramics – so-called Colono Ware with West African and Native American antecedents (Ferguson 1980) – as well as imported European ceramics, iron pots and kettles, and glass bottles. In addition to these well-preserved items we know from written and oral sources, as well as a few archaeological specimens, that slaves also used dried gourds for bowls and dippers, they carved wooden bowls and buckets, and they wove mats and baskets for use in their homes.

While the entire assemblage of containers and other utensils is important in analyzing the foodways of slaves, Colono Ware is especially significant. This ware is the major artifactual component of archaeological collections from slave quarters, comprising an average of 70 percent of all ceramics recovered.[3] Forty-eight percent of all ceramics from rural sites in the Colony is Colono Ware, while the ware comprises only 2.2 percent of the ceramics recovered from urban sites. Thus, the data indicate that Colono Ware was primarily a rural phenomenon associated with slaves, and that this domestically produced ceramic (Wheaton et al. 1983:225–50) was a major material component of the slave food system.

Combining these wares with unpreserved wooden, basketry and gourd utensils suggests a "container environment" that was dominated by handmade items similar to those of the African motherland of the majority of slaves. From birth, slave children were surrounded at mealtimes, not by the few pieces of slipware and stoneware bought for them by planters, but by traditionally styled earthenware made by their mothers or other African-American women. Although planters could buy exotic items, slave children could see the collective "mothers" of their lives making the things that nourished them every day.

In crafting Colono Ware, slave women produced artifacts that show little evidence of individual or group segmentation or hierarchy. From site to site the pottery is quite similar – plain and undecorated. Ceramic decoration implying segmentation appears only during the influx of Indian slaves resulting from raids on Spanish missions early in the eighteenth century. The evidence suggests that, except for the time when Indians were being brought into slavery, the ceramic ware emphasized the similarities of slaves and reinforced their common heritage and their differences from whites.

Not only were the artifacts of black foodways domestically produced and homogeneous, but the pattern of those foodways including the shape of the vessels, the foods prepared, the manner of preparation, and the etiquette of eating were different from the Georgian style and most similar to a generalized West African pattern. Small unrestricted bowls that average close to a liter in volume comprise about two-thirds of the entire collection of 67 reconstructed Colono Ware shapes recently inventoried from South Carolina sites (Ferguson, in press) (figure 2.1). Most of the remaining vessels are small jars that were charred in fires (figure 2.2). The high frequency of bowls in South Carolina is consistent with a pattern discovered by archaeologist John Otto (1984:67) from a nineteenth-century slave quarter in coastal Georgia. Although there was no Colono Ware in this primarily nineteenth-century assemblage, Otto's conclusion was that the imported British manufactured bowls used by slaves were part of a system of foodways similar to those of West Africa (Otto 1984:59–69, 85). My conclusions concur with and extend those of Otto.

Two of the most commonly occurring vessel forms in Africa in colonial as well as in recent times are cooking jars and serving bowls

Figure 2.1 Colono Ware bowl from Bluff Plantation, Combahee River, South Carolina. 7.8 cm tall

Figure 2.2 Colono Ware jar from West Branch of Cooper River, South Carolina. 12 cm tall

(Leith-Ross 1970; David and Hennig 1972:7–16; MacGaffey 1975:29). The jars commonly have rounded bases and flaring rims, occasionally with handles. Bowls are usually unrestricted and commonly used for drinking as well as for serving food. West Africans use these vessels for preparing and serving their general fare, which may be soup but is more commonly starch, such as millet, rice, or maize. These starches are often served with a vegetable relish to which meat or fish in small quantities is sometimes added. Cooks usually boil the starchy main dish in a large jar, while the sauce or sauces are cooked in smaller ones. This main dish is most often served in a large wooden, gourd, or ceramic bowl and smaller bowls filled with the sauces are placed near the central serving. Sitting on the ground, people eat the meal with their hands, taking a ball of the starchy main dish and dipping it into the relish.[4]

The handmade cookwares from colonial Carolina are generally consistent with this pattern. The volume distribution of jars is bimodal with a large size of approximately five liters appropriate for cooking the starchy main dish, and a smaller size averaging almost one and three quarters liters appropriate for cooking sauces.[5] In one case a perforated sherd has been recovered (Wheaton et al. 1983:233) that appears to me to be the basal portion of a type of perforated jar similar to those used in the northern portion of West Africa to steam *cous cous*, although it might also be for drying meat or other purposes (Park 1954:8; David and Hennig 1972:13; Dieterlen 1951:168; Leith-Ross 1970:28, 98, 176, 183).

Nine of the whole jars from South Carolina show evidence of having been used in fires, and many of these have thick encrustations of charring showing heavy use (figure 2.3). The shape of the jars, with generally rounded bases rather than the flat and tripodal bases of European vessels, is consistent with African and American Indian domestic technology rather than that of Europeans. This shape is well suited for use on three-stone hearths or hearths of three lumps of clay commonly found in West Africa.

Figure 2.3 Fragment of charred Colono Ware jar, Berkeley County, South Carolina. Approximately 5.5 cm tall

Earthenware pots generally cook slower and cooler than those of metal, and Blakely reports (1978:104) from the contemporary Hemba of the Congo that earthenware pots are preferred to metal ones for cooking manioc leaves because they cook more slowly. White Southerners, creolized through contact with their African and Indian slaves, showed a similar preference. In an 1828 cookbook, Virginia cook Mary Randolph (Randolph 1984:34–5) included a recipe for okra soup that called for cooking in an earthenware pipkin and serving over rice; and William Gilmore Simms (1970:361) wrote that many of the "old [white] ladies" insisted that okra soup "was always inferior if cooked in any but an Indian pot" and that an "iron vessel is one of the last which should be employed in the preparation of this truly southern dish." Importantly, both okra and rice were brought to the South from Africa, and both African and Indian slaves came from traditions of using handmade earthenware. Simms refers to earthenware as an Indian pot because by the mid-nineteenth century most African-American slaves had stopped making earthenware, and unglazed earthenware cooking jars and bowls were commonly acquired from itinerant Catawba Indians.

With rounded bases and unrestricted shapes the majority of Colono Ware bowls are similar in shape as well as size to those used in West Africa for warming and serving food (MacGaffey 1975:29; Prazan 1977:97; David and Hennig 1972:13). And the evidence for use is consistent with generalized West African practices – charring from cooking fires is rare and there is little evidence of cuts and wear from utensils. Native Africans would have eaten from bowls like these with their hands, and while there is no direct evidence that Carolina slaves ate from these bowls in this way, there is little evidence of utensil marks or wear.

Of the 45 bowls in the collection of whole vessels, only one shows evidence of cutlery marks, and evidence of other utensil wear in the soft fabric is evident on the interior bottom and rim of only three vessels – two of them from urban and cosmopolitan Charleston. The Colono Ware data show that on the rural plantations, colonial slaves were not eating like their European masters but like their African ancestors. Most colonial slaves probably ate similarly to Shadwick Hall's African grandmother who came to live on a Georgia plantation near the end of the slave trade. Hall said she

" . . . use tuh set down in the middle of the flo of uh house when she go tuh eat and she alluz eat out of a wooden bowl. Sometimes she use a spoon, but most of the time she jis eat with uh fingers" (WPA 1986:193–4).

Colono Ware vessels with similarity to European shapes are definitely in the minority in collections from South Carolina, and they are found where we might expect them – in urban centers and in rural areas where European influence was the greatest, such as near the kitchens of plantation houses. Two of the three plates in the collection are from Charleston; there is clear evidence of utensil wear on one of these plates. There is also a bowl from Charleston shaped like the pewter bowls of the eighteenth century. Vessels from the kitchen at Drayton Hall near Charleston are different from the majority of the ware in that there are shallow flat-bottomed pans similar to European pie pans. Archaeologist Lynne Lewis, who excavated this site, notes that Drayton Hall was not a working plantation but served "as a business management and country seat for the Drayton holdings" (Lewis 1978:11). It seems clear that in areas where there were European demands, pieces of Colono Ware were manufactured in European forms, but in the isolated communities of rural slaves, wares continued in the African form.

My conclusion is that the foodways of eighteenth-century African-American slaves in South Carolina were quite similar to those of West Africa and significantly different from those of European-Americans of the same time period. The pattern appears strong in the eighteenth century; Otto's evidence as well as some of the oral history of ex-slaves indicates that the pattern continued in some areas to the middle of the nineteenth century.

Thus, while the Georgian style prescribed using knives, spoons, and forks together with individual place settings of industrially manufactured flatware, African-American slaves appear to have been eating one-dish meals with their hands from cookware and dishes that had been domestically manufactured. The differences were not simply qualitative, they were differences of kind, indicating significantly different foodways in a different domestic environment. To the elite, this difference in kind was probably quite understandable; it emphasized the "obvious" dichotomy between European and "Negro" and exemplified the barbaric nature of Africans. The pressing question, however, is "What did this environment symbolize to African and African-American slaves?"

Looking at this faintly reconstructed environment, we may first recognize that the symbols are obviously not Georgian; and, at least to the degree that material symbols create ideology, we cannot expect African-American ideology to have been consistent with that of their Georgian-inspired owners. A striking feature of the collection of Colono Ware is *sameness*. Although there are differences in the quality of manufacture of vessels, there are few shapes and very little decoration. From the evidence, it seems that there was little difference in Colono Ware from plantation to plantation throughout the Low Country. There is no evidence of social segmentation or hierarchy being represented in the ceramics manufactured by slaves. The only evidence of similarity to

European forms is in urban areas and near the kitchens of main houses. In general, it seems that neither shape nor decoration was used extensively to define individual or group boundaries or status within the slave community. Colono Ware emphasizes similarity, not difference. The pottery is folk – traditional and regionally homogeneous.

In their foodways, slaves of South Carolina were not surrounded by an everyday symbolic environment that reinforced and explained their position in a hierarchy. They were within an ethnic environment that must have emphasized reciprocal relationships with one another, resourcefulness, competence and traditional ties to ancestral culture. This example of their symbolic world suggests no illusion to mask the contradictions. To the majority of slaves, the white elite must have been part of an alien world for which there may have been no well developed explanation, and without a generally accepted explanation of the social and economic differences between blacks and whites there must have been inefficiency in production. Thus, the building of an African-American culture, different in kind from that of Southern whites, maintained an unconscious resistance to slavery and the plantation system.

The result, I believe, was that Southern culture, including African-American culture, developed not at the direction of the elite but through a process of quasi-political negotiation – a conclusion similar to that presented by several historians (e.g., Genovese 1974; Blassingame 1979; Stuckey 1987; Sobel 1987). The exciting prospect of archaeology is that through an examination of the material record, such as the initial study presented here, we shall be able to look at the early stages of this negotiation from both sides.

ACKNOWLEDGEMENTS

My thanks to colleagues Joan Gero and Theodore Rosengarten for critically reviewing this paper, and to Carol Speight for her editorial assistance. Part of my research on colonial Carolina pottery was supported by a grant from the National Endowment for the Humanities.

NOTES

1   See Wood 1974; Littlefield 1981; and Morgan and Terry 1982 for a discussion of the demography, isolation, and relative autonomy of slaves in colonial South Carolina.

2 See Wood 1974:271–84 for examples of the violence of slavery in colonial South Carolina.
3 These percentages are an average from 23 South Carolina sites (Ferguson, in press).
4 For examples showing this pattern and its persistence through time, see: for the Kingdom of Mali, AD 1352, Oliver and Oliver 1965:13; the Gambia River, AD 1623, Jobson 1968:48–9; the Coast of Guinea, AD 1704, Bosman 1967:392; Sierra Leone, AD 1803, Winterbottom 1969:64–6; Angola, AD 1865, Monteiro 1968:288–9; Mossi, contemporary, Hammond 1966:57; Dukkawa of Northeast Nigeria, contemporary, Prazan 1977.
5 For African examples of similar vessels see David and Hennig 1972:11; Blakely 1978:25; Mangin 1921:70; Leith-Ross 1970.

REFERENCES

Aptheker, Herbert (1974) *American Negro Slave Revolts*. International Publishers, New York.
Blakely, Pamela (1978) *Material Culture in a Hemba Village*. Unpublished Master's thesis, Department of Folklore, Indiana University, Bloomington.
Blassingame, John W. (1979) *The Slave Community: Plantation Life in the Antebellum South*. Oxford University Press, New York.
Bosman, William (1967) *A New and Accurate Description of the Coast of Guinea: Divided into the Gold, the Slave, and the Ivory Coasts*. Frank Cass, London.
David, Nicholas and Hilke Hennig (1972) "The Ethnography of Pottery: a Fulani Case Seen in Archaeological Perspective." *McCaleb Module in Anthropology* 21, 1–29. Addison Wesley, Reading, MA.
Deetz, James (1977) *In Small Things Forgotten*. Doubleday, Garden City, NY.
Dieterlen, Germaine (1951) *Essai sur la Religion Bambara*. Presses Universitaires de France, Paris.
Ferguson, Leland (1980) "Looking for the 'Afro' in Colono-Indian Pottery." In *Archaeological Perspectives on Ethnicity in America*, ed. Robert L. Schuyler, pp. 14–28. Baywood, Farmingdale, NY.
——(In press) *Uncommon Ground: Archaeology and Colonial African-America*. Smithsonian Institution Press, Washington, D.C.
Genovese, Eugene D. (1974) *Roll, Jordan, Roll: the World the Slaves Made*. Pantheon Books, New York.
Gero, Joan M. (1983) *Material Culture and the Reproduction of Social Complexity: a Lithic Example from the Peruvian Formative*. Ph.D. dissertation, University of Massachusetts. University Microfilms, Ann Arbor.
Hammond, Peter B. (1966) *Yatenga: Technology in the Culture of a West African Kingdom*. Free Press, New York.
Hodder, Ian (1982) "Theoretical Archaeology: a Reactionary View." In *Symbolic and Structural Archaeology*, ed. Ian Hodder, pp. 1–16. Cambridge University Press, Cambridge.

Isaac, Rhys (1982) *The Transformation of Virginia, 1740–1790.* University of North Carolina Press, Chapel Hill.

Jobson, Richard (1968) *The Golden Trade or a Discovery of the River Gambra, and the Golden Trade of the Aeothiopians.* Dawsons of Pall Mall, London.

Leith-Ross, Sylvia (1970) *Nigerian Pottery.* Ibadan University Press, Ibadan.

Leone, Mark (1982) "Some Opinions About Recovering Mind." *American Antiquity* 47, 742–60.

——(1984) "Interpreting Ideology in Historical Archaeology: The William Paca Garden in Annapolis, Maryland." In *Ideology, Power and Prehistory*, eds Daniel Miller and Christopher Tilley. Cambridge University Press, Cambridge.

Lester, Julius (1968) *To Be a Slave.* Dell Publishing Co., New York.

Lewis, Lynne G. (1978) *Drayton Hall: Preliminary Archaeological Investigation at a Low Country Plantation.* National Trust for Historic Preservation, Charlottesville.

Littlefield, Daniel C. (1981) *Rice and Slaves: Ethnicity and the Slave Trade in Colonial South Carolina.* Louisiana State University Press, Baton Rouge.

McGaffey, Janet (1975) "Two Kongo Potters." *African Arts* 9(1), 29–31, 92.

Mangin, Eugene (1921) *Les Mossi: Essai sur les us et coutumes du peuple Mossi au Soudan Occidental.* Augustin Challamel, Paris.

Monteiro, Joachim John (1968) *Angola and the River Congo*, Vol. I. Frank Cass, London.

Morgan, Philip D. and George D. Terry (1982) "Slavery in Microcosm: a Conspiracy Scare in Colonial South Carolina." *Southern Studies: an Interdisciplinary Journal of the South* 21(2), 121–45.

Oliver, Ronald and Carolina Oliver (eds) (1965) *Africa in the Days of Exploration.* Prentice-Hall, Englewood Cliffs, NJ.

Otto, John Solomon (1984) *Cannon's Point Plantation, 1794–1860: Living Conditions and Status Patterns in the Old South.* Academic Press, New York.

Park, Mungo (1954) *Travels of Mungo Park.* E. P. Dutton, New York.

Prazan, Ceslaus (1977) *The Dukkawa of Northwest Nigeria.* Duquesne University Press, Pittsburgh.

Randolph, Mary (1984) *The Virginia House-Wife.* University of South Carolina Press, Columbia.

Simms, William Gilmore (1970) *The Wigwam and the Cabin.* AMS Press, New York.

Sobel, Mechal (1987) *The World They Made Together: Black and White Values in Eighteenth-Century Virginia.* Princeton University Press, Princeton, NJ.

Stuckey, Sterling (1987) *Slave Culture: Nationalist Theory and the Foundations of Black America.* Oxford University Press, New York.

Wheaton, Thomas R., Amy Friedlander and Patrick H. Garrow (1983) *Yaughan and Curriboo Plantations: Studies in Afro-American Archaeology.* Soil Systems, Inc., Atlanta.

Winterbottom, Thomas (1969) *An Account of the Native Africans in the Neighborhood of Sierra Leone*, Vol. I. Frank Cass, London.

Wood, Peter (1974) *Black Majority.* Alfred A. Knopf, New York.

Works Projects Administration (1986) *Drums and Shadows.* The University of Georgia Press, Athens.

3

The Continued Pattern of Dominance: Landlord and Tenant on the Postbellum Cotton Plantation

Charles E. Orser, Jr

Introduction

The relations between plantation owners and their slaves in the American South have been studied for years. Recent historians and anthropologists have shown, contrary to a current popular belief, that slaves did not have their culture destroyed by slavery and that they were not mindless dupes of the system. Rather, slaves resisted their bound condition and expressed their anger through both long-term, non-violent acts – work slowdowns, incomplete or inadequate labor, and feigned ignorance – and short-term, violent confrontations – revolts, uprisings, and insurrections (Aptheker 1969; Genovese 1974:587–660; 1979). When such acts of resistance occurred, slaveholders responded with vicious rapidity, as much to subdue their own fears as to smother revolution. Whether an act of perceived insolence was punished with a whipping, or whether an insurrection was quelled by hanging the leaders, the motive was always to keep the slaves in total subjection.

During the antebellum era on Southern plantations, planter dominance was met with slave resistance and slave resistance was met with planter dominance in a revolving cycle. Today, a popularly held image is that this cyclical process ceased to operate in 1865 when the Confederate States of America were formally defeated, and when some four million slaves were freed of their bondage. In actuality, even though black slaves were legally emancipated, they were not all freed from the plantation system.

The emancipation of the South's slave agriculturalists forms an important aspect of American history to which archaeologists must turn their attention. In this paper, the dominance of plantation landlords and the resistance of plantation tenants during the period from 1865 to 1935 is explored, and comments concerning the archaeological recognition of the dominance and resistance that occurred on Southern tenant plantations are presented.

The Continued Dominance of Cotton Planters after 1865

The most immediate problem facing plantation owners after 1865 was how to keep their landholdings together in the face of rumors that the Union Army planned to give each freed head of household "40 acres and a mule." Planters knew that to retain their wealth they had to put their plantations back into production with as little economic loss as possible. As a result, a number of systems designed to do this were experimented with immediately after the war (Orser 1986a).

The labor system preferred by many plantation owners was the wage-contract system. Under this system, freedmen worked under the specifications of a signed, legally binding labor contract expressly designed to put them, and to keep them, on plantations. These contracts were extremely restrictive and went so far as to set the length of their workday, establish a schedule of docking their pay for tardiness, require them to have their landlord's permission in order to leave the plantation, and levy stiff penalties on them for "insubordination" (Sitterson 1943:221–2; Williamson 1965:130–1). Although many kinds of contracts were written immediately after the war (Shlomowitz 1979:561–2), all of them were written to insure that plantation owners received the most labor for their money.

After a few years, many planters began to realize that in order to attract more workers to their estates they would have to agree to another system of land tenure. The system sought first by blacks and then agreed to by plantation owners was a system with a long history in the United States, sharecropping (Mendenhall 1937). In essence, sharecropping is a system wherein farmers receive a portion of the crop they produce in return for their labor. Even though sharecroppers do not own the crop they produce, freed slaves liked the concept of sharecropping because it presented an opportunity to be free from direct supervision and because it provided an agricultural return on their labor. Wage labor offered no agricultural return. Still, plantation owners were unwilling to give their sharecroppers too much freedom, and after the war, rules were enacted to control them. These rules were much like those established for wage hands and were every bit as restrictive. For example, on one plantation in the Mississippi Delta, these rules not only set the manner in which the crops would be be divided, but also contained a clause which maintained that the lease could be renewed only if the sharecropper acted in a way suitable to the landlord (Davis 1982:105). The landlord, of course, decided just how "suitable" a tenant was.

In addition to sharecropping, other forms of labor appeared on the South's postbellum plantations. The three most common kinds were share renting, standing renting, and cash renting.

In the share renting arrangement, the farmer supplied the labor, the work animals and their feed, the tools, the seed, and either three-quarters or two-thirds of the fertilizer. The landlord supplied the land, the housing, and the remainder of the fertilizer. The crop was divided between landlord and tenant according to the amount of fertilizer each had contributed. Many different varieties of share renting existed in the South between 1880 and 1935, some of which were peculiar to a particular region (Brannen 1924:34; Langsford and Thibodeaux 1939:15).

In the standing rent arrangement, the tenant paid the landlord with an agreed-upon amount of crop. The landlord agreed to supply the tenant only with land and housing and he theoretically took no part in dividing the crop the tenant produced. The standing rent tenant had a greater economic burden placed on him than did the sharecropper as he had to supply everything needed for farming. By the same token, however, he had greater opportunity to accumulate capital. For instance, whereas the standing renter who made four bales of cotton might have agreed to give one of them to the landlord, the sharecropper "cropping on halves" would lose two of them to the landlord. The following year, if eight bales were produced, the standing renter might still give one of them to the landlord, but the sharecropper would pay four bales as rent.

Cash renters had similar tenure arrangements with their landlords as did standing renters except that they paid their rent in an agreed-upon amount of cash. The landlord theoretically had nothing to do with the cash tenant's crop.

Once this tenure structure was established on the South's postbellum plantations, agricultural economists began to refer to it as the "agricultural ladder" (Spillman 1919). On the lowest rung of the ladder was the wage hand, and at the top was the independent owner-operator. Placed in between in ascending order were the sharecropper, the standing renter, and the cash renter. The goal envisioned by agricultural economists was that tenants should work to climb the ladder. Those who failed to climb it were "shiftless," "lazy," or "poor farmers."

Although the agricultural ladder was supposedly open to all farmers, overwhelming evidence exists to demonstrate that black tenant farmers had limited access to it. Black agriculturalists faced conditions that made their ascent up the ladder difficult at best. A survey of 11 counties in the Mississippi Delta and of 15 counties in the South Carolina Piedmont in

1930, compiled from published census records (United States Department of Commerce 1932), reveals that whites had control over greater values of land and buildings and of implements and machinery than did blacks. Black farmers, whether owners or sharecroppers, always commanded less property than did white farmers. What is more startling is that white cash renters controlled greater wealth than did black owners in both regions for both categories of property (table 3.1). In both land and buildings and implements and machinery, whites fared better than blacks.

Black agriculturalists, like their white counterparts, preferred the labor system that gave them the most freedom and the greatest opportunity for the accumulation of wealth. Although one economist has suggested that blacks preferred sharecropping because it gave them the chance to receive assistance from their more knowledgeable landlords (Reid 1977), comments made by tenant farmers disagree. For example, Nate Shaw, a tenant farmer in Alabama during the first half of the twentieth century, hated sharecropping because of the restrictions it placed on his ambitions to become a freer, more prosperous farmer. Shaw was further hampered in his plans because he was given the poorest land on the plantation to farm (Rosengarten 1984:102, 108–9). Sharecropping, however, was better than working for wages. As former tenant farmer Ed Brown said, "You couldn't join in the fun if you was on wages and your time belong to the bossman" (Maguire 1975:44). When not in the fields, wage hands were required to repair fences, to haul manure, to cut logs, or to do something else. None the less, Brown was cognizant that other systems of tenure were far better than sharecropping. For one year, in fact, Brown had worked as a standing renter. This arrangement, however, was terminated by his landlord when Brown sold his own cotton without consulting his landlord. Even though this sale was well within Brown's rights as a standing renter, legally in control of his own crop, his landlord did not approve of Brown's independence, and the following year the only arrangement Brown could negotiate with him was sharecropping (Maguire 1975:104).

Another kind of dominance exercised by planters involved the recognition by Southern courts that sharecroppers did not own their crops. In terms of law, sharecroppers were really wage hands who received crops in lieu of money (Applewhite 1954; Woodman 1979). As Ed Brown observed, in January, when he was breaking and turning the land with the help of his landlord's mule, the landlord would come by and ask him, "How is *your* crop, and how is you gettin' along turnin' *your* land?" In April the landlord would again inquire about Brown's crop, but by June the landlord would ask, "Is *our* cotton doin' pretty good?" By September, when cotton picking started, the landlord began to refer to, "*My* cotton, *my* corn, *my* crop" (Maguire 1975:55–9).

The timing between the landlord's statements about "his" crop and the nearing end of "furnishing time" are not coincidental. "Furnishings" were credits that local merchants, in collusion with landlords, would extend to tenants with the expectation that once the crop was harvested, the tenant would be able to pay his debt. Tenants were usually carried, or

Table 3.1 Mean land and building, and implement and machinery values in 1930, per farmer

	Land and buildings ($)	
	White	Black
Mississippi Delta[a]		
Owners	13,999.14	3,271.79
Cash renters	5,284.49	2,469.40
Sharecroppers	1,970.63	1,629.01
South Carolina Piedmont[b]		
Owners	4,109.02	1,909.45
Cash renters	2,770.39	1,403.59
Sharecroppers	1,714.94	1,292.85

	Implements and machinery ($)	
	White	Black
Mississippi Delta		
Owners	1,812.65	233.86
Cash renters	592.07	120.68
Sharecroppers	65.02	29.51
South Carolina Piedmont		
Owners	315.51	110.32
Cash renters	174.31	49.87
Sharecroppers	70.79	39.92

[a]Bolivar, Coahoma, Humphreys, Issaquena, Leflore, Quitman, Sharkey, Sunflower, Tallahatchie, Tunica, and Washington counties.
[b]Abbeville, Anderson, Cherokee, Chester, Fairfield, Greenville, Greenwood, Laurens, McCormick, Newberry, Oconee, Pickens, Spartanburg, Union, and York Counties.
Source: United States Department of Commerce (1932), *Agricultural Census*.

"furnished," until September or October. In some regions, a major source of income for landlords came from furnishing their tenants. In bad years tenants were given small advances and told to subsist as best they could, but in good years tenants could accumulate large debts because they were given large advances (Raper and Reid 1941:38–9).

Regardless of how much they were furnished, tenants usually saw a drastic cut in their incomes after their account was settled. The money tenants received after the settlement, called "cash after settling," already had the advances for food, clothing, farm supplies (including fertilizer), and interest subtracted (Woofter et al. 1936:86–7). Landlords on some plantations encouraged their tenants to spend their cash after settling on frivolous items in order to increase their tenants' dependence on them. The assumption these landlords made was that a tenant deep in debt would make a more obedient and, therefore, better worker, not to mention that as a debtor, the tenant now had the force of law against him. This system, exemplified by the crop lien, rightly has been termed "debt peonage" (Ransom and Sutch 1977:149–70).

Because sharecroppers did not own their crops, they were not the ones who divided it. As Ed Brown explained, because the landlord made the division, only he knew whether it had been made fairly. In the days of lynchings, Ku Klux Klan raids, and outright murder, a black tenant did not safely question the manner in which the landlord had divided his crop. In Brown's case, one landlord "took his share and all of mine and claim I owe him twenty-four dollars in addition" (Maguire 1975:72). This was the essence of debt peonage.

Tenant Resistance to Landlord Dominance

Given the institutionalized nature of landlord dominance after 1865, plantation tenants, particularly freedmen tenants, had little legal protection. Political and economic gains made in the South between 1865 and 1875 were repealed or weakened after 1875 to insure that blacks had little input into the structure of the "New South" (Cox and Cox 1973; Zinn 1980:193–205).

For freed blacks, as for enslaved blacks, much of their daily resistance was expressed in songs, folk tales, and language (Levine 1977). This verbal, non-violent form of protest was a way for blacks to shut whites out of their world; for them to have an identity largely removed from the "enforced personal feeling of inferiority" thrust upon them (DuBois 1935:9). Still, emancipated blacks also found other ways to respond to landlord dominance.

When formally freed, which sometimes did not happen until a Union soldier rode up and told them about emancipation, about half a million plantation blacks responded with a form of resistance that carried an unmistakable message: they readily deserted their plantation homes and their former masters to whom they had seemed so devoted as slaves. As one former slave from Monroe County, Mississippi, remembered, on the day that the slaves on her plantation heard about freedom, not one was left in the quarters by sundown (Rawick 1977–79: Supplemental Series 1, Vol. 7, p. 786).

Most former slaves, however, did not choose this form of resistance after emancipation, but preferred to stay in their antebellum plantation homes to see what was going to happen in the South. This decision to stay was based on a complex set of interrelated factors including personal circumstances, the generally poor or non-existent education of plantation blacks, the passing of strict vagrancy laws meant to keep blacks on plantations, and a widespread lack of training for anything but plantation agriculture. As former slave Lucy Donald of Rankin County, Mississippi, said, the slaves "didn't know what to do as they didn't know nothing but to farm, they hired out to the white farmers" (Rawick 1977–79: Supplemental Series 1, Vol. 7, p. 640). Presented with an inadequate but existing home within the slave quarters and promises of a share of that year's crop, most former slaves decided to stay on the plantations of their bondage for at least one year (Orser 1986b).

The contract system proved to be bad for black agriculturalists, however, and most resisted its restrictions by moving from plantation to plantation, breaking each successive contract, in search of fair terms. This movement by plantation farmers greatly upset plantation owners, because landless and largely propertyless freedmen could not be sued for breach of contract (Anonymous 1866, 1868). Planters took steps to blacklist freedmen who broke their contracts, and vagrancy laws stipulated that any vagrant – that is, any unemployed black – could be hired out to any landlord under any terms. None the less, freed slaves continued to resist, because as one former slave said, "One of the rights of bein' free was that we could move around and change bosses" (Rawick 1977–79: Supplemental Series 1, Vol. 8, p. 1348). To some, this movement "came to be regarded as the test of freedom" (Tebeau 1936:132). In the late nineteenth and early twentieth centuries, the movement of tenants from one plantation to another and even from one house to another on the same plantation was called "shifting." This frequent movement, although not unique to blacks but characteristic of farm tenancy in general, represents one kind of resistance to landlord dominance.

In a study of 93 selected plantation counties in 1920 (Brannen 1924:46–8, 74, Appendix D), 48.3 percent of all "share tenants" (sharecroppers and share renters) had lived on their farms for less than two years, 33.5 percent had lived there from two to four years, and only 18.2 percent had lived there for over five years. Among "cash tenants" (cash and standing renters), 30.0 percent had lived on their current farms less than two years, 33.8 percent from two to four years, and 36.2 percent for over five years. A comparison of blacks and whites revealed that as many as 53.2 percent of the whites had lived in their homes for less than two years, whereas 39.6 percent of the blacks had lived in their homes for this period. A similar study conducted in two cotton-producing counties in Georgia in the early 1930s showed that 23.1 percent of the white families had lived in their homes for one year, while 31.9 percent of the blacks had lived in their homes for this length of time. For sharecroppers, the average length of stay for whites was 2.4 years and for blacks 2.8 years; for cash renters 2.9 years for whites and 3.7 years for blacks (Raper 1936:59–61).

As the twentieth century progressed, the type of tenure became more important than did skin color as a factor for shifting. As sociologist Arthur F. Raper (1936:61) wrote, the "length of residence . . . varies with tenure class and farm conditions rather than with race." This conclusion was upheld by the author of another study on shifting who concluded that "the percentage of farmers in the lower tenure classes are found rather consistently in the categories showing shorter duration of farm occupancy" (Schuler 1938:183).

These studies of shifting suggest two things: first, that black tenant farmers may have moved less than they had immediately after the war, not because of their commitment to a particular piece of plantation land, but because they did not have equal access to the means of agricultural production – as a result, given the restrictions of debt peonage, black tenants were more limited in their physical movements because of white law and terrorism; second, that through time, white sharecroppers, who came to sharecropping through an entirely different set of circumstances than did blacks, suffered some of the same fates as black sharecroppers. In other words, much of the repression on postbellum plantations ran along class lines rather than along racial lines. Nevertheless, white sharecroppers were not lynched or run out of their homes.

The Archaeological Recognition of Resistance and Dominance

What is revealed through even this cursory examination of the South between 1865 and 1935 is that the plantation system was not dismantled as a result of the Civil War and that a pattern of dominance, established since the earliest days of plantation agriculture, continued throughout this period. The gap between what landlords received from the labor of

48   CHARLES E. ORSER, JR

their tenants and what tenants in turn received from the landlords is the
axis upon which a true understanding of the continued dominance of the
plantation pivots.

The distinction between the needs and wants of owners and those of
workers, and the relationship of this distinction to domination and
repression, has been explained by social philosopher Leszek Nowak
(1983). Nowak argues that society is composed of three "momentums" –
economic, political, and ideological – that each contain two classes of
people – owners and workers, rulers and ruled, and priests and followers
– who struggle against each other. This classic model of society is built
around a theory of power that maintains in essence that the relationship
within each struggle is identical. As such, the struggle of the ruled against
the rulers in the political moment is identical to that of the workers
against the owners in the economic moment.

Property within a society incorporating slavery and tenancy is
allocated according to a surplus value (that value produced by workers
but given to the owners) and a variable capital (that value left to the
workers). The gap that exists between these two values is termed the
"alienation of work" (Nowak 1983:36–7). A similar process appears in
the political moment, but results in civic alienation – the gap between the
autonomy of the rulers and the expected freedom of the ruled. In both
moments, a "threshold of class peace" is passed as the gap grows larger.
A period of revolutionary activity occurs when the gap increases to such
a point that the fear of retaliation appears less severe than the
continuation of the existing order.

During the antebellum period, the levels of work and civic alienation
between slaves and masters were high. The disparity between what slaves
received versus what they had a right to expect partly accounts for slave
resistance and explains one reason that freed slaves left their plantation
homes immediately after the war or shortly thereafter. The contract
system of labor was intended to keep the levels of work and civic
alienation high, with the freedom offered to slaves restricted so that the
threshold of class peace was not crossed.

The levels of alienation decreased between 1865 and roughly 1875
when Southern planters, as a conquered ruling class, were themselves
somewhat disenfranchised and thought that they might actually lose
their land to emancipated blacks. After 1875, however, the levels of civic
and work alienation increased to pre-war levels as Southern plantation
tenancy became more institutionalized. Within this framework, then, the
task of the archaeologist involves the recognition of this alienation and
the resistance that accompanied it. Although this recognition is
exceedingly difficult, tentative ideas about its identification can be
offered.

The material correlates of landlord dominance do seem to appear in archaeological deposits found on postbellum plantations. For example, at Millwood Plantation in Abbeville County, South Carolina – one of only two postbellum plantations extensively investigated in the American South, the other being Waverly Plantation in Mississippi (Adams 1980) – evidence for the superior economic position of the landlord exists (Orser 1988). A simple comparison of the building the landlord inhabited versus one that a tenant occupied demonstrates the gap between the two kinds of people.

Of the 28 building foundations investigated at Millwood, written records and oral information substantiated that one building foundation, designated Structure 1, was the home of the plantation landlord, while another foundation, designated Structure 17, represented the remains of a share renter's home (Orser et al. 1982:139–77, 313–31). The size and construction differentials between these structures are remarkable. Structure 1 measured 23 feet (7 meters) wide and 39 feet (11.9 meters) long, or 897 square feet (83.3 square meters) in size; Structure 17 was 14 feet (4.3 meters) wide and 39 feet (11.9 meters) long, or 546 square feet (51.1 square meters). Photographic evidence shows that Structure 1 was even larger, but no supporting archaeological proof could be found to document its full size. Even so, the relative size of these structures is revealed by the knowledge that one person lived in Structure 1 whereas as many as 10 might have lived in Structure 17 at one time. Furthermore, the landlord's house contained a fireplace at each end, while the tenant's house contained a central, double fireplace. On the interior, the landlord's house was divided into five separate rooms: a porch, a hall lined with books, a dining room, a combination office and living room, and a bedroom. A former occupant of Structure 17 said that her home contained only two actual rooms, a kitchen and a bedroom. The bedroom was divided into two separate bedrooms by some sort of partition. She said that this house was not "fine inside as the white people's house" but that it did share certain similarities to the landlord's house inside (Orser et al. 1982:577). Exactly what these similarities were cannot be determined, but as share renters their house was undoubtedly appreciably better than those of sharecroppers who lived in log, "bad houses." Photographic evidence suggests that the landlord's house was not a grand mansion, but merely a simple, clapboarded house. Still, one writer who had extensive first-hand knowledge of Millwood Plantation described it as "a long and very comfortable one story building" (Dundas 1949:15).

In addition to the construction of the houses, their location on the plantation undoubtedly also carries meaning within the plantation power system (Orser 1983; Orser and Nekola 1985). It can be assumed that the planter's home would be located where he could exert the most influence over the operation of the estate. At Millwood Plantation, Structures 1 and 17 seem to have been located according to some design of this nature. Photographic evidence shows that Structure 17 was located near a large barn and two crudely built outbuildings. Even though archaeological evidence for these buildings could not be found, their presence is to be expected at a share tenant's house because of his ownership of farm tools. Both photographic and archaeological evidence show that Structure 1 was located within a compound of buildings including three small sheds probably used to house the plantation's tools. The foundations of the landlord's outbuildings and the lack of physical evidence for the share tenant's outbuildings demonstrates the more substantial nature of the landlord's buildings.

In summary, house construction and placement on the plantation indicates the differential power held by a building's inhabitants. Although house placement and design could be shaped by a number of factors (Douglas 1972:514), this is one area that promises to provide abundant information about postbellum plantation dominance. Archaeologists must explore planter housing not in terms of how grand their homes were, but in terms of what information they convey about the role of planters in dominating their work-force.

One of the most tangible indicators of the decreased alienation of black agriculturalists in the South after 1865 was their movement out of the compact, uniform slave quarters and into single-family tenant dwellings. These buildings, although the property of the landlord and, as Nate Shaw said, just "a old common-built house" (Rosengarten 1984:102), were built some distance from the watchful eye of the landlord. The presence of these houses scattered across plantation lands was noted by inhabitants and travellers in the South after the war (Barrow 1881:832; Campbell 1879). At Millwood Plantation, for example, 66 tenant structures were tentatively identified on the over 10,000 acres (4,000 hectares) that comprised the plantation. Of these buildings, Structure 17 was closest to Structure 1, only 300 feet (91.4 meters), while the farthest was 4.5 miles (7.2 kilometers) from Structure 1. Most of the houses were located over two miles (3.2 kilometers) from the landlord's house. The presence of these houses across the plantation is only partially indicative of the struggle between tenants and landlords, however, because tenants could be dispersed across a plantation for the simple economic reason of putting them closer to their fields. The landlord had the power to place the tenants where he wanted them.

Other evidence for tenant resistance to landlord domination is harder to isolate in archaeological deposits. Plantation tenants had no power to sustain long-term resistance movements; such movements, like the drive to unionize into the Southern Farmers' Alliance, the Southern Tenant Farmers' Union, and the Sharecroppers' Union (Dyson 1982:86–7, 94–8, 150–67; Grubbs 1971; Schwartz 1976), were short-lived and would leave little readily recognizable archaeological evidence. As a result, archaeologists must be more creative in the search for indicators of tenant resistance. At this point, these indicators are unknown and can now be only guessed.

Conclusion

The continued dominance of landlords and the continued resistance of plantation agriculturalists on Southern plantations after 1865 is well documented and cannot be refuted. This process of daily interaction has been mentioned by historians and was given expression by writers during the postbellum era. Historians interested in dominance and resistance are finding new examples of the give and take between plantation inhabitants at every turn.

Archaeologists, however, face severe difficulties in their equally important search. for the material manifestations of this process. A significant problem is the simple one that only two postbellum tenant plantations have ever been excavated to any real extent. Another obviously related problem involves the reorientation of much of today's archaeological reasoning that must accompany the search for landlord dominance and tenant resistance. The postbellum plantation has been ignored, just as was its antebellum counterpart, for too long. Many contemporary historical archaeologists still look askance at the excavation of the postbellum plantation because of their failure to understand its importance. Further research by archaeologists, both archival and archaeological, is necessary before the material correlates of work and civic alienation can be identified. The postbellum tenant plantation offers a unique and rich environment for the examination of economic, political, and ideological alienation and struggle, and archaeologists must learn to isolate its indicators. This paper is only one small step in what will hopefully be a long field of inquiry of historical archaeology.

REFERENCES

Adams, William H. (ed.) (1980) *Waverly Plantation: Ethnoarchaeology of a Tenant Farming Community*. Heritage Conservation and Recreation Service, Washington, D.C.

Anonymous (1866) "What's To Be Done With the Negroes?" *DeBow's Review* 1(n.s.), 578.

——(1868) "How They Are Settling the Labor Question in Mississippi." *DeBow's Review* 5(n.s.), 224.

Applewhite, Marjorie Mendenhall (1954) "Sharecropper and Tenant in the Courts of North Carolina." *North Carolina Historical Review* 31, 134–49.

Aptheker, Herbert (1969) *American Negro Slave Revolts*. International Publishers, New York.

Barrow, David Crenshaw (1881) "A Georgia Plantation." *Scribner's Monthly* 21, 830–6.

Brannen, C. O. (1924) *Relation of Land Tenure to Plantation Organization*. United States Department of Agriculture, Bulletin 1269. Government Printing Office, Washington, D.C.

Campbell, George (1879) *Black and White: The Outcome of a Visit to the United States*. Chatto and Windus, London.

Cox, LaWanda and John H. Cox (eds) (1973) *Reconstruction, the Negro, and the New South*. University of South Carolina Press, Columbia.

Davis, Ronald L. F. (1982) *Good and Faithful Labor: From Slavery to Sharecropping in the Natchez District, 1860–1890*. Greenwood Press, Westport, CT.

Douglas, Mary (1972) "Symbolic Order in the Use of Domestic Space." In *Man, Settlement, and Urbanism*, eds Peter J. Ucko, Ruth Tringham, and G. W. Dimbleby, pp. 513–21. Schenkman, Cambridge, MA.

DuBois, W. E. B. (1935) *Black Reconstruction in America, 1860–1880*. Harcourt, Brace, and World, New York.

Dundas, Francis de Sales (1949) *The Calhoun Settlement: District of Abbeville, South Carolina*. F. de Sales Dundas, Staunton, VA.

Dyson, Lowell K. (1982) *Red Harvest: The Communist Party and American Farmers*. University of Nebraska Press, Lincoln.

Genovese, Eugene D. (1974) *Roll, Jordan, Roll: The World the Slaves Made*. Pantheon, New York.

——(1979) *From Rebellion to Revolution: Afro-American Slave Revolts in the Making of the Modern World*. Louisiana State University Press, Baton Rouge.

Grubbs, Donald H. (1971) *Cry from the Cotton: The Southern Tenant Farmers' Union and the New Deal*. University of North Carolina Press, Chapel Hill.

Langsford, E. L. and B. H. Thibodeaux (1939) *Plantation Organization and Operation in the Yazoo-Mississippi Delta Area*. United States Department of Agriculture, Technical Bulletin 682. Government Printing Office, Washington, D.C.

Levine, Lawrence W. (1977) *Black Culture and Black Consciousness: Afro-American Folk Thought from Slavery to Freedom*. Oxford University Press, New York.

Maguire, Jane (1975) *On Shares: Ed Brown's Story*. W. W. Norton, New York.

Mendenhall, Marjorie Stratford (1937) "The Rise of Southern Tenancy." *Yale Review* 27, 110–29.

Nowak, Leszek (1983) *Property and Power: Towards a Non-Marxian Historical Materialism*. D. Reidel, Dordrecht, Holland.

Orser, Charles E., Jr (1983) "The Spatial Organization of a Postbellum Plantation." Paper delivered at the 40th Southeastern Archaeological Conference, Columbia, South Carolina.

——(1986a) "The Archaeological Recognition of the Squad System on Postbellum Cotton Plantations." *Southeastern Archaeology* 5, 11–20.

——(1986b) "Out of Slavery: The Material Culture of Freedom." Paper delivered at the 10th Annual Symposium on Language and Culture in South Carolina, University of South Carolina, Columbia.

——(1988) *The Material Basis of the Postbellum Tenant Plantation: Historical Archaeology in the South Carolina Piedmont*. University of Georgia Press, Athens.

Orser, Charles E., Jr and Annette M. Nekola (1985) "Plantation Settlement from Slavery to Tenancy: An Example from a Piedmont Plantation in South Carolina." In *The Archaeology of Slavery and Plantation Life*, ed. Theresa A. Singleton, pp. 67–94. Academic Press, Orlando.

Orser, Charles E., Jr, Annette M. Nekola, and James L. Roark (1982) *Exploring the Rustic Life: Multidisciplinary Research at Millwood Plantation, A Large Piedmont Plantation in Abbeville County, South Carolina, and Elbert County, Georgia*. Report submitted to the National Park Service, Atlanta.

Ransom, Roger L. and Richard Sutch (1977) *One Kind of Freedom: The Economic Consequences of Emancipation*. Cambridge University Press, Cambridge.

Raper, Arthur F. (1936) *Preface to Peasantry: A Tale of Two Black Belt Counties*. University of North Carolina Press, Chapel Hill.

Raper, Arthur F. and Ira De A. Reid (1941) *Sharecroppers All*. University of North Carolina Press, Chapel Hill.

Rawick, George L. (ed.) (1977–1979) *The American Slave: A Composite Autobiography*. Greenwood Press, Westport, CT.

Reid, Joseph D., Jr (1977) "The Theory of Share Tenancy Revised – Again." *Journal of Political Economy* 85, 403–7.

Rosengarten, Theodore (1984) *All God's Dangers: The Life of Nate Shaw*. Vintage Books, New York.

Schuler, E. A. (1938) *Social Status and Farm Tenure: Attitudes and Social Conditions of Corn Belt and Cotton Belt Farmers*. United States Department of Agriculture, Farm Security Administration, and the Bureau of Agricultural Economics, Social Research Report 4. Government Printing Office, Washington, D.C.

Schwartz, Michael (1976) *Radical Protest and Social Structure: The Southern Farmers' Alliance and Cotton Tenancy, 1880–1890*. Academic Press, New York.

Shlomowitz, Ralph (1979) "The Origins of Southern Sharecropping." *Agricultural History* 53, 557–75.

Sitterson, J. Carlyle (1943) "The Transition from Slave to Free Economy on the William J. Minor Plantations." *Agricultural History* 17, 216–24.

Spillman, W. J. (1919) "The Agricultural Ladder." In *Papers on Tenancy*. Office of the Secretary of the American Association for Agricultural Legislation, Bulletin 2, pp. 29–38. University of Wisconsin, Madison.

Tebeau, C. W. (1936) "Some Aspects of Planter–Freedmen Relations, 1865–1880." *Journal of Negro History* 21, 130–50.

United States Department of Commerce (1932) *Agricultural Census of the United States: 1930, Agriculture, Volume II, Part 2, The Southern States.* Government Printing Office, Washington, D.C.

Williamson, Joel (1965) *After Slavery: The Negro in South Carolina During Reconstruction, 1861–1877.* University of North Carolina Press, Chapel Hill.

Woodman, Harold D. (1979) "Post Civil War Southern Agriculture and the Law." *Agricultural History* 53, 319–37.

Woofter, Thomas J., Jr, Gordon Blackwell, Harold Hoffsommer, James G. Maddox, Jean M. Massell, B. O. Williams, and Waller Wynne, Jr (1936) *Landlord and Tenant on the Cotton Plantation.* Works Progress Administration, Division of Social Research, Monograph 5. Government Printing Office, Washington, D.C.

Zinn, Howard (1980) *A People's History of the United States.* Harper and Row, New York.

4

Material Culture in Boston: The Black Experience

Beth Anne Bower

Ira Berlin's important article "Time, Space and the Evolution of Afro-American Society in British Mainland North America" criticizes historians' treatment of the African-American experience as an attempt to capture the essence of slave culture at the expense of appreciating the heterogeneous effects of time and place (Berlin 1980:44). Not only do historians fail to see regional and generational differences in African-American culture, they also too often fail to consider the diversity of African cultures whence these people came. As historical archaeologists increasingly involve themselves in the study of African-Americans, they would do well to heed Berlin's advice and be alert for variation in African-American culture.

The vast majority of work by historical archaeologists on African-Americans has focused on Southern slave and tenant plantations (e.g., Singleton 1985, 1988; Ferguson 1980; Otto 1984; Orser 1988). By comparison Northern African-American communities have received much less attention (e.g., Bower and Rushing 1980; Geismar 1982; Schuyler 1980; Baker 1980; Deetz 1977) with most of it concentrating on the nineteenth century. Obviously this Northern material record of freed laborers, servants, and maritimers is quite distinct from the slave plantation ways of life documented for the South, though no systematic comparison has been made. The Northern material record amplifies the picture of a complex, internally heterogeneous African-American culture actively constructing social institutions, symbolic systems and material worlds in the persistent context of a complex, shifting white racism found in the growing body of studies by historians (e.g., Jacobs 1968; White 1971; Horton and Horton 1979; Pleck 1979; Levesque 1976; Piersen 1988). However, the work of historical archaeologists and of historians is virtually silent on the seventeenth and eighteenth centuries, Green (1942) and Moore (1866) being the major exceptions. The documents hint of an equally, if differently, diverse way of life, suggestions that should guide historical archaeological investigations of this period.

In no place is an awareness of the disparateness of the Afro-American experience as important as in a major port such as Boston. The very size of Boston as well as its urban character makes the Afro-American experience complex. Boston's heterogeneity was based on markets for slaves and cheap, free black labor; secondly, these markets were nurtured by the Puritan founders' recognition that their prosperity hinged on the triangular trade which included slaves. Boston became a major slave trading center in New England, marketing people from all over Sub-Saharan Africa. The continual existence of Negro institutions of resistance continued to infuse diverse African experiences into New England life and to foster active resistance by Afro-American and some Anglo-Americans to the riches built on slavery.

The Seventeenth Century

It has been suggested that the Puritans never condoned slavery. Let me quote John Winthrop's brother-in-law, Emmanuel Downing, who hoped the war with the Narragansett Indians would be successful and deliver Narragansett prisoners:

> ... enough to exchange for Moores, which wilbe more gayneful pilladge for us than wee conceive, for I doe not see how we can thrive untill we gett into a stock of slaves sufficient to doe all our business. For our children's children will hardly see this great continent filled with people, soe that our servants will still desire freedom to plant for them selves, and not stay but for verie great wages. And I suppose you know verie well how wee shall maunteyne 20 Moores cheaper than one Englishe servant. (Moore 1866:10).

The Puritans clearly classed Africans and Indians as barbarians whose station was to serve the English.

The black experience in Boston began in 1638 when the Massachuesetts Bay Colony's ship, the *Desire*, brought back Africans from Providence Island in the West Indies. The Puritans of Providence Island had obtained the Africans by seizing Spanish ships, but the small island colony "feared that the number of negroes might become too great to be managed" and traded them to their New England partners for "cannibal negroes," the Pequod Indians (Moore 1866:6). With this event the forced immigration of thousands of Africans and Afro-Americans to Boston began.

The roundabout trip to Boston of the African slaves brought on the *Desire* is indicative of the early days of the slave trade. Throughout this ordeal, however, African values, language, and hierarchy survived. John Josslyn, an early visitor to New England, related his experience at the home of Samuel Maverick in Boston Harbor in 1639:

> Mr. Maverick's Negro woman came to the chamber window, and in her own country language, and tune sang loud and shrill, going out to her, she used a great deal of respect towards me, and willingly would have expressed her grief in English . . . whereupon I repaired to my host, to learn of him the cause, and resolved to intreat him in her behalf, for that I understood before, that she had been a Queen in her own country, and observed a very humble and dutiful garb used towards her by another Negro who was her maid. Mr. Maverick was desirous to have a breed of Negroes, and therefore seeing she would not yield by persuasions to company with a Negro young man he had in his house; he commanded him will'd she nill'd she to go to bed to her, which no sooner done but she kickt him out again. This she took in high disdain beyond her slavery, and this was the cause of her grief. (Josslyn 1833:28; Moore 1866:8)

This woman was probably one of the *Desire* slaves, but maintained her language and status while Maverick's slave.

There is little information on the number of slaves who were brought to Boston in the early decades of the city's growth. We do know that the Boston entrepreneurs jumped wholeheartedly into the slave trade – sometimes too enthusiastically for their peers. Two men were tried in Boston and their slaves returned to Africa, not because they had brought in slaves, but because evidence showed that the slaves had been captured on a Sunday (Moore 1866:29–30). During this time the slave ports mentioned are Angola, the Island of Maio (one of the Cape Verde Islands), and Guinea, all on the West Coast of Africa.

By the 1650s there were free black people living in and around Boston. In 1654, a black slave named Angola was purchased by a free black man, Sebastian Ken, also known as Bus Bus Negro of Dorchester (Suffolk County Registry of Deeds, II :297) for a bushel of peas and set free. Angola was given property in Boston by Governor Bellingham as a reward for saving his life (Suffolk County Registry of Deeds VII: 22). In the 1670s, the source of New England's slaves was East Africa; rivalry between the Dutch West India Company and the English Royal African Company forced New England slavers to go further for their quarry, thus for a few decades they went to East rather than West Africa (Greene 1942:21–2).

One additional influence on the formation of Afro-American culture in seventeenth-century Boston was Native Americans. The Puritans who founded Boston enslaved Native Americans who were captured during warfare or who violated Massachusetts law (Moore 1866:32). For example, Hugh Peter wrote to John Winthrop in 1637: "Mr. Endicot and my selfe salute you in Jesus Christ . . . Wee have heard of a dividence of women and children in the bay and would bee glad of a share, viz; a young woman or girle and a boy if you think good" (Moore 1866:4). Native Americans and Africans were classified in the same category by the Puritans – as barbarians. Slave owners often acquired both black and native American slaves, and encouraged the intermarriage of the races; because more African males were imported than females and female Native Americans were more likely to survive the wars,these unions probably occurred fairly often (Greene 1942:93–6, 200–9).

Where do we get the impression that Puritans possessed a distate for slavery? Two important sources are reports by Governors Randolph and Bradstreet that present an extremely low number of Afro-American slaves in seventeenth-century Boston. In 1676, Edmund Randolph responded to several heads of inquiry that there were "not above 200 slaves in the colony, and those are brought from Guinea and Madagascar" (Moore 1866:49). In May of 1680, Governor Bradstreet answered again:

> There hath been no company of blacks or slaves brought into the country since the beginning of this plantation for the space of 50 years. Only one small Vessell about two yeares since, after 20 months voyage to Madagascar brought hither betwixt 40 and 50 Negroes, mostly women and children . . . Now and then two or three negroes are brought hither from Barbadoes and other of his majestie's plantations and sold here . . . So that there may be within our government about 100 or 120. There are very few blacks borne here, I think not above [five] or six at the most in a year, none baptized that I ever hear of . . . (Moore 1866:49)

From these and similar statements, historians have concluded that the influx of Africans and Afro-Americans from the Caribbean to the colonies was insignificant in the seventeenth century. I would suggest, given the disparity in numbers between the two reports, that the governors were lying. Watkins and Hume have shown in their discussion of the "Poor Potter" of Yorktown that the colonial government was apt to tell the heads of inquiry exactly what they wanted to hear – that the North American colonies were not competing with the mother country (Watkins and Noel Hume 1967:76). The New England slavers had prudently stepped out of the way of the Royal Africa Company on the West Coast of Africa, and it is possible that the governors did not want to call attention to the extent of New England involvement in the trade. Further evidence to support this theory is the statement of a French

Protestant refugee in Boston in 1687: "You may also own negroes and negresses; there is not a house in Boston however small may be its means that has not one or two. There are those that have 5 or 6, and all make a good living" (Jennings 1947:87). Although this is probably an exaggeration, Gary Nash in The Urban Crucible (1979) states that by 1690 about 3 to 4 percent of the population, and about one out of nine families, owned at least one slave (Nash 1979:13–14). This, of course, does not take into account either free black people, of which there was a small colony at this time, or the children of slaves.

By the end of the seventeenth century, then, probably 5 to 6 percent of Boston's population was made up of both free and slave people of African descent. This community comprised Africans, native born Afro-Americans, Caribean born Afro-Americans, and mulattoes from both Native American and white unions. The records show that African influence could have come from both the East and West Coasts of Africa. Although clearly from a variety of backgrounds, individuals in Boston's black community, by virtue of its urban port location, had close contact which contributed to the emergence of Boston's Afro-American culture by the end of the seventeenth century.

The Eighteenth Century

The eighteenth century in Boston began with a crisis for the city's access to cheap labor. Governor Dudley's report of 1708 states: "In Boston, there are 400 negro servants, one half of whom were born here" (Moore 1866:26n). The city government was concerned about the behavior of non-white servants and slaves and passed a rash of laws restricting their activities, including curfews and penalties for striking a Christian, improper intercourse with whites, and miscegenation (Moore 1866:54). In the same year, Dudley accused the West Indies plantation owners of selling their worst servants and slaves to Bostonians, referring to them as "refuse" (Greene 1942:35).

White servants did not constitute a suitable source of labor. Thomas Moore wrote in 1722 that Boston's "masters will rather be burnt in their beds by [rebellious slaves] than suffer English servants to come hither to work" (Nash 1979:111). Not only did white servants tend to run away, but Boston's elite apparently dreaded the possibility that the servants, once free, would strive and possibly succeed in raising themselves to their master's social level (Nash 1979:111). There was no threat of social equality in the case of black slaves, for even free black men were doomed to the bottom of the white social strata by the color of their skin.

Faced with resistance from whites, local slaves and servants and competition in the slave market, New England slave holders took a new tack, turned to the importation of Yamassee Indians from South Carolina and renewed the importation of black slaves directly from Africa (Nash 1979:111). After importing what Nash estimates to be hundreds of Native Americans, the Bostonians determined that these were "Malicious, surly and revengeful" and banned their importation (Nash 1979:106). The influx of African slaves continued and Boston's black population quadrupled by 1742 while the entire population of the city only doubled.

The importation of African slaves waned in the late 1750s, but this did not signal a decline in a distinctive Afro-American culture. The large number of Africans who arrived in previous decades made their presence felt in contributions to black culture (Berlin 1980:52); in addition, the size of the African community gave new impetus to black freedom movements. At the same time within Boston's depressed economy the white working class, weary of competition, called for the end of slave labor. This led to the start of emancipation of many of Boston's slaves (Nash 1979:320–1).

America's War of Independence was the most disruptive influence on the black community in Boston in the eighteenth century. Black bondsmen and freemen were asked to choose sides, and when the Patriot side won, perhaps one-third of Boston's black population left with the British in 1776 (Quarles 1973:134). This loss was quickly replaced by rural Massachusetts and New England slaves who were freed as a result of their participation on the Patriot side. Emancipation for all slaves in Massachusetts followed soon after, and Boston became the City of Freedom for many still enslaved in the South. From the 1780s onward, Boston's native black population was augmented by both freed and escaped slaves from Southern states, primarily Virginia. In the 1790s there was an influx of refugees from the French West Indian colony of Haiti, and a colony of French Catholic Afro-Americans formed in Boston.

Through most of the eighteenth century, then, Boston's black community grew, reaching a peak in the 1740s at 8 percent of Boston's population (Nash 1979:107). In the eighteenth century we see an influx of Native Americans from the South, and a large influx of Africans, one source stating that over 23,000 black people were imported into Massachusetts in the 1750s and 1760s (Jennings 1947:86). These new immigrants were incorporated into the community, and by the time of the Revolution were actively petitioning for their freedom and for their own cultural institutions (Greene 1942:315). Disrupted, as were all Americans, by the American Revolution, Boston's black community received new immigrants from the rural North and the French Caribbean.

Conclusions and Prospects

The preceding discussion elucidates the complexity of the influences on Afro-American culture in Boston over time. This is in no way meant to push aside the profound impact that English culture had on Afro-Americans, but rather to remind us that Afro-American culture was neither uniform nor static. Much of what influenced the growth of this culture was the urban nature of Boston; the port of Boston contributed to the diversity of the culture while at the same time, because of its geography and settlement patterns, the city enabled Afro-Americans to be in close contact. Although the ratio of white people to Afro-Americans was high in Boston, we cannot necessarily assume that white culture would also have been overwhelming. Herskovits points out that it is not just in rural and remote Southern plantations that one can expect the retention of native culture, but that "the anonymity of city life is often conducive to carrying on outlawed customs and beliefs when they can be quietly pursued, or to furthering activities under a ban in disguised form" (Herskovits 1958:124). He adds that city dwellers had more access to wealth accumulation, which was prerequisite to certain rituals and cultural activities.

White Bostonians, more than any other Northern community, contributed to the emergence of the different Afro-American cultures in Boston over time. Bostonians clearly concerned themselves with separating "barbarians" from "Christians" in the seventeenth century and "negroes, mulattoes and Indians" from whites in the eighteenth century. This dogged racism, even after Emancipation by 1790, excluded all black people from white society. The Afro-American community responded by forming its own society, with its own customs, social strata, and institutions. This response to shifting but persistent racism is only vaguely found in seventeenth-century documents, coming to a sharper focus in the eighteenth century. There is a clear role here for historical archaeology to provide an understanding of these forerunners of the vibrant culture of the eighteenth century. To be successful, historical archaeologists must approach Boston's Afro-American culture history with an acute awareness of its diversity over time. We must be alert for a range of cultural influences including West African, East African, Caribbean, French West Indian, English, New England Native American, Southern Native American, and Southern Afro-American. We also must be prepared to look for Afro-American material culture and patterning on a wider variety of sites, and not identify as Afro-American only sites with Afro-American heads of household; and we must consider not only the influence of English culture on Afro-

Americans, but also the influence of black culture on the everyday lives of white Bostonians.

REFERENCES

Baker, V. (1980) "Archaeological Visibility of Afro-American Culture: An Example from Black Lucy's Garden, Andover, Mass." In *Archaeological Perspectives on Ethnicity in America*, ed. R. L. Schuyler, pp. 29–37. Baywood Publishing Co., Farmingdale, NY.

Berlin, I. (1980) "Time, Space and the Evolution of Afro-American Society in British Mainland North America." *American Historical Review* 85(1), 44–78.

Bower, B. A. and B. Rushing (1980) "The African Meeting House: The Center for the 19th Century Afro-American Community in Boston." In *Archaeological Perspectives on Ethnicity in America*, ed. R. L. Schuyler, pp. 69–75. Baywood Publishing Co., Farmingdale, NY.

Deetz, J. (1977) *In Small Things Forgotten*. Anchor Books, New York.

Ferguson, L. (1980) "Looking for the 'Afro' in Colono-Indian Pottery." In *Archaeological Perspectives on Ethnicity in America*, ed. R. L. Schuyler, pp. 14–28. Baywood Publishing Co., Farmingdale, NY.

Geismar, J. H. (1982) *The Archeology of Social Disintegration in Skunk Hollow: A Nineteenth Century Rural Black Community*. Academic Press, New York.

Greene, L. (1942) *The Negro in Colonial New England, 1620–1776*. Columbia University Press, NY.

Herskovits, M. (1958) *The Myth of the Negro Past*. Beacon Press, Boston.

Horton, J. and L. Horton (1979) *Black Bostonians: Family Life and Community Struggle in the Antebellum North*. Holmes and Meier Publishers, New York.

Jacobs, D. (1968) *A History of the Boston Negro from the Revolution to the Civil War*. Unpublished Ph.D. Dissertation, Boston University, Boston.

Jennings, J. (1947) *Boston, Cradle of Liberty: 1630–1776*. Doubleday and Co., Garden City, NY.

Josslyn, J. (1833) *An Account of Two Voyages to New England, made during the years 1618, 1663*. Massachusetts Historical Society Collections, Third Series. Boston.

Levesque, G. A. (1976) *Black Boston: Negro Life in Garrison's Boston, 1800–1860*. Unpublished Ph.D. Dissertation, State University of New York, Binghamton, NY.

Moore, G. H. (1866) *Notes on Slavery in Massachusetts*. D. Appleton and Co.; reprinted 1968, Negro Universities Press, New York.

Nash, G. B. (1979) *The Urban Crucible: Social Change, Political Consciousness and the Origins of the American Revolution*. Harvard University Press, Cambridge, MA.

Orser, C. E., Jr (1988) "Toward a Theory of Power for Historical Archaeology: Plantations and Space." In *The Recovery of Meaning: Historical Archaeology in the Eastern United States*, eds M. P. Leone and P. B. Potter, Jr, pp. 313–43. Smithsonian Institution, Washington, D.C.

Otto, J. S. (1984) *Cannon's Point Plantation, 1794–1860: Living Conditions and Status Patterns in the Old South.* Academic Press, Orlando.
Piersen, W. D. (1988) *Black Yankees.* University of Massachusetts Press, Amherst, MA.
Pleck, E. (1979) *Black Migration and Poverty.* Academic Press, New York.
Quarles, B. (1973) *The Negro in the American Revolution.* W. W. Norton and Co., New York.
Schuyler, R. L. (1980) "Sandy Ground: Archaeology of a 19th Century Oystering Village." In *Archaeological Perspectives on Ethnicity in America,* ed. R. L. Schuyler, pp. 48–59. Baywood Publishing Co., Farmingdale, NY.
Singleton, T. (ed.) (1985) *The Archaeology of Slavery and Plantation Life.* Academic Press, Orlando.
——(1988) "An Archaeological Framework for Slavery and Emancipation, 1740–1880." In *The Recovery of Meaning: Historical Archaeology in the Eastern United States,* eds M. P. Leone and P. B. Potter, Jr, pp. 345–70. Smithsonian Institution, Washington, D.C.
Watkins, M. and I. Noel Hume (1967) "The 'Poor Potter' of Yorktown." *United States National Museum Bulletin* 249(54), 73–112. Smithsonian Institution, Washington, D.C.
White, A. (1971) *Blacks and Education in Antebellum Massachusetts. Strategies for Social Mobility.* Unpublished Ph.D. Dissertation, State University of New York at Buffalo, NY.

5

The Northern Cheyenne Outbreak of 1879: Using Oral History and Archaeology as Tools of Resistance

J. Douglas McDonald, Larry J. Zimmerman, A. L. McDonald, William Tall Bull, and Ted Rising Sun

Introduction

The Northern Cheyenne people have long resisted domination by outside forces. They participated in active military resistance to Euro-American settlement during the latter half of the nineteenth century; since the mid-twentieth century they have fought against takeover of their lands in Montana by energy companies (Ashabranner 1982). This paper documents one of their many efforts to counter the dominant culture's telling of historical events about the Cheyenne.

The Cheyenne recently employed archaeology to document their own version of an important incident in their resistance to domination during the Cheyenne "Outbreak" from Fort Robinson, Nebraska, during the winter of 1879. For several generations, the Northern Cheyenne have heard, and some have accepted as truth, the white version of how the Outbreak occurred and which escape routes the Cheyenne chief Dull Knife's people took; however, the Northern Cheyenne oral history of the event differs substantially from that of the military. This paper will show how archaeology was used to bolster the case for the Cheyenne version of the Outbreak; at the same time, by example, we hope to show how archaeology and history are used for domination, but how they can also become tools of resistance.

History and Cheyenne Traditions of the Outbreak of 1879

During the summer of 1987, the Northern Cheyenne tribe of southeastern Montana collaborated on a project with archaeologists from the University of South Dakota Archaeology Laboratory in an effort to substantiate Northern Cheyenne oral history concerning the Cheyenne Outbreak from Fort Robinson on January 9, 1879. Dull Knife Memorial College, a community college on the Northern Cheyenne reservation, was in the process of acquiring a 365-acre plot of land near Fort Robinson (figure 5.1). The plot was of particular interest to the college in that the domain contained the escape route taken by Dull Knife's band during the Outbreak. The escape route had been a point of contention for years with white accounts establishing one route and Cheyenne accounts supporting alternative routes; the college hoped that the use of archaeology might shed some light on the controversy. Ultimately, the college and the Northern Cheyenne Tribe wish to construct a commemorative path along the escape route and perhaps build a visitors' center to tell their story.

That the versions of the escape story vary is not surprising. The flight of the Cheyenne from Indian Territory is an account of courage and daring, one that caused great confusion for the Euro-Americans of the period. That story bears retelling, especially where Cheyenne tradition differs from white history.

The flight from Indian Territory and the Outbreak

Considerable confusion surrounded the Medicine Lodge Treaty of 1867, ratified by Congress in 1868. The most significant misunderstanding, and the one that ultimately led to the Cheyenne Outbreak, was that many of the chiefs who signed the Treaty did not understand that they and their people were to be moved south to "Indian Territory," in present-day Oklahoma. In November of 1872, a party of chiefs from several Northern plains tribes traveled to Washington to express to President Grant their desire to stay in the North. Dull Knife and Little Wolf of the Northern Cheyenne were present at this meeting. Their firm refusal to move south forced Grant to allow them to stay, but only temporarily. However, with the Custer Massacre at Little Big Horn in 1876, Dull Knife and Little Wolf knew they were in for trouble despite the fact that they and their followers were not involved in the battle (Ashabranner 1982:37–9).

Fearing the repercussions that were sure to follow the defeat of Custer, Dull Knife and Little Wolf sought refuge along the Powder

River in the Big Horn Mountains. Soldiers under the command of General R. S. Mackenzie discovered and routed the Cheyenne, destroying their food supply and killing many horses. This was a significant defeat for the Cheyenne, for it was the loss of this battle that caused some among them to consider surrender for the first time. Under the leadership of Dull Knife, they eventually surrendered to General Mackenzie at Fort Robinson in western Nebraska in April, 1877. The government's desire was to consolidate the Northern and Southern Cheyenne tribes, although the tribes had by then evolved into somewhat different peoples, living in totally different environments. After much deliberation, the Cheyenne finally consented to move south for Indian Territory on what they considered a trial basis. The journey was a difficult one, taking 70 days.

Immediately upon their arrival at Darlington Agency (Fort Reno) near present-day Oklahoma City in August, 1877, the Cheyenne were racked with sickness. Exposure to the unfamiliar southern Indians, combined with exhaustion, insufficient food and clothing, and unfamiliar climate caused the deaths of many of their number. For the more than five thousand Indians living at the Darlington Agency at that time, only one doctor was stationed; he was given almost no medical supplies, and none arrived for nearly a year. Over two-thirds of the northerners were soon sick with fever and plague. That winter, 41 Northern Cheyenne died (Grinnell 1915:400–1; Report of Indian Commissioners for 1879; Sandoz 1953:11).

Mounting pressure from Dull Knife's and Little Wolf's people, combined with the chiefs' own miseries (Dull Knife had contracted pneumonia), caused them to flee north to their homeland in September of 1878. They made no secret of their desires and plans to leave. In council with the Indian Agent Miles, Dull Knife stated simply: "My friend, I am leaving," and left the room with his family. Little Wolf went so far as to ask that the soldiers allow the Cheyenne to travel a few days' journey from the post before setting after them. He said that some of his people wished to remain and they did not wish to bloody the ground of their future home. He stated that when the inevitable fighting began, he wanted it to begin away from their relatives and friends who had chosen to stay (Ashabranner 1982:42).

The 353 Cheyenne staged a remarkable running battle with the military never able to overtake them. Even though the Indians were still in extremely poor physical health, and had few horses, scant provisions, and relatively few firearms, they managed to elude the soldiers for many miles and had only four major encounters. After the band crossed the North Platte River in Nebraska, they split into two groups; one was led by Dull Knife, the other by Little Wolf. Little Wolf wished to return to the Powder River country, while Dull Knife mistakenly figured that they would be safe at the Red Cloud Agency near Fort Robinson; but he did not know that Red Cloud had been relocated to Pine Ridge. Little Wolf's band settled into the Sand Hills of northwestern Nebraska for a relatively peaceful winter. Dull Knife's people were not so lucky. In late October of 1878, the Third Cavalry from Fort Robinson located Dull Knife and persuaded him to surrender. The surrender was not without incident. When the young men learned that the group was being conducted to Fort Robinson, they incited the people to scatter and dig rifle pits for a "last stand," but eventually the entire group was rounded up and led to the fort.

On the way to Fort Robinson, a seemingly trivial event took place that would have disastrous consequences later. Leaf, the wife of Bull Hump (Dull Knife's son) jumped from a wagon and hid in the snow as the convoy moved past. Once the Indians were settled in, she entered the camp, disguised as a male Sioux scout, and convinced Bull Hump to come away with her. Dull Knife's people had a decent time for a month or so, having the run of the fort and permission to hunt (from which activity many feel that reconnaissance of the terrain was secretly conducted). One day, the cook discovered the absence of Bull Hump by having one cup too many at breakfast time. Although the cook kept Bull Hump's flight secret for a day, he finally alerted Captain Wessels, the commanding officer. Although both Bull Hump and Leaf were recaptured, the Cheyenne were locked into their barracks and told they would be sent south to Indian Territory again. Dull Knife flatly refused, and stated that they would all die before returning to the "land of sickness." Shortly thereafter, Wessels cut off the Indians' food rations in an attempt to starve them into submission, a plan that failed. He then cut off the water supply, but still the Cheyenne refused to consent to the journey south. After five days with no food, and three with no water (accounts vary on the exact number of days for both), and the imprisonment of Wild Hog, Crow, and Strong Left Hand – all three, influential leaders – the Indians had had enough.

On the bright, moonlit evening of January 9, 1879, Dull Knife's people broke from the barracks. Although they had only five rifles and an assortment of old pistols, they staged a running battle that saw nearly half of them killed and scattered along the way. They fought their way across the old parade grounds, down to the bridge over the White River, and headed upstream. Some of the young men carried saddles, and forged ahead to attempt the theft of horses from the Bronson Ranch on Dead Man's Creek (Sandoz 1953:204, 221, 225). However, Bronson's ranch, and those for miles around, had been alerted to the possibility of the breakout; therefore, all stock had been gathered and was under heavy guard.

At some point along the White River, approximately two and a half miles west of the fort, the Indians crossed the river again and headed for the sandstone bluffs. (It is at this point that the group crossed the land now owned by Dull Knife Memorial College on which the survey was conducted to ascertain the exact escape route.) They made their way to the cliffs and through one of two cracks in the rocks that would allow passage. Those who survived to the top of the ridge were pursued for eleven more days – much to the embarrassment of the soldiers – and finally killed in a small buffalo wallow on Antelope Creek, almost 25 miles from Fort Robinson. Only a handful lived from this "last stand" to be taken back to the fort.

Sixty-four Cheyenne were killed during the Outbreak. The surviving male leaders (Crow, Tangle Hair, Strong Left Hand, Wild Hog, and Porcupine) and their families were sent to Dodge City, Kansas, for trial; the remainder were sent to the Pine Ridge agency of the Sioux. Dull Knife and his family had escaped death by hiding in a cave. They later made their way, undetected, to the house of William Rowland, the half-Cheyenne interpreter for the fort, from where they were taken to the Pine Ridge agency. Eventually, the remnant of Dull Knife's band settled on the Tongue River Reservation in southeastern Montana (Stands in Timber 1967:236–7; Grinnell 1915:426–7).

Controversy over escape routes

The major concern of the Northern Cheyenne for this project was that the version of the escape consistently discussed by military and local history accounts designate an area for the escape routes of Dull Knife's band that is incongruent with Northern Cheyenne oral tradition. The military accounts, and even a roadside historical marker, all name the section marked Area C on figure 5.1 as the escape route. Area C is a long, barren ridge rising to a crest. The Cheyenne have long disputed this route; Rising Sun remembers his grandmother, who escaped in the Outbreak, showing him a route going through Areas A and B (figure 5.1) to the west-northwest following a drainage.

Archaeological Research

Fieldwork consisted of a joint venture involving a survey crew of four from the University of South Dakota Archaeology Laboratory and three representatives of Dull Knife Memorial College and the Northern Cheyenne Cultural Committee. Four days of intensive survey were conducted on the site. The fieldwork was coordinated with the

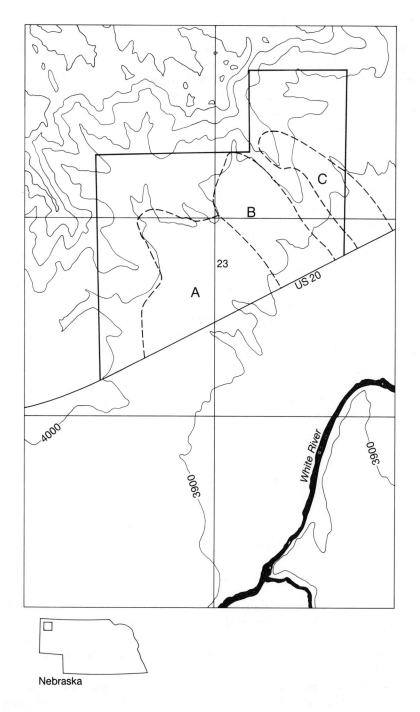

Figure 5.1 Survey project: Areas A, B, and C, near Fort Robinson, Nebraska

representatives of the Northern Cheyenne tribe who provided geographical guidance while maintaining the spiritual and religious integrity of the project. Prayers and story-telling were incorporated into the research being conducted by the USD crew, and both groups were satisfied with the special reverence paid to the land and artifacts recovered.

Primary field techniques during the survey consisted of visual inspection and periodic random shovel testing. These techniques were enhanced by three metal detectors, which were in constant use. Every metal target alert was investigated since it was assumed that the most diagnostic artifacts recovered would be spent ammunition, rounds shot by or at the escaping Cheyenne.

The project area was divided into three sections according to their geographical and ethnohistorical significance and the frequency and pattern of artifacts recovered (figure 5.1). The bare ridge that comprises Area C is, as stated above, the route presented by historians to the modern Northern Cheyenne as the escape route; no artifacts of any kind were recovered in Area C.

Areas A and B contain the two major drainages of the project area; these areas produced a number of artifacts possibly deposited during the Cheyenne Outbreak. There is abundant natural cover, and old photographs of the area suggest that the landscape was very similar to that of today. Areas A and B also coincide with the routes recounted by past elders of the Northern Cheyenne tribe who participated in the Outbreak.

Listing and discussion of artifacts found

The following is a listing and summary of all munitions recovered during the survey. All metal artifacts were discovered by metal detectors, and all were either on the surface, or at depths not exceeding 10 centimeters. Other artifacts were recovered, but most were of recent origin. The artifacts are listed according to the day they were recovered, and the area from which they were recovered.

June 23, 1987: artifacts from Area B

1 Two lead pistol balls, flattened from impact on one side. These balls appear to be 0.41 caliber, and show only slight oxidation.
2 One large rifle bullet, flattened on anterior end from impact. Bullet is 0.58 caliber, 512 grains, 33.2 grams and believed to fit Enfield Rifle. Bullet is very oxidized.
3 One rifle bullet, flattened on anterior end from impact. Bullet is 0.50 caliber, believed to fit broad range of rifles of that period, including the popular Sharp's model. Bullet is slightly oxidized.

4   Five deformed bullet fragments. These appear to be flattened pistol balls.

June 24, 1987: Area B

1   One 0.45 caliber, rimmed, Benet Cup (center-fire, inside primed) pistol cartridge casing. Benet Cup priming was discontinued in 1882. The 0.45 caliber was one of several standard army pistol issues of the time of the Cheyenne Outbreak.
2   One 0.50 caliber outside primed copper cartridge. Probably of later issue, due to external primer – used more commonly *after* 1882.

June 25, 1987: Area A

1   Four deformed lead bullet fragments, torn beyond recognition from impact. Each is heavily oxidized, showing extreme weathering.
2   Two 0.44 caliber lead pistol balls, 136 grains, 8.8 grams. These balls show signs of ramrod tamping and are extremely weathered and oxidized.
3   One undeformed 45–70 caliber hollow base bullet, 405 grains, 26 grams. The 45–70 carbine was standard infantry and cavalry issue during the later 1870s to mid–1880s. The triple basal rings identify the bullet as being from that time period.
4   One heavily oxidized and weathered 0.44 caliber lead bullet, 200 grains, 12.6 grams. believed to fit either Henry or Winchester rifles, or possibly a Colt revolver (of which the Cheyenne had several). Believed to fit a rim-fire cartridge.
5   One side-notched, straight based, triangular projectile point. Point is rather small, 22mm × 11mm (base width), unifacially flaked, made from white chert. This point could have been deposited at any time in probably the last 500 years, but was considered significant due to the context in which it was discovered. The point was recovered at the same level, and within several feet of all other artifacts (ammunition) in Area A.

June 26, 1987: Area B

1   One 0.50 caliber rifle ball, 173 grains, 11.2 grams. Shows evidence of ramrod tamping, very oxidized and weathered. May have come from a host of 0.50 caliber rifles of that era, of which the Sharp's was the most popular.
2   One deformed 0.58 caliber lead bullet, 512 grains, 33.2 grams, hollow base, triple basal grooves – identical to previously mentioned 0.58 caliber slug.

Field research conclusions

Taking into account all information gathered from every available source, the escape routes discussed in Northern Cheyenne oral history are more acceptable than that presented by the military and local historians. It is understood that no single article of information (the artifacts recovered, the ethnohistoric accounts, the available literature, etc.) is alone sufficient to reach this conclusion. But although other explanations for the types and distribution of artifacts are possible, the weight of all the types of evidence taken together dramatically favor Northern Cheyenne oral history.

Though seemingly trivial, this controversy takes on a much greater significance for the Northern Cheyenne than might be assumed. In essence, if they accept the white version, they must thereby accept that Dull Knife and his people made a very foolish mistake, one that seems totally out of the ordinary for all they know of him. The army claims the Cheyenne moved up the ridge to arrive at the sandstone cliffs: ethnohistoric accounts by grandchildren (Tall Bull and Rising Sun) of actual participants of the Outbreak dispute this as not only inaccurate, but illogical. On a moonlit night, why would people who are being hotly pursued "skyline" themselves, thereby presenting easy targets? It seems unlikely that a group of people who made a habit of successfully eluding the army on the open plains would behave in such a way, even when in flight and disarray. They speculate, but have no oral tradition to document it, that some of the "Dog Soldiers," whose job was to guard escape, might have acted as decoy to draw pursuers onto the ridge.

A more likely solution is offered by the present-day Northern Cheyenne. After failing to secure horses at the Bronson Ranch, the people struck straight north, across the White River at the mouth of Dead Man's Creek. Such a maneuver would reduce the necessary distance to travel without cover by nearly half and would provide them with cover in the draws on the *other side* of Area C. This scenario is supported by the lack of artifacts in Area C. There has been, to the best of anyone's knowledge, *no firm evidence* that the Indians fled up the exposed ridge in Area C; in none of the accounts of the official inquiry was it suggested that the Indians took this route. The map provided in the report of the Board of Inquiry (figure 5.2) sheds absolutely no light on exactly where the Cheyenne might have crossed the land now owned by Dull Knife Memorial College (DKMC).

There is therefore no reason not to accept the Northern Cheyenne version. First-hand ethnohistoric accounts by members of Dull Knife's band were available to the Cheyenne people as late as 1953, at which time the last known participant in the Outbreak still living (Ted Rising Sun's

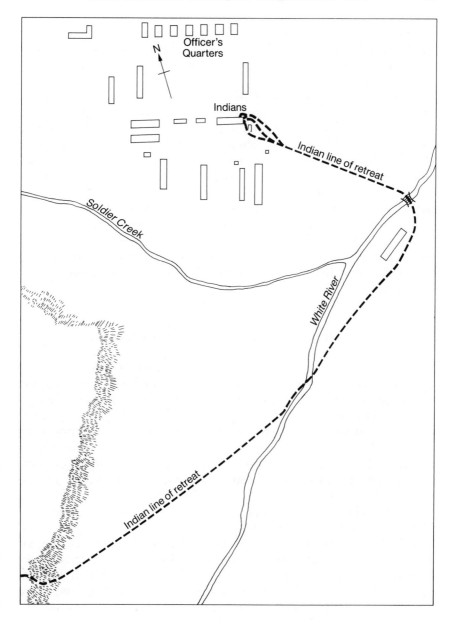

Figure 5.2 Hand-drawn map of Fort Robinson showing the flight of Dull Knife's band (after US Army Board of Inquiry, Feb. 1879).

grandmother) passed away. There are a number of Northern Cheyenne people alive today who were raised listening to accounts and stories of the Outbreak by several elders who were directly involved. Several of these people (Tall Bull, Rising Sun) are well acquainted with both the story and the terrain surrounding the Cheyenne Outbreak. It makes little sense to these people why the Indians would have chosen to expose themselves for such a long period of time on a moonlit night. Further, such a route would not have allowed for a rendezvous with the young men believed to have forged ahead to steal horses from the Bronson Ranch. This route is also incongruent with what the modern-day Cheyenne believe their people "would have done" – which must be taken as a serious point. The survey crew did recover artifacts in the areas considered as more favorable by the representatives of DKMC and the Northern Cheyenne tribe. Finally, several of the elders who participated in the Oubtreak spoke of using the natural cover of the land – trees, rocks, and washouts – as they ran. No such cover exists on Area C, nor do old photographs of the area indicate that there was any more cover at that time.

Oral History as a Form of Resistance

The results of this survey were met with skepticism by historians of the episode, who point out the inaccuracy of oral tradition and the difficulties of linking it to real events. Understanding their reluctance is difficult until one considers the investment that a people have in their version of history. The Cheyenne Outbreak is a quasi-classic story of the American West, well documented from the white point of view in book (Sandoz 1953) and film. To allow a challenge by Indians to the historical view undermines a vital tool of domination: the fact that *victors* write the history of events, especially of the subordinated group's efforts at resistance. This can be illustrated by examining how the Cheyenne Outbreak was treated in the film.

John Ford's classic Western film *Cheyenne Autumn* remains an important symbol of how the dominant society in America views Indians: as simply an interesting sidebar to American history. Indeed the whole telling of the *Cheyenne Autumn* story is done from the white perspective. The major part of the cast, even the Indians, is non-Indian; Gilbert Roland as Dull Knife and Ricardo Montalban as Little Wolf seem minor characters compared to Richard Widmark as the hero military officer who pursues the Northern Cheyenne as they escape from Indian Territory back to their homelands on the northern Plains, and who helps them eventually win freedom. Cheyenne women are

reduced to translators so that Carroll Baker, as a white Quaker, can tell
the story of the escape from the "inside." Indian children are reduced to
willing acceptors of white culture to show how white Indian-haters can
be converted. The end product is a moral tale of the Old West,
supporting America's "Manifest Destiny" and salving the American
conscience about the treatment of Indians. At the same time *Cheyenne
Autumn*, like many other films and books about Indian–white relations,
is a tool of domination.

The problems of perspective and historical license are common
enough in fiction and film, but do have the insidious effect, when such
errors are repeated often enough, of validating historical inaccuracies.
For the dominant society, even educated audiences capable of evaluating
the factuality of the particular case, succumb to the constant repetition
which reinforces dominant culture ideologies. Even for those in the
subordinate culture, the repeated structures can eventually become
accepted and the subordinated thereby participate in their own oppression.
Greater historical accuracy, one might think, should ameliorate the
problem, but such is not the case. History and its auxiliary science of
archaeology become part of the architecture by which people are
dominated.

Most people, including most archaeologists, might assume that the
history or prehistory they write is basically value-neutral, simply a
telling of events as they occurred at some time in the past. Few might
recognize that the historical disciplines themselves are products of
Western tradition and thereby can become tools for use in the
subordination of non-Western peoples. As products of their own
culture, many scholars cannot understand that even the concepts of time
and the past can vary substantially between cultures (Zimmerman 1987).
Versions of why and how events happened can be vastly different or
only slightly so, but with emphasis placed on different parts of the same
event. As a case in point, Native Americans have been profoundly
disturbed at archaeological constructions of an Indian past. At the broadest
level, for example, archaeologists believe that the idea that the Indians'
ancestors crossed the Bering Land Bridge sometime during the last
glaciation is founded on incontrovertible evidence. Many traditionally
oriented Indians, on the other hand, dispute an Asiatic origin and claim
that their people were created in place during some ancient time.

Since the 1960s many non-Indian notions and images of the American
Indian have changed substantially from earlier periods. Indian political
resurgence has defiantly claimed "the right once again [for Indians] to
make their own choices" (Cornell 1988:4). Among the many rights
claimed is the right to a control over the telling of their own past. That
there can be more than one version of the past, especially a version

differing from that constructed by members of the dominant society, is difficult for both Indians and non-Indians to comprehend.

For Indians, subjugation has kept the past of their oral traditions silent outside their own culture. Years of telling the story by white sources has added validity to white history, often co-opting Indians into the dominant society's version. Non-Indians created a version of Indian history told from the view of the "victors," a view that locked Indians into the period of the ethnographic present. For Indians, this has posed a real dilemma; as Deloria (1973:49) summarizes the problem, "the tragedy of America's Indians . . . is that they no longer exist, except in the pages of books."

Non-Indians mostly have viewed Indian peoples as natives or primitives. Following Gill (1982:2–5), non-Indians are involved in a complex ambivalence towards Indians. On one hand, Indians are everything non-Indians aren't and everything non-Indians despise; on the other, they are everything whites admire. Whites are sophisticated while the native is crude, naive and savage. At the same time, the native is the bringer of culture, the basic form of humankind, a wholly natural child of the earth and sky and part of the ecological system, and a prototype. The non-Indian image of Indian, therefore, is an image of a non-Indian self, insidiously forced on Indian people, making them conform to the expectations of non-Indians. Thus, the dominant society creates an ideological structure and imposes it on Indian peoples, coercing them into participating in their own oppression. In white construction of the history of Indian–white relations (cf. Rubertone 1989), nowhere is this more clearly seen than in the accounts of military confrontations between the groups. Historical accounts of battles written by whites contain elements of this ideological structure of ambivalence: Indians were despised as cunning, ruthless, and bloodthirsty savages, yet at the same time, admired as noble warriors with consummate skill, daring, strategy, and tenacity in the face of overwhelming white technological superiority and numbers. In the end, however, the stories of such battles are told from a white perspective.

Even when archaeology is employed to find the "truth" about battles, it usually seeks a white truth. For example, recent excellent archaeological work was done on the site of the Custer Battlefield in eastern Montana and widely publicized in the media. The analysis focused on armament, weapon types and numbers; the chronology of the Little Big Horn fight; the analysis of human remains; campaign equipment; and the Deep Ravine question as a way to guide research (Scott et al. 1989:8–9). From information about these issues, they hoped to be able to document a post-Civil War battlefield pattern. Every perspective in the volume is white, and virtually no effort is made to incorporate or corroborate a rather substantial Indian oral history about the episode, turning to it only when there is no other form of evidence. Every concern is about Custer and his men and their battle tactics. This is not to say that the Battle of the Greasy Grass (an Indian name for the same battle) report is bad archaeology; quite the opposite is true. The battle of the Little Big Horn report is a superior example of how white archaeology is used for white purposes.

Conclusion

At the same time, when history and archaeology are used by dominated groups, they can become tools capable of allowing the groups to free themselves from participation in the dominant ideology. The Northern Cheyenne were quite pleased with the results of the application of archaeological research to one of their concerns. They came to understand that their long-felt mistrust of archaeology might no longer be necessary. Both the archaeologists and the Northern Cheyenne learned that they can be natural allies, sometimes each possessing what the other needs.

The tribes need the knowledge of identification and preservation that are intrinsic to archaeology. This knowledge will allow them to research and preserve their own cultural and material history. The archaeologist needs access to lands, information, and materials controlled by the tribes. If a positive working relationship, based on mutual trust and a desire to fashion as complete a mosaic of the past as possible, including an Indian view, can be established, then historical and prehistorical "truth" need not be as elusive as it has been for both sides. If the methods of archaeology are applied directly by Indians, archaeology will become an even more effective tool for resistance, used to bolster oral history.

REFERENCES

Ashabranner, Brent (1982) *Morning Star, Black Sun*. Dodd, Mead and Company, New York.
Board of Indians Commissioners (1880) *Eleventh Annual Report of the Board of Indian Commissioners for the Year 1879*. Government Printing Office, Washington, D.C.
Cornell, Stephen (1988) *The Return of the Native: American Indian Political Resurgence*. Oxford University Press, New York.
Deloria, Vine, Jr (1973) *God is Red*. Delta Books, New York.
Gill, Sam (1982) *Beyond the Primitive: The Religions of Nonliterate Peoples*. Prentice-Hall, Englewood Cliffs, NJ.

Grinnell, G. B. (1915) *The Fighting Cheyennes*. Scribner Publishing, New York.

Rubertone, Patricia (1989) "Archaeology, Colonialism and 17th–Century Native America: Towards an Alternative Interpretation." In *Conflict in the Archaeology of Living Traditions*, ed. Robert Layton, pp. 32–45. Unwin Hyman, London.

Sandoz, Mari (1953) *Cheyenne Autumn*. McGraw-Hill Co., New York.

Scott, Douglas, Richard Fox, Melissa Connor and Dick Harmon (1989) *Archaeological Perspectives on the Battle of the Little Bighorn*. University of Oklahoma Press, Norman.

Stands In Timber, John (1967) *Cheyenne Memories*. Yale University Press, New Haven, CT.

Zimmerman, Larry (1987) "The Impact of the Concepts of Time and Past on the Concept of Archaeology: Some Lessons from the Reburial Issue." *Archaeological Review from Cambridge* 6(1), 42–50.

6

Landscapes of Inequality

Stephen A. Mrozowski[1]

Introduction

If you walk through the residential neighborhoods of most large cities in the United States you will see little if any space used for food production. There are gardens, of course; in fact in most modern cities space has been allotted for community or council gardens in addition to the numerous small plots found in the yards of some households. In the United States these gardens seldom provide more than a seasonal supply of fresh vegetables, herbs or flowers. From studies of modern gardeners in New England it does not appear that their activities could be classified as productive labor in a pure economic sense (Mrozowski 1987a). That little space is utilized for food production in most modern American cities says more about the land use practices which accompany urban capitalism in the United States than it does about modern urban centers on a global scale; in Hong Kong, for example, a distinctly capitalist city, large areas are allotted for household food production (Douglas 1983).

Modern American cities also differ from their pre-industrial predecessors in Britain and Europe, wherein large tracts of land were set aside for food production and other subsistence activities. In some cases these areas were immediately outside a city wall, but often they were within the boundaries of the community (Braudel 1981:484–7). Domestic space in Anglo-Saxon, Medieval and Post-Medieval towns in Britain was used for keeping livestock, kitchen gardening, activities relating to your occupation if you were a tradesman, as well as water and waste management (e.g., Platt 1975; Biddle 1976; Ashton and Bond 1987). The "Dark Earth" commonly found in Romano-British and Medieval towns has been attributed to market gardens (Macphail 1981:309–31). These pre-industrial, urban land use practices were reproduced in the New World; artisans living in the cities of New England utilized their

79

domestic space for a variety of purposes, including keeping pigs, gardening and activities related to their occupations (Mrozowski 1987b; Reinhard et al. 1986; see also Beaudry 1986; Pendery.1978).

By the end of the nineteenth century urban domestic space was no longer employed for productive activities. Where for centuries domestic space served as an area for work, now it performed more of an ornamental function. The same trend was also visible in the city as a whole where large tracts of land were set aside for parks; in addition, trees were purposely planted along residential streets as a way of tempering the brick and mortar of the city.

The reasons why this change took place were complex and global in scope. The impact on domestic space in urban communities was part of a larger transformation involving the emergence of a new spatial order of production in which work space was separated from domestic space. At the household level, production was being replaced by factory-based manufacturing. These changes also had ideological dimensions, what Braudel (1981:513–14) has called "a new state of mind" or what Harvey (1973:203) has referred to as "a way of life." In the city this state of mind or way of life was "predicated on, among other things, a certain hierarchical ordering of activity broadly consistent with the dominant mode of production" (Harvey 1973:203). The shift from mercantile capitalism to industrial capitalism involved the separation of work space from living space, thus a new urban landscape which was shaped by and in turn contributed to a new ideology.

This chapter examines the growth of urban society in New England during the eighteenth century and its transformation during the nineteenth century. I argue that the urban landscapes of eighteenth-century mercantile capitalism and nineteenth-century industrial capitalism were direct expressions of the spatial requirements of both economic regimes and the inequalities they engendered. In addition there emerged an urban ideology during the eighteenth century which was the antithesis of the agrarian mentalité present in New England's rural communities. Finally I argue that urbanization during the nineteenth century was predicated on a new set of spatial priorities which were influenced by both material and ideological forces and which shaped the urban landscape of the city at large, as well as the individual lots. The arguments are based upon data collected from studies conducted in Boston and Lowell, Massachusetts and Newport and Providence, Rhode Island.

The Evolution of an Urban Landscape

The evolution of the early modern urban landscape is inextricably linked with the development of the capitalist mode of production. Braudel puts it succinctly: "Capitalism and towns were basically the same thing in the West" (1981:514). In fact Braudel has argued that at the heart of every world-economy is a dominant capitalist city which serves as its "centre of gravity . . . as the logistic heart of its activity" (1984:27). However, urban landscapes don't change with every change in capitalist accumulation: "capital's needs at one moment in history are not necessarily consistent with later requirements" (Harvey 1982:403). The result is an urban landscape composed of the fixed capital accumulated during earlier periods of production which helped to stabilize a previous or present mode of production. The same landscape may, however, contain contradictory elements which could give rise to a new mode of production (Harvey 1973:203). For this reason it is imperative that the prerequisite conditions of the eighteenth century be considered as a point of departure for examining nineteenth-century urbanization in New England.

Colonization and Commercial Growth

Cities played a pivotal role in the colonization of New England. Mercantile capitalism depended upon shipping for the transportation of goods, people, and information to and from the New World. Several port communities emerged to organize this trade; in New England the major entrepôts included Boston in the Massachusetts Bay colony and Newport in Rhode Island.

It was the waterfront areas of both communities that first exhibited urbanization. With economic expansion and the influx of population efforts were made to begin constructing a commercial infrastructure. The most tangible products of this work were the wharves and warehouses that soon lined the waterfronts of both communities. A less visible, but equally important, change was the early filling of waterfront areas which resulted in the elimination of many wetland plant species and their replacement with new communities better adapted to the drier conditions (e.g., Kelso and Schoss 1983; Mrozowski 1985, 1987b). Land adjacent to the waterfront was subdivided in order to make space available for the many artisans, seamen and laborers whose work was tied to commercial shipping. The result was a pattern of mixed residential/commercial land use which characterized many of the seaport communities of eighteenth-

82   STEPHEN A. MROZOWSKI

century New England (e.g., Bradley 1983; Pendery 1978; Rubertone and Gallagher 1981; Perley 1924).

Commerce continued to fuel the expansion of New England's economy during the eighteenth century resulting in the accelerated growth of the region's port communities. This growth was distinctively urban in character so that although the areal extent of towns like Boston and Newport did not dramatically change, population density increased. One example of this is Newport's subdivision of its town common in 1706 to accommodate the growing number of newcomers who needed housing (Rudolph 1978:22). The subdivision of private land also accelerated during the first half of the eighteenth century (Mrozowski 1987b). By 1750 New England's urban villages were becoming densely populated communities experiencing some of the problems associated with the larger cities of the nineteenth century (see figures 6.1 and 6.2). For example, new acts were passed in 1707 to control the disposal of offensive waste from tanners in both Newport and Providence, suggesting they had become enough of a problem to require special legislation (Rhode Island Colonial Records Vol. IV:7–9, hereafter RICR). Analysis of soil from privies and yards suggests that intensive land use practices resulted in insanitary conditions in some households which contributed to the inhabitants becoming infected with a wide variety of parasites (Reinhard et al. 1986).

The wars between competing mercantile powers also helped shape the urban landscape. These conflicts meant increased wealth for some, but for many poor it meant great hardship. The ranks of the colonial militia who fought in these conflicts were filled primarily by farmers, laborers, indentured servants, and apprentices (Nash 1979:58). One result was increased population density in urban centers like Boston as the families of rural farmers migrated to the city; this increase in population put great pressure on Boston's housing. For the families of those who were killed, Boston became a temporary home, but limited housing meant over-crowding and the possible proliferation of makeshift dwellings. Low stocks of fuel led many to steal wood from fences and other structures. And a general lack of food may have resulted in the intensive exploitation of wild plants and animals, behavior which has been detected archaeologically on sites of this period in Newport (Mrozowski 1983; Reinhard et al. 1986).

Disease also gave a distinctive shape to the New England mercantile city. During the period 1738–42, for example, the Boston Selectmen's records are filled with cases concerning the outbreak of smallpox. One

Figure 6.1   Boston during the eighteenth century (courtesy of the Massachusetts Historical Society)

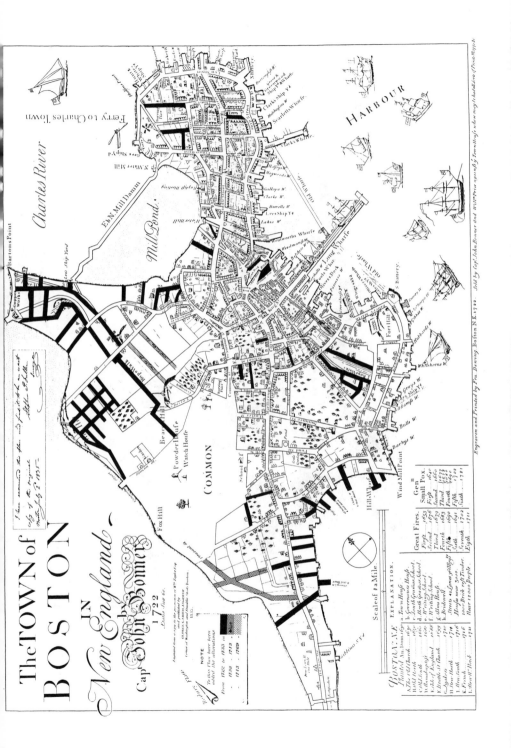

The TOWN of BOSTON IN New England ~ by Capt. John Bonner 1722

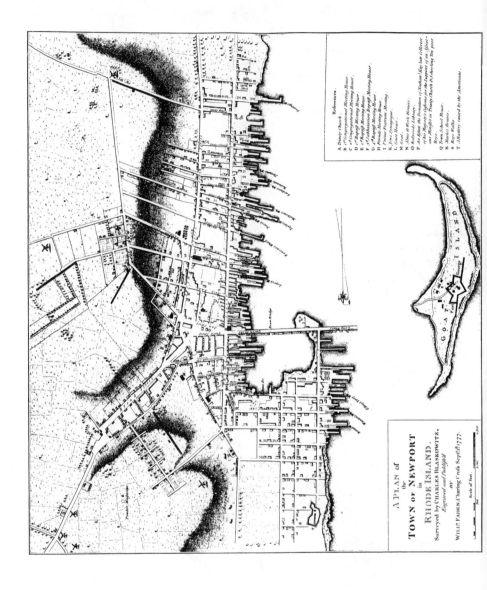

Figure 6.2 Newport, Massachusetts, in 1777 (courtesy of the Newport Historical Society)

aspect of this outbreak was the forced concentration of many of the ailing in the western part of the town (Records of the Boston Selectmen, 1736–1742).

The increased commercialization of the economy in New England's urban centers had a number of social consequences. For one, wealth became concentrated in fewer and fewer hands, as has been noted for Boston (e.g., Henretta 1965; Nash 1979), Newport (Rudolph 1978) and Providence (Cady 1957). This wealth concentration was related to emerging class distinctions that had an effect on the landscape. In Newport, for example, a petition set forth to the Colonial General Assembly in 1742 by "all the free-holders of the woods part of town" requested that the town be divided (RICR 1742, Vol. V:54), evidence of an emerging conflict between the farmers of the "woods part" of town and the "merchants and tradesmen" who resided in the "compact part of town":

> For as the compact part of said town consists chiefly of merchants and tradesmen, it would be their interest to make such suitable prudential acts for the better government of their affairs, so likewise as the woods part of said town consists of farmers, proper prudential laws and orders would be made suitable for their condition and circumstances without opposition, which, as yet hath not been observed.
>
> The petitioners also apprehend they are greatly injured being obliged to bear a greater proportion of the public charge and expense of said town . . . (RICR 1742, Vol. V:54–5)

A year later a separate community was established, called Middletown (RICR 1743, Vol. V:66–70).

Similar complaints were voiced by the farmers living in Providence, Rhode Island. Here again, agriculturalists were at odds with the merchants and artisans living in the more densely settled part of the community. Though this initial rupture failed to produce the sort of community fission that Newport experienced, none the less, by 1765 farmers in the northern portion of the town were successful in establishing a separate town which is today called North Providence (Cady 1957).

Both Rhode Island cases reveal the development of diverging societies; one distinctly urban and almost completely commercial, the other a more traditional agrarian society. The difference was clearly visible on the landscape. In the towns, land use was driven by a need for space along the waterfront. The resulting landscape was greatly compartmentalized with buildings, fences, small gangways, and yards used often for commercial activities. Rural households also used the space around their dwellings, traditionally called the croft (Anderson 1971), for work, but activities were more likely to have been associated with domestic production more than with commercial pursuits. Productive activities were found in the outlying fields or pastures known as the toft (Anderson 1971). Another difference was that on rural farmsteads the croft was traditionally the sphere of the women, while the toft, the fields and pastures, was worked by men. Among urban households such a distinction cannot be assumed. Until work space and domestic space were separated during the nineteenth century, urban yard space may have been utilized by both sexes.

Within the commercial cities, domestic land use varied according to occupation and wealth. Archaeological evidence gathered in Newport, for example, suggests that artisans relied upon their domestic space for productive activities which meant clutter and disease (Mrozowski 1987b; Reinhard et al. 1986). Merchants, by comparison, may not have utilized the space around their dwellings for activities relating to production (Mrozowski 1987b); instead, the evidence suggests well maintained yards that may have served an economic function as space for entertaining.

Although the Newport data represent only a small number of cases, the contrast between two occupational classes, merchants and artisans, is indicative of broader patterns. The violence which shook Boston periodically during the third quarter of the eighteenth century was not solely a reaction to British attempts to regulate the colonial economy. Nash (1979) has presented a strong argument for the growing class divisions which were polarizing Boston society. The image of an urban poor huddled in small impermanent shelters hurling human excrement at the coaches of the wealthy presents a romantic, and probably accurate, picture of what Boston was like during this period of revolutionary fervor.

New England cities on the eve of industrialization reflected the tensions and conflicts that were a part of mercantile capitalism. These tensions were manifest in a variety of ways: in the contrasting land use practices of urban artisans and the well-to-do and the growing division between urban and rural values. At the heart of the latter was an emerging urban ideology that saw land and resources merely as commodities to be exploited. Living in cities, urban dwellers appear to have seen the world differently from their rural brethren who still held to traditional agrarian values. It is the political conflicts between urban and rural populations which illustrate this most graphically. Under industrial capitalism these divisions would reveal an even more basic perceptual dichotomy between nature and society that would greatly influence the course of urbanization.

Another facet of nineteenth-century urbanization would be the landscapes of inequalities generated by a profit-minded economy and class distinctions which would become even more rigidly defined under the influence of industrial capitalism. In the planned industrial cities of Lowell, Massachusetts and Manchester, New Hampshire, class distinctions were institutionalized by a new landscape expressly suited for efficiency and control.

Industrialization

With the establishment of the Republic, great emphasis was placed on the development of native industry. The transformation of New England's economy from one based on mercantile capitalism to one rooted in industrial capitalism took place during the nineteenth century and resulted in the appearance of a new social order. Part of this process involved the transition from small-scale, shop-oriented manufacturing to full-blown, factory-based industry. This shift to mass production meant the consolidation of labor into larger units and a reorganization of the spatial ordering of cities as well. Most Americans involved in manufacturing sought to build a viable industry, but not necessarily one based on the English model. Writers of the period were at times candidly explicit regarding their reaction to British industrial cities. For example, upon his return from traveling in the English Midlands, Zachariah Allen (1832) wrote the following concerning Manchester: "God forbid, however fondly the patriot may cherish the hope of increasing the resources of his country . . . that there ever may arise a counterpart of Manchester in the New World" (reprinted in Kulik et al. 1982:7). As a result of this reaction to European industrialization, the landscapes of North American industrial capitalism look like a series of experiments. In some places, industry occurred in small rural villages of 100 workers, a practice known as "the Rhode Island System" (see Prude 1983). Company housing consisted of small cottage tenements; one-, two-, or four-family tenements were the most common. Scholars also note that "some companies staked out garden plots that mill village families could rent to raise part of their own food. Pasturage to support a family's cow could also be rented in some villages" (Parks and Folsom 1982:xxvii).

In striking contrast to these rural industrial villages were the large, planned industrial urban centers, the first and most notable being Lowell, Massachusetts. In 1830 Lowell was but an idea and a large expanse of pasture. Twenty years later it would be a thriving city of close to 20,000 (figure 6.3). The founders of the city, known as the "Boston Associates," had a vision of a benevolent but efficient community "dominated by the requirements of capital that shaped work and life

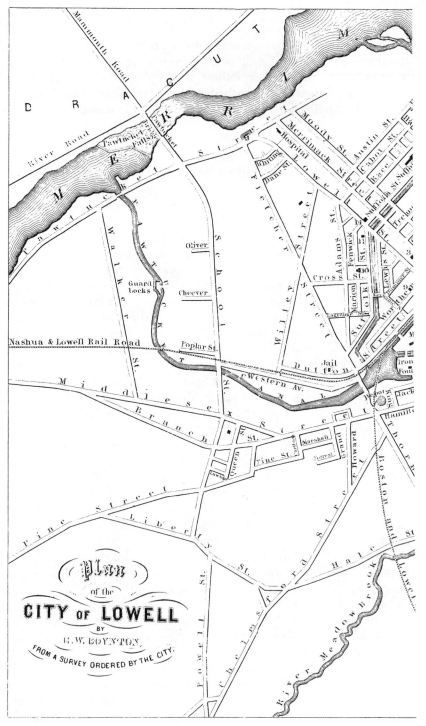

Figure 6.3 Lowell, Massachusetts, in 1845 (courtesy of the Lowell Historical Society)

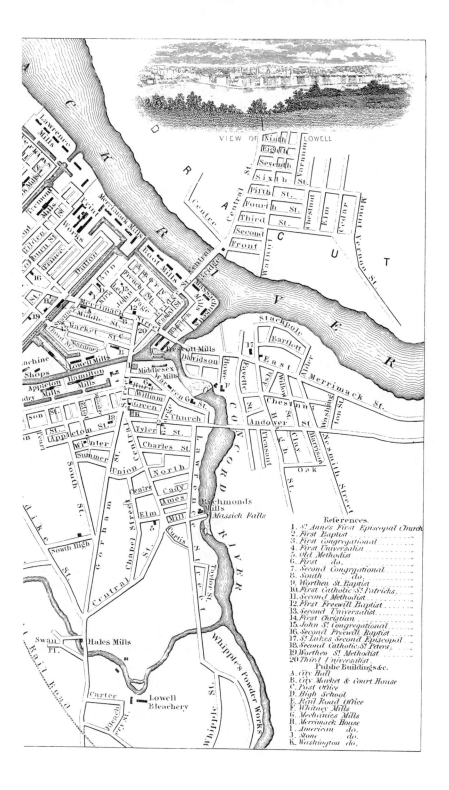

VIEW OF LOWELL

Ninth St.
Eighth St.
Seventh St.
Sixth St.
Fifth St.
Fourth St.
Third St.
Second St.
Front St.

Lawrence Mills

Merrimack Mills

Boot Mills

Prescott Mills
Davidson

Middlesex Mills

Hamilton Mills

Appleton Mills

Lowell Mills

Machine Shops

Lowell Bleachery

Hales Mills

Stackpole
Bartlett
East
Merrimack St.
Fayette
Chestnut
Andover St.
Oak St.

CONCORD RIVER

Richmonds Mills
Massick Falls

References.

1. St Anne's First Episcopal Church
2. First Baptist
3. First Congregational
4. First Universalist
5. Old Methodist
6. First do.
7. Second Congregational
8. South do.
9. Worthen St. Baptist
10. First Catholic St. Patricks
11. Second Methodist
12. First Freewill Baptist
13. Second Universalist
14. First Christian
15. John St. Congregational
16. Second Freewill Baptist
17. St Lukes Second Episcopal
18. Second Catholic St. Peters
19. Worthen St. Methodist
20. Third Universalist

Public Buildings &c.

A. City Hall
B. City Market & Court House
C. Post Office
D. High School
E. Rail Road Office
F. Whitney Mills
G. Mechanics Mills
H. Merrimack House
I. American do.
J. Stone do.
K. Washington do.

itself" (Gross and Wright 1985:15). The crux of the plan was the spatial arrangement of mill, workers' housing, and overseer's house (the mill agent): all three components of the system were within walking distance of one another. The resulting landscape was designed to function as a "strict system of moral police" (Miles 1846:128) as well as a means of deriving profits. By placing both work and living space under the control of the corporation, the founders of Lowell sought to construct a system analogous to the very machines upon which production was based. Workers and their housing merely became parts of the machine.

This dual concern for moral control and profit rested at the heart of corporate paternalism, the philosophy which formed the foundation not only of Lowell, but of other planned industrial communities as well (e.g., Hareven 1978; Candee 1985). Partially in response to concerns over industry's evolution in Britain and Europe, Lowell's founders hoped to answer critics with their system of "moral police." At the same time they sought to quell the reservations of the families of the young, mostly female operatives, who were to be the backbone of the factory system (see Dublin 1979, 1981). The reliance upon female labor was also calculated to answer those critics who saw industry as a drain on the agrarian labor force (see Parks and Folsom 1982). Though this part of the experiment would have only a short life, Lowell's founders were able to maintain control over the development of the city by concentrating their capital in a small number of large mill operations which were essentially identical to one another. This model, known as "the Waltham System." named after the Boston Associates' initial experiment in Waltham, Massachusetts, would be reproduced in a series of communities throughout New England (see Candee 1985).

Although previous archaeological investigations have been conducted in Lowell (e.g., Gorman et al. 1985; Schuyler 1974, 1976), the bulk of the information discussed in this paper is drawn from the Lowell Archaeological Survey Project which has focused on the Boott Cotton Mill operation (Beaudry and Mrozowski 1987a, 1987b).[2] To date excavations have been conducted at the former site of the Boott Mill Boarding Houses and at the Kirk Street Agent's House, the residence for the agents of both the Boott and Massachusetts Mills. The scope of the investigations of the Boott Mills has been interdisciplinary; however, the primary focus of this paper is the evolution of Lowell's urban landscape. What the results of this study suggest is that class distinctions built into the system developed at Lowell incorporated the landscape as an active agent in the reinforcement of these distinctions.

While the aim of corporate paternalism was the mutual wellbeing of both worker and owner, the ideal was governed by class distinctions as well as being subject to change over time. Class differences were expressed on the landscape in the form of contrasting architectural styles for mill workers' housing and agent's dwellings. The boarding houses were "typical of the better industrial and commercial architecture of the era" (Clancey 1987a:16) (figure 6.4). At the same time the building's exterior speaks to an economy of design which suggests that the houses were "perceived by their designers as industrial in character and not as transplanted and simplified examples of urban townhouses" (Clancey 1987a:16).

By contrast, the Boott Mills agent's house (figure 6.5) was more in keeping with stately brownstones of Boston. The agent's house is similar "in form and character to the city's corporate boardinghouse blocks of the same period, but its exterior facing materials – pressed brick with brownstone trim, and dressed granite at the foundation – are much higher quality" (Clancey 1987b:29). The same was true of the building's interior. Besides the time and money spent by the corporation on the agent's house, there is also evidence that efforts were made to redecorate the interior periodically to keep it fashionable and to provide the family with the latest in domestic technology (Clancey 1987b:29–42). The floorplan of the building also reveals the need for space for servants' quarters, another feature of the agent's status which contrasts with that of the workers themselves.

The buildings the company supplied for its workers and its agents reveal an adherence to strict class distinctions. The utilitarian nature of the boarding house design reflects its industrial purpose: to house company operatives. The agent's house needed to project a very different facade. Its location alone, strategically placed between the mill workers and the rest of the community, was part of the overall plan to use spatial organization to accentuate the hierarchical dynamics of the mill operation while at the same time insuring economy of effort.

The yard of the agent's house also discloses the class distinctions from the boarding houses; these operated at both the utilitarian and symbolic levels. Excavations conducted in the rear yard suggested that some domestic, utilitarian activities were probably carried out there. Unlike the front and side yards of the dwelling which were landscaped with loam, the rear yard contained large concentrations of domestic debris. The result of soils, pollen, macrofossils, and opal phytolith analysis (Kelso et al. 1987:93–128) seem to support an interpretation of contrasting uses of yard space around the dwelling. These same analyses also indicate a general trend "toward less soil disturbance and more complete ground cover dominated by grass" (Kelso et al. 1987:127), a trend opposite to that discerned at the boarding houses.

At the boarding houses exploratory botanical analysis suggests that early yards dominated by grasses gave way to a landscape increasingly dominated by weeds and vines (Mrozowski and Kelso 1987:151).

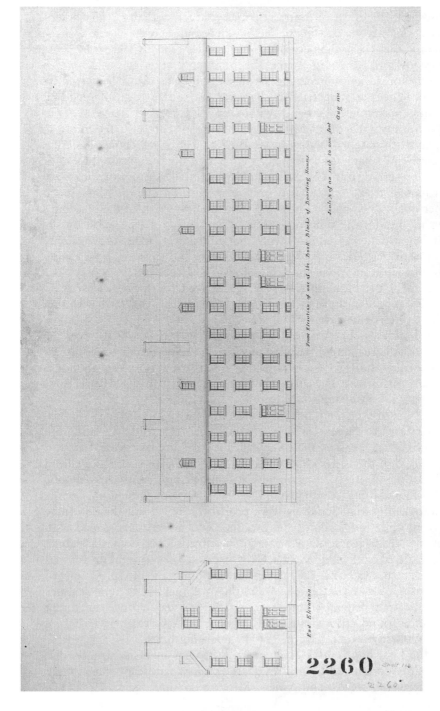

Figure 6.4 Original front elevation of the Boot Mills Boarding Houses, 1836 (courtesy of the Lowell Historical Society)

Figure 6.5 The Kirk Street Agent's House, Lowell, Massachusetts (photograph by Stephen A. Mrozowski)

Nightshade (*Solanum sps.*), an active colonizer of continuously disturbed soils, was represented prominently in both pollen and macrofossil remains. A large number of Solanum seeds were recovered from a brick feature that appears to be a terminal box for a downspout (Beaudry 1987:98). This suggests that vines of nightshade were probably growing on drainspouts as well as walls and fences. Most of the weeds represented in both pollen and macrofossil samples were ruderals, plants commonly found in continuously disturbed soils, indicating that the boarding house yards were intensively utilized.

The trend from well maintained, grass-dominated yards to those characterized by weeds is but one facet of a trend interpreted as a progressive lack of interest in the living conditions of mill operatives: "Always interested primarily in economic advantage, the corporations evolved from a public 'benevolent' paternalism through a begrudging paternalism to a time when they no longer took responsibility for the housing of their workers" (Bell 1987:68). These changes were manifest in a variety of areas. The mills themselves were poorly ventilated which resulted in problems with lung disease (Bell 1987:67). Water was supplied both by wells and by the canals of Lowell, but both archaeological and documentary evidence indicate that disease stemming from contaminated water supplies may have been at least partially caused by the continued use of wells and privies at the boarding houses (Bell 1987:63–4). So in spite of continuing efforts to control the daily lives of their workers (e.g., Bond 1987), the diverging trajectories of the boarding house and agent's house yards reveal different sets of priorities.

Further consideration of the agent's house yard also discloses how the landscape performed a symbolic role. The documentary evidence relating to the construction of the agent's house revealed that more fencing is mentioned in the records than would have been necessary to surround the perimeter of the site and divide the two rear yards (Robbins 1979). One possibility is its use for a garden or stable yard (Robbins 1979); an alternative answer is that the fencing was used to divide the front and rear yards of the duplex thereby forming a boundary between public and private space. If the rear yard was employed primarily for utilitarian purposes while the front and side yards served more of an ornamental function there may have been a conscious effort made to (1) divide the two spaces and (2) insure that the public space was visible while the private space was left private. The public expression communicated by the facade of the building was foregrounded by the ornamental front and side yards only, while the rear yard would have maintained a utilitarian character more in keeping with a pre-industrial use of yard space. From this perspective, the yards of the agent's house would represent a household in transition with the front yard representing a modern use of space, but with a rear yard still sharing some pre-industrial characteristics.

In many respects the agent's household represented a modern household with many of the latest innovations in domestic technology – gas lighting, for example. The contrasting uses of yard space serve to remind us, however, that change is a transitional process. Those who lived in the company boarding houses would not have had access to some types of innovation that the agents' families would have. The same appears to have been true for some of Newport's merchants and artisans. In either instance, contrasting landscapes are tangible products of the kinds of inequalities that were part of capitalism's legacy.

The new class order of industrial capitalism not only created totally novel landscapes; it also transformed the landscapes of mercantile cities. In older, established cities like Boston, nineteenth-century industrial capitalism brought the first purely residential neighborhoods as part of a new spatial order. One change was the growth of the communities' size. By the mid-nineteenth century, Boston was close to twice the size it had been a century earlier. The mechanism for this expansion was a series of massive operations in which mud-flats and swampy areas of the city were filled. These projects were funded by a small group of wealthy capitalists who then transformed the newly created space into planned developments. One aspect of this process was the use of a grid system for streets and a desire to mirror modern European cities, notably Paris. This same grid pattern was employed earlier in the Beacon Hill district of the city.

Both developments were planned as purely residential areas. This segregation of work space and living space is one of the characteristics of nineteenth-century urban development under the influence of capitalism. Warner's (1962) examination of Boston's suburban development clearly indicates that the spatial reordering of the community was a major contributing factor in the growth of modern Boston. The suburbs were home to the new middle class who sought to capture country living within horse-car distance of the city. Two interesting characteristics of these new, middle-class suburban households were that they often relied upon a single, male-generated income, and that the yard areas surrounding the dwellings were not designed to allow for much in the way of productive activities. This is probably due in large part to the shifting roles of middle-class women under the influence of industrial capitalism, which involved the replacement of productive activities with a new status, that of the moral arbiter of the domestic domain (e.g., Cott 1978; Hayden 1981; Strasser 1982; Mrozowski 1988). Of course, not all women were involved in this transition at this time. I believe it can be argued that this pattern first emerged in New England among the urban elite during the eighteenth century (Mrozowski 1988). The separation of entire classes of women from the work-force, a hallmark of capitalism, had now spread to include a new social group during the nineteenth century.

Another facet of nineteenth-century urbanization involved the growing separation of nature and society. In the same way that industrial capitalism resulted in the separation of work and domestic space, and of upper- and middle-class women from productive labor, there appears to have emerged a division between nature and society. Interestingly enough this division is expressed through efforts to socialize nature in the parks and tree-lined streets of nineteenth-century urban centers in both Europe (Hohenberg and Lees 1985) and the United States. Through the socialization of nature it was possible to mask the growing inequalities of urban living by suggesting them to be the result of natural forces. Inequality was viewed as the outgrowth of natural processes that resulted in an ordered society; thus the ordered society of the city, which included nature in the form of artificially maintained green spaces, was merely the product of nature itself. Though this division would manifest itself during the nineteenth century, its origins in the United States can be traced to emerging urban ideology of the eighteenth century so vehemently resisted by the farmers of the period.

Summary and Conclusions

In this paper I have traced the evolution of the urban landscape in New England under the influence of two economic regimes. Although mercantile and industrial capitalism shared many features, each relied upon a different form of economic integration which contributed to distinctive urban landscapes. The mixed residential/commercial landscape of eighteenth-century Boston was replaced by a spatial order characterized by the separation of work from the home. One effect was the eventual loss of the household's productive function. More effort was now placed on social reproduction among the upper and middle classes. Part of this process involved new roles for both men and women in the household: with production replaced by the factory, the space surrounding the dwelling which had, in traditional agrarian society, been the domain of the women, now was an extension of male status in a new social order. The urban landscape of present-day America is a product of this process. The yard and dwelling as symbolic status markers were now inseparable. Status was expressed through both architectural style and ornamental landscaping; on a grander scale this process was seen city-wide through the development of parks and other green space as part of the socialization of nature.

Though the landscape and the new social order is most clearly seen on the new industrial landscapes, such as that of Lowell, the archaeology of eighteenth-century Boston and Newport indicate that this process had its roots before industrial capitalism. Among merchants involved in an economic system based on mercantile capitalism, the yard space surrounding their dwellings was of little productive value. For the urban artisans of the period the same was not the case, as they relied heavily upon their domestic space for work space. Because of the intensive land use practices they employed to insure market participation, these artisans often lived in insanitary surroundings, highly conducive to the spread of disease. Disease, work, and wealth all merged in these landscapes of inequality.

In planned industrial cities like Lowell, these inequalities were incorporated into the landscape. Boarding houses were placed in close proximity to the locus of production. Policed by a system of corporate paternalism, these dwellings were quite different from the middle-class residence of their overseer. And as with the artisans of eighteenth-century Newport, disease was a part of the daily lives of the mill workers of Lowell.

The archaeology undertaken at the Agent's House serves as a reminder that change took place piecemeal, with earlier periods leaving their signature. The agents and their families were part of a major transition of the household, in which gender determined one's role in a new social order. Class, too, was important as it had always been in the past; whether one had access to the benefits of domestic technology was class-determined. Ironically, the women of many upper- and middle-class households were in the process of having their status lowered while the ideology of domesticity masked the transformation (Mrozowski 1988; Cott 1978).

The new domestic landscape of middle-class America which emerged during the nineteenth century was but one expression of a larger transformation which would produce the modern world as we know it. Though only part of the picture, the urban landscape reveals one way in which cultural values are materially expressed. The inequalities of a new social order were justified as being the product of natural processes. By socializing nature, urban elites were demonstrating their control of nature. At the symbolic level upper- and middle-class women shared a status similar to that of workers, their domination viewed as the natural expression of male superiority (see also MacCormack 1986:1–24). By transforming the domestic domain into an expression of male status, it was necessary that women accept their new role and relinquish their productive function to men. Obviously this was resisted by some, but the landscape of suburban Boston suggests that most eventually accepted what capitalism had fostered. For capitalism to succeed it was necessary that household production cease; in order for this to happen, an ideology had to evolve which would reinforce those who participated in the process. The source of that ideology was the commercial urban centers so instrumental in the rise of a capitalist world economy: cities composed of landscapes of inequality.

ACKNOWLEDGEMENTS/NOTES

1   I would like to thank Randall McGuire and Robert Paynter for their help; I would especially like to thank Robert Paynter for his editorial assistance. I would like to acknowledge both Mary C. Beaudry and Gerald K. Kelso for their continuing inspiration and energy on the Lowell Project. I would also like to acknowledge the fine work of Gregory Clancey, Kathleen Bond, Edward Bell, David Dutton, and David Landon who have served as the backbone of the Lowell Archaeological Survey Project.
2   The Lowell Archaeological Survey is a five-year project as part of a Cooperative Agreement between the Division of Cultural Resources, North Atlantic Region of the National Park Service in Boston, and the Center for Archaeological Studies at Boston University. Principals for the Project are Dr Stephen A. Mrozowski of the University of Massachusetts at Boston,

Supervisory Archaeologist for the National Park Service, and Dr Mary C. Beaudry of Boston University, who serve as research directors for the project. Dr Ricardo Elia of Boston University serves as Project Manager. Other Project personnel include Dr Richard Candee of Boston University who serves as the coordinator of the architectural research, and Dr Gerald K. Kelso, National Park Service, who serves as project palynologist. Donald Jones, Edward Bell, and Nancy Seasholes (Boston University) have served as Project archaeologists along with Research Assistants Edward L. Bell, Kathleen H. Bond, David Dutton, William Fisher, Gregory K. Clancey, and David Landon.

REFERENCES

Anderson, J. (1971) *A Solid Sufficiency: An Ethnography of Yeoman Foodways in Stuart England*. Unpublished Ph.D. dissertation, University of Pennsylvania.
Ashton, M. and J. Bond (1987) *The Landscape of Towns*. Alan Sutton, Gloucester.
Beaudry, M. C. (1986) "The Archaeology of Historical Land Use in Massachusetts." *Historical Archaeology* 20(2), 38–46.
——(1987) "Archaeological Testing at the Proposed Lowell Boarding House Park Site." In *Interdisciplinary Investigations of the Boott Mills, Lowell, Massachusetts*, Vol. I: *Life at the Boarding Houses*, eds M. C. Beaudry and S. A. Mrozowski, pp. 69–114. Cultural Resource Management Study No. 18, Division of Cultural Resources, North Atlantic Region, National Park Service, Boston.
Beaudry, M. C. and S. A. Mrozowski (1987a) *Interdisciplinary Investigations of the Boot Mills, Lowell, Massachusetts*, Vol. I: *Life at the Boarding Houses*. Cultural Resource Management Study No. 18, Division of Cultural Resources, North Atlantic Region, National Park Service, Boston.
——(1987b) *Interdisciplinary Investigations of the Boott Mills, Lowell, Massachusetts*, Vol. II: *The Kirk Street Agent's House*. Cultural Resource Management Study No. 19, Division of Cultural Resources, North Atlantic Region, National Park Service, Boston.
Bell, E. L. (1987) "A Preliminary Report on Health, Hygiene, and Sanitation at the Boott Mills Boarding Houses: An Historical and Archaeological Perspective." In *Interdisciplinary Investigations of the Boott Mills, Lowell, Massachusetts*, Vol. I: *Life in the Boarding Houses*, eds M. C. Beaudry and S. A. Mrozowski, pp. 57–68. Cultural Resource Management Study No. 18, Division of Cultural Resources, North Atlantic Region, National Park Service, Boston.
Biddle, M. (1976) "Towns." In *The Archaeology of Anglo-Saxon England*, ed. D. M. Wilson, pp. 99–150. Cambridge University Press, Cambridge.
Bond, K. H. (1987) "A Preliminary report on the Demography of the Boott Mills Housing Units #38–48." In *Interdisciplinary Investigations of the Boott Mills, Lowell, Massachusetts*, Vol. I: *Life at the Boarding Houses*, eds M. C. Beaudry and S. A. Mrozowski, pp. 35–55. Cultural Resource Management

Study No. 18, Division of Cultural Resources, North Atlantic Region, National Park Service, Boston.

Bradley, J. W. (ed.) (1983) *Archaeology of the Bostonian Hotel Site*. Massachusetts Historical Commission Occasional Papers in Archaeology and History No. 2, Boston.

Braudel, F. (1981) *The Structures of Everyday Life: Civilization and Capitalism 15th–18th Century*, Vol. I. Harper and Row, New York.

——(1984) *The Perspective of the World: Civilization and Capitalism 15th–18th Century*, Vol. III. Harper and Row, New York.

Cady, J. H. (1957) *The Civic and Architectural Development of Providence, 1636–1950*. The Book Shop, Providence.

Candee, R. M. (1985) "Architecture and Corporate Planning in the Early Waltham System." In *Essays from the Lowell Conference on Industrial History 1982 and 1983*, ed. R. Weible, pp. 17–43. Museum of American Textile History, Andover.

Clancey, G. K. (1987a) "The Boott Mills Boarding Houses and Adjacent Structures: The Evidence of Maps and Photographs." In *Interdisciplinary Investigations of the Boott Mills, Lowell, Massachusetts*, Vol. I: *Life in the Boarding Houses*, eds M. C. Beaudry and S. A. Mrozowski, pp. 15–33. Cultural Resource Management Study No. 18, Division of Cultural Resources, North Atlantic Region, National Park Service, Boston.

——(1987b) "An Architectural Study of the Kirk Street Agent's House." In *Interdisciplinary Investigations of the Boott Mills, Lowell, Massachusetts*, Vol. II: *The Kirk Street Agent's House*, eds M. C. Beaudry and S. A. Mrozowski, pp. 29–41. Cultural Resource Management Study No. 18, Division of Cultural Resources, North Atlantic Region, National Park Service, Boston.

Cott, N. F. (1978) *The Bonds of Womanhood: Women's Sphere in New England 1780–1835*. Yale University Press, New Haven, CT.

Douglas, I. (1983) *The Urban Environment*. Edward Arnold, London.

Dublin, T. (1979) *Women at Work: The Transformation of Work and Community in Lowell, Massachusetts, 1826–1860*. Columbia University Press, New York.

——(1981) *From Farm to Factory: The Mill Experience and Women's Lives in New England, 1830–1860*. Columbia University Press, New York.

Gorman, F. J., J. Cheney, M. B. Folsom, and G. T. Laden (1985) "Intensive Archaeological Survey of Post Office Square Garage Lowell, Massachusetts." Report submitted to the Division of Planning and Development, City of Lowell, Lowell, Massachusetts.

Gross, L. F. and R. A. Wright (1985) "Historic Structure Report – History Portion: Buiilding 6; The Counting House; The Adjacent Courtyard; and the Facades of Buildings 1 and 2. Boott Mill Complex, Lowell National Historical Park, Lowell, Massachusetts." Report prepared for National Park Service, Denver Service Center, Denver, Colorado.

Hareven, T. (1978) *Amoskeag: Life and Work in an American Factory City*. Pantheon Books, New York.

Harvey, D. (1973) *Social Justice and the City*. Edward Arnold, London.

——(1982) *The Limits of Capital*. Johns Hopkins University Press, Baltimore.

Hayden, D. (1981) *The Grand Domestic Revolution: A History of Feminist Designs for American Homes, Neighborhoods, and Cities*. MIT Press, Cambridge, MA.

Henretta, J. A. (1965) "Economic Development and Social Structure in Colonial Boston." *William and Mary Quarterly*, 3rd Series, 75–92.

Hohenberg, P. M. and L. H. Lees (1985) *The Making of Urban Europe 1000–1950*. Harvard University Press, Cambridge, MA.

Kelso, G. K., S. A. Mrozowski, and W. F. Fisher (1987) "Contextual Archaeology at the Kirk Street Agent's House." In *Interdisciplinary Investigations of the Boott Mills, Lowell, Massachusetts*, Vol. II: *The Kirk Street Agent's House* eds M. C. Beaudry and S. A. Mrozowski, pp. 97–127. Cultural Resource Management Study No. 19, Division of Cultural Resources, North Atlantic Region, National Park Service, Boston.

Kelso, G. K. and J. Schoss (1983) "Exploratory Pollen Analysis of the Bostonian Hotel Site Sediments." In *Archaeology of the Bostonian Hotel Site*, ed. James Bradley, pp. 67–76. Massachusetts Historical Commission Occasional Publications in Archaeology and History No. 2, Boston.

Kulik, G., R. Parks, and T. Penn (eds) (1982) *The New England Mill Village, 1790–1860*. MIT Press, Cambridge, MA.

MacCormack, C. P. (1986) "Nature, Culture and Gender: A Critique." In *Nature, Culture and Gender*, eds C. P. MacCormack and M. Strathern, pp. 1–24. Cambridge University Press, Cambridge.

Macphail, R. (1981) "Soil and Botanical Studies of the 'Dark Earth'." In *The Environment of Man: the Iron Age to the Anglo-Saxon Period*, eds M. Jones and G. Dimbleby, pp. 309–31. BAR British Series 87, Oxford.

Miles, H. A. (1846) *Lowell, As It Was, and As It Is* (1972 reprint edn). Arno Press, New York.

Mrozowski, S. A. (1983) "Examining the Urban Environment Through the Analysis of Floral Remains." *The Newsletter of the Conference on New England Archaeology* 3(2), 31–50.

——(1985) *Boston's Archaeological Legacy*. Boston Landmarks Commission, Boston.

——(1987a) *The Ethnoarchaeology of Urban Gardening*. Unpublished Ph.D. dissertation, Department of Anthropology, Brown University, Providence.

——(1987b) "Exploring New England's Evolving Urban Landscape." In *Living in Cities*, ed. E. Staski, pp. 1–9. Special Publication No. 5 of the Society for Historical Archaeology. Ann Arbor.

——(1988) "For gentlemen of Capacity and Leisure: the Archaeology of Colonial Newspapers." In *Documentary Archaeology in the New World*, ed. M. C. Beaudry, pp. 184–91. Cambridge University Press, Cambridge.

Mrozowski, S. A. and G. K. Kelso (1987) "Palynology and Archeobotany of the Proposed Lowell Boarding House Park Site." In *Interdisciplinary Investigations of the Boott Mills, Lowell, Massachusetts*, Vol. I: *Life at the Boarding Houses*, eds M. C. Beaudry and S. A. Mrozowski, pp. 139–51. Cultural Resource Management Study No. 18, Division of Cultural Resources, North Atlantic Region, National Park Service, Boston.

Nash, G. (1979) *The Urban Crucible*. Harvard University Press, Cambridge, MA.

Parks, R. and M. B. Folsom (1982) "Introduction." In *The New England Mill Village, 1790–1860*, eds G. Kulik, R. Parks, and T. Penn, pp. xxiii–xxxv. MIT Press, Cambridge, MA.

Pendery, S. R. (1978) "Urban Process in Portsmouth, New Hampshire: An Archaeological Perspective." In *New England Historical Archaeology*, Annual Proceedings of the Dublin Seminar for New England Folklife, ed. P. Benes, pp. 24–35. Boston University Scholarly Press, Boston.

Perley, S. (1924) *The History of Salem, Massachusetts*, Vol. I. Perley Salem, MA.

Platt, C. (1975) "The Excavations, 1966–1969." In *Excavations in Medieval Southampton, 1953–1969*, eds C. Platt and R. Coleman-Smith, pp. 232–330. Leicester University Press, Leicester.

Prude, J. (1983) *The Coming of the Industrial Order: Town and Factory Life in Rural Massachusetts*. Cambridge University Press, New York.

Records of the Boston Selectmen (1886) *Report of the Record Commissioners*. Records of the Boston Selectmen 1736 to 1742. Rockwell and Churchill, Boston.

Reinhard, K. J., S. A. Mrozowski and K. Orloski (1986) "Privies, Pollen, Parasites and Seeds: A Biological Nexus in Historical Archaeology." *The MASCA Journal* 4(1), 31–6.

Rhode Island Colonial Records (1857) *Records of the Colony of Rhode Island and Providence Plantations*, Vols. IV and V, ed. John Russell Bartlett. Knowles, Anthony and Co., Providence, RI.

Robbins, J. (1979) "Historic Structure Report, Architectural Data, Boott Cotton Mills and Massachusetts Cotton Mills Agents House, 67 and 63 Kirk Street, Lowell National Historical Park, Lowell, Middlesex County, Massachusetts." Draft Report, National Park Service, Denver Service Center, Denver, Colorado.

Rubertone, P. E. and J. Gallagher (1981) *Archaeological Site Examination: A Case Study in Urban Archaeology, Roger Williams National Monument*. Cultural Resource Management Study No. 4, Division of Cultural Resources, North Atlantic Region, National Park Service, Boston.

Rudolph, R. (1978) "18th Century Newport and its Merchants." *Bulletin of the Newport Historical Society*, No. 170, Vol. 52, parts 1 and 2.

Schuyler, R. L. (1974) "Lowellian Archaeology." *Society for Industrial Archaeology Newsletter*, Supplementary Issue No. 7, 3–4.

——(1976) "Merrimack Valley Project: 2nd Year." *Society for Industrial Archaeology Newsletter*, Supplementary Issue No. 8, 7–8.

Strasser, S. (1982) *Never Done: A History of American Housework*. Pantheon, New York.

Warner, S. B. (1962) *Street Car suburbs*. Harvard University Press, Cambridge, MA.

7

Building Power in the Cultural Landscape of Broome County, New York 1880 to 1940

Randall H. McGuire

In the first two decades of the twentieth century, capitalism in the United States faced a crisis born of the inherent contradictions in the system and the resistance of labor to existing class relations. In the political arena progressives and yellow journalists attacked the capitalists, and Congress legislated previously unheard of controls on business. Labor was militant and the black flags of anarchy and the red flags of socialism hung in many union halls. Most fundamentally, capitalism faced a realization crisis manifest in the great depression of the 1890s and the declining rate of profit in the last decades of the nineteenth century.

The crisis of the early twentieth century did not result in the long hoped for socialist revolution nor in a radical transformation of capitalism. Rather, capitalism evolved into a more mature form of monopoly capitalism which we still labor under today (Mandel 1978; Amsden 1979:15–17; Brodhead 1981). Important aspects of this transformation were the advent of consumerism and the renegotiation of capital–labor relations. This renegotiation preserved the essential capitalist relations of production while co-opting the socialist goals of labor. Integral to the transformation was the formulation of a new ideology of class relations which, rather than naturalizing class inequalities, denied the existence of class. The creation and modification of the cultural landscape in Broome County, New York both reflected and participated in this process of ideological transformation.

Late Nineteenth-Century Capitalism

Capitalist production in late nineteenth century America was based on the extraction of absolute surplus value (Amsden 1979:13). As discussed by

102

Marx (1906), increasing absolute surplus value involves the intensification of labor and the lengthening of the working day. Integral to the maintenance and intensification of this type of extraction was the existence of a dynamic reserve army of the unemployed which was constantly replenished by immigration from Europe. One of the main characteristics of this factory work-force was extremely high turnover averaging 100 percent a year (Slichter 1919:16; Nelson 1975:85–6). With the exception of a limited number of skilled workers the capitalist regarded labor as a replenishable resource to be consumed just as his factories consumed coal. Craft workers thus gained power and special status because of the skills which the capitalist required and they controlled. Unions gained real strength and permanency only among these aristocrats of labor. With the combined force of skills and organization, craft workers attained benefits which granted many of them the trappings of a middle-class lifestyle (Guerin 1979:57–61; Walkowitz 1978:102–10). The capitalist, however, constantly sought to deskill production and the proportion of skilled workers in the labor force declined throughout the late nineteenth century.

In addition to the reserve army of unemployed and the high turnover rates which worked against the organization of non-craft workers, coercion was central to the capitalist control of labor. The capitalist hired foremen to drive the workers on the shop floor through a combination of threats, abuse and often physical violence. The foreman hired the worker, fired the worker, supervised the work and in many cases could set the level of compensation (Nelson 1975:34–54). Capitalists did not hesitate to employ violence in the handling of strikes, and cases like the Homestead strike of 1892 where management fortified the mill and fought pitched gun battles with the strikers differed only in degree from the usual tactics for strikebreaking.

The nineteenth-century capitalist reaped enormous profits but little of this reached the mass of workers. Throughout the later half of this period most workers lived in conditions of poverty, working 10 to 16 hours a day and sending their children into the mills and factories to survive (Walkowitz 1978:102–7; Tentler 1979; Guerin 1979). Workers could afford few of the products of their labor and maintained very low levels of consumption, especially of durable goods (Ewen 1976; Matthaei 1982:235).

The class relations of the late nineteenth century were rationalized (for the elite) and obscured (from the workers) by an ideology that equated society with nature and derived the apparent inequalities from the characteristics of individuals. The writings of authors such as Conwell (1905) and Sumner (1963) proclaimed this ideology of Social Darwinism and the gospel of wealth. Social Darwinism provided a model for the social world derived from the natural world. Life was a struggle for survival and success and only the fittest would survive: in the natural world this led to the improvement of the species, also a desirable process in society. Success was attainable by all. Its determinates lay in the characteristics of the individual: hard work, thrift, intelligence, sobriety, cleanliness and a little luck guaranteed success. Failure resulted from a lack of these qualities or, more importantly, their opposite: laziness, extravagance, stupidity, slovenliness, and drunkenness. The "gospel of wealth" proclaimed that wealth was the emblem of success, the reward of a good life and personal ability.

The forms and appearances of late nineteenth-century reality reinforced and validated this ideology. Clear material differences delineated those who had succeeded and were the most fit from those of lesser character and ability who had failed. The failures lived in squalid quarters, possessed little or nothing of value, wasted what little they earned on strong drink, frequently were without work and violated the sanctity of the home by sending their women and children into the mines, mills, and factories. The ideology both originated in the stark material differences between classes and perpetuated these differences.

The cultural landscape figured prominently in this ideology. It was both a model of and a model for social action. It fulfilled the expectations of the ideology and guaranteed the continuance of the relations which created the reality. Even in the paternalistic company towns, where the capitalist installed his workers in clean, family-oriented dwellings for their own betterment, the form, substance, and spatial relationships of homes and other edifices clearly reflected each individual's position in the factory order (Nelson 1975:90–5; Walkowitz 1978:48–75).

The Maturation of Capitalism in the Early Twentieth Century

The workers of the late nineteenth century did not bend to their yoke willingly but resisted in violent strike after violent strike. Three main periods of labor unrest stand out, the late 1870s, the early 1890s and finally after the turn of the century from 1905 to 1919. By the early 1900s the distinct segregation of classes, abuse of workers, and conflict with capitalists had produced the strongest and most radical militancy in the history of American labor (Amsden 1979; Guerin 1979).

During the first two decades of the twentieth century unions called not only for the improvement of working conditions, increased wages, and shorter hours but also for the establishment of a socialist economy. When the Industrial Workers of the World (IWW) won the American Woolen Company strike in Lawrence, Massachusetts, in 1912, the strikers celebrated by singing the Internationale (Guerin 1979:79). The Bolshevik revolution in 1917 further radicalized workers and for the first time the capitalists were faced with the reality of a socialist revolution. Radicalism peaked in the strikes of 1919 when both the railroad workers and the United Mine Workers called for the nationalization of their respective industries. These strikes were brutally put down with the arrest, deportation, imprisonment, and execution of suspected radicals.

The industry of the late nineteenth century had been built primarily on the production of the means of production and secondarily on the production of consumer goods for the middle and upper classes (Ewen 1976:24; Mandel 1978:184–92). By the end of the century these markets had been saturated and capitalism faced a realization crisis. The industries of the USA, in order to survive, had to produce far more than the market which existed for their products. This crisis revealed itself in the great depression of 1893 and the falling rate of profits from 1873 to the 1890s (Mandel 1978:83, 120–1).

Resolution of the crisis of the early twentieth century lay in two interrelated movements which altered the system of production in the United States without compromising the essential relations of capitalism (Brodhead 1981). The first of these is what Antonio Gramsci called "Fordism," marked by the introduction of assembly line mass production and a shift to the extraction of relative surplus value. The second movement was an ideological movement which sought to restructure production in the form of an industrial democracy.

In 1910 Henry Ford reorganized his Highland, Michigan plant along an assembly line and by 1914 had cut the assembly time for an automobile chassis from 12.5 hours to 33 minutes (Chandler 1967:26–7; Meyer 1981). Mass production involved the use of highly specialized single purpose machines with equally highly specialized and easily trained workmen to produce goods at rates that seem astronomical when compared to late nineteenth-century production (Ewen 1976:23–4). The capitalist extracted increasing amounts of relative surplus value by replacing skilled workers with machines. Mass production dehumanized labor while offering workers greater material benefits for their labor. Principles of scientific management sought to fully integrate the worker with the machines so that human and machine worked in perfect synchronization (Nelson 1975:55–79). The worker became little more than an extension of the machine in this ultimate dehumanization of the productive process. Ford drew workers to his plants with the famous promise of $5.00 a day and, more importantly, he sought to make products for consumption by the workers, thereby transforming them into consumers (Ewen 1976).

This transformation of the productive process also necessitated a renegotiation of the relationship between capital and labor. Capital no longer depended on the workers solely as a source of human energy; it now also depended on them for markets (Ewen 1976:23–39; Edsforth 1987:19). Capitalists expressed this new relationship in terms of a functionally integrated circle beneficial to all: "They [workers] have time to see more, do more and incidentally buy more. This stimulates business and increases prosperity, and in the general economic circle the money passes through industry again and back into the workman's pocket" (Ford 1929:17).

For the worker to consume, the material conditions of the working class had to be modified (Ewen 1976). Consumption required the worker to have leisure time and therefore a shorter working day. Higher pay rates would give the worker more to spend and time payment plans and credit would stretch that buying power further. The capitalist stressed home ownership by workers to increase consumption, and modern advertising techniques were developed to encourage and educate the workers in their new role. These innovations co-opted some of the demands of the nineteenth-century labor movement, such as the eight-hour day; they also required a transformation of the highly mobile, erratically employed labor force of the late nineteenth century into a stable, continuously employed population.

This transformation of the relationship between capital and labor and of the material conditions of labor created the new markets required to overcome the realization crisis but it also undermined capital's traditional means of controlling labor. Scientific management centralized hiring in personnel departments and reduced the power of the shop foreman (Nelson 1975:55–101). Having a vast reserve army of the unemployed would be counter-productive because its members would not have the money to be consumers. Violent actions against labor engendered bad feelings toward companies and alienated consumers. All in all, these changes favored a shift in labor control from coercion to manipulation (Ewen 1976:26; Filene 1924; Carver 1926; Edsforth 1987).

The ideological basis for this shift lay in the notion of an industrial democracy. John Leitch (1919:1) wrote, "Have we not talked rather too much about working people as a class and too little of them as human beings?" The concept of an industrial democracy reformulated the mystification of the capitalist relationship by denying the reality of class stratification. The industrial reformers of the early twentieth century blamed the abuses, poverty, violence, and exploitation of the nineteenth century not on capitalism, but on deviations from the democratic principles which had founded the United States (Carver 1926; Allen 1952).

Not only were labor and capital functionally and beneficially linked in the economy, but also a social revolution was afoot (Allen 1952). "It is a revolution that is to wipe out the distinctions between laborers and capitalists by making laborers their own capitalists and by compelling most capitalists to become laborers of one kind or another" (Carver 1926:9). These reformers preached that success in industry required that the capitalist do away with the social and material differences that set him apart from his workers. They also called for the creation of worker councils and company unions. These later reforms did not secure widespread favor but did enhance the ideological shift.

The advocates of industrial democracy drew the form and substance of their new ideology from the past. The late nineteenth century was portrayed as a short-term quirk in the democratic growth of the country. Thomas Nixon Carver (1926:261–2), a Harvard economist, wrote: "To be alive to-day, in this country, and to remember the years from 1870 to 1920 is to awake from a nightmare." The prophets of an industrial democracy remade the colonial past in places like Colonial Williamsburg to sanctify their vision and avidly advocated the Colonial Revival movement in architecture and design. The imagery of a naturally set order was replaced by a vision of a mythic past. However, this new ideology did not abandon all the conceptual baggage of the late nineteenth century; the cult of individual achievement remained a key facet of the mystification. Success and failure still sprang from the abilities of individuals, but the definition of success changed. In a democratic society, where all were partners in industry, success was a relative phenomenon. Whereas in the tenets of Social Darwinism all men had the opportunity to succeed, in the industrial democracy all men could gain some degree of success.

The ideology of industrial democracy both arose from and created the reality of the 1920s. The identification of success with conspicuous consumption was inherited from the past. With the spread of mass production conspicuous consumption became possible for much of the working class. A form of commodity fetishism had been created which confused material things with human relations: once the availability of things changed, the illusion of change in human relations was created (Edsforth 1987:35). In *Middletown* of the 1920s working-class housewives described how in their childhood classes had existed in the community because only the rich had cars, washing machines, and their own homes, but now everyone had these things and only differences of degree remained (Lynd and Lynd 1929:82–3). Class had seemingly melted away. The cultural landscape was an active participant in the creation of this new ideology. The Colonial Revival movement in architecture and design begat a new metaphor for the wealthy, a metaphor that down played ostentatiousness and reinforced the mythic past of the industrial democracy. The capitalist aided the illusion of classlessness by modifying the landscape to create the image of equality and continuous gradation.

In the industrial democracy the fetishism of commodities, which replaced relations of stratification with things, became the answer to the socialist alternative. In 1934 a delegation of Soviet shoe producers toured the Endicott-Johnson shoe factories in Broome County, New York. A company history published the next year noted that the Soviets were shocked by the number of workers' automobiles surrounding the factory and they exclaimed "All these belong to workers? . . . Impossible! in Russia only officials have cars" (Inglis 1935:111). At that moment, in those factories, men, women, and teenagers labored as extensions of specialized machines doing one small task in the shoe-making process over and over again, several hundred times a day.

The Transformation of the Cultural Landscape in Broome County

The ideological shift that ensued in the early twentieth century is clearly visible in the cultural landscape of Broome County, New York. The contributions to the landscape by two of the most prominent capitalists in the history of the county, Jonas M. Kilmer and George F. Johnson, provide a basis for looking at how that landscape served as both a model for and a model of social action.

The cultural landscape of Broome County was not just a passive vessel collecting meaning from the action of people. The elites of Binghamton consciously used the landscape to reinforce their view of the world and to give reality to that view. The opacity of the reality so created gave form and substance to the ideology. However, it affected the day to day experience and consciousness of the working class in ways never intended by its creators: in ways of resistance. The landscape also provided the physical environment structuring interaction. Physical proximity has a strong effect on the extent and nature of interaction between individuals and groups. The landscape can be manipulated to invite interaction between groups in some contexts and discourage it in others; it can be used to link the activities of the home with those of work or to sharply split them. The landscape is not simply backdrop and props, it is the stage of human action.

In the history of Binghamton no one ever totally rebuilt the cultural landscape. People sought (and still seek) to shape it to their purposes, but at no time did anyone have the means to totally destroy what had gone before and replace it with their own vision. Each new addition to the landscape entered into a dialogue with the past, a dialogue which reinterpreted the past in terms of the new ideal. The opposition between the new forms and the old creates a tension and a continuing dynamic not totally controlled by those who create the landscape.

The industrial history of Broome County reflects well the general trends seen in the nation as a whole. Manufacturing grew to be the main economic activity in the county after the Civil War. The largest city in the county, Binghamton, became a center for cigar production along with a variety of other industries; among them, glassblowing, metalworking, furniture making, and patent medicines were also present. Most of these industries experienced wild fluctuations in prosperity during the late nineteenth century and few firms lasted more than a decade (McGuire and Osterud 1980).

Through the nineteenth and into the early twentieth century the Irish and migrants from rural Pennsylvania made up the majority of the work-force. Turnover in the plants was great and the work-force highly mobile: less than 50 percent of the people counted in the 1880 census appear in the 1890 census. Wage levels were relatively low with an 1880 average annual wage of $351 for all workers, both manufacturing and white-collar: Walkowitz (1978:103), in his study of the upstate New York Town of Troy, estimated that in 1880 a yearly income of $365 would be needed to support a family of four.

During the late nineteenth century labor became more and more militant in Binghamton. The glassblowers' union struck often and in 1890 the cigar workers walked out of every factory, paralyzing the community (McGuire and Osterud 1980). By the start of the twentieth century many saw Binghamton as a center for the radical union, the Knights of Labor, and a hotbed of labor unrest.

Jonas M. Kilmer came to Binghamton in 1878 after 18 years as a merchant in New York (Bothwell 1983:68–72). He became a partner with his brother in the production of Dr Kilmer's Swamp Root Cure and in 1893 he bought his brother out, taking on full ownership of the company. He also expanded his ventures by publishing a newspaper, the *Binghamton Press*, and establishing a bank. At the turn of the century he was probably the wealthiest man in the county. He died in 1912 passing on a sizeable financial empire which his son consolidated and expanded through the first half of the twentieth century. The *Binghamton Press* ran a full front page obituary for him and proclaimed his occupation as "capitalist." A few old people in the community today remember Jonas Kilmer and he lives on in a handful of myths. All of the tales relate to the power and opulence of his life. Rooms in his mansion were wallpapered with tooled elephant hide and in the last decades of his life he is said to have walked the streets with a riding quirt in his hand.

In the 1880s Kilmer built a new factory for the production of the swamp root cure (figure 7.1). He located it prominently on one of

Figure 7.1 Jonas Kilmer's Swamp Root Cure Factory, Binghamton, New York (photograph by R. H. McGuire)

Binghamton's main streets in a position where it dominated the view from the passenger depot for the railroad; thus one of the first things a visitor to the community would see was Kilmer's industrial palace. Kilmer had the plant faced and embellished with granite. A bank of large, bronze framed, display windows, now bricked up, pierced the first floor. Behind this ornate facade lay a rambling assortment of brick buildings which housed the activities of several hundred workers.

In 1904 Kilmer still retained control of his financial empire and in that year his son ordered the erection of the 12-storey Binghamton Press building as a lasting memorial to his father (figure 7.2). Located in the center of town this ornate tower was the most prominent building in Binghamton, validating Kilmer's claim to fame in the community. Local legend says that the Kilmers held up construction of the building until the nearby Security Mutual building was completed; they then added several floors to their building to make it taller than the new Security Mutual building. The Binghamton Press building dominated the city's skyline until the 1960s when a state office building rose to compete with it, and it still dominates the horizon from many vistas.

Kilmer built his mansion on the west side of the Chenango River, away from his factory, businesses, and workers (figure 7.3). The house sat at the end of a mansion row near the Kilmers' extensive horse farm. Built of stone in a late Victorian chateau style the building confronted

Figure 7.2 The Binghamton Press Building, Binghamton, New York (photograph by R. H. McGuire)

Figure 7.3 The Jonas Kilmer Mansion, Binghamton, New York (photograph by R. H. McGuire)

Figure 7.4 Late nineteenth-century tenement building, Binghamton, New York (photograph by R. H. McGuire)

people approaching it from town with two massive towers, giving the air of a fortification. Facing the horse farm the roof falls off in a much more gentle country style. The mansion holds many stained-glass panels and has bas relief carvings on its face. The structure is even today a grand expression of opulence, power, and success in late nineteenth-century America.

The working class of nineteenth-century Binghamton lived in housing markedly different from Kilmer's castle. They occupied multiple family houses and tenements across the river and downtown from the homes of Kilmer and other local capitalists. The majority of these buildings were overcrowded wooden fire traps lacking in basic comforts (figure 7.4). There could be little doubt in nineteenth-century Binghamton as to who were the fit and the unfit. The squalor and crowded condition of the working-class neighborhoods clearly showed why their occupants had failed in the struggle for success.

Kilmer had prepared well in advance for his death in 1912. In 1893 he had a major part in the founding of a new rural cemetery in Binghamton, Floral Park. Here the new wealthy manufacturers of Binghamton could create a landscape where their positions and power would endure for the millennium. Equally important, the cemetery was a park where the masses could view the social relations of their world sanctified for eternity (McGuire 1988). On the highest point in this cemetery Kilmer built his mausoleum (figure 7.5). This building is the grandest mortuary monument erected in Binghamton and larger than the apartments in which many of Kilmer's workers would have lived.

In his manipulation of the cultural landscape of Binghamton Kilmer realized and reinforced the late nineteenth-century ideology of class relations. He and his fellow capitalists built a city clearly divided into class boroughs. The conditions in these boroughs were the reality that the ideology of Social Darwinism demanded. Kilmer's factory and the Binghamton Press building were status offerings in Kilmer's competition with other capitalists and the fact that no others raised comparable structures cemented Kilmer's position as the leading capitalist of his time. Finally, in the cemetery, Kilmer gave form to a landscape that he hoped would perpetuate his success and the class relations of his day for eternity.

The segregation of the working class into their own boroughs facilitated class solidarity. Men and women from the same households worked side by side on the shop floor; at the end of each day they returned to a common neighborhood, so that class, work, and family networks all overlapped. In 1890 the working class of the community united when the cigar workers, all on the same day, walked out of every cigar factory in town. They turned the ideology of Social Darwinism on its head. They protested that wages had decreased to the point that they were *forced* to send their wives and daughters into the factories. These workers did not belong to a union and the solidarity of the strike sprang from the informal networks of family and neighborhood (McGuire and Osterud 1980:61). The unions that followed the strike built on these networks.

In 1881 George F. Johnson came to Binghamton as a foreman in the Lestershire boot and shoe factory where he rose to the post of assistant superintendent. In 1890 the company moved its plant to farmland west of the city of Binghamton and away from the labor turmoil of that community. In that same year the company went broke and one of its creditors, Henry B. Endicott, took control of the factory. Endicott had no interest in running the plant and he put George F. Johnson in charge of the operation. In 1897 Johnson became a partner and in 1899 the company was renamed the Endicott-Johnson company. Endicott died in 1919 leaving Johnson in full control of the company, and Johnson set about to realize his vision of an industrial democracy in Broome County.

From the early 1900s until the 1930s the Endicott-Johnson company boomed. By 1934 it had 29 factories in Broome County employing 19,000 people, over 60 percent of the Broome County manufacturing work-force (Inglis 1935). The company engaged in all stages of the shoe

Figure 7.5 The Kilmer Mausoleum, Johnson City, New York (photograph by R. H. McGuire)

manufacturing and marketing process from the tanning of the leather to the retail sale of the shoes.

Johnson brought his family into the operation starting in the 1890s: first his two brothers, Harry L. and Fred, and then in the early 1900s he put his son in charge of the tanning plant and his nephew Charles in charge of the shoe factories. The Johnsons lived amongst their workers, went by their first names and mixed with the workers at picnics and sporting events. The Johnson family provided a metaphor for the company; all workers were told that they were part of the Endicott-Johnson family.

Throughout its history the Endicott-Johnson company sought to forestall worker unrest and unionism. The original Lestershire factory had been built to the west of Binghamton to remove workers from the influence of Binghamton's union work-force. After World War I the company had to deal with high turnover rates and demands for higher wages; it reacted to these problems by instituting a system of welfare capitalism designed to keep wages at low levels, to build worker loyalty to the company and to maintain a stable, dependable, work-force in Broome County (McGuire and Osterud 1980:78; Zahavi 1983). The welfare system had several facets. The company provided free medical care, inexpensive cafeterias for noon meals, and public farmer's markets; it made many highly visible donations to the communities in the county, among them, parks and carousels. To encourage a stable labor force the company bought up broad tracts of land in the county, hired contractors and built large numbers of single-family homes which were then sold back to the workers, priority in these sales being given to workers with large families (Zahavi 1983). The company's policies were built around the image of the family and encouraged workers through company propaganda, free maternity care and other means to have large families.

As the company grew during the early 1900s Johnson built two industrial villages west of Binghamton. These sites removed the workers from the union influence of Binghamton but, more importantly, they allowed Johnson to construct a new cultural landscape, to create the surface reality necessary for his industrial democracy. Johnson built these communities with a definite image in mind: "my picture of a real factory was the shop out in the open country, with the homes of the workers around it in a little village" (Inglis 1935:25). He argued that workers and employers should live as friends and neighbors in a community of mutual interest (Inglis 1935:97); he thus created a cultural landscape that mystified the reality of class relations at Endicott-Johnson by denying the existence of class differences and class interests.

The first of these communities, eventually named Johnson City, grew up around the original Lestershire factory, while the second, Endicott, was located about four miles further west. The map of Johnson City shows how Johnson integrated the factories, parks, churches, workers' homes, and the homes of his own family in a single whole (figure 7.6). No clear spatial distinction was made in the community between work and home, boss and worker, or industry and leisure. Endicott was even a truer rendition of this plan because Johnson controlled more of the construction in this town.

Although not visible on a map, the community was split into ethnic enclaves. At least a third of the company's work-force were immigrants and the children of immigrants, and most of the rest were migrants from rural Pennsylvania. A total of more than 18 ethnic groups were present and most of these had their own neighborhood or block. Johnson favored this division through the use of zoning ordinances, by building churches and halls for ethnic associations and by encouraging ethnic floats and the wearing of ethnic dress in company parades and celebrations. However, the company did not group workers by ethnicity on the shop floor (the only exception to this pattern occurred in the tannery where most of the workers were Italians). In the shoe plants work groups were multi-ethnic and workers spoke English; when they returned to their neighborhoods they lived with fellow ethnics and spoke their native tongue.

Every working-class family had multiple members, men, women, and teenagers, in the factories (McGuire and Woodsong 1990). The jobs in the factories were segregated by sex, however, so that men and women did not work together.

The cultural landscape of the Endicott-Johnson (EJ) villages united all workers in the EJ family and maintained highly visible differences only within the work-force itself. The networks of home, neighborhood, and work intersected but by and large did not overlap. The spatial and conceptual locus of this intersection was the EJ family.

The factories themselves were utilitarian buildings set back from major roads (figure 7.7). The company built each factory so that the output of one plant passed as directly as possible to the next. Production inside was scientifically organized to minimize any wasted motion and maximize the flow of the product. All of the EJ plants differ markedly from Kilmer's industrial palace.

Johnson erected a variety of buildings as part of his welfare capitalism scheme, many of which remain in use today: these include the Ideal Hospital in Endicott, Your Home Library in Johnson City, and Recreation Park in Binghamton. Johnson left no monument to himself in the form of an elaborate building and, after the factories, the largest edifices he built were for the welfare capitalism program. But many monuments to Johnson do exist in Broome County: in Recreation Park

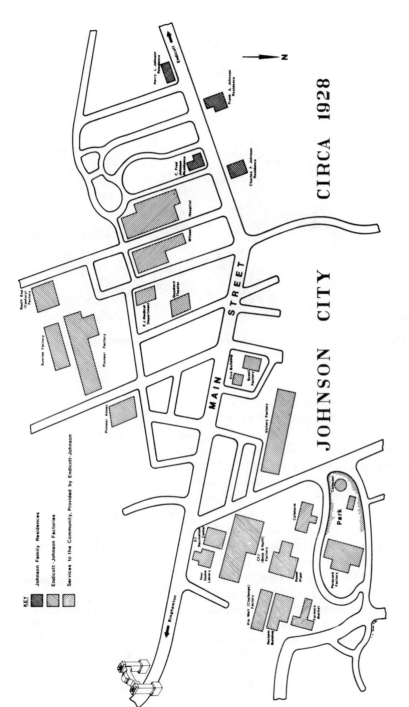

Figure 7.6 Map of Johnson City, New York

Figure 7.7 An Endicott-Johnson Shoe Factory, Johnson City New York (photograph by R. H. McGuire)

the city of Binghamton erected a bronze statue to Johnson at the dedication of the park, and EJ workers placed a bronze plaque on a granite boulder near Your Home Library in Johnson City. The most prominent monuments are two granite arches erected by the EJ workers at the eastern boundaries of both Johnson City and Endicott (figure 7.8).

These monuments are in fact complex statements of social relations which the appearance and a surface perception of the monuments mask. The EJ company often maneuvered workers to gain expressions of worker loyalty and appreciation to the company. In 1916, when Johnson introduced the eight-hour day, the workers staged what the official company history referred to as a massive spontaneous parade through Endicott to Johnson's home (Inglis 1935:158). The company provided the paraders with a souvenir pamphlet published at company expense. Johnson encouraged shop supervisors to pass around loyalty petitions when he expected worker unrest (Zahavi 1983:615). In the early 1920s shop supervisors also intitiated the construction of the granite arches in Johnson City and Endicott, soliciting funds from workers on the shop floors (Bothwell 1983:75).

George Johnson's home no longer stands in Endicott but the company history described it:

The house is of frame construction, of generous size, in plain Colonial style, with a broad porch, well shaded, and it is painted in Colonial Yellow tint. Wide beds of flowers surround it. Compared with the mansions of most captains of industry, this home of the chief of a $36,000,000 corporation is of Spartan simplicity. The establishment is a model of comfort, without a trace of show, a sort of big brother to the many E. J. Workers homes that lie close at hand. (Inglis 1935:118).

The homes of several of the other members of the Johnson family still stand including that of Charles F. Johnson Jr, the nephew of George, Vice-President of the company and supervisor of all the shoe manufacturing plants. This home, on the main street of Johnson City, is also a Colonial Revival style house (figure 7.9). It differs from the homes sold to the EJ workers primarily in its size. Most of the EJ workers' homes were craft style bungalows and box-like four-by-fours but many also were simple Colonial Revival structures, the Johnsons' homes in smaller scale (figure 7.10). The Johnsons chose the styles and plans for the workers' housing.

In company photographs and descriptions these working-class dwellings looked solidly middle-class. They had neatly manicured lawns and a car in every drive. The company literature did not show the large gardens and pens for geese, goats, or rabbits that lay in each backyard. The

Figure 7.8 The Endicott-Johnson Arch, Endicott, New York (photograph by R. H. McGuire)

Figure 7.9 The Charles F. Johnson Home, Johnson City New York (photograph by R. H. McGuire)

Figure 7.10 Endicott-Johnson built workers' homes, Endicott, New York (photograph by R. H. McGuire)

workers turned their backyards into small farms because their wages did not allow them to meet all of their needs (McGuire and Woodsong 1990). To partake of the consumer society they had to engage in subsistence production on their 50 × 150 foot city lots.

When Johnson built his new industrial villages he also provided for a cemetery, which would recreate for eternity Johnson's industrial community. In the center was an area reserved for the Johnson family and the resting place of George F. Johnson himself (figure 7.11). Johnson's welfare programs included provisions to help workers purchase plots in this cemetery, and markers, so that Johnson lies resting today surrounded by the graves of his workers (figure 7.12) – the beneficially integrated community preserved for eternity.

Figure 7.11 The Grave of George F. Johnson, Endwell, New York (photograph by R. H. McGuire)

The cultural landscape that George F. Johnson created entered into a dialogue with that left by Jonas Kilmer and the other capitalists of his time, a dialogue which validated the new ideology. Even though Johnson located his industrial democracy outside of Binghamton, in part to obtain a tabula rasa upon which he could leave his mark, Binghamton remained close at hand and in sharp contrast to his industrial villages.

One of the major messages of industrial democracy to the working class was that the socialist revolution was not needed because industrial

Figure 7.12 Endicott-Johnson workers' graves, Endwell, New York (photograph by R. H. McGuire)

democracy had already wrought a revolution in the United States. The company history said of George Johnson: "Karl Marx urged labor to take capital by the throat and seize its rights; George F. Johnson has taken labor by the hand and led the way to their mutual welfare" (Inglis 1935:288). No stronger validation existed in Broome County for this statement than the contrast between the tenements of the east side and the EJ workers' bungalows, or between the castle of Jonas Kilmer and the Colonial Revival homes of the Johnsons. But what this contrast and apparent change masked was the lack of any real change in the capitalist nature of relations in the factory. The material demands of the late nineteenth-century labor movement had been met to the advantage of capital, but labor had lost far more than it had gained. Mass production meant a de-humanization of labor, as workers became little more than extensions of their machines. Workers lost control of their actions on the shop floor, and their actions off the shop floor were increasingly manipulated by the welfare policies of their bosses or by advertising which sought to redefine their most basic perceptions of self (Ewen 1976; Edsforth 1987).

The Endicott-Johnson company's policies succeeded in forestalling strikes and union activity until the late 1940s; workers did, however, resist authoritarian supervisors and changes in work discipline. When grievances arose the multi-ethnic shop floors were quite capable of shutting down the floor and demanding to talk to one of the Johnsons. The workers used EJ's welfare capitalist philosophy to negotiate with the company, turning the company ideology back on itself so that the company had to either give in or openly deny the ideology (Zahavi 1983). For example, in the depth of the depression the company laid off workers in the tannery. The president and officers of an Italian fraternal and beneficial organization, the Sons of Italy, went to George Johnson. They said: "*Padron*, when we came here you promised us a square deal. If we worked well for the company the company would take care of us. The men you laid off have families and you must keep your part of the deal to care for them." These Italian workers had incorporated the company philosophy into their own ethnic framework and used the reciprocal implications of the philosophy to resist a company action. The men in question were called back to work, but a general work slowdown was imposed in the tannery.

However, the EJ workers' power to use the company's ideology to resist and negotiate their wants with the company did not give them the power to alter the company's position in a world economy. During the depression the company started to slowly dismantle the welfare programs of its founder. A multinational corporation bought the company in the 1940s; in the 1950s the company started losing production to the Orient and by the end of the 1960s EJ had shrunk to only a handful of manufacturing plants in the county.

REFERENCES

Allen, Frederick Lewis (1952) *The Big Change*. Harper Brothers, New York.
Amsden, John (1979) "Introduction." In *100 years of Labor in the USA* by Daniel Guerin, pp. 1–30. Ink Links Ltd, London.
Bothwell, Lawrence (1983) *Broome County Heritage*. Windsor Publications, Woodland Hills, NY.
Brodhead, Frank (1981) "Social Control." *Radical America* 15(6), 69–78.
Carver, Thomas Nixon (1926) *The Present Economic Revolution in the United States*. Goerge Allen and Unwin, London.
Chandler, Alfred Dupont (1967) *Giant Enterprise, Ford, General Motors and the Automobile Industry*. Random House, New York.
Conwell, Russell H. (1905) *Acres of Diamonds*. Random House, New York.
Edsforth, Ronald (1987) *Class Conflict and Cultural Consensus*. Rutgers University Press, New Brunswick.
Ewen, Stuart (1976) *Captains of Consciousness: Advertising and the Social Roots of the Consumer Culture*. McGraw-Hill, New York.
Filene, Edward A. (1924) *The Way Out: A Forecast of Coming Changes in American Business and Industry*. Nelson Doubleday, New York.

Ford, Henry (1929) *My Philosophy of Industry*. Coward-McCann Inc., New York.

Guerin, Daniel (1979) *100 Years of Labor in the USA*. Ink Links Ltd. London.

Inglis, William (1935) *George F. Johnson and His Industrial Democracy*. Endicott-Johnson Co., Endicott, NY.

Leitch, John (1919) *Man to Man: The Story of Industrial Democracy*. B. C. Forbes Co., New York.

Lynd, Robert S. and Helen Merrell Lynd (1929) *Middletown*. Harcourt, Brace and Co., New York.

Mandel, Ernest (1978) *Late Capitalism*. Verso, London.

Marx, Karl (1906) *Capital*, Vol. I. Modern Library, New York.

Matthaei, Julie A. (1982) *An Economic History of Women in America*. Schocken Books, New York.

McGuire, Randall H. (1988) "Dialogues with the Dead: Ideology and the Cemetery." In *The Recovery of Meaning*, ed. M. P. Leone and P. B. Potter, pp. 435–80, Smithsonian Institution Press, Washington, D.C.

McGuire, Randall H. and Cynthia Woodsong (1990) "Making Ends Meet: Unwaged Work and Domestic Inequality in Broome County New York 1930–1980." In *Work Without Wages: Comparative Studies of Housework and Petty Commodity Production*, eds J. L. Collins and M. E. Gimenez, pp. 169–92. State University of New York Press, Albany.

McGuire, Ross and Nancy Grey Osterud (1980) *Working Lives: Broome County New York, 1800–1930*. Roberson Center for the Arts and Sciences, Binghamton, NY.

Meyer, Stephen III (1981) *The Five Dollar Day*. State University of New York Press, Albany.

Nelson, Daniel (1975) *Managers and Workers: Origins of the New Factory System in the United States 1880–1920*. University of Wisconsin Press, Madison.

Slichter, Sumner H. (1919) *The Turnover of Factory Labor*. B. C. Forbes Co., New York.

Sumner, William Graham (1963) *Social Darwinism: Selected Essays*. Prentice-Hall, Englewood Cliffs, NJ.

Tentler, Leslie Woodcock (1979) *Wage Earning Women*. Oxford University Press, New York.

Walkowitz, Daniel J. (1978) *Worker City, Company Town*. University of Illinois Press, Urbana.

Zahavi, Gerald (1983) "Negotiated Loyalty: Welfare Capitalism and the Shoeworkers of Endicott Johnson, 1920–1940." *Journal of American History* 70(3), 602–20.

8

"Employees Must Be of Moral and Temperate Habits": Rural and Urban Elite Ideologies

LouAnn Wurst

Introduction

Now, sir, the men who are shrewd enough to make money are shrewd enough to see that they had better create a good moral atmosphere in the communities where they have made investments. They know that stocks and bonds and mortgages are all the more valuable for being within the sound of the church-going bell . . . (Goodykoontz 1939:35)

This passage, originally published in the *Home Missionary* in 1864, not only suggests an interesting correlation between business and standards of morality, but also implies the active role of the elite in formulating and enforcing this morality. At face value, this passage can be viewed as a blatantly instrumentalist statement of ideology.

Recent critiques of the conception of ideology (Patterson 1985; Larrain 1983; McGuire 1988) have emphasized that there are two very different conceptualizations of ideology. The first sees it as positive, as the totality of forms of social consciousness (McGuire 1988; Larrain 1983). While this is a highly pervasive view of ideology, it has been criticized since it equates ideology with the anthropological concept of culture (McGuire 1988). The second view, on the other hand, refers to a negative conception, where ideology serves to mystify real social contradictions and contribute to their reproduction (Patterson 1985; Larrain 1983). The combination of both of these positions leads to a functional, instrumental explanation of ideology as nothing more than a device or tool that one class uses to exploit another (McGuire 1988). The first view of ideology contributes the notion of a uniform cross-class consciousness, where the ideology is never pierced or challenged by dominated groups.

Abercrombie et al. (1980) have proposed an alternative view of ideology that tries to avoid this inherent instrumentalism. They have noted that in three major historical periods, the "dominant ideology," or the ideology of the dominant class, has served mainly to integrate the dominant class rather than subvert the subordinate classes, who in turn, either reject or reinterpret that dominant ideology. They conclude that a dominant ideology is a weak tool since it is often fractured and contradictory. Thus, the simplistic idea that ideology is something that the dominant class does to exploit the lower classes cannot be totally substantiated.

For our purposes, ideology will be defined as that subset of culture that is involved in power relations (McGuire 1988). This allows us both to get around the problem of equating culture with ideology and also to avoid an instrumentalist position by allowing not only different ideologies, but also different interpretations of the "dominant ideology" by different classes. This view also suggests that different sets of power relations will be involved in different ideological relations. Thus, different ideologies can exist side-by-side and more than likely in situations of conflict.

This paper will explore a conflict between the elite ideological structures of two different economic and power structures. Specifically, this case study deals with the conflict between rural and urban manufacturing. The conflict involves the collapse of rural manufacturing and the resultant domination of urban industry in Broome County, New York. I will focus on the ideology of the rural elite which stems from the religious movement of the Second Great Awakening during the first three decades of the nineteenth century. This movement entailed a radical change in Protestant theology and activated widespread moral and social reform movements.

Although the religious changes and activism of the Second Great Awakening occurred throughout the nation, most historians consider the area west of the Catskill and Adirondack Mountains (primarily around Rochester, Syracuse, Rome, and Utica) to be the areas most impacted by this religious enthusiasm. Cross (1950) has called this geographic area the "Burned-Over District." Even though Broome County falls within the geographic boundaries of the "Burned-Over District," the Second Great Awakening was not considered particularly strong in the area; Cross (1950) refers to Broome County as a "cold" area in terms of revival impacts.

Although the enthusiasm generated by the Second Great awakening may not have been very strong in the Binghamton area, a set of gravestone symbols associated with Second Great Awakening religion is present. Gravestones, then, become a very important medium through which to study the causes and factors of the Second Great Awakening for several reasons: (1) if it were not for the gravestone symbolism, we would never even associate the Awakening with Binghamton; (2) given that the Awakening is explicitly concerned with changes in the conception of salvation, gravestones are an appropriate material form to express these changes; (3) gravestones are easily dated; and (4) since gravestones are visible on and constitute a part of the built landscape, the symbolism can be seen as not only signifying the ideology of the Awakening, but also as playing an active role in creating and reproducing this ideology (McGuire this volume; Miller 1984; Parker Pearson 1982).

In order to interpret who is using the ideology of the Second Great Awakening and why, the location and dates of the gravestones become extremely important. The symbolism does not appear on gravestones in the Binghamton area until 30 to 40 years after the Second Great Awakening (mean date 1866). Also, the gravestone symbolism is rarely found in the urban cemeteries of Binghamton, but is commonly found in the cemeteries of the small agrarian and village communities that surround Binghamton (Wurst 1986). Another important aspect of the gravestone symbolism is that it occurs in very low frequencies: out of 1,644 gravestones examined from rural cemeteries, dating between 1800 and 1900, only 119, or 7.24 percent of the total stones had Second Great Awakening symbolism on them. The vast majority of nineteenth-century gravestones are undecorated.

The gravestone data in conjunction with historical information on the Second Great Awakening provide access to the ideology of the rural elite. A comparison with urban gravestones in Binghamton shows that this rural ideology was both in active conflict with the dominant ideology of the urban elite and yet also shared many characteristics with it.

The Religion of the Second Great Awakening

The Second Great Awakening is defined here as an ideology; this is contrary to most scholarship on the subject, which defines it as a specific historical event. This position allows consideration of the gravestone symbolism which would normally fall outside of traditional conceptions of the Second Great Awakening. The proposed ideology can be identified by a set of characteristic features involved in power relations (e.g., Johnson 1978).

The two most important characteristics of Protestant religion at this time were a shift in the theological conception of salvation and the widespread use of revival methods. The change in the theology of salvation entailed a shift from the Calvinist doctrine of the predestination of the elect, to an Arminian concept of salvation, where individuals control their own salvation (Adams 1801). For the Calvinist, the elect, those destined for salvation, were preordained from eternity. Individuals not elected could not change their fate, and attempts to repent sin were not considered signs of salvation, but rather as arising from mere selfish fear. The elect, on the other hand, could not avoid salvation regardless of their sins (Weisberger 1958:43). Arminianism by contrast, implies that the individual can attain salvation purely by faith and belief in Jesus Christ. This doctrine states that "election and reprobation are conditional, depending partly on the behavior of the sinner" (Weisberger 1958:43). Even though the Methodists accepted this doctrine during the First Great Awakening, it is only during the Second Great Awakening that this conception of salvation became predominant and spread to other Protestant groups (McLoughlin 1978:114).

With Arminianism, the emphasis of Protestant religion became the active conversion of sinners, an approach that would have been blasphemous and inconsistent under Calvinist doctrines. To accommodate these goals, revival techniques called the "New Measures" by Charles Grandison Finney, the most notable evangelist of the Second Great Awakening, came into general use. One of the most important of the "New Measures" was the concept of social prayer, which transformed prayer into a public and intensely social event (Johnson 1978:97). Finney (1960) advised that preaching must be direct, grounded in common experience, colloquial in manner, and repetition must be frequent. A radical new practice was to call on sinners out loud and by name instead of using the commonly accepted third person (Cross 1950). Other New Measures included allowing women to pray and exhort when men were present (McLoughlin 1978:124), protracted prayer meetings, lasting sometimes as long as a month, and the use of the "anxious seat" or "mourner's bench" (Carwardine 1972). The anxious seat was probably the most controversial of the New Measures. It consisted of a special bench or pew that was located at the front of the congregation to which sinners were asked to come for special prayers and to be encouraged by the ministers and the other converted church members (Carwardine 1972; McLoughlin 1978).

The effects of all of these New Measures was to make the conversion experience both social and visible. Since under the Arminian doctrine individuals had control over their own salvation, the only way to be converted was from within, by individual choice. This implied that those who were not converted actively chose not to be. The result was an intense moral and religious missionary movement that attempted to convert the entire world, an ideal made possible, though optimistic, by the newly accepted doctrine of salvation. Finney himself said that "if they were united all over the world, the Millennium might be brought about in three months" (Finney 1876). The coming of the Millennium, the reign of heaven on earth, was the logical and inevitable result of the conversion of everyone on earth.

The idea that a return to uncompromising personal standards was necessary for the coming of the Millennium was directly related to the emphasis on conversion (Johnson 1978). Challenges were made against immoral practices such as intemperance, slavery and the breaking of the Sabbath. A whole rash of moral and social reform societies dedicated to furthering the Millennium came into existence; by far the most common and popular of these were temperance associations (Gusfield 1963), home missions, Bible distribution and tract societies (Goodykoontz 1939; Brooks 1900), and Sunday Schools (LaQueur 1976; Cross 1950). Social reform organizations were most active in prison and insane asylum reform, relief for the poor, and school reform movements (Rothman 1971; Katz 1968; Crandall 1969; Mohl 1971; Rosenberg 1971).

Revivalism became accepted practice as a result of the Second Great Awakening, but did not remain static throughout the nineteenth century. Initially, conservative members of society considered revivals an irrational frenzy of emotional enthusiasm (Bell 1977; Cross 1950). By the 1830s evangelists and revivals became an accepted part of life (Weisberger 1958). Handbooks and manuals such as Finney's *Lectures On Revivals Of Religion* (1960), which listed all that one needed to know in order to "get up" a successful revival, ritualized the techniques. By the turn of the twentieth century, evangelists had gained a reputation much as we know them today.

During the Second Great Awakening, revivals were predominantly a rural phenomenon, having little success in the cities (Bell 1977; Rosenberg 1971; McLoughlin 1978; however, see Carwardine 1972). It has been said that "Finney prolonged his meetings, not only into the small hours of the morning, but for day after day, so that all business was brought to a standstill" (Miller 1965:24). This method was fine in rural areas at times when there was little work to do, but revivals practiced like this were not effective in urban commercial and industrial areas that did not operate with slack work periods.

Revival methods had changed by the 1850s to make them compatible with "modern" urban business practices. This change is exemplified by the "Businessmen's Revival" of 1857–8 (McLoughlin 1978), which was characterized by its urban nature and that "it relied upon businessmen, business methods and the business outlook" (Bell 1977:169). Instead of the protracted revival meetings of Finney's day, the "characteristic feature of these revivals was the noonday prayer meeting, in which thousands of people met for an hour of services and prayer in the midst of their work day" (Bell 1977:178). The "Businessmen's Revival" and the revival meetings of Dwight L. Moody and Ira Sankey from 1875 to 1885 (McLoughlin 1978) transformed revival practices to accommodate them to the urban industrial setting.

This survey of the changes in revival practice during the nineteenth century brings to light some problems involved in viewing the Second Great Awakening as a static historical event. By defining the Awakening as an ideology with its key characteristics being personal salvation and individual morality, we can look at the changes and reinterpretations of these characteristics through time even though these changes fall outside of the traditionally accepted bounds of the Second Great Awakening.

Manufacturing and the Second Great Awakening

Johnson (1978) presents one of the most detailed explanations of the Second Great Awakening. Johnson identifies a rural elite of people who processed local raw materials into finished goods either for sale to people in the countryside or for export (1978:17). Using church records, diaries, and other historical sources from the Rochester area, Johnson was able to demonstrate that it was this rural elite who had attended, and in fact initiated, the revivals of the Second Great Awakening. He attributes their activity to a loss of social control.

According to Johnson, the loss of social control by the rural elite was due to the breakdown of the apprenticeship system, the increasing separation of work and living spaces and the creation of class-based neighborhoods. Because of these changes, workers were no longer living in the houses of their employers, which freed them from the immediate discipline exerted by the older, household-centered relations of production (1978:48). For Johnson, then, the ideology of the Second Great Awakening and the revivals and social and moral reform associations, initiated and controlled by the rural elite, provided them with the means of imposing new standards of work discipline and moral behavior which functioned as an important social control. The rural elite also used the ideology of the Second Great Awakening to mitigate the effects of increased separation of the classes and the potential for open class conflict. The Awakening ostensibly recreated society into two groups that obscured the class structure, the saved and the non-saved or Christians and non-Christians. According to Johnson, this realignment helped eliminate open class conflict during this time by creating a "class" composed of both workers and employers who were preceived as having the same interests.

Johnson's analysis shows that the rural elite were soon joined at revivals by large numbers of wage earners (1978:119). The workers accepted the new standards of labor discipline because the ideology incorporated democratic ideals, specifically that social mobility hinged on moral habits, hard work and temperance. Church-goers were twice as stable as non-church-goers in terms of long time residency, and the relationship between occupational advance and church membership was strong throughout the entire wage-earning population (1978:122).

Johnson argues that church membership "induced habits and attitudes that fit comfortably with a market economy and disciplined work environment" (1978:124). Along with this went a healthy dose of coercion. Employers began to demand the personal piety of employees, and insisted on seeing them in church (Johnson 1978:121). In some cases, conforming to the ideals of the Awakening was a prerequisite for obtaining employment. For example, job advertisements from Rochester state: "none need apply except those of moral habits and the best of workmen"; "employees must be of moral and temperate habits"; or "none but temperate men need apply" (Johnson 1978:122).

The Gravestone Symbolism

By 1850, the previously universal urn-and-willow gravestone decoration was no longer being used in Broome County and a whole new set of gravestone symbols took its place. Many of these symbols transcend the Second Great Awakening and continue as Christian religious symbols up to the present. The most common gravestone symbols associated with the Second Great Awakening ideology are the one-way sign, or index finger pointing toward heaven, clasped hands, the Bible, the laurel wreath, the anchor, and the flag. Thse symbols will all be discussed individually.

The one-way sign is by far the most common symbol in the Broome County area, being found on 45 percent (54 stones) of the stones with Second Great Awakening symbolism (figure 8.1). This symbol is a warning and lesson to all that pass by that Jesus Christ is the one way to salvation (Olderr 1986). Through this symbol the gravestone indicates that the buried individual has gone to Jesus and proclaims to all others that it is not too late to follow the same path. Epitaphs frequently accompanying this symbol, "Gone to heaven," "At rest in heaven," and "At rest," make this connection even clearer. These sentiments, expressing assurance of salvation and warning others to follow the same path, would have been unthinkable and even blasphemous under the Calvinist doctrine of predestination of the elect.

Figure 8.1 Gravestone showing one-way sign (photograph by LouAnn Wurst)

Clasped hands represent 11.76 percent (14 stones) of the gravestone symbols (figure 8.2). Hands in general represent "the corporal manifestation of the inner state of the human body" (Cirlot 1971) and often appear with other Second Great Awakening symbols. Two hands joined together signifies mystic marriage (Cirlot 1971) or union, brotherhood and alliance (Olderr 1986). On a tombstone, clasped hands also symbolize farewell and welcome (Olderr 1986). In Holmes and Barber's (1854) *Religious Emblems*, Christian Faith is portrayed as Truth and Hope with joined hands while Love stands in the background (figure 8.3).

The anchor represents 10 percent of the sample or 12 stones (figure 8.4). The symbolism of the anchor derives directly from the Bible: "We who have taken refuge in him might be strongly encouraged to seize the hope which is placed before us like a sure and firm anchor" (Heb.6:19). The anchor symbolizes hope of heaven or salvation with the apostle Paul as the anchor (Holmes and Barber 1854). The anchor also signifies the ship as the Church of God and emphasizes missionization, literally of other peoples and cultures, but more importantly within the community, and the necessities of moral and social reform. One epitaph on a gravestone with an anchor is "We are drifting on the tide but she has gained the shore."

Figure 8.2 Gravestones decorated with clasped hands (photograph by LouAnn Wurst)

The Bible symbolizes the intensely individualistic nature of Second Great Awakening religion. The idea that every man was his own preacher was the major impetus for Bible Distribution Societies; it became essential for every individual to read and interpret the Bible rather than accept traditional Calvinist doctrine. The Bible was used to signify this individualized religion as opposed to the strict organization of Calvinism (Weisberger 1958). The Bible carved on the gravestone comprises 9.24 percent of the sample, or 11 stones (figure 8.5).

The last symbol exclusively of the Second Great Awakening ideology that occurs in any frequency, 12.6 percent (15 stones), is the laurel wreath. The laurel wreath has been a common symbol of victory since the Romans. On gravestones, in the seventeenth and early eighteenth centuries laurel wreaths were sometimes found encircling a death's head carving, symbolizing the victory of death. In the nineteenth century, however, this symbol is usually found alone or encircling the one-way sign. The meaning of this symbol has changed to the victory of the soul (Stannard 1977; deVries 1974).

Other symbols of the Second Great Awakening are usually made up of combinations of the above: hand on the Bible (6.72% or 8 stones); hand holding a broken rose (2.54% or 3 stones); hand holding a broken chain (0.84% or 1 stone); and a hand holding a flag (0.84% or 1 stone). The flag is also a symbol of victory, in this case non-military (Olderr 1986).

All of these symbols emphasize not only salvation but the assurance of salvation, one of the basic characteristics of Second Great Awakening belief. Common epitaphs on gravestones with these decorations make the idea of assurance even clearer: "At Rest"; "Gone Home"; "Gone to Heaven"; "Blessed are the dead that die in the Lord"; and "Meet Me in Heaven." Thus death became the final arbitrator of salvation:

> death! what art thou to the Christian's assurance? Great hour of answer to life's prayer – great hour that shall break asunder the bond of life's mystery – hour of release from life's burden – hour of reunion with the loved and lost – what mighty hopes hasten their fulfillment in thee . . . Oh! Death! the Christian's death! What art thou but the gate of life, the portal of heaven, the threshold of eternity! (Dewey 1885).

Till we all come in the unity of the Faith. Ephes. iv. **13.**

Figure 8.3 Illustration portraying Christian faith (taken from Holmes and Barber 1854:13). Note that all the Second Great Awakening gravestone symbols are present

Figure 8.4 Gravestone showing anchor in conjunction with a boat and Masonic eye (photograph by LouAnn Wurst)

Figure 8.5 Gravestone with a hand holding a Bible (photograph by LouAnn Wurst)

The gravestone symbols and epitaphs make this message clear. As the following epitaph shows, there is always a chance for salvation as long as there is life:

> Dear Jesus, Dear Jesus,
> Her last words
> Her only hope

Methodology

A comparison of rural and urban cemeteries was performed as an outgrowth of the Binghamton Gravestone Project (McGuire 1988; Clark 1986). The most important difference between the urban (Binghamton) and rural/country data sets is that decoration in general, and the Second Great Awakening symbolism specifically, appeared to be more common in the rural cemeteries than in the urban gravestone sample throughout the nineteenth century. The data themselves substantiated this; out of a total of 634 nineteenth-century gravestones collected from Protestant cemeteries in Binghamton, none of the stones had Second Great

Awakening symbolism on them. In the rural cemeteries collected for the Project, only five gravestones out of 366, or 1.36 percent, had the symbolism.

Data were collected from 11 rural cemeteries in Broome County. Information recorded included: the kind of symbolism, the form and material of the gravestone, the name and dates of the individual(s) buried there, any epitaph (if legible), and any information from associated graves (for example, if the stone with symbolism is the wife's, and the husband's is undecorated, or if the symbolism occurs on an obelisk, with whose name is it associated, etc.). Often it was not possible to collect all this information since some stones were illegible due to erosion, buried or sunk into the ground, or broken. When any of these situations arose, as much information as possible was collected.

To determine the frequency of the symbolism, a 100 percent sample of nineteenth-century marble stones in the cemeteries was collected for comparative pruposes. For this sample, only the date of the stone and whether or not it exhibited Second Great Awakening symbolism was recorded. The dates of the stones themselves were collected in five-year intervals (1850 to 1855, etc.). This 100 percent sample of all marble stones was collected for nine rural cemeteries.

The gravestone data (table 8.1) indicate that the Second Great Awakening symbolism does in fact occur in low frequency. The symbolism in Broome County ranges from 3 to 14 percent of the total nineteenth-century stones per cemetery, having an average of 7.23 percent for the entire sample. The mean date of the Second Great Awakening symbolism in Broome County is 1866.

Information on the occupations of individuals and families using the symbols was essential to interpret the gravestone data in Broome County. Occupational information for rural areas is sometimes difficult to obtain; city and suburban directories for Binghamton and Broome County were begun in the 1850s, but the information for rural areas is remarkably sketchy. Most of the earliest directories list only the individual names for each area, sometimes including the address. The only directories that consistently list the occupations for rural areas are Boyd's 1869 and Williams' 1889 Directories. While these contain valuable information, most of the individuals in the rural sample were dead before 1869.

Federal Manuscript Censuses were also consulted in order to collect occupational information for the rural sample. However, the Manuscript Census reports practically everyone as a farmer. While this is undoutedly true, the censuses tend to ignore additional economic activities.

The Broome County histories (Wilkinson 1967; Smith 1885; Lawyer 1900; Seward 1924) were the most valuable source of occupational

Table 8.1 The gravestone sample, Broome County

Cemetery	Total stones	Total decorated (N/%)	Mean date	No. with occupational information (N/%)
Upper Lisle	229	32 (14)	1861	3 (9.4)
Glen Aubrey	75	8 (10.66)	1875	0 (0)
Maine	234	7 (3)	1864	1 (14)
Windsor	235	12 (5)	1864	10 (83)
Allentown	52	4 (7.7)	1855	0 (0)
U. Center	144	9 (6)	1867	1 (11)
Riverside	318	17 (5.3)	1867	7 (41)
Vestal	152	8 (5.3)	1871	5 (62.5)
Kattellville	205	10 (5)	1865	5 (50)
Deposit	n/a	8	1866	5 (62)
Port Crane	n/a	4	1873	2 (50)
Totals	1644	119	1866	

information. These local histories give a detailed account of the first settlers in each town and village, discussing the most prominent citizens, businessmen, and "Factors" in the area's history. Some individuals present in the gravestone sample were discussed in these histories as farmers, but the very fact of their being mentioned suggests a more prominent social position than we would normally ascribe to farmers. While it is certainly true that these histories enumerate only the most powerful citizens in terms of society and economy, and is hence incredibly biased, almost all of the occupational information on the sample was obtained from these sources. Since most of the individuals in the gravestone sample were included in these sources, the sample itself is biased to the inclusion of rural elites.

Out of a total gravestone sample of 107 stones with Second Great Awakening symbolism on them, data on the occupations were collected for 42 heads of households, representing 68 stones including wives, children, etc. This represents 64 percent of the sample. The occupations obtained, along with the number of heads of households practicing each, are listed in table 8.2. Individuals practicing 28 (66.66 percent) of the 42 occupations owned or operated rural industries or manufacturing establishments. The exceptions are the four "Prominent" merchants, the storekeeper, the inventor, the six preachers, and the two doctors or dentists. However, these occupations can still be considered elite in the sense that they represent the most powerful and/or wealthy individuals in a rural community. Assuming this, the overwhelming majority of individuals who used Second Great Awakening symbolism on their gravestones belonged to the class of rural elite.

The Rural Elite in Broome County

The initial economy of Broome County was based on the extraction and processing of local raw materials (McGuire and Osterud 1980; Osterud 1983). During the first three decades of the nineteenth century, timber was the major marketable commodity and lumbering was the leading

Table 8.2 Occupational information of individuals with Second Great Awakening Symbolism on gravestones

No. of individuals	Occupation
3	lumber and flour mills
1	grist mills
1	carriage maker
3	tanner and currier
1	manufacturer of well curbs
4	"Prominent" merchant
1	flour/grist/sawmill; store and hotel
1	tannery; churn, firkin, tub, and barrell factory
1	land agent
1	blacksmith
10	farmer
1	carpenter
6	preacher, minister
1	harness maker
1	inventor, Windsor Bridge Co.
2	surgeon, dentist, doctor
1	steam sawmill and blacksmith shop
1	sawmill and rake factory
1	grist mill and prominent merchant
1	storekeeper
Total 42	

sector of the economy (Osterud 1983:47). Lumbering and clearing the land was the obvious prerequisite for agricultural pursuits.

Small manufacturing and commercial enterprises developed rapidly throughout Broome County after 1820. These manufacturing concerns processed local raw materials into finished goods for export and for sale in Broome County. High transportation costs during this period made the finishing of raw materials into transportable products essential to the economy of the area. The most important of these manufacturers were saw, grist, and flour mills, distilleries, asheries, tanneries, blacksmith shops, and wagon makers.

The rural industries that developed encountered difficulties due to changes in inland transportation. The Chenango Canal, completed in 1836, connecting Binghamton with Utica, had only a limited initial impact on rural manufacturers and artisans since traffic on the canal was seasonal, cargo space was limited, and transport was costly. The primary impact of the canal was to consolidate Binghamton's position as the commercial center for the Broome County area (McGuire and Osterud 1980:36). The Erie Railroad accelerated this consolidation in 1849, and finally, and efficiently, connected Binghamton with the national market network (Bothwell 1983).

As Binghamton's position solidified, non-agricultural manufacturing concerns became concentrated and centralized in the city to take advantage of these transportation routes (McGuire and Osterud 1980:35). Developments in production machinery, new forms of power, and the rail system reduced manufacturers' need to be located near raw materials and increased the demand for access to capital and labor. Since these were rare in rural areas, industry and manufacturing became centralized in urban areas (Gibb 1985:14). Rural industry and manufacturing establishments were unable to compete with their urban counterparts and were either forced into extinction or survived by shifting their strategy to rural retail and repair shops (Gibb 1985).

The decline of rural industry seems to have accelerated after mid-century. In 1845, the Federal Census of Manufacturers listed 179 sawmills in the county and by 1872, only 109 remained (Hough 1872). This is due in part to the decrease in available lumber as well as to the centralization and expansion of extant lumber and sawmills. After mid-century many rural manufacturers began to close down. One of the largest tanneries in the county, employing 26 people, was shut down in 1872.

In sum, production of non-agricultural goods became centralized in urban areas where there was direct access to capital, labor, and transportation. This necessarily effected the demise of rural industry and manufacturing, since rural areas did not have access to these requirements.

The class of the rural elite, who owned and operated these industries, suffered at the hands of the emergent urban industrial elite. With the elimination of its industry and manufacturing, rural Broome County took on the appearance of a homogeneous agricultural area.

Gravestones and Decline

As this survey of the position of the rural elite in Broome County shows, we cannot interpret the use of the Second Great Awakening symbolism as a confirmation of Johnson's explanation; the situation is much more complex. To review, Johnson interprets the Second Great Awakening and the religious and social reform movements as the means whereby the rural elite could maintain and intensify their control over the labor force with the advent of large-scale manufacturing and the competitive market economy. In Broome County the symbolism occurs (mean date 1866) just when the rural industry in that area is in a state of collapse, and it is associated with those people who have the most to lose (both power and money) by these changes in the economic structure. This is a very different situation from that described by Johnson. The symbolism on the gravestones in Broome County appears to be a situation where the symbolism of a movement that originally gave the class of the rural elite its power and stability (according to Johnson) is being recouped and materialized at the time when that class is experiencing its greatest economic stress.

This idea can be strengthened by comparing the frequency of the symbolism among the different cemeteries collected in Broome County. For example, the cemeteries that have the highest frequency of symbolism (more than 10 percent), Glen Aubrey and Upper Lisle, are located in communities that had exclusive reliance on the extractive economy, and as communities, were devastated by the centralization of industry and manufacturing in Binghamton. In 1855, Upper Lisle contained a gun shop, harness shop, sawmill, two blacksmith shops, a carpenter shop, two hotels, a tannery, grist mill, two stores and a last factory (Gifford and Wenig 1855). By 1908, the only industries located in Upper Lisle were a cheese and butter factory, a grist mill and a sawmill (*Plat Book of Broome County* 1908). The effects of the decline of rural industry and manufacturing in Upper Lisle can be summed up by saying: "Forty years (1860–1900) have wrought many changes in the condition of the affairs of Upper Lisle, and the hamlet people no longer can enjoy their old-time prestige" (Lawyer 1900:760).

The same state of affairs seems to have existed in Glen Aubrey. Among other industry, a large tannery was located in the village. In

1855, the Glen Aubrey Tannery had a real property value of $15,000 and had produced $122,500 worth of leather; the tannery also owned 21 company houses for its employees (Greenmun 1976). When the tannery closed down operations in 1872, 26 employees worked for them. It is curious that an operation of this scale is barely mentioned in the histories of Smith (1885) and Lawyer (1900). We can, perhaps, assume that the rural industries in Glen Aubrey were so reduced in importance by the time these histories were written that it was not even mentioned.

The cemeteries that have the lowest frequency of symbolism (5 percent or less), on the other hand, are Kattellville, Maine, Windsor, Riverside, Vestal, Port Crane, and Deposit. All of these communities, with the exception of Kattellville, served as commercial centers for the larger rural region. This is not to suggest that industry was not an important sector of the economy, or that these communities did not face the same problem with the centralization and concentration of industry in Binghamton. Discussing the village of Lisle, Lawyer says:

> For more than three quarters of a century Lisle has been an agricultural and industrial town, and during the last thirty years (1870–1900) agriculture in a great measure has replaced all other business pursuits. This does not come from the fact that the industrial resources of the town are exhausted, but rather indicates that manufacturing industries have gradually withdrawn and removed to the larger commercial centers where labor is more easily secured and where transportation facilities are better. (Lawyer 1900:684).

Even though these communities suffered the same decline in rural extractive industries, the towns seem to have been commercial centers for the surrounding rural areas. Lawyer noted that Maine was the "chief center of trade in the town for more than half a century" (Lawyer 1900:713).

One other important factor that seems to have mitigated the effect of the loss of rural industry was the railroad(s). The village of Deposit was located along the Erie Railroad line and contained an important railroad station. Beginning in the 1850s, businesses were moving from old locations to be closer to the station, or establishing new businesses in the area (Lynch 1976). The villages of Lisle and Whitney's Point are both located along the Syracuse and Binghamton Railroad line. This railroad began operations in 1854, and appears to have been an economic boost to both of these communities.

The economic structure of these villages as commercial centers is very different from that for areas that relied exclusively on agriculture and rural industry. The commercial sector of the economy may have acted as a buffer against the stress of the collapse of rural industry. This may have circumvented the need for the material expression of Second Great Awakening symbolism, explaining the low frequency, and may also explain why the cemeteries located in these villages are more "urban" in character than the other cemeteries in the sample. The commercial "factors" in these communities would be more likely to follow urban examples of material culture than to align themselves materially with a declining class.

Rural versus urban

The best way to understand the differences between nineteenth-century rural and urban cemeteries is to view them as material manifestations of different ideological strategies followed by different groups. The Second Great Awakening has been identified as an ideology that served the rural elite. Since the urban elite were involved in different power relations we can assume that their ideology was different from that of the rural elite. This is substantiated by the material differences of each group as exemplified by the gravestones.

The rural elite, as well as just about everyone else in rural areas, practiced the religion of Evangelical Protestantism. It was important that distinctions between the rural elite and common people should be played down. The industries owned and operated by the rural elite were tied very closely to the rural producers – both because of the demand for raw materials and for a market to dispose of the finished goods. Johnson notes that in Rochester, those "who entered the country trade without meeting its cultural and behavior standards" were soon forced out of business (1978:21).

The strategy practiced by the rural elite was one of minimizing, ignoring, or playing down class differences between elites and non-elites. This strategy was followed in the attendance of the same churches (or at very least the same denomination); it is also evident in the community cemetery, which portrays little differentiation in the size, shape, or material of gravestones, except for the Second Great Awakening symbolism, between elite and non-elite groups.

In urban areas, specifically Binghamton, the reverse of this situation is true. Urban elites seem to have followed a strategy of strict and active class separation, in religion as well as in the cemeteries. Binghamton's urban elite, including those who organized and were buried in Spring Forest, Binghamton's grandest cemetery, were Episcopalians. The American Anglican or Episcopalian Church has a long history of being the church of the landed aristocracy, and later of the urban elite (Sanford 1904; Goodykoontz 1939; Mullen 1986; Konolige and Konolige 1978; Hodges 1906). Even within recent decades the vast majority of America's business elite belonged to the Episcopal Church (Keller 1963).

Episcopalianism was the only Protestant denomination that actively rejected the social/religious morality of the Second Great Awakening. The Episcopalians' approach to religion has always been one of separation:

> the standard image of the successfully and socially prestigious average Episcopalian congregation seems to fly in the face of any talk of the travail of assimilation . . . Episcopal theology has always marched to a drummer different from that of the rest of Protestantism . . . The historical question for American Episcopalians has always been how to keep their church intellectually distinct while being socially assimilated. (Mullen 1986:x)

Episcopalianism in the nineteenth century followed a policy of isolationism; they did not join in the missionary works of their Protestant compatriots, nor did they engage in moral reform organizations (Goodykoontz 1939:103). A strict policy of segregation of the urban elite from non-elite groups was maintained.

This policy of separation was also carried out in the cemeteries. Spring Forest was created by the urban Episcopalian elite of Binghamton, giving them a medium within which to emphasize and maintain the distinction between the classes. With the organization of the new cemetery, small marble tablet gravestones began to give way both to large family markers and to the use of granite as a material. These prestigious cemeteries of the nineteenth century were used in ways analogous to modern parks, for walks, picnics, and outings. Grave markers and monuments were erected with the knowledge that they would be seen and commented on; they were very visible public statements (McGuire 1988). Even granite as a material was important for ostentatious display, since at this time it was much more expensive than marble and evoked connotations of permanence, progress, and modernity (Wurst 1985).

Economically, the urban elite were not tied to other social classes in the same way as the rural elite. Industry and manufacturing became centralized in urban areas in order to have direct access to capital, labor, and transportation. Production in urban areas was based on the extraction of absolute surplus value, which involved both the intensification of labor and the lengthening of the work day. This implied a reserve army of unemployed laborers and a high labor turnover (Amsden 1979; Marx 1906). The material distinctions between the urban elite and the laboring classes both grew out of and created these relations of production since the urban elite accrued large profits but the laborers could afford few of the products they manufactured and thus maintained low levels of material consumption (McGuire 1984:4).

These class relations were rationalized by a complex ideology formulated by and used to reinforce the position of the urban elite. Developed after the Civil War, this ideology, referred to as Social

Darwinism or the gospel of wealth, maintained that the real and material differences between the classes derived from inequalities in the characters of individuals. This determination was considered immutable since it was based on scientific principles, and the emphasis was secular and thus more "rational" (Conwell 1905; Sumner 1963). The basic tenet of this ideology is that success was attainable by all, and was determined by the individual's character. Those individuals who succeeded did so because of hard work, thrift, intelligence, sobriety, and cleanliness (McGuire 1988). On the other hand, the fate of the common laborer was naturalized because they lacked these characteristics; they did not work hard enough or they drank and squandered money.

It is not surprising, then, that the differences between the urban elite and the laboring classes were actively stressed both socially and materially. The urban elites were not tied to or dependent on other social classes as a source of raw materials or as a market for finished products in the way the rural elite were, so there was not the same incentive to minimize class distinctions. It is only with the development of mass production, based on non-elite groups as consumers, that this urban ideology changes to actively minimize class distinctions (see McGuire 1984).

Even though the roots of the ideology of the urban elite are distinct from the ideology of the Second Great Awakening propagated by and for the rural elite, there are interesting similarities between them. The most prominent of these is the concept of the attainability of success based on individual characteristics. Even the characteristics emphasized by each of these ideologies are the same: sobriety, thrift, hard work, and morality. The very name "gospel of wealth" suggests strong alliances between the two ideologies. The major difference between them is in the stated goal; for the ideology of the Second Great Awakening, the ultimate goal was success in the afterlife, heaven, whereas the ideology of the urban elite emphasized material success and wealth.

Conclusion

This analysis has shown that in Broome County during the second half of the nineteenth century two different ideologies existed side by side: the ideology of the rural elite stemming from the religion of the Second Great Awakening, and that of the urban elite whose emphasis was both scientific and secular (Hofstadter 1944). Although these two ideologies shared many similar characteristics, the implications of each for the social and material relations between elite and non-elite groups were very different. The rural elite ideology actively minimized or ignored class differences while the urban elite strove to accentuate those differences.

Given this analysis, it becomes impossible to view ideology in simplistic functional terms. The classes of rural and urban elite, as well as their ideologies, did not exist in isolation but in conflict. The loss of power experienced by the rural elite was directly related to the rise of the urban elite. Even though there are similarities between the two ideologies, I think it is significant that the rural elite, at their demise, are materially symbolizing the major difference between them, the religious aspects.

ACKNOWLEDGEMENTS

This research was part of the Binghamton Gravestone Project, and would not have been possible without the help of everyone involved in that project. I would especially like to thank Randy McGuire, Lynn Clark, and Mark Cassell for their help. Any errors are, of course, my own.

REFERENCES

Abercrombie, N., S. Hill and B. Turner (1980) *The Dominant Ideology Thesis.* Allen and Unwin, London.
Adams, Hannah (1801) *A View of Religions.* Manning and Loring, Boston.
Amsden, John (1979) "Introduction." In *100 Years of Labor in the USA,* by Daniel Guerin. Ink Links Ltd, London.
Bell, Marion L. (1977) *Crusade in the City: Revivalism in Nineteenth Century Philadelphia.* Bucknell University Press, London.
Bothwell, Lawrence (1983) *Broome County Heritage.* Windsor Publications, Woodland Hills, NY.
Boyd, Andrew (pub. and compiler) (1869) *Boyd's Binghamton Directory for 1869-70.* Albany, New York.
Brooks, Charles Wesley (1900) *A Century of Missions in the Empire State.* American Baptist Publication Society, Philadelphia.
Carwardine, Richard (1972) "The Second Great Awakening in the Urban Centers: An Examination of Methodism and the 'New Measures'." *Journal of American History* 59, 327-40.
Cirlot, J. E. (1971) *A Dictionary of Symbols.* Philosophical Library, New York.
Clark, Lynn Marie (1986) *Ethnicity in Binghamton Cemeteries.* MA Thesis, Department of Anthropology, State University of New York, Binghamton.
Conwell, Russell H. (1905) *Acres of Diamonds.* Random House, New York.
Crandall, John C. (1969) "Patriotism and Humanitarian Reform in Children's Literature, 1825-1860." *American Quarterly* 21, 3-22.
Cross, Whitney R. (1950) *The Burned-Over District: The Social and Intellectual*

History of Enthusiastic Religion in Western New York, 1800–1850. Harper and Row, New York.

deVries, A. D. (1974) *Dictionary of Symbols and Imagery.* North Holland Publishing Co., Amsterdam.

Dewey, Orville (1885) "Death as the Gate of Life." In *The Home Beyond of Views of Heaven and its Relation to Earth,* ed. Dr Samuel Fallows, p. 105. Fairbanks and Palmer, Chicago.

Finney, Charles Grandison (1876) *Memoirs of Rev. Charles G. Finney, written by himself.* A. S. Barnes, New York.

——(1960) *Lectures on Revivals of Religion.* Harvard University Press, Cambridge, MA.

Gibb, James (1985) *Centralization and Cultural Transformation Processes: The Archaeology of Wagon Shops and Other Artisan Shops.* Master's Thesis, State University of New York at Binghamton.

Gifford, Franklin and E. Wenig (1855) *Map of Broome County from Actual Surveys.* A. D. Gallop and Co., Philadelphia.

Goodykoontz, Colin Brummitt (1939) *Home Missions on the American Frontier.* Caxton Publishers, Caldwell, ID.

Greenmun, Kathleen (1976) "Town of Nanticoke: A Brief History." In *Historical Essays on the Sixteen Towns of Broome County.* Broome County American Revolution Bicentennial Commission, Broome County, NY.

Gusfield, Joseph R. (1963) *Symbolic Crusade: Status, Politics and the American Temperance Movement.* University of Illinois Press, Chicago.

Hodges, george (1906) *Three Hundred Years of the Episcopal Church in America.* W. Jacobs Co., Philadelphia.

Hofstadter, Richard (1944) *Social Darwinism in American Thought.* University of Pennsylvania Press, Philadelphia.

Holmes, William and John W. Barber (1854) *Religious Emblems: being a series of emblematic engravings with written explanations, miscellaneous observations and religious reflections, designed to illustrate Divine Truth, in accordance with the cardinal principles of Christianity.* Henry Howe, Cincinnati, OH.

Hough, Franklin B. (1872) *Gazetteer of the State of New York.* Andrew Boyd, Albany, NY.

Johnson, Paul E. (1978) *A Shopkeeper's Millennium.* Hill and Wang, New York.

Katz, Michael B. (1968) *The Irony of Early School Reform: Educational Innovation in Mid-Nineteenth Century Massachusetts.* Harvard University Press, Cambridge, MA.

Keller, Suzanne (1983) *Beyond the Ruling Class: Strategic Elites in Modern Society.* Random House, New York.

Konolige, Kit and Frederica Konolige (1978) *The Power of Their Glory, America's Ruling Class: The Episcopalians.* Wyden Books, New York.

LaQueur, Thomas Walter (1976) *Religion and Respectability: Sunday Schools and Working Class Culture 1780–1850.* Yale University Press, New York.

Larrain, Jorge (1983) *Marxism and Ideology* Macmillan Press, London.

Lawyer, William S. (1900) *Binghamton: Its Settlement, Growth and Development and the Factors in its History 1800–1900.* Century Memorial Publishing Company, Boston, MA.

Lynch, Margaret R. (1976) "Brief Historical Review of the Town of Sanford." In *Historical Essays on the Sixteen Towns of Broome County*. Broome County American Revolution Bicentennial Commission, Broome County, NY.

Marx, Karl (1906) *Capital*, Vol. I. Modern Library, New York.

McGuire, Randall (1984) "Elite Responses to Resistance." Paper presented at the meetings of the Society for Historical Archaeology, Boston.

——(1988) "Dialogues with the Dead: Ideology and the Cemetery." In *The Recovery of Meaning in Historical Archaeology*, eds M. P. Leone and P. B. Potter. Smithsonian Institution Press, Washington, D.C.

McGuire, Ross and Nancy Grey Osterud (1980) *Working Lives: Broome County, New York 1800–1930*. Roberson Center for the Arts and Sciences, Binghamton, New York.

McLoughlin, William G. (1976) *Revivals, Awakenings and Reform: An Essay on Religion and Social Change in America*. University of Chicago Press, Chicago.

Miller, Daniel (1984) "Modernism and Suburbia as Material Ideology." In *Ideology, Power and Prehistory*, eds Daniel Miller and Christopher Tilley. Cambridge University Press, New York.

Miller, Perry (1965) *The Life of the Mind in America*. Harcourt, Brace and World, New York.

Mohl, Raymond (1971) *Poverty in New York, 1783–1825*. Oxford University Press, New York.

Mullen, John (1986) *Episcopal Vision/American Reality: High Church Theology and Social Thought in Evangelical America*. Yale University Press, New Haven, CT.

Olderr, Steven (1986) *Symbolism: A Comprehensive Dictionary*. McFarland and Company, New York and London.

Osterud, Nancy Grey (1983) *Strategies of Mutuality: Relations Among Women and Men in an Agricultural Community*. Ph.D. Dissertation, Brown University, Providence.

Parker Pearson, Michael (1982) "Mortuary Practices, Society and Ideology: An Ethnoarchaeological Study." In *Symbolic and Structural Archaeology*, ed. Ian Hodder. Cambridge University Press, New York.

Patterson, Thomas (1985) "Culture and Ideology: Alternate Concepts or Different Methods." Paper presented at the 1985 RATS Meetings, Department of Anthropology, State University of New York at Binghamton.

Plat Book of Broome County (1908) North West Publishing Company, Des Moines, IA.

Rosenberg, Carroll Smith (1971) *Religion and the Rise of the American City: The New York City Mission Movement, 1812–1870*. Cornell University Press, Ithaca.

Rothman, David J. (1971) *The Discovery of the Asylum: Social Order and Disorder in the New Republic*. Little and Brown Co., New York.

Sanford, Elias Benjamin (ed.) (1904) *A Concise Cyclopedia of Religious Knowledge*. The S. S. Scranton Co., Hartford, CT.

Seward, William Foote (ed.) (1924) *Binghamton and Broome County, New York: A History*. Lewis Historical Publishing Co., New York.

Smith, H. P. (ed.) (1885) *History of Broome County*. D. Mason and Co., Syracuse, NY.

Stannard, David E. (1977) *The Puritan Way of Death*. Oxford University Press, Oxford.

Sumner, William Graham (1963) *Social Darwinism: Selected Essays*. Prentice-Hall, Englewood Cliffs, NJ.

Weisberger, Bernard A. (1958) *They Gathered at the River: The Story of the Great Revivalists and Their Impact Upon Religion in America*. Quadrangle Books, Chicago.

Wilkinson, J. B. (1967) *The Annals of Binghamton of 1840*. The Broome County Historical Association, Binghamton.

Williams, J. E. (compiler and pub.) (1889) *Williams' Directory of Broome and Chenango Counties for 1889*. Binghamton, New York.

Wurst, LouAnn (1985) "Style and Technology: A View From the Cemetery." Paper presented at the American Anthropological meetings, Washington, D.C.

Wurst, LouAnn (1986) *A Rope of Sand: Second Great Awakening Symbolism on the Gravestones of the Rural Elite in Broome County, New York*. Master's Thesis, State University of New York at Binghamton.

9

Artifacts and Active Voices: Material Culture as Social Discourse

Mary C. Beaudry, Lauren J. Cook, and Stephen A. Mrozowski

The only way to preserve the fantasy of the inarticulate masses is never to listen to members of the masses when they are articulate.
Henry Glassie *Passing the Time in Ballymenone* (1982)

The anthropological mode of history . . . begins from the premise that individual expression takes place within a general idiom.
Robert Darnton *The Great Cat Massacre and Other Episodes in French Cultural History* (1984)

Transformation and *mediation*: the two most essential characteristics of human social life.
Anthony Giddens *A Contemporary Critique of Historical Materialism* (1981)

Material Expressions of Culture

A common theme connecting interpretations of the material record of the past is how people engage the material world in cultural expression in the negotiation of everyday life. The relationship of behavior to the material world is far from passive; artifacts are tangible incarnations of social relationships embodying the attitudes and behaviors of the past. "The underlying premise [of material culture study] is that objects made or modified by man reflect, consciously or unconsciously, directly or indirectly, the beliefs of the individuals who made, commissioned, purchased, or used them and, by extension, the beliefs of the larger society to which they belonged" (Prown 1988:19).

150

Historical archaeologists have long acknowledged the pivotal role material culture studies play in their research (see Ferguson 1977); James Deetz, perhaps the field's most creative exponent of artifacts as cultural message-carriers,[1] has even proposed that historical archaeology is best thought of as "the science of material culture" (Deetz 1977a:12). Few historical archaeologists have heeded his call; meanwhile, the past decade has witnessed the emergence and growth of material culture studies as a strongly interdisciplinary field in its own right.[2]

Material culture studies in historical archaeology have for the most part been conducted within the research paradigm that until recently dominated the field – logical positivism/logical empiricism (see Gibbon 1989) – and researchers have purposely avoided the issue of meaning while criticizing the few who grappled with understanding the cognitive aspects of artifact use in the past. Hence we are burdened with a positivist legacy that produced a literature replete with descriptive studies providing details on artifact identification, typology, and chronology[3] linked either to constructing often quite colorful culture histories or "explanatory models" that were unstintingly empiricist in nature. The recent surge of interest in "the recovery of meaning" stems both from dissatisfaction with the old paradigm as well as from the inexorable penetration of new intellectual trends from literary theory, history, and anthropology past the barriers of a lingeringly intransigent positivism into the mainstream of archaeological thought.

Those who look for meaning in the archaeological record approach it from a variety of theoretical perspectives, including structuralism, cognitive semiotics, economic theory, Marxism, and critical theory. For many historical archaeologists, new, post-positivist[4] approaches offer an opportunity for interpretation and explanation of social differentiation that was impossible under the generalizing mode of the old paradigm, with its overriding concern for statistical regularities. A new concern for intensive, often prosopographic detail in carefully framed case studies does not signal the emergence of a new particularism. This move, according to Hodder (1987a:2), has come about because many have recognized that "historical explanation . . . involves an attempt at particular and total description, and it does not oppose such description to explanation and general theory. Rather, our generalising anthropological concerns can progress only through an adequate description, and hence understanding, in our terms, of the particular."

While Hodder's statement seems to fly in the face of much of what has been dogma in historical archaeology, attention to recent intellectual trends reveals that once again archaeologists have fallen victim to what Leone (1972) once referred to as "paradigm lag."[5] Paynter (1984) has noted that positivist epistemology has been largely discredited by prehistorians and others (cf. Hodder 1986; Shanks and Tilley 1987; Leone et al. 1987; Wylie 1989; but see also Earle and Preucel 1987), yet far too many historical archaeologists seem to be operating within a paradigm that others have forsaken. Only the most extreme and reductionist of pattern-seekers could find any merit in the bizarre lengths to which South's pattern analysis (South 1977, 1978)[6] and Miller's economic scaling (Miller 1980) have been taken. This sort of objectification lies outside of the realm of a truly anthropological investigation and in fact reduces historical archaeology to a most dry and impersonal sort of economic history.

Recent trends in anthropological thought and in the social and human sciences as a whole involve a shift away from "totalizing frameworks" (Marcus and Fischer 1986:9):

> social thought in the years since [the 1960s] has grown more suspicious of the ability of encompassing paradigms to ask the right questions, let alone provide answers, about the variety of local responses to the operation of global systems, which are not understood as certainly as they were once thought to be under the regime of "grand theory" styles. Consequently, the most interesting theoretical debates in a number of fields have shifted to the level of method, to problems of epistemology, interpretation, and discursive forms of representation themselves . . .

Social theorists have become more and more concerned with appropriate and adequate levels of description as well as with problems of representation; much of the intellectual content of recent thought in anthropology, archaeology, and the human sciences in general is derived from theories of interpretation developed in the fields of philosophy and literary criticism (cf.Hunt 1989; Rabinow and Sullivan 1979, 1987). A self-critical mode and careful consideration of "such issues as contextuality, the meaning of social life to those who enact it, and the explanation of exceptions and indeterminants rather than regularities in phenomena observed" (Marcus and Fischer 1986:8) characterize the new "experimental" trend in both anthropology and archaeology.

In this essay we advocate blending an interpretive approach, normally applied to "symbolic" aspects of culture, with the archaeologist's necessary focus on things material and particular. Geertz (1980:135) points out that part of our intellectual legacy from the nineteenth century is a notion that " 'symbolic' opposes to 'real' as fanciful to sober, figurative to literal, obscure to plain, aesthetic to practical, mystical to mundane, and decorative to substantial." Our approach attends both to the materiality of the data – their substantive and functional roles – as well as to the ideological roles. Our concern for the "situatedness" of the data prompts us to focus on context – archaeological, historical, institutional, and behavioral context – while avoiding the tendency to treat meaning and context as static, suspended in time. The archaeological record encodes time and encodes change over time; hence we can derive from it evidence of historical process and cultural change.

Interpretive approaches in anthropology are characterized by attention to belief systems or world views and by a concern for meaning within its cultural and historical contexts; culture is seen as meaningfully constituted, cultural facts as observations subject to multiple interpretations.[7] Yentsch (n.d.:7) notes that in interpretive studies

> the focus is on historical moments and repetitive events that convey information about a specific culture. The emphasis is on small-scaled and detailed examinations of specific, varied expressions of cultural meaning, on a small range of human activity that tells of ordinary social action, on the day-to-day behavior that in its particularity and complex texture reveals the meaning that gave form to peoples' lives in a given time and place.

Attention to historical and cultural context allows human beings an active role in creating meaning and in shaping the world around them; they are seen to interact with their environment rather than simply react to it. Material culture is viewed as a medium of communication and expression that can condition and at times control social action. Our version of an interpretive approach involves combining several recent trends in the human sciences: semiotics and the study of symbolism; sociological and anthropological theories of social action and social discourse; and detailed construction of the historical and cultural context of artifact use through a critical reading of cultural texts.

Artifact as Text and Symbol

In semiotic terms, meaning is said to be signified by a particular signifier (a word, a written character, an image, or an object).[8] This relationship between representation and meaning, signifier and signified, is known as a sign. For example, red roses signify passion, and when used intentionally to do so, they constitute a sign of passion (Barthes 1957:197–8). A symbol is an arbitrary sign, such as a red traffic signal – there is no particular reason that a red traffic signal should be a sign to stop, except that that meaning has been assigned to it by society (Hawkes 1977:129). The function of the symbol is one of linkage in the process of communicating about the unknown by means of the known (the symbol itself). That is, properties assigned to the symbol by consensus may be transferred by the observer to the situation in which the symbol is employed. The symbol and the symbolized are not seen as being in a static cognitive relationship, but rather articulate with one another as components of a shifting and dynamic relationship (Turner 1974:25–30). Symbols are signs used in a communicative, semiotic process. Objects often function as symbols and have been approached semiotically by scholars (Krampen 1979).

While particular objects and their symbolism vary among cultures, the use of objects as symbols is pan-cultural. Attempts on the part of prehistorians to identify symbols and symbolic domains in the material culture of pre-literate populations (e.g., Hodder 1987b; Shanks and Tilley 1982; Shennan 1982) are predicated on the universal role that the relationship between symbolic action and object-symbols plays in social interaction. Csiksentmihalyi and Rochberg-Halton argue quite persuasively that our interaction with certain categories of objects as material entities is inextricable from our interaction with them as symbols. The domestic objects that clutter our living space may be viewed as "meaningful only as part of a communicative sign process and are active ingredients of that process" (Csiksentmihalyi and Rochberg-Halton 1981:173). As symbols, artifacts fix on their owners and users certain culture-specific attributes – in effect, they serve as "the visible part of culture," by "making firm and visible a particular set of judgements in the fluid processes of classifying persons and events" (Douglas and Isherwood 1979:66–7). Through an analysis of the use of material items in facilitating judgement, classification, and self-expression we can begin to understand the ways in which individuals constructed their cultural identity.

Construction of cultural identity is first and foremost a public act of mediation between self and other; often workers and members of subordinated groups (e.g., slaves, Native Americans, women) find room for self-expression not so much in work as during off-work hours. The role of leisure activities, or those activities that are not considered work, is important to self-definition and self-expression. While the importance of work in the process of self-definition is undeniable, there is a considerable support for the contention that it is through leisure, or at least non-work, activities that the greater part of self-definition and self-expression takes place (Pieper 1952; Huizinga 1970; Godbey 1981:98, 123–5) – people "create strong and complex selves by investing their psychic energy in activities that are usually called 'leisure'" (Csiksentmihalyi and Rochberg-Halton 1981:48). In a capitalist, industrialized society the working class will not control the means of production, but its members will express themselves individually and as a subculture through other components of what Csiksentmihalyi and Rochberg-Halton (1981:49) call "the means of action." They define the means of action as "any object or sign that allows a person to 'make his self manifest'" (including, where applicable, the means of production).[9]

Social psychologists tell us that the process of classifying others and assessing their intentions and motives is a transitory, swift, and necessary component of public interaction. Through a staggering variety of signs (including objects), gestures and postures, we communicate to those with whom we interact, telling them who we are and what we are doing: "Everyone knows of course, that the individual necessarily provides a reading of himself when he is in the presence of others. Gender, age, class, state of health, ethnicity will all be conveyed, in the main unwittingly" (Goffman 1971:127). Those social psychologists specializing in urban interaction emphasize that these presentations of self occur in the arena of the street (cf. Sennett 1978:164–6). Lyn Lofland refers to this process of classification of others as "appearential ordering," a term that stresses both the classificatory function of the activity and its reliance on appearance as the criterion of judgement. In such a "problematic world of strangers" as the city, "all the city dweller had to go on, to know anything at all about these other people, was the information he could glean by looking at them . . . City life was made possible by an 'ordering' of the urban populace in terms of appearance and spatial location such that those within the city could know a great deal about one another by simply looking" (Lofland 1973:22).

The process of "decoding" the appearance of others is based on the interpretation of visible symbols encoded primarily in forms of dress and other bodily adornments (jewelry, hair styles, etc.) as well as in behavior (Praetzellis et al. 1987). The Victorian context was marked by a "miniaturization" of visible symbols, in which appearential ordering turned on the smallest details of dress or appearance (Sennett 1978:165–8).

The power of material symbols to communicate often lies in their use "out of context" – that is in contexts other than those in which the dominant cultural tradition would apply them. An extreme example would be the "punk" usage of safety pins as earrings rather than as fasteners. Such recycling of the mundane in a symbolic context is informative to the initiated (cf. Barthes 1981:58).

> The tensions between dominant and subordinate groups can be found reflected in the surfaces of subculture – in the styles of mundane objects which have a double meaning. On the one hand, they warn the "straight" world in advance of a sinister presence – the presence of difference – and draw down upon themselves vague suspicions, uneasy laughter, "white and dumb rages." On the other hand, for those who erect them into icons, who use them as words or curses, these objects become signs of forbidden identity, sources of value. (Hebdige 1979:2–3)

Style, then, communicates subculture, and is instrumental in group definition and boundary maintenance. Ethnic and class subcultures wield style as a tool to identify those who "belong" and occasionally as a weapon to annoy those who do not.

Belonging – group identity, group membership – is inevitably linked to relations of power and to social differentiation. Too often historical archaeologists interested in the relations of power have failed to heed E. P. Thompson's (1978:157) call to examine class from the bottom up, or Henry Glassie's (1978:86) exhortation to study people "from the inside out." Hence in part the method we employ arises from a reaction against what we perceive as the limitations of an approach to artifact use in relations of power that seems to permit only the powerful to make statements with artifacts.[10] This has come about through the application of Marxist-derived critical theory employing Althusser's dominant ideology thesis to case studies in historical archaeology. It is an approach that has found an ever-growing body of critics.

From the Artifacts of Hegemony to Artifacts in Hegemonic Discourse

In a particularly well-published example of class analysis of material culture outside the workplace, Mark Leone and others at Historic Annapolis, Inc., have explored the ideological function of William Paca's garden (Leone 1984, 1986, 1987, 1988a, 1988b; Leone et al. 1989).[11] Paca was a lawyer and jurist, a signer of the Declaration of Independence, and the Governor of Maryland from 1782 to 1785 – by any standard, he was a member of that colony's economic and cultural elite (Malone 1946:123–4). Analysis of Paca's reconstructed formal garden has centered around the symbolism of power over nature, as a metaphor for power relations in society. In a critique of the role of ideology in the work of Marxian archaeologists, Ian Hodder (1986:61–70) uses Leone's research on the Paca Garden to illustrate four problems in the treatment of ideology:

1 "There is no indication anywhere that the same material culture may have different meanings and different ideological effects for different social groups" (Hodder 1986:65). The assumption is that all of Annapolis shared Paca's view of the garden.
2 There is a tendency to oppose social reality and ideology, with the latter falsifying, "naturalizing or masking inequalities in the social order" (Hodder 1986:65). Rather than obscuring Paca's elite status, his garden would appear instead to emphasize it.
3 Insufficient attention is paid to the specific historical context in which the garden is supposed to have served its ideological function.

4   The linkage between the functions of ideologies and their purported
    products is not well drawn. "One is left with the question, where
    does the particular ideology . . . come from?" (Hodder 1986:69). For
    example, the principles of perspective that Leone sees as serving the
    social function of legitimating Paca's dominant position in society are
    within a historical tradition of landscape construction that can
    ultimately be traced back to the Classical world. These concepts of
    order may have played a role in creating Paca's aspirations, as much
    as they were a tool for realizing them.

These problems with the treatment of ideology have important
implications for an archaeology of social class. In regard to the first
problem, one of the most disconcerting features of analyses of Paca's
garden is their treatment of the role of ideology in class relations. They
rely on the "Dominant Ideology Thesis," drawn from Louis Althusser's
(1971) essay on the function of ideology on the state level, which holds
that the ideologies of the dominant groups in society are imposed on
submissive groups. This thesis denies subordinate groups the ability to
formulate their own ideologies and has been found to be subject to many
exceptions when measured against historical situations (Abercrombie et
al. 1980; Miller 1987:162–3; McGuire 1988:439–40; Rojek 1989:100–1).
The result is a "trickle down" model of relationships between the classes,
a model that tends to deny the very existence of a working-class culture.[12]
    The problem seems to be that Leone's analyses have examined only
Paca and his activities and motivations, ignoring those of the "ruled."
But we must be careful not to equate the powers of artifacts with the
power of their owners or users; further, there is no reason to assume that
gardens, or other artifacts, are capable of serving only one symbolic
function, and a good deal of reason to assume that they can mediate a
variety of meanings, often simultaneously.[13] It is clear that the
"dominant ideology thesis" implies a degree of social control on the part of
elites that makes it particularly unsuitable as a model for class relationships
in developed, industrialized societies – even less so in pre-industrial societies
or ones still strongly enmeshed in an economic system characterized by
barter rather than exchange of cash (cf.Giddens 1981:55).
    Other critiques of the dominant ideology thesis in historical archae-
ology draw on a wide range of scholarship in other fields that likewise
find the approach unsatisfactory. Martin Hall (n.d.:11) critiques both the
structuralist program employed by Deetz as well as Leone's use of the
dominant ideology thesis, noting that Abercrombie et al. (1980) "have
tracked the notion of dominant ideology through feudalism, early
capitalism, and advanced capitalism, and have found it wanting." Those
authors found that dominant ideologies were often inconsistent and

seldom had great effect on subordinate classes; in medieval times the peasantry was "kept in order by brute force rather than ideological subtlety" (Hall n.d.:11), while under early capitalism, domination was achieved through economic forces (ibid.). Hall suggests that Annapolis gardens can be reinterpreted without the notion of false consciousness or masking ideologies; instrumentation, garden design, and fashion in dishes and other material goods can be seen as "a means whereby the elite incorporated themselves as a class" (ibid.:12). He points out that if we elect to view "ideology, vested in material culture . . . as a way in which the large planters of the Tidewater convinced themselves of their position in life" (ibid.:13), we approach James Scott's (1985) concept of ideology as a bridge channeling the material world into ongoing social discourse, "constituting and reconstituting existence with the semiotic power of 'texts without words', with the reading of artifacts as ideology, expressing actors' views of their relationships between themselves and others" (ibid.:14). Hall uses Scott's concept of ideology and his notion of "everyday resistance" to reinterpret the material culture of slave life in the plantation South and to offer insight into the archaeological record of slave dwellings at the Cape of Good Hope in South Africa.[14] He does so by incorporating into the paradigm the concept of discourse, drawn from Foucault (1972), with its emphasis on the importance of the sign.[15] When the material world and the actions of those who create it, come into contact with it, and use it for whatever ends, are all seen as statements in a discourse, it is the ambiguity arising out of the multiple meanings material objects carry – the polysemic status of artifacts – that provides the point of entry for explanation. Hall's complementary use of "the varied texts of official records, kitchen refuse, and literary impression" illustrates a way of approaching "artifacts as integral parts of the statements through which people create and re-create themselves, and these statements as integral parts of discourses that create and re-create one another" (Hall n.d.:26).

    What we seek, then, is a class-based model of relationships within and between subcultures that is flexible enough to account for the accommodations of interest that in fact occur among and between social classes and ethnic groups (and that can be demonstrated to have occurred in the historical past). One framework that appears to have the potential to subsume complex processes of cultural change involving class, ethnic, and gender groups has been used extensively by British students of popular culture (e.g., Bennett et al. 1981, 1986; Hargreaves 1989). This is the notion of "cultural hegemony," adapted from the work of the Italian Marxist, Antonio Gramsci. Gramsci was expressly concerned with the tendency of "scientific" Marxism to view ideology as a passive reflection of an economic substructure, rather than as a "real" entity, active in its own right. According to Gramsci, members of social classes put forth competing ideologies, centered around what they perceive to be their own interests. Class relationships consist of the negotiation of these ideologies in the cultural arena. Symbols may be adopted and manipulated by the members of different groups, in a process through which each group "seeks to negotiate opposing class cultures onto a cultural and ideological terrain which wins for it a position of leadership" (Bennett 1986:xv).

"Hegemony," then, is an ever-shifting "prevailing consciousness," negotiated among interest groups, that is internalized or accepted to varying degrees by members of those groups (Boggs 1976:39). Raymond Williams (1977:110) sees hegemony as transcending what is traditionally defined as ideology, to include experience as well:

It [hegemony] is a whole body of practices and expectations, over the whole of living: our senses and assignments of energy, our shaping perceptions of ourselves and our world. It is a lived system of meanings and values – constitutive and constituting – which as they are experienced as practices appear as reciprocally confirming. It thus constitutes a sense of reality for most people in the society, a sense of absolute because experienced reality beyond which it is very difficult for most members of the society to move, in most areas of their lives. It is, that is to say, a "culture," but a culture which has also to be seen as the lived dominance and subordination of particular classes.

Discussions of "lived" hegemonies, then, must involve detailed examination of the historical contexts in which they arose and operated.

Constructing Historical and Ethnographic Context

To suggest, as do Leone and Potter (1988a:12–13), that it is possible to confuse the documentary record with the ethnographic record is to confuse etic and emic perspectives (cf.Schuyler 1978; see also Melas 1989). The ethnographic record is the product of the ethnographer and as such is an etic document. Yentsch (1988b:152–3) notes that the documentary record can be approached from both etic and emic perspectives; this is possible because documents are created with words. Hence we can analyze them as reflective of past semantic systems: "the way pre-modern people used and structured their language, or the words they used in [documents], reveals more about the [past] than appears if the words are taken at face value. . . . The words in the [documents] are residual pieces of a bygone world-in-action in which they played a major role" (Yentsch 1988b:153). To use documents to generate archaeological expectations or to attach functions to artifacts is certainly akin to the use of ethnographic data by prehistorians. But is this all historical archaeologists do with documents? The answer is no; the use of the written word in historical archaeology in the construction of context and history is far more developed than Leone and Potter (1988a:11–12) suggest (cf. Beaudry 1988a; Schmidt and Mrozowski 1983).

Leone and Potter subscribe to the erroneous view that the archaeological record and documentary record were produced by "people who usually had no direct connection with one another" (1988b:14). Making direct, one-to-one match-ups between producers of documents and excavated artifacts is of limited utility under any circumstances; documents do, in point of fact, encode connections among people at many levels: face-to-face relations of kin, family, household, neighborhood, and community; impersonal relations of power between factory owners and workers, and so forth. For instance, documents that record commercial connections provide an emic window on the social relations of production (cf.Paynter 1988). It goes without saying that documentary analysis (in addition to and in distinction to "historical research") is integral to the study of material life in historical times, and we contend that it is in fact a vital element in all historical archaeological research. It is vital for constructing context.

Context is where meaning is located and constituted and provides the key to its interpretation. Recovery of meaning is predicated on recovery of context because context not only frames meaning by tying it to actual situations and events, but it is inextricably bound up with meaning. The existence of a context implies the presence of meanings functioning within it, and, conversely, meanings cannot exist in the absence of context. While we can talk about meaning taking place "out of context," we are not implying the absence of context, but rather that the context of use is not the usual or expected context. Often it is in unusual or unexpected contexts that meaning is renegotiated or redefined.

Analysis of cultural texts gives us insight into peoples' attitudes toward the world around them – an integral component of the recovery of meaning as well as of explanation of the archaeological record. Historical archaeologists have the means at hand to inject into their etic, objective studies of the past an emic, culturally sensitive perspective; interpretive analysis, with its concern for meaning and for folk classification and perception, offers a framework for textual analysis aimed at recovering folk meaning. It does so by taking an analytical and ethnographic approach to documents, an approach labeled variously "historical ethnography" (cf.Yentsch 1975; Schuyler 1988; Beaudry n.d.) and "documentary archaeology" (cf. Beaudry 1988a).

In essence, what we seek is the "full and inclusive context" which

Taylor indicated should be our primary interest (Taylor 1948:32). As Schmidt and Mrozowski note, the construction of cultural context is the way in which cultural meaning may be added to archaeology and to any patterns that may be deduced from archaeological evidence: "We must carefully research different historical documents and the literature of history to derive constructs that can be synthesized to build a complex cultural context for our archaeological excavation, be it a shipwreck, an Iron Age factory site in Tanzania, or a colonial privy . . . If we fail to do this, then we overlook cultural contexts that tell us most about behavior" (Schmidt and Mrozowski 1983:146–7). Despite claims to the contrary (i.e., Leone 1988a; Leone and Potter 1988a:14–18), this sort of approach *does not* confuse the documentary record with the ethnographic record or render the one equivalent to the other; rather, it permits a critical, intepretive, and culturally sensitive approach to historical documents with the aim of avoiding over-objectification of its subject matter. And while some perhaps are tempted to extend to such an approach the dismissive label "eclecticism" (e.g. Orser 1988:314–15), it can be said in its favor that an interpretive approach, because it is receptive to differing perspectives, manages to avoid the pitfalls of the doctrinaire application of modern radical political thought inherent in what Orser and others propose as a more "unified" (we would say *rigid*) theoretical perspective tied to the dominant ideology thesis.

There is a persistent "fear of the emic" that is likely a residue of positivism. Many historical archaeologists retain the bias toward documents acquired during their training in prehistory, and some researchers remain oblivious to the possibilities for sophisticated and sensitive analysis of both the material and documentary records. South quite clearly continues to consider archival sources as no more than straightforward documentation, as historical background or as verification: "historical archaeology offers tremendous potential for controlling archaeological variables against the background of historical documentation" (South 1988:38–9). Leone and Potter's (1988b:12–14) suggestion that we treat the documentary and archaeological records as wholly distinct bodies of data, testing one against the other, offers a perspective not very different from South's partitive approach.[16]

Others remain so suspicious of documents as to recommend they be relegated to a minor role in interpretation. Rubertone (1989:32), for example, claims that "the archaeology of seventeenth-century Native America serves as a source of information on Indian history that exists independent of written accounts produced by European observers." Preferring the "unwritten record" for what it reveals about Native American resistance to European domination, Rubertone dismisses documents because "partisan observers wrote to serve their own best interests and in doing so have omitted from the written evidence how the Narragansett Indians struggled to preserve their independence."[17] This suspicion of documents, this notion that the biases of those who recorded them cannot be analyzed and interpreted but in fact will inevitably taint the researcher, is as naive as it is counter-intuitive and unproductive. In another instance, Ashmore and Wilk (1988:5) impute strange power to documents, dreading that the increased sophistication in deciphering ancient texts will lure Mesoamerican archaeologists away from material evidence and hence bias their conclusions. They feel that each source has "special uses" (and presumably, in the case of texts, these are limited) but do acknowledge that if material and textual sources are examined critically, they "can even be employed together as complements" (ibid.). Ashmore and Wilk nevertheless state uncategorically that "archaeologists should continue to *rely* on the more direct material evidence" (ibid. emphasis added).[18]

Analyzing written sources from both etic and emic perspectives (or, as some students of material culture put it, from both producer and user perspectives) can resolve this dilemma over what to do with documents. For, as Michael Ann Williams (1990; see also Williams 1986) asks, should we refuse to study women's roles in households and women's use of household space just because we "know" that in historical times houses were "male" artifacts because men built them? Can we assume that a producer controls how users perceive and employ the artifact? Certainly not in the case of texts, unless one assumes that reading merely constitutes "a submission to textual machinery" (Chartier 1989:156). To a certain extent our critical reading of documents is an "appropriation," an interpretation "outside of the text" (ibid.:157) that incorporates attention to the motivation of the producer, to the actions or response of the intended audience, and to our intentional use of the text in constructing our own narrative of interpretation. The synthesis we seek cannot be accomplished through a partitive and reductionist scheme whereby the documentary record is ignored, treated uncritically, or set wholly apart from other sources of evidence.

To move away from the attitude that the use of documents is a literal exercise in obtaining only the information intentionally conveyed by those who recorded them, we need to approach the documentary record as a body of texts (as anthropologists and folklorists do with tales, myths, etc.) and be mindful that our reading is in fact an interpretation of someone else's perceptions. Even our own perceptions cannot be taken at face value (cf.Beaudry 1980b:5). For linguists, a text is any record of a language event. This can be recalled, sound-recorded, written, or printed; it is both a physical thing and a semantic unit. The crucial aspects of texts are *content, form,* and *situation.* Situation, the "environment in which texts comes to life" (Gregory and Carroll 1978:3–4), has constant features that allow us to look for variations in the formal or substantial aspects of texts. Assuming, for instance, a reasonable degree of shared language used among a given body of, say, Anglo-American records, we may examine how information recorded varied either in its internal meaningful structure in a synchronic fashion, or how differences over time and space reflect changes in attitudes, availability of consumer goods, or contact between people of differing social, economic, or cultural backgrounds.

E. P. Thompson (1963:9–10) points out that research into social relations of class "must always be embodied in real people and in a real context" and advocates that documents be "scrutinized upside-down" (Thompson 1978:157). The implication is that documents, even those produced by members of the superordinate class, can be unintentionally revealing about otherwise disenfranchised or inarticulate members of society.[19] Such ethnographically and contextually sensitive data can be extracted through critical analysis of documentary texts in combination with material culture analysis. But looking at history from the "bottom up" *or* from the "top down" is insufficient, and an emic perspective aims to study meaning "from the inside out." Henry Glassie conveys this with eloquence and power in his stunning work *Passing the Time in Ballymenone*, and we quote him at length.

In the ceili, makers of tea and chat create the community. In the street, cattle mart, and public house, they buy and sell, watch and march, listen and sing, and form the crowd, the population of their region. . . . And beyond that . . . you have seen them, a little lost, standing alone in wordless confusion, country people, dressed neatly, poorly, on the streets of big cities.

That is where the politicians and their agents, the false scholars, want them: weak, bewildered, and, above all, silent. The man who is a learned educator at the fireside, a sparkling wit in the ceili, a bold singer in the pub, becomes, in the gigantic milieu of the nation, silent, nearly nothing, a follower for a politician's doctrine, a statistic for a scientist's scheme, a member of the inarticulate masses. The idea is evil. . . . [T]o support a frantic equation of power and wealth with intelligence and verbal skill, the false scholar contrives a pyramidal picture of society with kings and madmen at its peak, a silent majority at its spreading base. Then reality is ordered to trickle down from top to bottom, from power to weakness, wealth to poverty, intelligence to stupidity, invention to imitation, light to obscurity, texts to silence. Even scholars who strive to be democratic sometimes accept the ugly metaphor and propose to study things from the bottom up. Society is not peaked like a pyramid or layered like a cake. It is composed of communities simultaneously occupying space and time at the same human level. . . . All seem reasonable from within, strange from without, silent at a distance. The way to study people is not from the top down or the bottom up, but from the inside out, from the place where people are articulate to the place where they are not, from the place where they are in control of their destinies to the place where they are not. (Glassie 1982:85–6)

Carmel Schrire, a prehistorian who has turned to historical archaeology to examine issues of contact between native South Africans and Dutch colonialists, came quickly to the realization that archival sources interact with archaeological data; she points out that the success of an archaeological study of the impact of colonialism on indigenous people "hinges on its ability to dig as deeply into the archives as into the sands of an abandoned settlement by analyzing words and artefacts that encode a day's meal, a month's shipment of meat to an outpost, and a century's colonial policy enacted by the servants of the great Dutch East India Company" (Schrire n.d.: 2). We argue that this is as true for any other endeavor in historical archaeology as it is of Schrire's work at a seventeenth-century Dutch outpost in South Africa.

Archaeological Context

We have discussed at length the importance of context in assigning meaning to material culture, but the archaeological record as context requires corresponding attention. Especially in urban communities, archaeological deposits often result from rapid depositional episodes (see, e.g. Carver 1987; Beaudry 1986; Mrozowski 1984; Praetzellis et al. 1980). In cities, these rapid depositional events can be the consequence of household-level transitions (Mrozowski 1984; Beaudry and Mrozowski 1987b) or community-wide changes in waste and water management facilities (Honerkamp and Council 1984; Beaudry 1986; Praetzellis et al. 1988). The very structure of the archaeological record can also reveal past behavioral dynamics.

Historical archaeology cannot really be a "science of material culture" in the sense Deetz implied, nor can it be merely "material culture with dirt on it." Archaeological sites are complex matrices: understanding their internal structure, formation, and the relationships among site sediments, depositional processes, and artifacts in the matrix is a vital component of archaeological research (cf.Schiffer 1987; Binford 1976, 1979, 1981). Just as documents are not best used as background context to test against artifacts, artifacts are not best used when considered independent of the contexts from which they were recovered. The historical archaeologist must perform contextual analysis in its most comprehensive and inclusive form. Even a fairly straightforward example helps illustrate the power of contextual analysis arising from merging complementary control of both archaeological and historical contexts.

The presence of beverage alcohol containers at the Lowell boarding houses is undeniable evidence of liquor consumption, but the discovery of empty bottles in a cache beneath a privy floor is evidence of deliberate concealment – of clandestine disposal presumably following upon clandestine drinking. Situating this archaeological observation in a historical context constructed with the aid of company documents dealing with restrictions on alcohol consumption in the boarding houses (Bond 1989a), we create a behavioral link whereby the ordinary fragments of backyard refuse begin to speak for the seemingly inarticulate. The close contextual analysis of artifacts provides a counterpoint or subtext to writings of middle- and upper-class observers and reformers, subtly raising the volume of workers' voices so they can be heard above those who speak to us in such loud chorus through written texts.

Artifacts and Multiple Voices:[20]
Examples of Artifact Discourse Analysis

As noted above, a model based on cultural hegemony rather than dominant ideology has several advantages. First, it does not equate economic or political domination with social or cultural domination. For example, while elites may control much of the economic and political structures, it may be the bourgeoisie that has the most influence on the prevailing consciousness. Second, cultural hegemony is seen as based on control through consensus rather than coercion; this requires consideration of the *accommodations* reached by parallel, or even opposing, interests, as well as the equally important areas of conflict that are more easily and more often studied (Stedman Jones 1977:163). Third, and most important, hegemony is not seen as ever being complete (Boggs 1976:40). Initiatives and contributions emerge that are alternative and oppositional to existing hegemonies, although usually framed in the same terms of discourse, and some of these may be negotiated into hegemonic positions (Williams 1977:114). Thus, contributions from the working classes may find acceptance, or at least toleration, by the bourgeoisie and elites. This allows working-class ideology and working-class culture creative, active roles in the social process, rather than viewing them as dictated by and distilled from the ideologies and cultures of politically or economically dominant groups.

The idea of cultural hegemony is fully compatible with the communication-centered model for material culture that was outlined above, and therein lies its usefulness to archaeology. An important dimension of material culture is its communicative function, and much of that function takes place in the day-to-day negotiation of hegemony. The eighteenth-century merchant with his matching dishes and symmetrical house and grounds, and the twentieth-century "punk" with his safety pins and engineer's boots are equally involved in those negotiations, and much of what is recovered archaeologically may be seen as the product of hegemonic discourse, intentional or otherwise. In fact we may see the range of items available at any given time, with their varying moral and symbolic values, as extensions of contemporary hegemony – or even as a "material hegemony" that is every bit as shifting and fluid through time as is cultural hegemony.

A class-based archaeology based on cultural hegemony permits us to interpret our material in its communicative and symbolic aspects, and opens up new avenues for inquiry. For example, if Georgianization was the cultural contribution of the merchant class during the eighteenth century, as several archaeologists have recently proposed (Leone 1988b; Harrington 1989), then it may be viewed as an element in hegemonic discourse. While we could simply note that Georgianization occurs fairly universally across that class, it would be much more interesting and informative to go beyond this normative viewpoint to examine the ways in which other classes and cultural groups adopted, changed, or rejected the Georgian world-view and its associated material culture – to examine where Georgianization came from, how it became hegemonic in the eighteenth century, what it meant and how those meanings changed over time, how and by what it was superseded in the hegemony, when and why it re-entered the hegemony in "revivals," and what remains of it today.

The examples of material culture analysis we offer here are drawn from our recent collaborative research into the Boott Mills boarding houses of nineteenth- and twentieth-century Lowell, Massachusetts (Beaudry and Mrozowski 1987a, 1987b, 1988, 1989). Excavation focused on the rear yards of Boott units No. 45, a "typical" boarding house where workers dwelt, and No. 48, a tenement for supervisory personnel. The residents of the boarding house constituted a corporate household; the tenement was in effect an apartment lived in by a single, usually quite small, nuclear family who at times may have taken in boarders. From the backlots we recovered impressive quantities of everyday objects – buttons, beads, clay pipe fragments, bottle glass, costume jewelry, ceramics, hair combs, marbles, animal bones – left behind by the hundreds of mill employees who inhabited these houses during their operation. Perhaps it is ironic that so many who spent hour upon hour laboring in the mills producing fortunes for others would leave such a humble legacy of buttons, glass "gems," and liquor bottles. For while the archaeological and documentary record provide testimony to the power of corporate paternalism and of the boarding house system, those same data evoke expression, if not of resistance, of personal aspirations and self-expression. Despite the fact that limited economic means placed genuine impediments in the way of the material wants of Lowell's mill workers, evidence of adaptive behavior – of the creation of subculture – is visible. It is visible in the use of medicines more desirable for their alcohol content than their efficacy in curing illness (Bond 1989b), in humble aspirations to middle-class status reflected in the selection and use of household ceramics by tenement dwellers (Dutton 1989), and in the deliberate choices made by working women in buying and wearing less costly imitations of expensive jewelry and hair ornaments (Ziesing 1989). It is also expressed in the use of white clay pipes as expressions of class affiliation and even of class pride.

Discourse through tobacco-related material culture

An important element of the Lowell study sought to view tobacco use as an element of hegemonic discourse between classes and ethnic groups, as well as between men and women. The focus was on the nineteenth and early twentieth centuries (Cooke 1989). While tobacco use may seem a minor area in which to approach major issues of class relations, those relations penetrated daily life and were interwoven with its threads. Class provided, and provides, contours for the surfaces of everyday activities and interactions, such that its operation may be seen in the most mundane and trivial actions.[21]

The episodes of tobacco use found in the historical record were analyzed along three major dimensions (after Mercer 1986:54, who modified the procedure from Foucault 1972:50–5). The first of these is the *site* of use – the position, in space, in time, and in social context, in which the episode occurs. The second dimension considered is that of the *status* of the event – who the actors are, and their relative positions in structures of authority. Finally, the *subjectivities* of the behavior – the meanings that are conveyed – are considered wherever they are accessible.

Analysis of documentary sources written during the nineteenth and early twentieth centuries indicates an increasing association of short-stemmed white clay pipes with working-class men. Irish immigrants, African-Americans, and other ethnic groups were also associated with their use to varying degrees. Women, at least middle- and upper-class women, were not supposeed to smoke at all in the Northeast, particularly in public.

Nineteenth-century smoking emerges from contemporary documents as an activity devoid of overtones of class conflict – unlike the consumption of alcohol – until one looks at the role that smoking played in class-based conflicts over the use of public space. Smoking, like drinking, some team sports, and displays of sexuality, was not politely carried on in public places – streets, parks, restaurants, etc.[22] While smoking itself could be seen, and was seen, as a behavior that united classes, its indulgence by members of certain classes, ethnic groups, and genders in the social context of public space imbued it with subversive meanings and discomforting overtones when viewed by middle- and upper-class writers. Smoking thus found expression in the negotiation of both class- and gender-linked hegemonies, often by serving as an expression of identity and intrusive presence.

The materials used were crucial to the context of the smoking act, signalling the class, ethnic background, or perception of gender relations on the part of the smoker. The combined use of documents and excavated artifacts allows us to recover past contexts and actions, and the meanings that linked them. The pipe collection from the Boott Mills tenements and boarding houses shows evidence that the working-class smokers who lived there broke the stems of certain types of white clay pipes to shorten them before use. Within the context of contemporary behavior, such actions were clear expressions of membership in the working classes. Ethnic identity is clearly manifest in the presence in the collection of pipes bearing Irish political slogans, such as "Home Rule," and the names of such Irish martyrs as Wolfe Tone. Documents produced for the most part by middle- and upper-class writers can be combined with material evidence for working-class actions to reveal working-class meanings.

Discourses of control and defiance

Kathleen H. Bond's (1989a) detailed analysis of Boott Company correspondence brought into focus a number of areas of conflict between workers and management; many of the problems arose over worker behaviors the company officials found unacceptable because they eroded profitability or because certain public behaviors were destructive of the image the corporation wished to project. In a number of instances, boarding house keepers found themselves rebuked for trying to eke out extra profits for themselves by circumventing company rules about who to board and how to collect rents, or for permitting drinking on the premises. Aberrant worker behavior, especially public drinking and rowdiness, were, however, the prime target of supervisory wrath. Bond notes that the internally consistent themes of the correspondence reveal that company attempts at control of the work-force were consistently ineffectual; she links this with evidence from the archaeological excavations to illustrate the contradictory nature of company "concern" for workers (Bond 1989a:35):

> The information gleaned from the letters – that the boardinghouse yards were messy, that the overall condition of the backlots was poor, and that workers consumed alcohol in the units – concurs with the archeological evidence. In some instances the letters were even written to or about individuals who lived in the units investigated archeologically. The neat, orderly image of the mills that the owners took pains to present, however, is made all the more hollow by the archeological evidence. The archeology helps to strip off the façade of neatness and order; in so doing, it exposes management's attempts to regulate workers' behavior without taking equal responsibility for workers' lives. Managers, however, could not completely eliminate certain behavior. They could only "purify our corporation by discharging the offenders" and remain vulnerable, at least in a small way, to workers' attempts to retain control of their lives.

Much of the evidence to which Bond refers exists in the form of beverage alcohol containers in the backlots (Bond 1989b); apart from these, however, there were large numbers of patent medicine bottles, purported remedies for a wide variety of ailments, all with extremely high alcohol content. It is clear that drinking was prevalent despite unremitting efforts of the corporation to eliminate and prevent it. Bond (1989a:29) observes that "workers drank for a variety of reasons – ethnic customs, as means to promote working-class solidarity, and to temporarily escape from the realities of poverty – it was behavior the workers chose for themselves. If a worker wished to drink whiskey, no amount of 'moral' lecturing would change that fact." The archaeological record is testimony to the fact that the discourse between workers and managers about who controlled workers' leisure behavior in the boarding houses was played out endlessly in small acts of everyday resistance in ways over which management ultimately had very little control indeed.

Discourse through household ceramic use

The management policy of the Lowell corporation involved paternalism, but it was a paternalism without rights. It was in leisure behavior and off-work time, as well as personal dress and comportment, that individual workers expressed themselves and signaled the affiliations of ethnicity, subculture, and class.

Quite intriguing to consider in this regard is the use of tea wares and comparatively elaborate table settings by tenement residents. Dutton (1989) found that this contrasted with the patterning of the boarding house ceramic assemblage and can be linked to household composition – corporate versus nuclear household – as well as to cultural values. Aside from tea- and coffeeware, the two ceramic assemblages were remarkably similar (tables 9.1 –9.3). Undecorated whitewares dominated both collections with smaller percentages of transfer printed and handpainted ware present. The increased availability of ceramic tableware types and forms in the late nineteenth century lessens the number of observed differences between ceramic assemblages of households with similar financial means.

The ceramic assemblages recovered from the boarding house and tenement backlots at Lowell reflect two late nineteenth-century working-class households in similar economic circumstances but with different household composition. Ceramic purchasing patterns reflect attempts at economy while providing the necessary forms for food service and consumption. The tenement residents sought to emulate middle-class dining habits by including more vessels in a table setting per person even though these were unspecialized in function. This suggests that for the tenement, vessel function was versatile and that particular forms served in capacities other than their intended use. At the boarding house, however, the keeper provided only the basics for food service and consumption. Complete meals were served to individuals on a single

Table 9.1 Summary of ceramics by ware type

	Tenement		Boarding house	
Ware type	No.	%	No.	%
Bennington	0	0.00	1	0.52
Creamware	1	1.16	5	2.61
Earthenware	0	0.00	1	0.52
Pearlware	2	2.32	1	0.52
Porcelain	11	12.79	8	4.18
Redware	12	13.95	12	6.28
Stoneware	3	3.48	11	5.75
Whiteware	56	65.11	149	78.01
Yellow ware	1	1.16	3	1.57
Total	86	100.00	191	100.00

Table 9.2 Summary of ceramics by vessel type

Vessel form	Tenement No.	%	Boarding house No.	%
Ale bottle	1	1.16	0	0.00
Bowl	18	20.93	50	26.17
Chamber pot	1	1.16	0	0.00
Crock	1	1.16	2	1.04
Cup	13	15.11	22	11.51
Flower pot	3	3.48	5	2.61
Gravy boat	0	0.00	1	0.52
Jar	4	4.65	4	2.09
Jug	0	0.00	1	0.52
Plate	10	11.62	30	15.70
Platter	3	3.48	10	5.23
Pot	4	4.65	1	0.52
Saucer	18	20.93	36	18.84
Tea pot	0	0.00	1	0.52
Wash basin	0	0.00	1	0.52
Unidentified	11	12.79	26	13.61
Total	87	100.00	190	100.00

plate with little in the way of accessories (e.g., vegetable dishes, bread plates, and salad plates). Hence the tenement household emulated mainstream middle-class dining rituals by adapting its limited ceramic assemblage to reproduce as closely as possible a middle-class table service, while the boarding house keeper, concerned with providing a service for her boarders, eschewed such refinements in vessel function.

Recent work of other historical archaeologists provides us with the means for understanding the nature of these differences and the reasons for them. Wall (1987) was able to demonstrate through the analysis of a series of ceramic assemblages from eighteenth- and nineteenth-century New York City that such tablewares closely reflect a new set of values that emerged as urbanization and industrialization took place (see also Mrozowski 1988, who ties the widespread values of the nineteenth century to developments in eighteenth-century American cities). Ceramic assemblages from late in the second quarter of the nineteenth century tend to reflect a set of ideals that developed more or less as a response to changing social conditions brought about by industrialization and the emergence of the middle class. Chief among these values was the notion of separation of the home and the workplace, with woman's sphere being at home and proper work for women being running a household (but not necessarily physically engaging in housework). This notion of striving for refinement and middle-class status through adoption of middle-class standards for polite entertaining and social display, especially through tea drinking, is of interest in that it adds a dimension to ceramic analysis beyond economic considerations. It is obvious that ceramics were often symbols as much as they were everyday objects; historical archaeologists are increasingly willing to interpret their ceramic assemblages in light of the multiple functions they served in order to place their use in its proper cultural context: Burley (1989) and Yentsch (this volume) are especially fine examples of such analyses. Such studies bring women into focus, revealing how, especially in nineteenth-century homes, women influenced the nature of the household. An example from Fort Independence in Boston, Massachusetts, makes this clear and provides insight into the Lowell case.

Clements (1989) found that critical differences occurred between the ceramic and glassware not so much in the assemblages of officers versus

Table 9.3 Summary of ceramics by decoration

Decoration	Tenement		Boarding house	
	No.	%	No.	%
Decal	1	1.16	4	2.09
Dipped	0	0.00	3	1.57
Edged	6	6.97	11	5.75
Gilded	9	10.46	8	4.18
Handpainted	9	10.46	8	4.18
Lead glazed	6	6.97	10	5.23
Molded	9	10.46	29	15.18
Overglazed	1	1.16	0	0.00
Salt glazed	1	1.16	5	2.61
Sponge	3	3.48	6	3.14
Transfer print	12	13.95	32	16.75
Undecorated	28	32.55	74	38.74
Wash	1	1.16	1	0.52
Total	86	100.00	191	100.00

enlisted men but between married and bachelor officers. Deposits from households of married officers had by far the greater proportion of serving/entertaining vessels (e.g., fine dinner wares of blue-and-white transfer-printed pearlware or of Canton porcelain, in forms such as tureens, platters, vegetable nappies, tea wares, etc.). Both assemblages had drinking vessels – stemware and tumblers – but deposits from the bachelors' quarters had significantly more vessels related to alcohol consumption than to tea and coffee drinking or even to food consumption (probably because bachelor officers ate in the mess hall). In deposits from married officers' quarters other, non-food related artifacts, most notably toys, enhance the image of families and the activities families carry out. The presence of women and children hence had an unmistakable effect on the archaeological record; the stabilizing influence of women was not lost on the US Army, which encouraged its officers to marry. This afforded them respectability as well as stability, something the military valued highly in its early years when it was faced with public opposition to a standing army and fear – especially in major urban centers – of the possible ill effects of bringing large numbers of unattached, transient males into the community.

The Fort Independence example comes to life when we read the lament of the fort's unmarried physician, who complained of the instability of his life as well as remarking on the favor with which his superiors viewed the married state. Marriage, married life, and the need to maintain a social life in keeping with middle-class values would have been an important part of daily life for officers at an early nineteenth-century military post. Yet not all members of the garrison would adhere to such views; at a highly stratified military post it is far from surprising to find differences of rank reinforced materially. Solidarity among ranks was promoted through material culture use just as it was used to differentiate between ranks, yet much of the material difference perceived archaeologically reflects the fact that married officers maintained conventional households while unmarried officers and enlisted men did not.

It seems likely that the differences between ceramic assemblages at the Lowell Boott Mills boarding house and tenement can similarly be attributed to the differences in household makeup. While women were present and perhaps outnumbered males in both households, married women whose families rented Boott tenements could aspire to stable family life and could put into practice the values linked to the domestic ideology of the nineteenth century through the structure of meals and entertaining in the home, especially through the ritual of tea-time. While many of the same values found expression in the "professional" management of the boarding houses by their keepers (Landon and

Beaudry 1988; Landon 1989), purchase and use of ceramics was contextually quite different in the two households – boarding house residents, be they mill girls or immigrants, did not participate in discourse through ceramic selection and use, though they regularly ate off dishes provided by the keeper.[23] Tenement dwellers, because they were responsible for their own purchases, could and did make active use of ceramic items, not only in self-expression, but also in attempting to create new identities. Viewed in this way, ceramics from historical sites can be interpreted as elements in social discourse and their purchasers as active participants in such discourse. Here the discourse is embedded in the household and in family life and hence functions in a different social context than expression of working-class values through pipe-smoking or drinking in public.

Conclusion

The material record, or at least that portion of it that came from the backlots of what were once the Boott Mills boarding houses, can be viewed as part of a hegemonic discourse that has much to tell us that is not illuminated by the documentary record, as well as much that is. The material adds a texture, a *reality*, to the surfaces of the past that are revealed in print, filling out what Raymond Williams (1977:110) called "the whole substance of lived identities and relationships." Material is not seen here as just a passive product of economic behavior, but as an instrumental component of symbolic actions. The fact that symbolic behaviors are ephemeral makes their material traces that much more important.

At Lowell, our aim has been to go beyond economics, chronology, and spatial distribution in the analysis of ordinary residues of daily life such as bottle glass, clay pipe fragments, and pottery sherds. Blessed with rich documentary sources and a data-laden archaeological record, we have been able to delve deeply into the interpretation of meaning in material culture while maintaining a strong connection with the empirical. This combination enables us to construct context in its most comprehensive form. As Mary Douglas (1973:11–12) noted in commenting on Bourdieu's (1973) analysis of the "complexity and richness" of the rules organizing space in and around the Berber house, "if the author had limited himself to one system of signs, say furniture, or the house without the outside, or the whole material culture without the supporting rites and proverbs which he cites, he would have missed these meanings." Attention to cultural and historical contexts as well as to archaeological contexts from both etic and emic perspectives attunes us to the multiple meanings artifacts have for their users. By analyzing cultural texts, written or otherwise, from "the inside out," we can begin to reconstruct meaning in the active voice, in the multiple voices of the "silent majority" whose past discourse through artifacts reveals they were not so inarticulate after all.

NOTES

1   As early as 1967, Deetz proposed in his monograph *Invitation to Archaeology* that we conceive of artifacts as akin to elements of language, offering a formulation of *factemes* and *formemes* as the material culture equivalents of morphemes (words) and phonemes (meaningful sounds). While few, Deetz among them, have made explicit use of his scheme, a number of scholars have used linguistic models as the basis for material culture analysis (e.g., Glassie 1976; Beaudry 1978, 1980a, 1980b, 1980c, 1988b; Yentsch 1988b), and many more have applied the structuralist paradigm derived from linguistics (e.g., Deetz 1977b; Yentsch n.d., 1988a, 1988c, 1990, and this volume). See Tilley 1989 for a recent discussion of language theory and material culture analysis in archaeology.

2   For discussions of the growth and direction of material culture studies, see Prown 1988; Upton 1983; St George 1988a; Roberts 1985; Wells 1986. Anthologies of material culture studies include Bronner 1985; Quimby 1978; St George 1988b; Schlereth 1980, 1982, and 1985; see also the journal *Material Culture*.

3   For instance, Noël Hume (1969) provides a comprehensive descriptive guide to identifying artifacts of the colonial period; Stone (1974) employs the type-variety method to establish a typology for the thousands of artifacts recovered from the site of Fort Michilimackinac in Michigan; Harrington (1954), Binford (1962), and Walker (1965, 1967, 1977, 1983) all provide ways of dating sites and their levels by the clay pipes in them – Binford's use of a straight-line regression formula is in keeping with the best efforts of the New Archaeology to derive laws through quantification and formulaic approaches to data analysis; South (1977, 1978, 1979), pays homage to Binford, building on the comprehensive descriptive groundwork laid by Noël Hume, by offering a formula for ceramic dating, a discussion of site structure in historical archaeology, and a battery of ahistorical, statistically derived patterns based on "neutral" artifact groupings that in the long run have proved to be devoid of ethnographic import (cf.Yentsch 1989).

4   While most refer to recent trends as "post-processual" (cf. Leone 1986; Hodder 1989b), we find the appellation misleading and inaccurate. Self-styled post-processualists claiming to do "archaeology as long-term history" (e.g., Hodder 1987a) or "historical anthropology" (e.g., Little and Shackel 1989) are for all intents and purposes looking at process; post-processualism, as we understand it, rejects the strictly empiricist paradigm

of the New Archaeology (cf.Gibbon 1989; Courbin 1988) in order to pursue a concern for ideology, symbolism, and meaning, and for power in society. Hodder (1989b:70) explains that the term denotes a general post-modernist/post-structuralist trend in archaeology to break down the old dichotomy between "on the one hand, normative, culture-historical, idealist archaeology and, on the other hand, processual, cultural ecological, and materialist archaeology." Our own interest in the negotiation of meaning with and through artifacts is a processual approach of sorts; we suggest that archaeologists do themselves a disservice by seeming to eschew an interest in cultural and historical process when in fact what they are rejecting is not process but an unhealthy positivism. These remarks may seem mere cavilling, but concern with the interpretation of cultural texts ought inevitably to spark an awareness of the significance and power of language, especially of labels.

5   Not all of our most influential thinkers in historical archaeology would agree. In a recent publication (1988a) Deetz indicates that his interest in broad patterns of cognitive structure reflected in material culture has been influenced to a certain extent by critical theory (a perspective Deetz notes was presaged by Walter Taylor in *A Study of Archeology*, first published in 1948). Deetz states that archaeologists use "material culture as the primary data base for the construction of context" (1988a:18). This is decidedly something of a departure, for attention to context has never been a strong point of structuralist analysis; what is more, the statement points to the prehistorian's preference for material over documentary context (see note 18). (Sahlins' (1981, 1985) revised structuralism, which incorporates structure with a concern for historical time depth, has regrettably had very little influence in archaeology to date; a recent volume (Hodder 1989a) concerned with meaning, symbolism, and material culture contains a total of 25 essays, only one of which cites Sahlins.) Deetz denies that there is any need for concern over paradigm lag in the field of archaeology (for which he prefers the neologism *archaeography* – this after castigating certain of his colleagues for committing a similar offense by introducing the term *ethnoarchaeology* (1988a:18): "Why invent a new term, when two older ones do the job? Once combined, the terms cannot help but run together in ways that are not productive."). Deetz's new term is a lexical buttress for his opinion that theory resides only in ethnology, which is arguable given the fact that many of the theories employed in archaeology are borrowed from disciplines outside of anthropology and that some theory does in fact arise from the practice of archaeology itself. It would also seem that the denial of paradigm lag is at least an implicit denial of the relevance or validity of any other than Deetz's "culture as mental construct" paradigm (1988a:22; see also Deetz 1989). But, lip service to recent trends notwithstanding, Deetz has not given up interest in the search for broad cultural patterns; his recent interpretation of patterning in the distribution of Colono ware in the American South (1988b) is a particularly elegant and provocative example of his use of the "pure" structuralist paradigm. Martin Hall (n.d.:3) rightly notes, however, that "the results of this synchronic,

decontextualized method of structuralism seem often to be brilliant descriptions awaiting explanations."

6   Peña and Peña (1988) provide an especially apt exposé of the shortcomings of pattern analysis.

7   See, for example, Geertz 1982, 1983; Leach 1982; Wagner 1975; Taylor 1979; Yentsch n.d., 1988a, 1988b, 1988c, 1989, 1990; Yentsch et al. 1987; Beaudry and Mrozowski 1989 is an example of a full-scale, monograph-length interpretive case study.

8   As William Sturtevant (1964:107) noted, "material culture resembles language in some important aspects: some artifacts – for example, clothing – serve as arbitrary symbols for meanings." This means that material culture can be conceptualized within the semiotic notion of signs: "semiology aims to take in any system of signs, whatever their substances and limits, images, gestures, musical sounds, objects, and the complex associations of all of these, which form the context of ritual, convention or public entertainment: these constitute, if not language, at least systems of signification" (Barthes 1964:9). Hence semiotics is characterized by the conscious treatment of all aspects of human life, verbal and nonverbal, written or otherwise, as texts amenable to critical analysis (cf. Heath 1974; Coward and Ellis 1977). For a seminal discussion of "object language" and nonverbal communication, see Kruesch and Kees (1956:96–159).

9   According to Giddens (1981:51), this involves a measure of control over resources of "allocation" rather than resources of "authorization"; workers seldom control the means of production, but they do maintain a high degree of control over produced goods: "Allocation refers to man's capabilities of controlling not just 'objects' but the *object-world*. Domination from this aspect refers to human domination over nature. Authorisation refers to man's capabilities of controlling the humanly created world of *society itself*." What is critical to understanding the use of material culture – produced goods – in the definition of self and in the creation of subculture, ethnic identity, or in "everyday resistance" is the recognition that people transform the meaning of goods through their actions: "At the heart of both domination and power lies the *transformative capacity* of human action, the origin of all that is liberating and productive in social life as well as all that is repressive and destructive" (Giddens 1981:51).

10 Much of what we see today in the study of social inequality, of meaning conveyed through artifact production and use, or of artifacts in social discourse, superimposes new concepts onto old ways of doing things. In their practice of material culture analysis, some historical archaeologists (and others: cf. the essays in Hodder 1989a) continue to seek out the "one right way," and not a few evangelists preach the narrow path of theoretical righteousness. Our discussion of the construction of context, below, addresses the consequences of this continued insistence on "paradigmatic purity" (cf. Deetz 1983).

11 It should be noted that other principals (i.e., Dent and Yentsch) in the Annapolis research have quite different analytical and theoretical approaches. See, for example, Yentsch n.d., 1988c, 1990; Yentsch and McKee 1987.

12   This largely negative perspective on power relations is criticized by
      Giddens (1981:51), who notes that "the tendency to regard domination as
      inherently negative, and as intrinsically inimical to freedom of action on the
      part of those subject to it, is closely related politically to the idea that power
      is inherently *coercive*, and that its use inevitably implies the existence of
      conflict. Neither of these ideas withstands close scrutiny; each usually
      reflects the assumption that power is not an integral and primary aspect of
      social life." He further points out that the basic premise of an alternative
      theory of power set forth by Foucault, although it "does not see power as
      inherently coercive and conflictful," views social life as essentially formed
      by struggles for power. Such a perspective renders inarticulate those not in
      power except in terms of resistance and conflict, as reactive rather than
      active. If we consider E. P. Thompson's (1963, 1978) observation that class
      (ethnicity as well) exists only when it is articulated, we begin to understand
      why the dominant ideology thesis makes it impossible to examine artifacts
      as elements in social discourse. Martin Hall (n.d.:13) comments that
      Leone's interpretation of the adoption of individual place settings by
      Annapolitans comes across "almost as if the possession of matching
      tableware turned the worker into an automaton, as if the capitalist had won
      the struggle for ideological control as soon as he had persuaded his laborer
      to adopt good table manners."

13   Meaning is "negotiable, interpenetrating, and fluid" (Beeman 1976:575);
      when objects are used as a way of creating meaning, of communicating on a
      nonverbal level, meaning is not embedded in artifacts themselves but is
      assigned or attributed to objects by individuals operating in group-specific
      cultural contexts (see, e.g., Wobst 1977; Hodder 1989a, 1989b).

14   Larry McKee's work on slave life on nineteenth-century Virginia plantations
      similarly explores the manipulation of material culture as a form of
      discourse between planter and slave (1987, 1988, n.d.); see also Upton 1985.

15   O'Brien (1989) provides a cogent discussion of Foucault's contributions to
      historical method as well as an evaluation of his critics.

16   South's (1979) article on site structure was his last major push forward with
      an extrapolation of one of Binford's ideas into historical archaeology. His
      long silence opened the door for Leone to appropriate the same formula for
      success by rushing in with an adaptation of Binford's middle-range theory,
      set forward initially in Leone and Crosby (1987) and further developed in
      Leone (1989) and Leone and Potter (1988b). The proposal is "disingenuously
      reductionist" (cf.Yentsch 1989), for it involves treating documentary and
      archaeological data as analytically and epistemologically separate. Rather
      than critically analyzing both as elements of discourse, we are enjoined to
      test one against the other to flush out and resolve ambiguities. There is
      certainly merit in this procedure, but it fails as a method for documentary
      analysis because it does not move beyond the etic or descriptive grid
      derived from superficial treatment of documents. What is more, and this is
      truly insidious, this version of middle-range theory has very little to do
      with Binford's emphasis on using middle-range theory as a medium for
      understanding the structure of the archaeological record by developing

inferences, usually through ethnographic analogy, "aimed at the isolation of organizational variables characteristic of past systems" (Binford 1987:449). In essence, what Leone and his colleagues propose is a method that fails to treat either the documentary or the archaeological record with the analytical thoroughness both richly deserve and that the recovery of meaning requires.

17 This cannot be interpreted as anything other than a rationalization for not using documents critically, for it is far from an accurate representation of what can be gleaned from the primary sources. It is not in fact altogether clear that Rubertone has consulted primary sources, although much of the recent literature on the archaeology of Native American–European interaction makes excellent use of documents and material evidence in combination to examine not just resistance but deliberate construction of cultural identity by Native Americans (e.g., Bradley 1987; Bragdon 1988; Brenner 1988; Crosby 1988; Hamell 1983, 1987; Merrell 1988, 1989).

18 Perhaps the strong urge to remain a prehistorian in the face of textual evidence stems from what seems to be an underlying worry that adding documents into the equation calls for a critical approach not otherwise necessary because material evidence is somehow more direct than texts and hence more reliable, less in need of critical analysis.

19 Beaudry (1980a, 1980b) proposes that documents such as probate inventories can be treated as "eliciting contexts" from which the researcher can recover information on nonliterate or "semi-literate" segments of society. In a study of "heated" speech (profanity, slander, and insults), St George (1984) analyzed court records to reconstruct speech performances; his interpretations bring to light many aspects of social relations in seventeenth-century Massachusetts that recorders never intended to reveal. Rhys Isaac's (1988) discussion of the manipulative behavior of Landon Carter's slaves through a critical reading of Carter's own diary is a particularly splendid example of textual analysis. Isaac turns the intentions of the "partisan observer" literally "inside out" to reveal the nature of Carter's less-than-successful efforts to control his slaves and to command respect from them.

20 The concept of "multiple voices" is drawn from Mascia-Lees et al. in the Autumn, 1989, issue of *Signs*; we are grateful to Anne Yentsch and Suzanne Spencer-Wood for bringing this article to our attention.

21 Social and cultural historians have increasingly focused on everyday life and on private and public ritual as the nexus of social action (e.g., de Certeau 1984; Davis 1983; Darnton 1984; Larkin 1988). In great measure this outgrowth of Marxist and Annales schools of social history is a result of the increasingly strong influence of anthropological thought within history as well as cross-fertilization between the two disciplines. We argue here that historical archaeologists need to follow the lead of material culture specialists (e.g., Mackiewicz 1990) by becoming aware of and receptive to these trends. Perhaps we can look forward to a "reanthropologicization" of historical archaeology.

22 Class conflict over leisure behavior in public places was pervasive in the urban Northeast, and remains so today. Roy Rosenzweig (1983) uses

holiday celebrations, public park policy, and legislative control of saloons to trace the course of this conflict in Worcester, Massachusetts, during the late nineteenth and early twentieth centuries.

23   We found this to be true as well of ceramic use by residents of the Kirk Street Agents' House, who were near the top of the economic and social hierarchy in Lowell. The vessel forms did not differ greatly from those found at the boarding houses, nor did the cuts of meat represented by faunal remains (see Beaudry and Mrozowski 1987b), yet we infer from the cultural context that mealtimes at the two sorts of households were vastly different in quality, character, and symbolic import.

REFERENCES

Abercrombie, Nicholas, Stephan Hill, and Brian S. Turner (1980) *The Dominant Ideology Thesis*. George Allen and Unwin, London.

Althusser, Louis (1971) "Ideology and Ideological State Apparatuses (Notes Towards an Investigation)." In *Lenin and Philosophy and other Essays*, ed. Louis Althusser, pp. 127–86. Monthly Review Press, New York.

Ashmore, Wendy and Richard R. Wilk (1988) "Household and Community in the Mesoamerican Past." In *Household and Community in the Mesoamerican Past*, eds Richard R. Wilk and Wendy Ashmore, pp. 1–27. University of New Mexico Press, Albuquerque.

Barthes, Roland (1957) "Le mythe, aujourd'hui." In *Mythologies*, ed. Roland Barthes, pp. 191–247. Editions du Seuil, Paris.

——(1964) *Elements of Semiology* (1967 edn). Hill and Wang, New York.

——(1981) *Le grain de la voix, entretiens 1962–1980*. Editions du Seuil, Paris.

Beaudry, Mary C. (1978) "Worth its Weight in Iron: Categories of Material Culture in Early Virginia Probate Inventories." *Quarterly Bulletin of the Archeological Society of Virginia* 33(1), 19–26.

——(1980a) *"Or What Else You Please to Call It": Folk Semantic Domains in Early Virginia Probate Inventories*. Ph.D. dissertation, Brown University, Providence; University Microfilms International, Ann Arbor.

——(1980b) "Analysis of Semi-Literate Text." Paper presented at the Annual Meetings of the Society for Historical Archaeology, Albuquergue, NM.

——(1980c) "Pot-Shot, Jug-Bitten, Cup-Shaken: Object Language and Double Meanings." Paper presented at the Annual Meetings of the American Anthropological Association, Washington, D.C.

——(1986) "The Archaeology of Historical Land Use in Massachusetts." *Historical Archaeology* 20(2), 38–46.

——(1988a) ed. *Documentary Archaeology in the New World*. Cambridge University Press, Cambridge.

——(1988b) "Words for Things: Linguistic Analysis of Probate Inventories." In *Documentary Archaeology in the New World*, ed. Mary C. Beaudry, pp. 43–50. Cambridge University Press, Cambridge.

——(n.d.) "Ethnography in Retrospect: The Archaeology of Everyday Life in

Historical Times (A Review Essay)." In *Material Culture, World View, and Culture Change*, eds Mary C. Beaudry and Anne E. Yentsch. The Telford Press, Caldwell, NJ, forthcoming.

Beaudry, Mary C. and Stephen A. Mrozowski (eds) (1987a) *Interdisciplinary Investigations of the Boott Mills, Lowell, Massachusetts*. Vol. I: *Life at the Boarding Houses: A Preliminary Report*. Cultural Resources Management Study 18. US Department of the Interior, National Park Service, North Atlantic Regional Office, Boston.

——(eds) (1987b) *Interdisciplinary Investigations of the Boott Mills, Lowell, Massachusetts*. Vol. II: *The Kirk Street Agents' House*. Cultural Resources Management Study 19. US Department of the Interior, National Park Service, North Atlantic Regional Office, Boston.

——(1988) "The Archeology of Work and Home Life in Lowell, Massachusetts: An Interdisciplinary Study of the Boott Cotton Mills Corporation." *IA, the Journal of the Society for Industrial Archeology* 14(2), 1–22.

——(1989) *Interdisciplinary Investigations of the Boott Mills, Lowell, Massachusetts*. Vol. III: *The Boarding House System as a Way of Life*. Cultural Resources Management Study 21. US Department of the Interior, National Park Service, North Atlantic Regional Office, Boston.

Beeman, William O. (1976) *The Meaning of Stylistic Variation in Iranian Verbal Interaction*. Ph.D. dissertation, University of Chicago.

Bennett, Tony (1986) "Introduction: Popular Culture and 'the Turn to Gramsci.'" In *Popular Culture and Social Relations*, eds Tony Bennett, Colin Mercer, and Janet Woolacott, pp. xi–xix. Open University Press, Milton Keynes.

Bennett, Tony, Colin Mercer, and Janet Woolacott (eds) (1981) *Culture, Ideology, and Social Process*. Batsford Academic and Educational Ltd, London.

——(1986) *Popular Culture and Social Relations*. Open University Press, Milton Keynes.

Binford, Lewis R. (1962) "A New Method for Calculating Dates from Kaolin Pipe Stem Fragments." *Southeastern Archaeological Conference Newsletter* 9(1), 19–21.

——(1976) "Forty-seven Trips: A Case Study in the Character of Some Formation Processes of the Archaeological Record." In *The Interior Peoples of Northern Alaska*, ed. E. S. Hall, Jr, pp. 299–381. National Museum of Man, Mercury Series 49. Ottawa.

——(1979) "Organization and Formation Processes: Looking at Curated Technologies." *Journal of Anthropological Research* 35, 195–208.

——(1981) "Behavioral Archaeology and the 'Pompeii Premise.'" *Journal of Anthropological Research* 37, 255–73.

——(1987) "Researching Ambiguity: Frames of Reference and Site Structure." In *Method and Theory for Activity Area Research: An Ethnoarchaeological Approach*, ed. Susan Kent, pp. 449–512. Columbia University Press, New York.

Boggs, Carl (1976) *Gramsci's Marxism*. Pluto Press, London.

Bond, Kathleen H. (1989a) " 'that we may purify our corporation by discharging the offenders': The Documentary Record of Social Control in the Boott Boardinghouses." In *Interdisciplinary Investigations of the Boott Mills, Lowell, Massachusetts.* Vol. III: *The Boarding House System as a Way of Life,* eds Mary C. Beaudry and Stephen A. Mrozowski, pp. 23–36. Cultural Resources Management Study 21. US Department of the Interior, National Park Service, North Atlantic Regional Office, Boston.

——(1989b) "The Medicine, Alcohol, and Soda Vessels from the Boott Mills." In *Interdisciplinary Investigations of the Boott Mills, Lowell, Massachusetts.* Vol. III: *The Boarding House System as a Way of Life,* eds Mary C. Beaudry and Stephen A. Mrozowski, pp. 121–40. Cultural Resources Management Study 21. US Department of the Interior, National Park Service, North Atlantic Regional Office, Boston.

Bourdieu, P. (1973) "The Berber House." In *Rules and Meanings: The Anthropology of Everyday Knowledge,* ed. Mary Douglas, pp. 98–110. Penguin, Harmondsworth.

Bradley, James W. (1987) *Evolution of the Onandoga Iroquois: Accommodating Change, 1500–1655.* Syracuse University Press, Syracuse, NY.

Bragdon, Kathleen (1988) "Material Culture of the Christian Indians of New England." In *Documentary Archaeology in the New World,* ed. Mary C. Beaudry, pp. 126–31. Cambridge University Press, Cambridge.

Brenner, Elise M. (1988) "Sociopolitical Implications of Mortuary Ritual Remains in 17th-Century Native Southern New England." In *The Recovery of Meaning: Historical Archaeology in the Eastern United States,* eds Mark P. Leone and Parker B. Potter, Jr, pp. 147–81. Smithsonian Institution Press, Washington, DC.

Bronner, Simon J. (1985) *American Material Culture and Folklife: A Prologue and Dialogue.* UMI Research Press, Ann Arbor.

Burley, David V. (1989) "Function, Meaning and Context: Ambiguities in Ceramic Use by the *Hivernant* Métis of the Northwestern Plains." *Historical Archaeology* 23(1), 97–106.

Carver, Martin O. H. (1987) "The Nature of Urban Deposits." In *Urban Archaeology in Britain,* eds John Schofield and Roger Leach, pp. 9–26. Council for British Archaeology Report No. 61.

de Certeau, Michel (1984) *The Practice of Everyday Life.* University of California Press, Berkeley.

Chartier, Roger (1989) "Texts, Printings, Readings." In *The New Cultural History,* ed. Lynn Hunt, pp. 154–75. University of California Press, Berkeley.

Clements, Joyce (1989) *The Maturation of the American Military: A Case Study from Fort Independence, Boston, 1800–1820.* MA thesis, Department of Anthropology, University of Massachusetts, Boston.

Cook, Lauren J. (1989) "Tobacco-Related Material Culture and the Construction of Working Class Culture." In *Interdisciplinary Investigations of the Boott Mills, Lowell, Massachusetts.* Vol. III: *The Boarding House System as a Way of Life,* eds Mary C. Beaudry and Stephen A. Mrozowski, pp. 209–30. Cultural Resources Management Study 21. US Department of the Interior, National Park Service, North Atlantic Regional Office, Boston.

Courbin, Paul (1988) *What is Archaeology? An Essay on the Nature of*

Archaeological Research. (Trans. Paul Bahn.) University of Chicago Press, Chicago.

Coward, Rosalind and John Ellis, (1977) *Language and Materialism: Developments in Semiology and the Theory of the Subject*. Routledge and Kegan Paul, London.

Crosby, Constance A. (1988) "From Myth to History, or Why King Philip's Ghost Walks Abroad." In *The Recovery of Meaning: Historical Archaeology in the Eastern United States*, eds Mark P. Leone and Parker B. Potter, Jr. pp. 183–209. Smithsonian Institution Press, Washington, D.C.

Csiksentmihalyi, Mihalyi and Eugene Rochberg-Halton (1981) *The Meaning of Things: Domestic Symbols and the Self*. Cambridge University Press, Cambridge.

Darnton, Robert (1984) *The Great Cat Massacre and Other Episodes in French Cultural History*. Basic Books, New York.

Davis, Natalie Zemon (1983) *The Return of Martin Geurre*. Harvard University Press, Cambridge, MA.

Deetz, James J. F. (1967) *Invitation to Archaeology*. Natural History Press, New York.

——(1977a) "Historical Archaeology as the Science of Material Culture." In *Historical Archaeology and the Importance of Material Things*, ed. Leland G. Ferguson, pp. 9–12. Special Publication Series 2. Society for Historical Archaeology, Tucson, AZ.

——(1977b) *In Small Things Forgotten: The Archaeology of Everyday Life in Early America*. Anchor Books, New York.

——(1983) "Scientific Humanism and Humanistic Science: A Plea for Paradigmatic Pluralism in Historical Archaeology." *Geoscience and Man* 22, 27–34. Louisiana State University, Baton Rouge.

——(1988a) "History and Archaeological Theory: Walter Taylor Revisited." *American Antiquity* 53(1), 13–22.

——(1988b) "American Historical Archeology: Methods and Results." *Science* 239 (22 January 1988), 362–67.

——(1989) "Archaeography, Archaeology, or Archeology?" *American Journal of Archaeology* 93, 429–35.

Douglas, Mary (1973) "Introduction." In *Rules and Meanings: The Anthropology of Everyday Knowledge*, ed. Mary Douglas, pp. 9–13. Penguin, Harmondsworth.

Douglas, Mary and Baron Isherwood (1979) *The World of Goods*. W. W. Norton, New York.

Dutton, David H. (1989) "Thrasher's China or Colored Porcelain: Ceramics from a Boott Mills Boardinghouse and Tenement." In *Interdisciplinary Investigations of the Boott Mills, Lowell, Massachusetts*. Vol. III: *The Boarding House System as a Way of Life*, eds Mary C. Beaudry and Stephen A. Mrozowski, pp. 83–120. Cultural Resources Management Study 21. US Department of the Interior, National Park Service, North Atlantic Regional Office, Boston.

Earle, Timothy K. and Robert W. Preucel (1987) "Processual Archaeology and the Radical Critique." *Current Anthropology* 28(4), 501–38.

Ferguson, Leland G. (ed.) (1977) *Historical Archaeology and the Importance of*

Material Things. Special Publication Series 2. Society for Historical Archaeology, Tucson, AZ.

Foucault, Michel (1972) *The Archaeology of Knowledge and the Discourse on Language*. Tavistock, London.

Geertz, Clifford (1980) *Negara: The Theatre State in Nineteenth-Century Bali*. Princeton University Press, Princeton, NJ.

——(1982) *The Interpretation of Culture*. Basic Books, New York.

——(1983) *Local Knowledge: Further Essays in Interpretive Anthropology*. Basic Books, New York.

Gibbon, Guy (1989) *Explanation in Archaeology*. Basil Blackwell, Oxford.

Giddens, Anthony (1981) *A Contemporary Critique of Historical Materialism*. Vol. 1: *Power, Property and the State* (1987 edn). University of California Press, Berkeley.

Glassie, Henry (1976) *Folk Housing in Middle Virginia: A Structural Study of Folk Artifacts*. University of Tennessee Press, Knoxville.

——(1982) *Passing the Time in Ballymenone: Culture and History in an Ulster Community*. University of Pennsylvania Press, Philadelphia.

Godbey, Geoffrey (1981) *Leisure in Your Life: An Exploration*. Saunders College Publishing, Philadelphia.

Goffman, Erving (1971) *Relations in Public: Microstudies of the Public Order*. Harper and Row, New York.

Gregory, Michael and Susanne Carroll (1978) *Language and Situation: Language Varieties and Their Social Contexts*. Routledge and Kegan Paul, London.

Hall, Martin (n.d.) "Small Things" and "The Mobile, Conflictual Fusion of Power, Fear and Desire." In *Material Culture, World View, and Culture Change*, eds Mary C. Beaudry and Anne E. Yentsch. The Telford Press, Caldwell, NJ, forthcoming.

Hamell, George R. (1983) "Trading in Metaphors: The Magic of Beads." In *Proceedings of the 1982 Glass Trade Bead Conference*, ed. Charles F. Hayes III, pp. 5–28. Research Records 16. Rochester Museum and Science Center, Rochester, NY.

——(1987) "Mythical Realities and European Contact in the Northeast during the Sixteenth and Seventeenth Centuries." *Man in the Northeast* 33, 63–87.

Hargreaves, Jennifer (1989) "The Promise and Problems of Women's Leisure and Sport." In *Leisure for Leisure: Critical Essays*, ed. Chris Rojek, pp. 130–49. Routledge, New York.

Harrington, Faith (1989) "The Emergent Elite in Early 18th Century Portsmouth: The Archaeology of the Joseph Sherburne Houselot." *Historical Archaeology* 23(1), 2–18.

Harrington, J. C. (1954) "Dating Stem Fragments of Seventeenth and Eighteenth Century Clay Tobacco Pipes." *Quarterly Bulletin, Archaeological Society of Virginia* 9(1), not paginated.

Hawkes, Terence (1977) *Structuralism and Semiotics*. University of California Press, Berkeley.

Heath, . (1974) *Vertige du déplacement*. Fayard, Paris.

Hebdige, Dick (1979) *Subculture: The Meaning of Style*. Methuen, London.

Hodder, Ian (1986) *Reading the Past: Current Approaches to Interpretation in Archaeology*. Cambridge University Press, Cambridge.
——(1987a) "The Contribution of the Long Term." In *Archaeology as Long-Term History*, ed. Ian Hodder, 1–8. Cambridge University Press, Cambridge.
——(1987b) "The Contextual Analysis of Symbolic Meanings." In *The Archaeology of Contextual Meanings*, ed. Ian Hodder, pp. 1–10. Cambridge University Press, Cambridge.
——(ed.) (1989a) *The Meanings of Things: Material Culture and Symbolic Expression*. Unwin Hyman, London.
——(1989b) "Post-Modernism, Post-Structuralism, and Post-Processual archaeology." In *The Meanings of Things: Material Culture and Symbolic Expression*, ed. Ian Hodder, pp. 64–78. Unwin Hyman, London.
Honerkamp, Nicholas and R. Bruce Council (1984) "Individual Versus Corporate Adaptations in Urban Contexts." *Tennessee Anthropologist* 9(1), 22–31.
Huizinga, Johan (1970) *Homo ludens: A Study of the Play Element in Culture*. J. & J. Harper, New York.
Hunt, Lynn (ed.) (1989) *The New Cultural History*. University of California Press, Berkeley.
Isaac, Rhys (1988) "Ethnographic Method in History: An Action Approach." In *Material Life in America, 1600–1860*, ed. Robert Blair St George, pp. 39–61. Northeastern University Press, Boston.
Krampen, Martin (1979) "Survey of Current Work on the Semiology of Objects." In *A Semiotic Landscape: Proceedings of the First Congress of the International Association for Semiotic Studies, Milan, June 1974/Panorama sémiotique: Actes du premier congrès de l'Association Internationale de Sémiotique, Milan, juin 1974*, eds Seymour Chatman, Umberto Eco, and Jean-Marie Klinkenburg, pp. 158–68. Mouton, The Hague.
Kruesch, Jurgen and Weldon Kees (1956) *Nonverbal Communication: Notes on the Visual Perception of Human Relations* (1972 edn). University of California Press, Berkeley.
Landon, David B. (1989) "Domestic Ideology and the Economics of Boarding-house Keeping." in *Interdisciplinary Investigations of the Boott Mills, Lowell, Massachusetts. Vol. III: The Boarding House System as a Way of Life*, eds Mary C. Beaudry and Stephen A. Mrozowski, pp. 37–48. Cultural Resources Management Study 21. US Department of the Interior, National Park Service, North Atlantic Regional Office, Boston.
Landon, David B. and Mary C. Beaudry (1988) "Domestic Ideology and the Boardinghouse System in Lowell, Massachusetts." Paper presented to the Annual Meeting of the Dublin Seminar on New England Folklife, Durham, NH.
Larkin, Jack (1988) *The Reshaping of Everyday Life 1790–1840*. Harper and Row, New York.
Leach, Edmund (1982) *Social Anthropology*. Oxford University Press, New York.
Leone, Mark P. (1972) "Issues in Anthropological Archaeology." In *Contemporary Archaeology: A Guide to Theory and Contributions*, ed. Mark P. Leone, pp. 14–27. Southern Illinois University Press, Carbondale.
——(1984) "Interpreting Ideology in Historical Archaeology: Using the Rules

of Perspective in the William Paca Garden in Annapolis, Maryland." In *Ideology, Power, and Prehistory*, eds Daniel Miller and Christopher Tilley, pp. 25–35. Cambridge University Press, Cambridge.

——(1986) "Symbolic, Structural and Critical Archaeology." In *American Archaeology Past and Future: A Celebration of the Society for American Archaeology 1935–1985*, eds David J. Meltzer, Don D. Fowler, and Jeremy Sabloff, pp. 413–38. Smithsonian Institution Press, Washington, D.C.

——(1987) "Rule by Ostentation: The Relationship Between Space and Sight in Eighteenth-Century Landscape Architecture in the Chesapeake Region of Maryland." In *Method and Theory for Activity Area Research: An Ethnoarchaeological Approach*, ed. Susan Kent, pp. 604–33. Columbia University Press, New York.

——(1988a) "The Relationship Between Archaeological Data and the Documentary Record: 18th Century Gardens in Annapolis, Maryland." *Historical Archaeology* 22(1), 29–35.

——(1988b) "The Georgian Order as the Order of Merchant Capitalism in Annapolis, Maryland." In *The Recovery of Meaning: Historical Archaeology in the Eastern United States*, eds Mark P. Leone and Parker B. Potter, Jr. pp. 235–61. Smithsonian Institution Press, Washington, D.C.

——(1989) "Issues in Historic Landscapes and Gardens." *Historical Archaeology* 23(1), 45–7.

Leone, Mark P. and Constance A. Crosby (1987) "Epilogue: Middle-Range Theory in Historical Archaeology." In *Consumer Choice in Historical Archaeology*, ed. Suzanne M. Spencer-Wood, pp. 397–411. Plenum Press, New York.

Leone, Mark P., Elizabeth Kryder-Reid, Julie H. Ernstein, and Paul A. Shackel (1989) "Power Gardens of Annapolis." *Archaeology* 42(2), 35–9, 74–5.

Leone, Mark P. and Parker B. Potter, Jr (eds) (1988a) *The Recovery of Meaning: Historical Archaeology in the Eastern United States*. Smithsonian Institution Press, Washington, D.C.

——(1988b) "Introduction: Issues in Historical Archaeology." In *The Recovery of Meaning: Historical Archaeology in the Eastern United States*, eds Mark P. Leone and Parker B. Potter, Jr, pp. 1–22. Smithsonian Institution Press, Washington, D.C.

Leone, Mark P., Parker B. Potter, Jr, and Paul A. Shackel (1987) "Toward a Critical Archaeology." *Current Anthropology* 28(3), 283–302.

Little, Barbara and Paul A. Shackel (1989) "Scales of Historical Anthropology: An Archaeology of Colonial Anglo-America." *Antiquity* 63(240), 495–509.

Lofland, Lyn H. (1973) *A World of Strangers: Order and Action in Public Space.* Basic Books, New York.

McGuire, Randall H. (1988) "Dialogues with the Dead: Ideology and the Cemetery." In *The Recovery of Meaning: Historical Archaeology in the Eastern United States*, eds Mark P. Leone and Parker B. Potter, Jr, pp. 435–80. Smithsonian Institution Press, Washington, D.C.

McKee, Larry (1987) "Delineating Ethnicity from the Garbage of Early Virginians: the Faunal Remains from the Kingsmill Plantation Slave Quarter." *American Archeology* 6(1), 31–9.

——(1988) *Plantation Food Supply in Nineteenth Century Tidewater Virginia.* Ph.d dissertation, University of California, Berkeley.

——(n.d.) "The Ideals and Realities Behind the Design and Use of Nineteenth-Century Virginia Slave Cabins." In *Material Culture, World View, and Culture Change*, eds Mary C. Beaudry and Anne E. Yentsch. The Telford Press, Caldwell, NJ, forthcoming.

Mackiewicz, Susan (1990) *Philadelphia Flourishing: The Material World of Philadelphians, 1682–1760.* Ph.D. dissertation University of Delaware, Newark.

Malone, Dumas (ed.) (1946) *Dictionary of American Biography.* Charles Scribner's Sons, New York.

Marcus, George E. and Michael M. J. Fischer (1986) *Anthropology as Cultural Critique: An Experimental Moment in the Human Sciences.* University of Chicago Press, Chicago.

Mascia-Lees, Frances E., Patricia Sharpe, and Colleen Ballerino Cohen (1989) "The Postmodernist Turn in Anthropology: Cautions from a Feminist Perspective." *Signs* 15(1), 7–33.

Melas, E. M. (1989) "Emics, Etics, and Empathy in Archaeological Theory." In *The Meanings of Things: Material Culture and Symbolic Expression*, ed. Ian Hodder, pp. 137–55. Unwin Hyman, London.

Mercer, Colin (1986) "Complicit Pleasures." In *Popular Culture and Social Relations*, eds Tony Bennett, Colin Mercer, and Janet Woolacott, pp. 50–68. Open University Press, Milton Keynes.

Merrell, James H. (1988) "The Indians' New World: The Catawba Experience." In *Material Life in America, 1600–1860*, ed. Robert Blair St George, pp. 95–112. Northeastern University Press, Boston.

——(1989) "Some Thoughts on Colonial Historians and American Indians." *The William and Mary Quarterly* 46(1), 94–119.

Miller, Daniel (1987) *Material Culture and Mass Consumption.* Basil Blackwell, Oxford.

Miller, George L. (1980) "Classification and Economic Scaling of Nineteenth Century Ceramics." *Historical Archaeology* 14, 1–40.

Mrozowski, Stephen A. (1984) "Prospect and Perspective on an Archaeology of the Household." *Man in the Northeast* 27, 31–49.

——(1988) "'For Gentlemen of Capacity and Leisure': The Archaeology of Colonial Newspapers." In *Documentary Archaeology in the New World*, ed. Mary C. Beaudry, pp. 184–91. Cambridge University Press, Cambridge.

Noël Hume, Ivor (1969) *A Guide to Artifacts of Colonial America.* Alfred A. Knopf, New York.

O'Brien, Patricia (1989) "Michel Foucault's History of Culture." In *The New Cultural History*, ed. Lynn Hunt, pp. 25–46. University of California Press, Berkeley.

Orser, Charles E., Jr (1988) "Toward a Theory of Power for Historical Archaeology: Plantations and Space." In *The Recovery of Meaning: Historical Archaeology in the Eastern United States*, eds Mark P. Leone and Parker B. Potter, Jr, pp. 313–43. Smithsonian Institution Press, Washington, D.C.

188   MARY C. BEAUDRY ET AL.

Paynter, Robert (1984) "Social Dynamics and New England Archaeology." *Man in the Northeast* 27, 1–11.

——(1988) "Steps to an Archaeology of Capitalism: Material Change and Class Analysis." In *The Recovery of Meaning: Historical Archaeology in the Eastern United States*, eds Mark P. Leone and Parker B. Potter, Jr, 407–33. Smithsonian Institution Press, Washington, D.C.

Peña, J. Theodore and Elizabeth S. Peña (1988) Review of *The Archaeology of Slavery and Plantation Life*, ed. Teresa Singleton. *American Journal of Archaeology* 92, 153–5.

Pieper, Joseph (1952) *Leisure, the Basis of Culture*. Pantheon, New York.

Praetzellis, Adrian, Mary Praetzellis, and Marley Brown III (eds) (1980) *The Archaeology of the Golden Eagle Site*. Anthropological Studies Center, Sonoma State University, Rohnert Park, CA.

——(1987) "Artifacts as Symbols of Identity: An Example from Sacramento's Gold Rush Era Chinese Community." In *Living in Cities: Current Research in Urban Archaeology*, ed. Edward Staski, pp. 38–47. Special Publication Series 5. Society for Historical Archaeology, Pleasant Hill, CA.

——(1988) "What Happened to the Silent Majority? Research Strategies for Studying Dominant Group Material Culture in Late Nineteenth-Century California." In *Documentary Archaeology in the New World*, ed. Mary C. Beaudry, pp. 192–202. Cambridge University Press, Cambridge.

Prown, Jules David (1988) "Mind in Matter: An Introduction to Material Culture Theory and Method." In *Material Life in America, 1600–1860*, ed. Robert Blair St George, pp. 17–37. Northeastern University Press, Boston.

Quimby, Ian M. G. (ed.) (1978) *Material Culture and the Study of American Life*. W. W. Norton, New York.

Rabinow, Paul and William M. Sullivan (eds) (1979) *Interpretive Social Science: A Reader*. University of California Press, Berkeley.

——(1987) *Interpretive Social Science: A Second Look*. University of California Press, Berkeley.

Roberts, Warren E. (1985) [Untitled essay on material culture studies.] *Material Culture* 17, 89–93.

Rojek, Chris (1989) "Leisure and 'The Ruins of the Bourgeois World.'" In *Leisure for Leisure: Critical Essays*, ed. Chris Rojek, pp. 92–112. Routledge, New York.

Rosenzweig, Roy (1983) *Eight Hours for What We Will: Workers and Leisure in an Industrial City, 1870–1920*. Cambridge University Press, Cambridge.

Rubertone, Patricia E. (1989) "Archaeology, Colonialism and 17th-century Native America: Towards an Alternative Interpretation." In *Conflict in the Archaeology of Living Traditions*, ed. Robert Layton, pp. 32–45. Unwin Hyman, London.

Sahlins, Marshall D. (1981) *Historical Metaphors and Mythical Realities: Structure in the Mythology of the Sandwich Island Kingdom*. University of Michigan Press, Ann Arbor.

——(1985) *Islands of History*. University of Chicago Press, Chicago.

St George, Robert Blair (1984) "Heated Speech and Literacy in Seventeenth-Century New England." In *Seventeenth-Century New England*, eds David D.

Hall and David G. Allen, pp. 275–309. University Press of Virginia, Charlottesville.

——(1988a) "Introduction." In *Material Life in America, 1600–1860*, pp. 3–13. Northeastern University Press, Boston.

——(ed.) (1988b) *Material Life in America, 1600–1860*. Northeastern University Press, Boston.

Schiffer, Michael B. (1987) *Formation Processes of the Archaeological Record*. University of New Mexico Press, Albuquerque.

Schlereth, Thomas (ed.) (1980) *Artifacts and the American Past*. American Association for State and Local History, Nashville, TN.

——(1982) *Material Culture Studies in America*. American Association for State and Local History, Nashville, TN.

——(ed.) (1985) *Material Culture: A Research Guide*. University Press of Kansas, Lawrence.

Schmidt, Peter R. and Stephen A. Mrozowski (1983) "History, Smugglers, Change, and Shipwrecks." In *Shipwreck Anthropology*, ed. Richard A. Gould, pp. 143–71. University of New Mexico Press, Albuquerque.

Schrire, Carmel (n.d.) "Digging Archives at Oudepost I, Cape, South Africa." In *Material Culture, World View, and Culture Change*, eds Mary C. Beaudry and Anne E. Yentsch. The Telford Press, Caldwell, NJ, forthcoming.

Schuyler, Robert L. (1978) "The Spoken Word, the Written Word, Observed Behavior, and Preserved Behavior: The Contexts Available to the Archaeologist." In *Historical Archaeology: A Guide to Substantive and Theoretical Contributions*, ed. Robert L. Schuyler, pp. 267–77. Baywood Press, Farmingdale, NY.

——(1988) "Archaeological Remains, Documents, and Anthropology: A Call for a New Culture History." *Historical Archaeology* 22(1), 36–42.

Scott, James (1985) *Weapons of the Weak: Everyday Forms of Peasant Resistance*. Yale University Press, London.

Sennett, Richard (1978) *The Fall of Public Man*. Vintage Books, New York.

Shanks, Michael and Christopher Tilley (1982) "Ideology, Symbolic Power and Ritual Communication: A Reinterpretation of Neolithic Mortuary Practices." In *Symbolic and Structural Archaeology*, ed. Ian Hodder, pp. 129–54. Cambridge University Press, Cambridge.

——(1987) *Social Theory and Archaeology*. University of New Mexico Press, Albuquerque.

Shennan, Stephen (1982) "Ideology, Change, and the European Early Bronze Age." In *Symbolic and Structural Archaeology*, ed. Ian Hodder, pp. 155–61. Cambridge University Press, Cambridge.

South, Stanley (1977) *Method and Theory in Historical Archaeology*. Academic Press, New York.

——(1978) "Pattern Recognition in Historical Archaeology." *American Antiquity* 43(2), 223–30.

——(1979) "Historic Site Content, Structure, and Function." *American Antiquity* 44, 213–37.

——(1988) "Santa Elena: Threshold of Conquest." In *The Recovery of Meaning: Historical Archaeology in the Eastern United States*, eds Mark P. Leone and Parker B. Potter, Jr, pp. 27–71. Smithsonian Institution Press, Washington, D.C.

Stedman Jones, Gareth (1977) "Class Expression versus Social Control? A Critique of Recent Trends in the Social History of 'Leisure'." *History Workshop* 4, 162–70.

Stone, Lyle M. (1974) *Fort Michilimackinac 1715–1781: An Archaeological Perspective on the Revolutionary Frontier.* Michigan State University Press, East Lansing.

Sturtevant, William C. (1964) "Studies in Ethnoscience." *American Anthropologist* 66(3), 99–131.

Taylor, Charles (1979) "Interpretation and the Sciences of Man." In *Interpretive Social Science*, eds Paul Rabinow and William M. Sullivan. University of California Press, Berkeley.

Taylor, Walter W. (1948) *A Study of Archeology* (1967 edn). Southern Illinois University Press, Carbondale.

Thompson, E. P. (1963) *The Making of the English Working Class* (1966 edn). Vintage, New York.

——(1978) "Eighteenth-century English Society: Class Struggle Without Class?" *Social History* 3(2), 133–65.

Tilley, Christopher (1989) "Interpreting Material Culture." In *The Meanings of Things: Material Culture and Symbolic Expression*, ed. Ian Hodder, pp. 185–94. Unwin Hyman, London.

Turner, Victor (1974) *Dramas, Fields, and Metaphors: Symbolic Action in Human Society.* Cornell University Press, Ithaca, NY.

Upton, Dell (1983) "The Power of Things: Recent Studies in American Vernacular Architecture." *American Quarterly* 35, 262–79.

——(1985) "White and Black Landscapes in Eighteenth-Century Virginia." *Places* 2(2), 59–72.

Wagner, Roy (1975) *The Invention of Culture* (1981 edn). University of Chicago Press, Chicago.

Walker, Iain C. (1965) "Some Thoughts on the Harrington and Binford Systems for Statistically Dating Clay Pipes." *Quarterly Bulletin, Archeological Society of Virginia* 20(2), 60–4.

——(1967) "Statistical Methods for Dating Clay Pipe Fragments." *Post-Medieval Archaeology* (1967), 90–101.

——(1977) "Clay Tobacco-Pipes, with Particular Reference to the Bristol Industry." *History and Archaeology* (Parks Canada, Ottawa), 11A–D.

——(1983) "Nineteenth-Century Clay Tobacco Pipes in Canada." In *The Archaeology of the Clay Tobacco Pipe.* VIII: *America*, ed. Peter Davey. BAR International Series 175. Oxford.

Wall, Diana diZerega (1987) *At Home in New York: Changing Family Life Among the Propertied in the Late Eighteenth and Early Nineteenth Centuries.* Ph.D. dissertation, New York University.

Wells, Camille (1986) "Old Claims and New Demands: Vernacular Architecture Studies Today." In *Perspectives in Vernacular Architecture*, II, ed. Camille Wells, pp. 1–10. University of Missouri Press, Columbia.

Williams Michael Ann (1986) "The Little 'Big House': The Use and Meaning of the Single-Pen Dwelling." In *Perspectives in Vernacular Architecture*, II, ed. Camille Wells, pp. 130–6. University of Missouri Press, Columbia.

——(1990) "Pride and Prejudice: Understanding the Appalachian Boxed House." Lecture to the Boston University American Studies Program, January 26, 1990, Boston, MA.

Williams, Raymond (1977) *Marxism and Literature*. Oxford University Press, Oxford.

Wobst, H. M. (1977) "Stylistic Behavior and Information Exchange." In *For The Director: Research Essays in Honor of James B. Griffin*, ed. Charles E. Cleland, pp. 317–42. Anthropological Papers of the Museum of Anthropology 61. University of Michigan, Ann Arbor.

Wylie, Alison (1989) "Gender Theory and the Archaeological Record: Why Is There No Archaeology of Gender?" Paper presented at the Annual Meetings of the Society for American Archaeology, Atlanta, Georgia.

Yentsch, Anne E. (1975) *Understanding Seventeenth- and Eighteenth-Century Families – An Experiment in Historical Ethnography*. Unpublished Master's Thesis, Department of Anthropology, Brown University, Providence.

——(1988a) "Legends, Houses, Families, and Myths: Relationships between Material Culture and American Ideology." In *Documentary Archaeology in the New World*, ed. Mary C. Beaudry, pp. 5–19. Cambridge University Press, Cambridge.

——(1988b) "Farming, Fishing, Whaling, Trading: Land and Sea as Resource on 18th-Century Cape Cod." In *Documentary Archaeology in the New World*, ed. Mary C. Beaudry, pp. 138–60. Cambridge University Press, Cambridge.

——(1988c) "Some Opinions on the Importance of Context." Paper presented at the 22nd Annual Meetings of the Council for Northeast Historical Archaeology, Québec.

——(1989) "Access and Space, Symbolic and Material, in Historical Archaeology." Paper presented at the 22nd Annual Chacmool Conference, Calgary, Alberta.

——(1990) "The Calvert Orangery in Annapolis, Maryland: A Horticultural Symbol of Power and Prestige in an Early 18th-Century Community." In *Earth Patterns: Essays in Landscape Archaeology*, ed. William M. Kelso, pp. 169–87. University Press of Virginia, Charlottesville.

——(n.d.) "The Use of Land and Space on Lot 83, Annapolis, Maryland." In *New Perspectives on Maryland Archaeology*, eds R. J. Dent and B. J. Little. Special Publication of the Maryland Archaeology Society, forthcoming.

Yentsch, Anne E. and Larry McKee (1987) "Footprints of Buildings in Eighteenth-Century Annapolis." *American Archeology* 6(1), 40–50.

Yentsch, Anne E., Naomi Miller, Barbara Paca, and Dolores Piperno (1987) "Archaeologically Defining the Earlier Garden Landscapes at Morven: Preliminary Results." *Northeast Historical Archaeology* 16, 1–30.

Ziesing, Grace H. (1989) "Analysis of Personal Effects from Excavations of the Boott Mills Boardinghouse Backlots in Lowell." In *Interdisciplinary Investigations of the Boott Mills, Lowell, Massachusetts*. Vol. III: *The Boarding House System as a Way of Life*, eds Mary C. Beaudry and Stephen A. Mrozowski, pp. 141–68. Cultural Resources Management Study 21. US Department of the Interior, National Park Service, North Atlantic Regional Office, Boston.

10

The Symbolic Divisions of Pottery: Sex-related Attributes of English and Anglo-American Household Pots

Anne Yentsch

Introduction

Objects and metaphors

People communicate with metaphors. English metaphors include those of pottery: a "drinking-pot" is a man who imbibes heavily (Beaudry 1980); a "honey-pot" is a woman who openly expresses a strong degree of sexuality to attract men (Fraser 1985). Not only the English, but also the New World Indians used the imagery of pots to describe people, speaking of pregnant women as becoming pot-shaped or as "big-pots" (Levi-Strauss 1988:181). By taking the neutral word *pot* and attaching to it adjectives with culturally attributed masculine and feminine connotations, people speak about behavior and relationships between men and women. Yet, people do not speak with words alone. Men and women also use the world of objects to convey information through the use of analogy. In metaphorical analogies, one or more attributes of a person, animal, plant, or object correspond to one or more attributes of something else; by speaking of one, men and women speak indirectly of the other. In nonverbal communication even something as common as a household pot can have a metaphorical or symbolic association existing side by side with its ostensible utilitarian function. This chapter uses household pots to illustrate the ways in which pottery could serve as metaphors through which people "spoke" about social relationships, the roles of men and women, the ways in which social class arbitrarily divided men from women, woman from woman, man from man, and the boundary between culture and nature.

The argument builds on ideas expressed by James Deetz (1972, 1977). In "Ceramics from Plymouth: The Archaeological Evidence" (1972), Deetz considered change in the ceramic assemblages from coastal New England sites between the seventeenth and the late eighteenth centuries. He associated the appearance of matched sets of ceramic vessels with the rise of individualism discussed by historians, and observed in architectural plans of Virginia folk houses (Glassie 1975). Despite Deetz's plea that ceramics be understood in terms of their utilitarian *and* symbolic functions, the possibility that household ceramics had symbolic values of equal importance with or parallel to their more pragmatic use as food and beverage containers has not been widely explored by historical archaeologists in the United States (Deetz 1977:50).

The symbolism of pottery and porcelain vessels is a consequence of (a) the social rank of the people who use the vessels, (b) the social space wherein the vessels are used and/or stored, and (c) access to them. The latter reflects the ease with which they may be acquired which is, in turn, a combination of availability, price, and a family's purchasing power. Critical to understanding the symbolism associated with different functional sets of household ceramics are the uses of domestic space. The appearance of specific ceramic forms and ware-types in different household areas is not accidental; rather, ware-type, decoration, and form signal who uses particular vessels and what their uses are. Both the who and the what are related to the cultural restrictions of household space.

In this chapter, the discussion of common and uncommon pots is cast in a structuralist framework because structuralist analyses highlight how people were able to use the symbolic language of objects to speak of other aspects of daily life, reinforcing social principles with physical analogies. The symbolic messages were not only conveyed by those ceramic vessels that were used for display, but were reiterated by the differential use of pots. The impact of those used in display was heightened as they were cast against the background of those in daily use. The result was a cultural division of pottery which can be seen as repeating a series of binary discriminations highly visible in food use (i.e., hot/cold, wet/dry), and in spatial designations (i.e. inner/outer, heaven/earth), and in social rank (higher/lower). The two basic divisions of concern are the culturally defined dichotomies of culture/nature and male/female: the ways in which foods and pottery relate to them are schematically outlined in figures 10.1A and 10.1B. Integral to the analysis is a concern with the symbolic expression of relationships of dominance and subordination. The analysis indicates that ceramic vessels were elements in boundary maintenance. Over time, as cultural boundaries in English and Anglo-American society were more sharply

Masculine Culture Heaven Ritual Public	Feminine Nature Earth Secular Private
Elite Englishman (*Dominant social group*) Instrumental social action	Women, children, servants (*Subordinate social groups*) Expressive social action

Figure 10.1A Basic cultural categories used to classify social space, food, and pottery

Divisions of space

Public space: market area Cultivated land: farm, field Built access: road, bridge, walk	Private space: household area Uncultivated land: forest, marsh Natural access: ocean, river, creek

Divisions of food[1]

Courtly cuisine (mysterious)
  transformations of nature)
Cooked foods
Exotic foods
  Swans and blackbirds
  Wild boar or deer
  Whales, porpoises, sturgeon
  Rice-based potage
  Peaches and oranges
  Almonds
  Oriental spices
    Cinnamon, nutmeg, etc.
Exotic beverages
  Wine, tea, coffee, chocolate
	Daily cooking (everyday
	  transformations of nature)
	Raw foods
	Common foods
	  Geese, hens, partridges
	  Beef and pork
	  Herring or mackerel
	  Cereal-based potage
	  Apples and pears
	  Walnuts
	  Potherbs
	    Parsley, rosemary, thyme
	Common beverages
	  Beer, ale and cider

Divisions of pottery

Display pottery
  Plates, chargers, harvest jugs
Experimental use (ca. 1680)
  Tea and coffee pots, punch bowls
Exotic ware: porcelain, delft
Finely hand-painted decoration
Visual appearance: white-toned
	Utilitarian pots
	  Butter pots, crocks, storage jars
	Customary use (ca. 1680)
	  Dish, mug, jug
	Basic ware: earthen and stone
	Trailed or combed decoration
	Visual appearance: earth-toned

[1] See the work of Levi-Strauss (1958, 1965), Douglas (1972), and Goody (1982) for detailed discussions of the categories and transformations of food. See Wilson (1974), Henisch (1976), and Mennell (1985) for information on specific food items.

Figure 10.1B Analytic classifications of space, food, and pottery that align with the basic dichotomies shown in figure 1A

defined, earth-toned vessels became the primary vessels used in the foodways system in social spaces assigned to women, while white-toned vessels were increasingly used to denote status in social display, an element of the food domain that traditionally fell within the masculine sphere of activity.

As Macfarlane (1988:195) notes, concepts of power and property were merged in the medieval English world. Power was mysteriously and indirectly expressed in different forms of property of which the lowly household pot is one small example. The hierarchical relationships that constituted the social structure of the culture were repetitively illustrated within different cultural domains. In a manner akin to mythic thought, these illustrations constituted a number of statments set side by side. Levi-Strauss views myth as a series of texts and writes: "Imagine a text, difficult to understand in one language, translated into several languages; the combined meaning of all the different versions may prove richer and more profound than the partial, mutilated meaning drawn from each individual version" (1988:171). These domains included and used elements of material culture to reinforce the principles whereby they were organized; these principles included beliefs about the proper roles of men and women. In studying the masculine and feminine symbolism of a common class of artifacts found in the archaeological record, and thinking of them as metaphorical statements about the society at large, an archaeologist begins to see the wide range of ethnographic information conveyed by objects. Such research expands discussion of archaeologically recovered ceramic vessels beyond the readily observable attributes of form, material, temper, glaze, decoration, distribution, and economic value by placing artifacts within their social context.

If an archaeologist can and does separate masculine and feminine domains of culture within the archaeological record, what does she learn? Does it shed new light on a culture or open up different avenues for study? As I thought of artifacts as being either masculine or feminine, it became clear that as Schuyler (1980) and Handsman (1984) noted earlier, there is very little discussion of women's lives in the archaeological literature. A number of imaginative, sensitive, and informative books and articles have been written about women in English and Anglo-American society using historical resources (Amussen 1985, 1987; Cahn 1987; Cott 1977; Hanawalt 1986; Mertes 1988; Nicholson 1986; Norton 1980; Stansell 1987; Ulrich 1982, to name but some). There are very few (Deagan's (1973, 1983) work on Spanish sites, and Wall (1987) are exceptions) that have dealt with women's lives as seen through the archaeological record. Yet the bulk of any domestic assemblage is food-related refuse, and the foodways system *was* an institution in which women were deeply involved (see table 10.3); and although men controlled ceremonial food consumption, within household space women were primarily responsible for its production. When historical archaeologists ignore the data available from artifact analysis that contains information about gender, about the relations between men and women, and about the activities characteristic of each, they dispossess women from their past. Society is depersonalized; the fact that all cultures have male and female members can be ignored. Inevitably the analysis is biased towards one segment – the politically dominant segment – of the society.

It is not simply that women are overlooked. Archaeologists are also beguiled into ignoring many provocative aspects of men's lives. Men in the past, as men do today, spoke to each other about themselves, their power, their prestige, and rank in the same terms, using the same metaphors of pottery and of space, as they did about the relationships between men and women. This was surprising to learn, but perhaps it should not have been, for Marc Bloch concluded after a study of ritual that there were many examples where *gender symbolism was used as the basis for all types of ideological schemes* (1985:46). Starting with a consideration of relations between men and women, the symbolism in pottery inevitably leads one to look at how space is used and then to consider different facets of men's lives and their relationships with each other. This occurs because the axes in the prestige structure that patterned male–female relationships in terms of deference, respect, and obedience on the one hand and condescension, disregard, and authority on the other guided relationships between individuals of the same sex belonging to different status groups as well (Ortner and Whitehead 1982).

Gender and space

The relation between gender and space helps explain differences in vessel form, decoration, and function in earth-toned and white-toned medieval and post-medieval pottery. As space was reorganized making new areas in houses and yards more isolated and private (i.e., feminized), the symbolic attributes of artifacts normally used within these areas went from either gender-neutral or masculine to feminine. Household pots, predominantly earth-toned, became associated with women's tasks and with subordinate activities in the hierarchical food system. In this, their earth-toned colors aided, for natural lands were traditionally viewed as feminine. There was a cultural repertoire of symbols that described male and female qualities and activities as derivative aspects of either culture or nature. By extension, other earth-toned vessels also came to be associated with subordinate positions.

In feudal English society, a major social bond was the relation between subordinate men and those above them, including that of "lord and man, a relation implying on the lord's part protection and defense; on the man's part protection, service, and reverence, the service including service in arms" (Maitland 1919:143–4, quoted in Macfarlane 1988:196). This might be viewed as the primary hierarchical public relationship. A primary private relationship was the social bond between a man and his wife, implying on the man's part protection and defense, on the woman's part, service and reverence, the service including a wide range of domestic chores. Although elements of these relationships changed over time, women still held subordinate roles in Anglo-American families (Norton 1980:3). While there were gradations of rank among women, and some women possessed extraordinary economic, social, or political power, female hierarchy is collapsed here to facilitate discussion of male/female relationships. Women are treated as one set of individuals – a social group subordinate, for the most part, to adult Englishmen.

Similarly, the gradations that existed in rank among servants and slaves are not germane. Of course they used their material culture to express nuances of rank among themselves. But the basic argument still holds – that women, indentured servants, and slaves as social groups held lower positions in the hierarchically organized New World communities than did male free-holders, and that their respective positions were denoted by the objects they used.

Once one understands the masculine and feminine attributes of household space and customary male and female roles within the household, the dual role of ceramic objects (i.e., utilitarian and symbolic) is easier to perceive. For example, domestic or inner space (i.e., feminine space) parallels and mirrors community or exterior space (i.e., masculine space) while men's and women's roles within the home reiterate other positional relationships among men of differing social status in the wider community (cf.those between English nobility and ordinary men described by Maitland). Within the home domestic space can be thought of as public or private, ceremonial, commercial, domestic, or even defensive. Often it is classified by its use (i.e., as an activity area), and by the access people have to it. Use can be inferred from the artifact assemblages associated with specific areas as illustrated in table 10.1, which clearly shows (1) variations in the ceramic assemblage from different rooms at Corotoman that relate to (2) public and private uses of household space. Similar information drawn from probate inventory data is presented in table 10.2 for the Thomas Bordley residence in Annapolis, Maryland. Archaeologists are perhaps less aware of the way social relationships are organized by space within the home than of the role of space in organizing the activities of a community.

Table 10.1 Location of ceramic vessels found at Corotoman[a]

Room	White-toned vessels	Earth-toned vessels
Parlor		Pudding pans Serving jugs Drinking jugs
	Plates (delft, porcelain) Bowls (delft, porcelain) Tea bowls (porcelain) Chocolate cups (white salt-glaze)	
Central hall or passage		Basins Chamber pots Milk pans Pudding pans Storage pots Serving jugs Drinking jugs Mugs and drinking pots
	Porringers (delft)	
Chamber		Basins Chamber pot Mugs
Chamber closet		Basin Bottles Serving jug
	Plate (delft)	

[a] Corotoman was Robert "King" Carter's home on the Rappahannock River in Tidewater Virginia. The house burned down in 1729 providing an excellent sealed context for the finds (unpublished data provided by Alice Guerrant, personal communication 1980, and Conrad M. Goodwin, personal communication July 1988).

An Overview of Gender-related Use of Space

Certainly there was a sexual division of labor in medieval and post-medieval cultures, but the primary association of women with unpaid domestic labor and men with monetarily supported labor is a product of capitalism. The medieval woman's economic sphere was limited when compared with her father's, husband's, brother's, and son's. She rarely

Table 10.2 Placement of ceramic vessels in the Thomas Bordley House, Annapolis, Maryland, based on a room-by-room probate inventory of 1727

| Room | White-toned vessels[a] | | Earth-toned vessels | |
	Form	Use	Form	Use
Inner room	Custard cups	Tea consumption		
	Sugar dish	Tea consumption		
	Punch bowl	Wine consumption		
Parlor	Tea cups and saucers	Tea consumption		
	Dishes	Social dining		
	Plates	Social dining		
	Bowls	Social dining		
	Plates (delft)	Social dining		
	Saucers (delft)	Social dining		
Passage	Custard cups	Tea consumption		
Parlor Chamber	Custard cups	Tea consumption		
	Punch bowl	Wine consumption		
Kitchen			Stone pots	Storage
			Earthen pots	Storage
			Stone jugs	Ale/beer
			Earthen pans	Baking
			Chamber pots	Hygiene

[a] All the vessels are Chinese porcelain unless noted otherwise.

took part in activities that extended beyond the spatial boundaries defined by the location of her home and immediate neighborhood. While the eighteenth century saw the extension of cash labor to women, paid tasks were done as piecemeal labor within the home. In this they supplemented the small monies a woman might earn by selling her butter, eggs, or cheese at market.

Additionally, a man's professional life and his private life were merged because household buildings and family lands formed the major work areas for both sexes. Thus both men's and women's work was closely tied to household space. It is these qualities of family life that Deetz (1977) had in mind when he described seventeenth-century New England families as possessing organic solidarity; divisions between production and consumption, income-producing labor and reciprocal or domestic labor, work and home, public and private life differed radically from modern divisions which emphasize the separation of these domains. Neither regional lifestyles nor rural–urban variations created sufficient difference to alter the dominant, underlying form of medieval and post-medieval culture. There was an inescapable aura of organic unity between a household's living space and the physical terrain, emphasized by the natural building materials drawn from the regional environment. The bounds between activity areas were blurred; segmentation of activities was minimal. Workshops, warehouses, and offices might be parts of domestic establishments; animals might be kept within a household's building walls, and grain crops were frequently stored in house lofts.

Craftsmen and artisans residing in towns blended income-producing and domestic activity inside their houses and in their yards with minimal spatial distinctions (Yentsch and McKee 1987). There was social heterogeneity. Rich and poor households mingled together within town and city neighborhoods. Residential location, in contrast to size and style of house, was not a meaningful status indicator either in England (Reed 1983:146) or in America. Because there were few clearly defined, mutually exclusive social spaces, the emblems of rank were individually specific (i.e., clothing and personal utensils identified an individual's rank).

Elite households in the Old and New Worlds differed from average households because they were larger and contained individuals with more extensive kinship ties as well as a range of servants and, in the New World, slaves. An elite household entertained a constant flow of people whose visits were simultaneously friendly, social, and professional. It also provided social services to the community. In other words, wealthy families lived in larger, more complex households whose functions were multi-faceted, often including commercial or administrative governmental elements not found in the average household. Within such households, the economic and political domains were fused.

Until the mid-eighteenth century, few households had rooms set aside as public rooms where visitors were separated from the household. As Hamilton writes, "People ate, met, talked, slept, made love and made deals all in the same rooms" (1978:34). The endless succession of guests made demands on the household for provisions far above those of other households. The merging of social space reiterated the merging of power, property, economic, and social relationships. Although possessing greater complexity, undifferentiated space and a co-mingling of people and activities was as characteristic of wealthy households as it was of poorer ones throughout the seventeenth century and into the early years of the eighteenth century.

In English medieval culture, the marked spatial boundary was between the sacred and the profane, not between public and private. Women's work spilled over into public space when women sold butter, cheese, milk, eggs, and poultry at local markets. Feminine domains included the dairy, springhouse, hen house, and kitchen garden; and farmers' wives occasionally brought grain to the mill. As shown in table 10.3, women were in charge of many of the processes which transformed raw plant materials and the by-products of domesticated animals into usable goods: milk to butter and cheese, flax and wool to yarn, malt and other grains to ale, plants (pot vegetables and herbs) to soup and medicine. Still, their use of public space was episodic. Men, however, routinely used community or public space and were the individuals who traversed less settled reaches of the countryside. Men controlled the transformation of wild and domestic animals into edible meats through their mastery of the butchery process. As artisans and craftsmen, they were also in charge of the more mysterious transformation of metal ores into usable objects.

The allocation of space into masculine and feminine domains described above continued in Anglo-America. Domestic space was not highly differentiated, nor were activity areas restricted to a single activity. St George (1982) suggests that the parlor inside the house was masculine space while the hall comprised feminine space; to my mind, the hall might better be described as "unmarked" space because it was used by people of both sexes and all ages for a broad range of activities and daily tasks. It was also the center of household sociability. As the seventeenth century progressed domestic space was reclassified; the space represented by a hall was increasingly referred to as the kitchen. Presumably this change in nomenclature was accompanied by a separation of hall and kitchen activities. By the early eighteenth century most cooking areas were removed to a back room, often in a lean-to addition to the central house.

Table 10.3 Major phases in the cycle of food use among English communities

Food or beverage	Activity area	Characteristic activities	Workers	Domain
Phase 1: Food procurement				
Fish	Oceans, rivers, etc.	Seining, fishing	Men	Male
Crabs and shellfish	Creeks and bays	Gathering, trapping	Men	Male
Wild meats	Forests or marshes	Hunting, trapping	Men	Male
Wild birds	Fields and marshes	Hunting, trapping	Men	Male
Marketable grains	Farm fields	Tillage	Men	Male
Marketable fruits	Orchards	Harvest	Men	Male
Domestic meats	Farm pastures	Animal husbandry	Men	Male
Domestic poultry	Barnyard	Animal husbandry	Women	Female
Dairy products	Barn or barnyard	Milking/egg collection	Women	Female
Kitchen vegetables	House garden	Kitchen gardening	Women	Female
Cultivated herbs	House garden	Kitchen gardening	Women	Female
Spices (exotic)	Outside community	Sale/trade	Men	Male
Wines, hard liquors	Outside community	Sale/trade	Men	Male
Phase 2: Food preparation and storage				
Step 1. Initial processing				
Meat	Farm yard	Butchery	Men	Male
Grains	Barn, barnyard, mill	Winnowing, milling	Men	Male
Kitchen vegetables	Kitchen	Washing/drying	Women	Female
Herbs	Kitchen	Washing/drying	Women	Female
Dairy products	Kitchen or dairy	Curd separation, etc.	Women	Female

	Location	Activity	Performed by	Gender
Step 2. Initial storage				
Meat	Smokehouse, cellar	Curation	Men?	Male?
Grains	Barns, house lofts	Curation	Men?	Male?
Dried herbs	Kitchen	Curation	Women	Female
Root crops	Kitchen cellars	Curation	Women	Female
Butter, cheese	Dairy, springhouses	Curation	Women	Female
Step 3. Meal preparation and brewing				
All foodstuffs	Kitchen	Roasting, baking, etc.	Women	Female
Ale, beer, cider	Kitchen	Brewing	Women	Male
Tea, coffee, cocoa	Dining areas	Brewing	Women	Male
Step 4. Storage of prepared foods and beverages				
Meats	Springhouse?	Curation	Women	Female
Vegetables	Kitchen	Curation	Women	Female
Fruits	Kitchen	Curation	Women	Female
Baked goods	Kitchen	Curation	Women	Female
Phase 3: Household food distribution				
Food and beverages	Kitchen and work area	Serving	Women	Female
Food and beverages	Formal dining areas	Serving	Women or young men	Male
Meat	Formal dining areas	Carving	Adult men	Male
Phase 4: Food consumption				
Daily meals	Kitchen or work area	Food consumption	Household	Female
Feasts	Formal dining areas / Exterior public spaces	Social display	Family and guests	Male
Phase 5: Refuse disposal				
All garbage	Interior house	Cleaning	Women	Female

Aries (1962) contends that the concept of private, familial space did not develop until the 1500s and then spread slowly. Sixteenth- and seventeenth-century paintings show a blending of domestic and social activities within houses and within the same room. Late seventeenth-century room-by-room inventories, whether from England, New England, or the Chesapeake, provide additional evidence of the way activities merged within single rooms. There are also, however, a series of townscapes by Dutch genre painters, including Tenniers, that show men engaged in games or other social activities outside the house while women remain in doorways or near the doorsteps. The association of women with interior, or private space, and men with exterior, or public space, is given symbolic meaning in these and other contemporary paintings. It was repeated in Jacob Cats' 1628 admonition "The husband must be on the street to practice his trade, The wife must stay at home to be in the kitchen" (quoted in Schama 1987:400). The idea is perhaps most vividly expressed in New Jersey Governor William Livingstone's essays of 1790 which praised as a cultural ideal the American women who "enjoyed happiness in their chimney corners" (quoted in Norton 1980:5).

The way in which English and European culture was reorganized from the time of the Renaissance has been described by a number of historians. Different lines were drawn between culture and nature (Thomas 1983); boundaries between time, space, activities, and events became more finely drawn, readily distinguishable, and less easily crossed. The symbolic content of space was critical because it was a major axis organizing, separating, or conjoining activities. Since the reorganization emphasized the asymmetry that characterized relationships between men and women as well as other perceived differences, some objects became more associated with women's activities than with men's activities and vice versa. To the extent that objects denoted attributes of social space, their metaphorical roles had to change as the culture changed its use of space.

The Symbolism of Space: Its Relation to Gender-based Activities and Events

Gender ideology is frequently expressed in association with the nature/culture dichotomy (Ardener 1972; Barnes 1973; Ortner 1972; Rosaldo 1987). Feminist anthropologists, using structuralist theory, have argued the presence of a universal opposition between domestic, or feminine, and public, or masculine, roles. Rosaldo's earlier work also notes the way in which sex-related uses of space effectively create social distance and thereby emphasize the boundaries between male and female activities (1974:27). Reiter wrote of the public and private domains occupied by men and women in southern France, observing a sexual geography governing the use of space (1975:256); she based her designations of social space on (a) the type of activity occurring in a given area, and (b) the gender of those associated with the activities. Reiter's analysis indicates that women's tasks and social gatherings normally occurred in private (i.e., familial) areas of the community. Men, however, operated in more public, supra-familial, formal spheres. This could be seen in their dominance of economic and political activities, and their participation in church affairs.

Men's work exists in a wider domain than does the work of women. Women's work primarily occurs within the realm of the household; kinship plays a larger role in organizing household activities than it does in the outside community. Within the household, one's role is as often ascriptive as it is achieved; in the larger community, the positions of men *vis-àvis* their economic, political, and church roles are achieved. Rieter (1975) reviewed the anthropological and historical literature, concluding that all state societies appear to organize a division between public and private sectors in which public functions are seen as masculine and private ones as feminine. Within the public sphere, men control the information, the rituals, and the personal ties concerned with group structure and alliances between groups in addition to administering economic, political, and religious affairs.

The use of space Reiter described in present-day France is analogous to the use of space in earlier Anglo-American communities: market space was public and hence masculine while household space was private and hence feminine. In my opinion, these cultural divisions were given added emphasis by parallel divisions of each of these two domains. In other words, public space was not wholly public for it also contained a private component; private space was not wholly private for it also contained a public component. Within the context of the community, household space was private. Within the context of the house, some spatial areas were more private than others. The arrangement of space within the home can be discerned by listing or observing the participants and the type of activities they engage in within particular domestic areas using either archaeological or inventory data.

In any culture where men's work areas primarily fall within family space (defined as a house and its associated grounds), formal or ritual dinners (i.e., feasts) are a major means whereby a household relates to the wider community. Feasts are times when alliances and reciprocal relations between kin and guests are negotiated or established. The use of special foods and beverages and their accoutrements at feasts is but one indication that these events fall within the masculine sphere of a household's social action. At such events, the display value of food is more important than its nutritional value; the latter is incidental to the underlying symbolism and the expression of rank (Douglas 1972).

Throughout the eighteenth century, elite men went to considerable effort to obtain prestigious dinner wares from overseas and to insure that elaborate foods were part of the dining rituals enacted under their sponsorship. In Annapolis, the prestigious and politically well-connected Calvert family served a wide range of wild and domestic birds at their table to supplement the more common beef, pork, and mutton dishes, and ate chicken more frequently than their neighbors (Reitz 1988). The wider (as demonstrated by the species list) and more extensive use (demonstrated by the minimum number of animals) of wild and domestic birds for food, and the elaborate ceramics used in their home indicate a participation in ritual dining. As members of the first national Congress meeting in 1784 in war-time Annapolis, Thomas Jefferson and James Madison also hired a French chef to insure their ceremonial meals possessed the proper flair; the staff of General George Washington made consistent efforts to procure prestigious ceramics for his war-time staff dinners (Detweiler 1982:63–80). But it is not just the effort to procure expensive tablewares or serve high-style food that by itself justifies the ascription of social dining to the masculine domain of household activity; rather, it is the degree or intensity of social display involved/expressed in the total flow of social behavior within one area of the house as opposed to another.

There is some element of display involved in everyday meals, but the degree of display intensifies with the formality of the meal, with the number or importance of the guests, and with the importance of the event that a formal meal celebrates. The nonverbal information that is conveyed in the social performance that constitutes formal dining is normally patterned and orderly. The social space occupied by this use of food has more masculine attributes than the household areas used for food storage or preparation; the furnishing and utensils of the former space are, *ipso facto*, more masculine than the furnishings and utensils of the household areas where food is stored and prepared, and where everyday food is eaten. In the social space assigned to ritual dining, what takes place belongs within the realm of domestic (and often conspicuous) consumption whereas the activities in areas where utilitarian food use is the norm are associated with the realm of domestic production.

If one wants to describe a household's social spaces in terms of the power designated to them (i.e., in terms of the relative status of people, events, and material objects associated with such spaces), there was minimal allocation of power to spaces assigned to cooking and food storage. The utensils used in these areas included the pottery vessels today known as "coarsewares" that were often purchased from local craftsmen. These areas were peripheral to the space used for ceremonial sociability; the individuals most closely associated with food production were not necessarily *ever* present in the rooms used in ceremonial food display.

Southern families who could do so removed the "working hearth" from their homes and confined cooking tasks to kitchen lean-tos, to basement kitchens, or to kitchen/slave quarters erected in the yard. Cooking was also removed from the central hearth in New England homes in the eighteenth century. Over time, instead of the central, multi-purpose familial hearth familiar to most colonists of the early years of English settlement, two or more developed: an isolated cooking hearth located within feminine social space, and hearths in parlors, chambers, offices, and so on, that supplied warmth and light, but whose fires were peripheral to food preparation. This arrangement of hearths that emerged in eighteenth-century homes created social distance. The separation of the cooking hearth from the main ceremonial eating area distanced the people and activities associated with the cooking hearth from the people and activities associated with ritual dining. The separation of social spaces formerly co-mingled also enabled a household to limit access to its display areas, thereby making entry a privilege and itself the sign of status. Doorways to these areas functioned as social thresholds. Low-status individuals such as peddlers, apprentices, servants, and African slaves were expected to enter the house and/or transact their business with household members in regions of the house and yard distant from the rooms used for entertainment and leisure activities (Glassie 1975; Neiman 1978; Upton 1988).

Some scholars argue that the rationale for the presence of outbuildings in the Southern colonies, such as kitchens, dairies, wash houses, and the like, was solely economic (Walsh, personal communication). Others argue that the rationale was comfort (i.e., separating "hot" activities from cooler ones, especially in summer). Whatever the reason, by separating bound labor or slave labor from the household, the distancing of the food processing areas also separated the women of a family from the main house for significant portions of time on a daily or weekly basis. As a routine event, predictable and repetitious, the separation came to be perceived as reasonable and natural.

As the spaces where women prepared food were distanced from the areas used for social display where men entertained and/or conducted their economic and political affairs, the position of women in the information networks shifted, and their access to these became constricted. To the extent that women were not actual participants in ritual dining they lost power, for their social ties with particular sets of individuals within the community became more diffuse, and their knowledge of external events became filtered and indirect. It is through such processes that otherwise ordinary events are made mysterious and individuals appear more powerful than they may actually be.

Hierarchy in Ceramic Vessels

The social scaling of activities associated with a household's activity areas provides an approach to foodstuffs that subsumes the concept of cuisine. Food can be identified with phases in the food cycle and classified according to the space and means whereby it was (1) obtained, (2) introduced into the household domain, (3) transformed from raw product into edible meal, (4) distributed, and (5) consumed. As foodstuffs pass through these phases, different implements are necessary and the individuals who handle the food or oversee its use hold different status positions related to each phase of the cycle. Although it is technically possible for a woman or a man to grow a plant, dry it, cook it, serve it, and then eat it, nevertheless, if he or she does so, the role is different at each step and accorded different status. The information in table 10.3 indicates that the more usual succession was for men to obtain food (a) if its source was distant *vis-à-vis* the home or (b) if its production in the home held the potential for sales of surpluses in distant markets. If men were instrumental in obtaining food, as is the case for most meats, then they also handled its initial processing and perhaps supervised its storage. Primarily, however, women take over the activities related to food preparation and storage (i.e., during Phase 2 of the food cycle, especially in its later steps). Food and beverages then remain within the feminine domain until they become elements in formal meals or in food served outside the home. One means of marking the different steps in the food cycle and of separating the status positions involved was a visual difference in the utensils used to move or store foodstuffs; most pottery containers appear among household utensils at points in the food cycle where women become involved. Further, variations in the ceramic utensils keep pace with the progress of foodstuffs throughout the cycle until, as food refuse, it is returned to nature.

Each era has its own core of significant symbols which express the organizing principles of a culture. Perhaps because ceramics were not readily available nor used in large quantities, they seem to have been peripheral or value-neutral in the set of meaningful symbols used to indicate hierarchy in medieval food use. Descriptions of English ceramic assemblages in British site reports (Cunningham and Drury 1986; Fox and Barton 1986) indicate that two forms – cooking pots and pitchers/ jugs – were dominant at domestic English sites of the late medieval period. Starting in the sixteenth century, as cultural space was reorganized and pottery became more widely available, in addition to silver and pewter vessels, ceramic utensils also became an integral part of the symbolic inventory that surrounded the use of food in social display.

As food preparation and storage were separated from other food-related activities, the boundaries between this phase of food use and other familial activities, especially food consumption, were increasingly distinguished both by the space wherein they took place and the tools necessary to them. This had an additional impact on the way in which ceramic objects were classified: as the lines between activities were more clearly defined, the objects associated with different activities had to contain characteristic features that could be easily seen as belonging to a single phase of food use. For example, when household space was less differentiated, there was an overlap in the materials used for household pots. Differently formed vessels made of identical earthenware fabrics with similar, if not identical, glazes were used for cooking and serving food, for storing, distributing, and consuming beverages. This overlap disappeared with time. The start of the trend is readily seen in figures 10.2 and 10.3 which illustrate the increasing diversification of ceramic assemblages at an English site from 1400 to ca. 1670. Note that the trend is even more apparent in Chesapeake sites dating to 1620–50 (figures 10.4 and 10.5).

Prior to New World colonization, the use of specific English vessel forms was a consequence of food use following one of two traditions: a folk tradition used in yeoman households, and an elite or courtly tradition (Mennell 1985). At harvest time, large meals prepared by yeoman households were feasts: performances illustrating the rights and

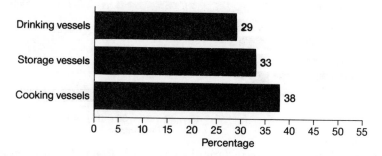

Figure 10.2 Percentage of vessel forms by functional category for assemblages from Moulsham Street deposits dating between 1400 and 1500 (data compiled using the illustrations in Cunningham and Drury 1986)

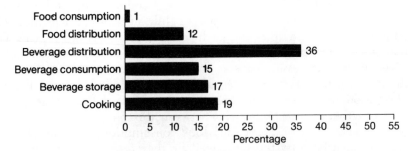

Figure 10.3 Percentage of vessel forms by functional category for assemblages from Moulsham Street deposits dating to ca.1670 (data compiled using the illustrations in Cunningham and Drury 1986)

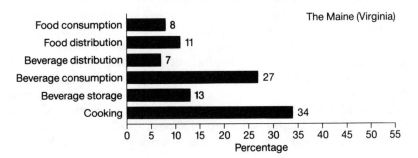

Figure 10.4 Percentage of vessel forms by functional category for an assemblage from The Maine dating 1618–1626 (data based on ceramic analysis by Merry Abbitt-Outlaw and shown on minimum vessel lists in Yentsch, Bescherer, and Patrick (forthcoming))

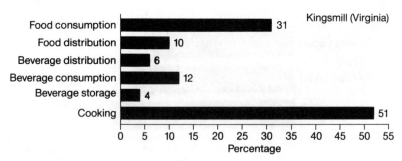

Figure 10.5 Percentage of vessel forms by functional category for an assemblage from Kingsmill dating 1625–1650 (data based on ceramic analysis by Merry Abbitt-Outlaw and shown on minimum vessel lists in Yentsch, Bescherer, and Patrick (forthcoming))

obligations of the family to servants, non-resident kin, and neighbors helping with the harvest. As a rule, however, ritual dining was an occasional event in the average English household. Its use centered around rites of passage such as weddings, christenings, deaths, and/or religious holidays and fast days. In contrast, the meals of elite families were routinely used as a mechanism to display their wealth and power. In either case, different vessels symbolically associated with variations in social rank were used and in their variation provided a parallel to the variation in the use of spices, exotic foodstuffs, meat sources and cuts as well as in the complexity of the recipe, preparation time required, and availability of prepared dishes.

Divided on the basis of form, each vessel belonged to a set of similarly used vessels with status gradations expressed through material, glaze, and design motif. For example, the basic form of a tankard or plate was the same whether it was made of gold, silver, horn, pewter, or earthenware. Its material (for example, silver versus stoneware) was the first attribute which signified its position in the vessel hierarchy with further refinements in status designation made on the basis of more subtle variations in material and decoration within each basic type (i.e., stoneware vessels such as Westerwald, Nottingham, or Scratch Brown tankards were distinguishable within the stoneware class of tankards by their color, glaze, and decorative embellishments; more vivid distinctions existed among ceramic plates, and their decoration was primarily based on additive techniques).

Prestigious foods and beverages used in the courtly tradition were frequently served in special purpose vesels. Some, such as chafing dishes, were distinguished by form while others were distinguished by material, as in the case of a recipe for an Elizabethan trifle that was seasoned with sugar and ginger and then served in a "silver piece or bowl" (Wilson 1974:169). Many courtly dishes had no counterpart in the folk tradition until, in the eighteenth century, as their use trickled down and their value shifted, consumption became commonplace and the vessels associated with them became widely available. Teawares are perhaps the best example of this trend as it is encountered in the archaeological evidence left on Anglo-American sites.

The relative position of each vessel in the hierarchy indicated the relative status of the individuals involved in the production and consumption of the foods or beverages contained within it. The social principle of rank was reinforced by the physical analogy (Douglas 1986). The mechanism through which this occurred was the association, at its most basic level, of specific types of food with either food production or food consumption, i.e. with either the feminine or masculine sphere of food use. Further, the use of these principles over and over again as meals were served throughout the year reinforced the organizing principles, grounding them in events that were so ordinary and repetitious they were taken for granted, appearing as natural as the rising and setting of the sun.

How did this occur? It is my belief that initially neither men nor women were defined by the ceramics they owned. Men made pots for male and female use. Overall, medieval English pottery was probably gender-neutral or quasi-masculine. Ceramic vessels were used in undifferentiated household space, although it was space controlled by men. Men gave their cups/mugs/jugs names such as "Crumpledud," "Peregrin," and "The Grete Grubbe" (Thrupp 1962:147), thus distinguishing drinking vessels from ordinary household pots. Decorative motifs on these vessels included masculine hunting scenes and male figures (Rackham 1948). Earthenware jugs, whose spouts were decorated with masculine faces, were popular. The continuation of this tradition is visible in the faces/masks on seventeenth-century Bellarmine jugs.

Objects often acquire symbolic meaning through their association with the people who use them. It is improbable that medieval cooking pots were viewed as masculine objects for they were used by women or household servants. Cooking pots were probably not objects to which power accrued. Access to them was not limited; their use was not mysterious. They were used daily and routinely in readily accessible service rooms. From the onset, cooking vessels were either plain or had minimal decoration carved into their fabric (a subtractive process) in contrast to the drinking vessels which were decorated in additive styles as early as the fourteenth century.

There existed a division of medieval pottery, based on vessel form and decoration, wherein vessels used in food preparation and consumption were set apart from those used in beverage consumption. The boundary was not elaborately marked and consisted of basic distinctions in form and contrasting means of decoration (additive versus subtractive). The composition of the body (i.e., paste or fabric), the hue of the lead glaze (often similar despite variation in vessel form), and stylistic simplicity blurred the distinction. As a category, these pottery vessels had attributes that linked them to the natural world. The use of red, red-brown, and buff clays with lead glazes, and sometimes green or greenish-yellow decoration, created pots with varied earth tones that had a visual resemblance to the colors of earth, field, and forest, thereby setting the vessels close to nature on the culture–nature continuum. The functional association of earthenwares with the transformation of food from its raw, natural state to a cooked form reiterated their visual position on the nature–culture axis.

The metaphorical link between pottery and nature was commented on by Deetz (1983, 1988). The classificatory link between women and nature has been written about by many (see review in Ortner 1972). Ceramic decoration illustrated the intermingling of human social relationships, man–animal relationships, and the deep penetration of the natural world into the cultural domain. The decorations on earth-toned serving dishes seen in the late seventeenth century were complex and included intertwining plants, mythological monsters, and anthropomorphic animals. With the start of the eighteenth century, however, the decorative motifs change; serving dishes are moved closer to the domain of culture than nature.

Rye (1976) observed of Papuan pottery that its dark hues were more practical or heat-efficient for cooking pots, but any recognition by Englishmen of a link between cooking efficiency and color tone is difficult to establish. English archaeologists (Cunningham and Drury 1986; Fox and Barton 1986) describe finely potted vessels with white pastes found in contexts dating to the 1560s. By the eighteenth century, the technology to produce utilitarian wares in whiter tones had existed for more than 100 years. White slips appear on drab gray-bodied English stoneware drinking vessels by 1710. Beautifully intricate wheel-engraved, brown-dipped white stoneware mugs were reportedly made by Dwight as early as 1680–90 (Oswald et al. 1982:31). Yet stoneware cooking or storage vessels were produced in the dark-toned tradition of earlier earthenwares long into the nineteenth century.

How can one explain the persistence of dark-toned hues on cooking utensils? Thinking about the problem in terms of technological advances or market availability produces what Firth (1975:26) calls a "disjunction – a gap between the overt superficial statement of action and its underlying meaning." On the surface, the presence of dark-toned cooking vessels seems neither sensible nor necessary. The observation that there is a fairly sharp boundary between earth-toned and white-toned vessels present by the late seventeenth century that becomes increasingly well defined with time also suggests that something of greater significance than market availability is at work. Distinctive because of the sharp, simple color contrast, the division of ceramic vessel forms by ware types indicates an emergent separation of activities between Phases 2 and 3 of the food cycle that further separates Phase 4 from earlier phases.

The earth tones of seventeenth-century ceramics stand in contrast to the whiteness of later ceramic assemblages; the preference was a cultural one, although technological and economic factors also were active. Deetz (1988) was one of the first historical archaeologists to point out that pure white ceramics were available as oriental porcelain and tin-enameled cups, plates, and chargers by the early seventeenth century and that they were

Anne Yentsch

used in New World homes, albeit sparsely. However, in this era such
vessels were not central elements within the foodways system. By
ca.1680–90, the cultural preference for white vessels increases; its
influence on the household of Governor William Drummond can be
seen in the number of white-toned vessels from his occupational phase at
Governor's Land in Tidewater Virginia (see table 10.4). At Governor's
Land, earth-toned vessels were less frequently used to distribute food,
consume food, consume traditional beverages, or sip tea than were their
white counterparts. Looking at this assemblage in comparison with its
early seventeenth-century predecessors in Virginia (deposits from The
Maine, Kingsmill Tenement, Pasbehay Tenement, and from Martin's
Hundred) indicated that the overall percentage of white-toned vessels
was 50 percent, or double the average, 26 percent, for the earlier sites
(Yentsch, Bescherer and Patrick, forthcoming).

Table 10.4 Percentage of white-toned ceramics recovered from two
deposits at the Drummond Site ca.1680–1710

Functional vessel class	Percent of assemblage represented by delft or porcelain	Percent within class
Food preparation and storage	0	0
Food distribution	7	50
Food consumption	15	94
Beverage storage (bottles)	0	0
Traditional beverages	10	59
Teawares	18	100

Source: Unpublished data provided by Merry Abbitt-Outlaw and Alain Outlaw,
courtesy of the Virginia Research Center for Archaeology, Historic Landmarks
Commission.

The trend toward whiter vessels was accompanied by a restriction of
earth-toned pottery to vessel forms used in unprestigious tasks. The
increased use of the whiter wares in food distribution and consumption
was also accompanied by an elaboration of individual forms through size
variation (introducing a qualitative difference among, for example,
plates) and through sheer number. In this the households of the gentry
led the way, as can be seen in a series of tables that (a) list the vessels in
terms of their primary color tone for two different sets of eighteenth-
century deposits at the Calvert site in Annapolis, Maryland (where

earlier governors of the Province lived)) (table 10.5) and (b) in related data that contrast the ceramic holdings of the Calvert family as recovered archaeologically with vessel forms sold by merchants in the Chesapeake (tables 10.6 and 10.7; see also Patrick 1990).

The greater elaboration in pottery and porcelain accompanied an increased spatial differentiation within houses, as described earlier. Within wealthy households, two or more social spaces were set aside: kitchens, and rooms where formal dinners were held. White-toned vessels became associated with the masculine sphere of household food use, i.e., with food used to establish and promote prestige through ceremonial display. Earth-toned vessels were dissociated from this realm of behavior.

As symbols, ceramic vessels were part of a prestige structure associated with food use. Their differential use by various status groups was a mechanism by which one status group was set apart from another: thus to study variation in ceramic assemblages is to study the archaeology of inequality. A structural analysis is especially helpful in highlighting the way in which particular elements of the prestige structure existed and provides a framework for considering form, dominant color tone, and decoration.

The first and most obvious opposition is the duality posed by color. Glassie (1975) equates white with distance from nature, therefore with artificiality, and, following from its association with something artificial, to culture rather than nature. The analogy can be extended. As nature is equated with feminine properties, so then is culture equated with masculine properties (Ortner 1972). Equally useful are other binary discriminations used to analyze food: Bourdieu's (1979) formality/ informality, exotic/homely, and experimental/traditional as well as Sahlins' (1976) social dimension of outer and inner.

Using Bourdieu's oppositions and noting the social space in which food vessels were used reveals that the wares found in formal dining spaces were whiter than those used in less prestigious informal contexts, where earth-toned vessels were the norm. To the extent that formal dining, social pomp, and conspicuous consumption were means of expressing power, of establishing reciprocal relationships, and of forming and strengthening alliances between households, they fell within a masculine domain. While women might participate in ritual dining and could enhance their own power through their orchestration and support of conspicuous food consumption, their benefits were merely derived; men controlled this cultural domain.

Formal designs on white-toned vessels were an important element in ritual dining. Chinese armorial porcelain is the example *par excellence* of the use of dinner wares to convey status information. Armorial porcelain

Table 10.5 Vessel forms represented in the preliminary minimum vessel list for the Calvert Site in Annapolis, Maryland. The list was compiled by Anne Yentsch and Karen Bescherer (Yentsch, Bescherer, and Patrick, forthcoming)

	Earth-toned vessels		White-toned vessels		Total
	N	%	N	%	N
Food processing, preparation, and storage vessels					
Dairy processing					
Milk pans	18	100	–		18
Beverage storage					
Bottles	13	87	2	13	15
Food storage					
Butter pots	29	100	–		29
Jars/crocks	56	100	–		56
Olive jars	3	100	–		3
Cooking utensils					
Baking pan	2	100	–		2
Colander	1	100	–		1
Cooking pots	5	100	–		5
Mixing bowls	11	100	–		11
Pipkins	2	100	–		2
Pudding pans	20	100	–		20
Food distribution					
Bowls, assorted			50	100	50
Chargers/platters	0		19	100	19
Condiment jars	1	10	9	90	10
Dishes, assorted	17	30	40	70	57
Fruit baskets	–		2	100	2
Salts	–		10	100	10
Sauce boat	–		1	100	1
Saucers	–		15	100	15
Scallop shells	–		2	100	2
Tureens	–		1	100	1
Food consumption					
Porringers	4	66	2	33	6
Plates, dessert	–		2	100	2
Plates, small	–		13	100	13
Plates, soup	–		8	100	8

	Earth-toned vessels		White-toned vessels		Total
	N	%	N	%	N
Plates, assorted	–		8	100	8
Plates, generic	–		102	100	102
Beverage distribution and consumption					
Punch bowls, assorted					
sizes	–		75	100	75
Traditional beverage distribution					
Jugs	13	100	–		13
Jug, ornamental (bear)	–		1	100	1
Pitchers	1	20	4	80	5
Traditional beverage consumption					
Cans	2	100	–		2
Caudle pots	1	100	–		1
Drinking pots	5	100	–		5
Posset pots	–		1	100	1
Cups	1	9	10	91	11
Mugs	82	84	16	16	98
Tankards	2	11	16	89	18
Tea, coffee, chocolate					
Tea bowls and saucers	1	>1	168	<99	169
Teapots	1	7	14	94	15
Coffee or chocolate					
pots	–		3	100	3
Capuchins	1	33	2	66	3
Cream pots, etc.	–		4	100	4
Sugar pots, etc.	–		6	100	6
Other beverage					
Wine cups	–		2	100	2
Other					
Basins	–		12	100	12
Cosmetic jar	–		2	100	2
Drug pots or jars	–		3	100	3
Galley pots	–		28	100	28
Ginger pot	–		3	100	3
Flower pots	2	100	–		2
Chamber pots	12	57	9	43	21

Table 10.6 Table ceramic forms available in Chesapeake stores (1759–1775) and located at the Calvert site (ca.1720–ca.1790)[a]

Type	Calvert	Allason	Dixon	Hamilton	Hammond	Coffing
Serving						
Dish	X	X	X	X	X	X
Tureen	X		X	X		
Platter	X	X	X	X		
Salad bowl	X					
Sauce boat	X	X	X	X	X	
Butter boat plate	X		X	X	X	
Pickle stand	X			X		
Fruit dish/ basket	X	X	X	X		
Mustard pot	X		X	X		
Pepper caster			X			
Table cross (cat)		X				
Salt cellar	X	X		X	X	
Teapot	X	X	X	X	X	
Coffee/choc- olate pot	X		X	X		
Milk pot/ cream jug	X	X	X	X	X	
Sugar bowl/ dish	X	X	X	X	X	
Sugar box	X	X		X		
Slop bowl	X		X	X	X	
Punch bowl	X	X	X	X		
Punch strainer			X			
Water pitcher	X	X	X	X		
Consuming						
Dinner plate	X	X	X	X	X	X
Soup plate	X			X		
Dessert plate	X					
Twifler plate	X	X				
Breakfast plate	X		X	X		
Teacup and saucer	X	X	X	X	X	
Coffee cup/can	X	X		X		

Type	Calvert	Allason	Dixon	Hamilton	Hammond	Coffing
Breakfast cup	X		X			
Cup/mug	X	X	X	X	X	
Drinking bowl	X	X	X			
Wine cup	X					
Porringer	X	X	X	X		X

[a] For these purposes, only form and not ware type is explored. Data are based on archaeological evidence for Calvert Site; annual store inventory for the shops of Allason (Falmouth, Virginia), Dixon (Port Royal, Virginia), and Hamilton (Piscattaway, Maryland); and store ledgers for Hammond (Annapolis, Maryland) and Coffing (Annapolis, Maryland).
Source: Patrick 1990.

was specially ordered (Howard 1974). The drawings of each coat-of-arms had to be transported from England to China where an armorial set was hand-painted as per the drawing; the porcelain was then shipped thousands of sea miles to its destination. A man whose household served food on armorial porcelain demonstrated his access to distant trade networks. But even the use of simpler, white-toned vessels such as Queen's ware cream-colored plates served to mark a family's social rank.

Using Bourdieu's analytical strategy, vessels can be ranked as experimental or traditional, exotic or homely. Earth-toned vessels were traditional. The basic continuity of form over the centuries, despite the small alterations so useful in dating sherds, is testimony of this quality. To the extent that men, as producers of pottery, permitted no radical experimentation with their form, control was retained over the domain wherein they were used/consumed. The designs that embellished earth-toned vessels were traditional English motifs; no one could associate these vessels visually with the exotic (i.e., "attractively strange or unusual"). In contrast, refined earthen and stone wares as well as porcelains often were produced in exotic, experimental forms as were many of the foods and beverages contained within them.

Sahlins' concept of "inner" refers to something closer to nature; he describes things associated with outer domains as more civilized (1976). In this context, one can interpret "more civilized" as the equivalent of "more masculine." Given the etiquette of the seventeenth and eighteenth centuries, it is appropriate to say that formal dining areas were more civilized and further from nature than kitchens, pantries, or other food preparation areas, and that this was a progressive evolution from earlier standards of civilized behavior (Elias 1939). The proliferation of knives, forks, and spoons; of specialized drinking vessels; small, medium, and large plates; and specialized serving containers such as soup tureens and

Table 10.7 Cooking, storing, and other ceramic forms available in Chesapeake stores (1759–1775) and located at the Calvert site (ca.1720–ca.1790)

Type	Calvert	Allason	Dixon	Hamilton	Hammond	Coffing
Cooking						
Pot	X				X	X
Pan	X				X	X
Bowl	X	X	X	X	X	X
Basin	X		X			
Pudding pan	X					
Patty pan	X		X	X		
Pie pan	X					
Colander	X					
Storing						
Jug	X	X	X	X	X	
Jar/canister	X	X	X		X	
Bottle	X	X	X	X		
Butter pot	X	X	X	X	X	
Pickle pot	X		X			
Venison pot			X			
Milk pan	X	X	X	X	X	X
Other						
Wash basin	X	X	X	X	X	
Chamber pot	X	X		X	X	
Galley pot	X					
Pill slab	X					
Tile	X					
Candlestick	X					
Flower pot	X					
Garniture	X			X		
Dolls' dish	X					

[a] For these purposes, only form and not ware type is explored. Data are based on archaeological evidence for Calvert Site; annual store inventory for the shops of Allason (Falmouth, Virginia), Dixon (Port Royal, Virginia), and Hamilton (Piscattaway, Maryland); and store ledgers for Hammond (Annapolis, Maryland) and Coffing (Annapolis, Maryland).
Source: Patrick 1990.

sauce boats that one sees in the eighteenth century is generally taken as an indication of "civilized dining" and is usually presumed to accompany a more elaborate table etiquette. It would be erroneous to conclude that the increased degree of gentility these items represent is symbolic of their feminization.

Other Elements of the Prestige Structure of Pottery

Variation in ceramic assemblages

In a context where the status gradations were wide-ranging, greater variety and elaboration in pottery existed. In a context where status gradations were simpler, there was less need for variation or elaboration. It is this principle that underlies the homogeneity in New England assemblages which contain much smaller quantities of delft or porcelain than those found in the South. Compare, for example, the contents of two rural Massachusetts assemblages with those from equivalent sites in the Chesapeake as shown in table 10.8. Overall there is greater use of white-toned vessels in the Chesapeake. This distinction is also visible in sherd counts: quantities at Massachusetts sites range between 3 and 15 percent of the total sherd count; quantities at Chesapeake sites range between 3 and 41 percent in the seventeenth and between 15 and 52 percent in the eighteenth century (Yentsch 1990:39, figure 6).

Southern households could be simple or highly complex, extended beyond the confines normally provided by kinship lines. In elite Southern society, food was prepared by slave cooks who were usually women (Walsh 1986, personal communication). In wealthy households, the activities associated with Phases 2, 3, and 5 of the food cycle were assigned to female servants or household slaves (females or young, adolescent males). Adolescent boys, as house slaves, might also serve food.

The use of adolescent males is important because the passage of food from preparation areas to dining areas brought food out of one domain and into another where free men who were neither kin nor household members might be present. A structuralist would say that it was appropriate for adolescent boys instead of girls to bring food into dining areas for the young men brought it out of private, intensive space where it was transformed from its raw or semi-processed natural state into an element of cuisine, and carried it into public, extensive space where it became part of social display. Their ambiguous sexual status (neither adult male nor child) paralleled the ambiguity of the transitional passage from one area to another. As exotic intermediaries, they increased the

Table 10.8 The representation (%) of white-toned ceramics (delft, porcelain, or white salt-glazed stoneware) in different functional categories from late seventeenth- and early eighteenth-century assemblages from coastal Massachusetts, lower Maryland, and Tidewater Virginia

	New England sites		Chesapeake sites					
Functional vessel class	Wellfleet	Howland	Utopia*	Pettus*	Compton*	Clifts IV	Hicks	Calvert
Food preparation and storage	0	0	0	0	0	0	0	0
Food distribution	7	11	33	82	25	60	24	71
Food consumption	27	47	71	97	75	66	100	100
Beverage storage (bottles)	0	0	0	0	n.a.	0	0	0
Traditional beverages	0	9	31	17	0	35	3	33
Punch bowls and teawares	100	100	n.a.	100	n.a.	100	100	99

* Denotes the late 17th-century sites.
Sources: Bragdon (1988) for New England; Outlaw and Friedlander (1989) for Compton; the remainder is based on minimum vessel lists provided in Yentsch, Bescherer, and Patrick (forthcoming). Further information on the assemblages from these sites is also provided in Yentsch (1990, 1992).

ritual value of the food. They gave to it qualities similar to those imparted by French chefs in the homes of British nobles and in the Annapolis kitchens of American statesmen like Jefferson.

Mediation between the sphere of food preparation and storage and that of food consumption was also provided by the serving utensils used to distribute food. Initially a distinction was made between utilitarian vessels used to hold liquids (German stoneware bottles and their earthenware equivalents) and those used to serve beverages; this can be seen in archaeological assemblages of the 1400s (Lewis 1978). By ca.1680 the decorative slipwares and incised graffito derivatives marked the vessels used for serving both liquids and solids. By ca.1740, the sign that one had crossed the boundary between one domain of food use and another included the visual distinction between earth-toned and white-toned vessels and other stylistic variations serving to elaborate this elemental, visual difference.

The teawares

Pottery could set apart one man from another, and one household could be distinguished from another by the quality of the ceramics used to serve those who were guests. This occurred whether or not men were present: women, in their role as hostesses, functioned as representatives of the household. Hence the teawares – Chinese porcelain, delft, and elegant salt-glazed copies of Chinese forms – did not lose their masculine association initially when used by women. By serving, a woman paid homage to her family and guests while simultaneously, by her rank, denoting the status of the household. The situation is analogous to Henry II's homage to his son which he marked by serving his son himself at the son's coronation, and it is also analogous to the manner in which young men marked the rank of their elders by serving them in medieval dining halls. As a woman's social network was formed by kinship lines, eighteenth-century women who took tea together usually were relatives or near neighbors. In almost all social situations, it was the man of the house who invited non-kin into a home, and a wife honored him by serving them.

This is demonstrated in the tea ceremony. By ca.1680, teawares began to enter the archaeological record (Yentsch 1990:figure 8; 1992:figure 9), but at this time tea was a masculine beverage. The tea ceremony, surrounded by social pomp, became a focal element in women's lives by ca.1740. Because of its association with women, some might think of the tea ceremony as feminine and hence suggest that the white-toned tea bowls, saucers, pots, and creamers used to serve it indicate that these vessels had no masculine symbolism. However, in the late seventeenth century tea was an exotic beverage consumed by elite men in tea-houses. As tea was assimilated into the household beverage system, women began to consume it and took over the role of brewing and serving it to their men, replicating the pattern of its distribution in the tea-houses. Through the use of high-status teawares, women conveyed the social status of their household to their kin or neighbors who might visit on an informal basis and to others in the community who were invited for more formal occasions. Women increased their power by their organization of such social rituals. As the eighteenth century progressed, tea became a political symbol (Breen 1986) and a beverage whose use cross-cut the social hierarchy. As this occurred, tea pots and tea cups appeared in a variety of wares decorated in motifs associated with the folk tradition and with daily food. Whereas between 1680 and 1720 tea was a prestigious masculine beverage, as it was popularized in the mid-eighteenth century it was also feminized – a trend strongly manifested in its nineteenth-century use. Fashion was the mechanism by which teawares were transferred from one side of the oppositional binary structure to the other.

It is this which explains the short production span for agate, tortoiseshell, clouded, and green wares made by Whieldon and Wedgwood in the 1750s and 1760s. What they attempted was the transfer of earth-toned colors and the fruit/flower motifs of the earlier folk tradition to vessel forms separate from the folk tradition. Teawares were members of the masculine domain of pottery whereas the earth-toned colors and folk motifs were components in the feminine domain. The pottery these ingenious entrepreneurs created formed a mixed metaphor that carried a contradictory social message: the result was a visual insult. White salt-glazed vessels in many of the very same forms, produced in the same molds, were popular because their color and style was consistent with the symbolism associated with ceremonial food consumption. This ritual use of food involved men as individuals, and women as mothers, wives, and daughters, but not as individuals in their own right. Fashion trends in marketing, as markers of upward social mobility, were most successful when they flowed with the basic principles in the prestige structure rather than against them. Had the production of Whieldon-Wedgwood wares been delayed until the early nineteenth century, their popularity might have been greater for by that time tea was thoroughly assimilated into the folk tradition.

Cultural expressions of social inequality are often complex and may be partially masked by being situated in a context where they appear unnecessary. Teawares were objects denoting the status of a household although they were used by women. On the surface, and due in part to the fact that tea in the United States did become feminized at a later point in time, eighteenth-century teawares appear to the modern observer to wear a feminine guise. However, they were used to convey information about social rank within the household to family members and to guests through the highly formalized tea ceremony. This was a ceremony in which women played an important role, but its focus was not the feminine actors involved in it: rather, it was the conveyance of information about the household, the gathering of information about others, and the maintenance of group alliances. Hence teawares fell within the masculine domain of beverage use. Further, objects that were seemingly masculine could be used to set apart one man from another through the incorporation of feminine elements into their decoration. This follows Bloch's premise that gender symbolism may often form the basis for ideological divisions that are not gender-bound (1985).

The Metaphor of Pottery

In summary, a basic separation – an element in the social structure of each family – was the separation between men's and women's roles. Earth-toned and white-toned pottery marked this taken-for-granted separation. Simply put, men and women were not created equal. The use of white-toned vessels that were symbols associated with social display (and therefore with elite and powerful men) did not penetrate feminine space. If such vessels had done so, this would have introduced an internal inconsistency into the symbolic system by equating feminine space or, among slave owners, Afro-American space with the highest level of the social structure. The use of coarse earthenwares and stonewares in this area was, however, consistent with the social structure and its subordinate placement of those who worked in such activity areas. The use of white ceramic vessels in food preparation would have inverted the social order by equating culture with nature, men with women.

The relational statements expressed by variation in food vessels about the social hierarchy also enabled members of the culture to make statements about the use of space and the use of food by speaking of these indirectly through the metaphor of pottery. Thus the oppositions expressed in spatial boundaries between activity areas were reinforced and replicated in the division of pottery that simultaneously also substituted, metaphorically, for the different uses to which food was put. The break between two food traditions – the courtly and the folk – emphasized the two-tiered structure of the society (Yentsch 1991). The elite food tradition was built on a complex labor base, and required the use of scarce resources, elaborate utensils, and time-consuming procedures; the cooking techniques associated with haute cuisine were mysterious, for knowledge of these was restricted. The daily meals of ordinary people, on the other hand, utilized a small labor pool (often only mothers and daughters), drew on readily available foodstuffs with a seasonal base, and used procedures that minimized labor requirements. Knowledge of food preparation techniques for everyday food was passed from one generation of women to the next and might be shared outside the kin group.

The differences between the two types of food use (for social display and for daily sustenance) provided a series of visual boundaries between sets of individuals that were integral to the social organization. Man's authority over the natural world was seen to be virtually unlimited – the natural world was something he might use "for his profit or for his pleasure" (Day 1620:213, quoted in Thomas 1983:21); by creating asymmetrical relationships among individuals, relationships based on dominance and subordination, categories of people were created within the culture who might be used for profit or for pleasure. One way of establishing the legitimacy of these relationships was to situate certain of them within the natural world: one means of doing so was to define different types of activities and objects as existing closer to nature than others. This was accomplished by attributing to them qualities that were culturally defined as feminine.

The prestige structure, consisting of food and food-related objects such as pottery vessels, was not simply a division between male and female domains. It distinguished between men of different social rank, providing gradations of social worth that extended across ethnic and racial lines. It was based on the idea that qualities in an individual were defined by contiguity: that is to say, that by working in an area socially defined as closer to nature than another with tools that were perceived as belonging on the nature side of the culture–nature continuum, one also became symbolically associated with nature. Ideologically this legitimated the use or misuse of such individuals for another's proft or pleasure because it placed them lower in the hierarchy of beings, which itself was part of the political and social model for social action. This ideological division was not gender-bound, but it made use of gender symbolism in household space, in household food, and in household pottery as one of its legitimizing mechanisms.

ACKNOWLEDGEMENTS

I would like to thank Carole Carr, Jim Deetz, Conrad Goodwin, Gary Wheeler Stone, and, especially, Mary C. Beaudry and Lorena Walsh, for their helpful comments and criticisms on earlier versions of this paper. Work on the Calvert ceramics was funded, in part, by Grant RO-21482-87 from the National Endowment for the Humanities.

REFERENCES

Amussen, Susan D. (1985) "Gender, Family, and the Social Order, 1560–1725." In *Order and Disorder in Early Modern England*, eds Anthony Fletcher and John Stevenson, pp. 196–217. Cambridge University Press, London.
——(1987) *An Ordered Society: Gender and Class in Early Modern England*. Basil Blackwell, Oxford.
Ardener, Edwin (1972) "Belief and the Problem of Women." In *The Interpretation of Ritual*, ed. J. LaFontaine. Tavistock, London.
Aires, Phillipe (1962) *Centuries of Childhood*. Penguin, London.
Barnes, J. A. (1973) "Genetrix:Genitor–Nature:Culture?" In *The Character of Kinship*, ed. Jack Goody. Cambridge University Press, London.
Beaudry, Mary C. (1980) "Pot-Shot, Jug-Bitten, Cup-Shaken: Object Language and Double Meanings." Paper presented at the American Anthropological Association Meetings, Washington, D.C.
——(n.d.) *Domestic Pursuits: Historical Archaeology of American Households*. Telford Press, Caldwell, NJ (forthcoming).
Bloch, Maurice (1985) "From Cognition to Ideology." In *Power and Knowledge* ed. Richard Fardon, pp. 21–48. Scottish Academic Press, Edinburgh.
Bourdieu, Pierre (1979) *La Distinction*. Le Minuit, Paris.
Bragdon, Kathleen (1988) "Occupational Differences reflected in material culture." *Documentary Archaeology*, ed. M. C. Beaudry, pp. 83–91. Cambridge University Press, Cambridge.
Breen, Timothy (1986) "Baubles of Britain: the Meaning of Things." Paper presented at the Washington, D.C. Historical Society Meetings, March 20–21, 1986.
Cahn, Susan (1987) *Industry of Devotion: the Transformation of Women's Work in England, 1500–1600*. Columbia University Press, New York.
Cott, Nancy F. (1977) *The Bonds of Womanhood: "Women's Sphere" in New England, 1780–1835*. Yale University Press, New Haven, CT.
Cunningham, C. M. and P. J. Drury (1986) *Post-medieval Sites and Their Pottery: Moulsham Street, Chelmsford*, Chelmsford Archaeological Trust Report No. 54.
Day, John (1620) *Day's Descant* (quoted in K. Thomas (1983) *Man and the Natural World*. Allen Lane, London).
Deagan, Kathleen (1973) "Mestizaje in Colonial St. Augustine." *Ethnohistory* 20(1), 55–65.
——(1983) *Spanish St. Augustine: the Archaeology of a Colonial Creole Community*. Academic Press, New York.
Deetz, James (1972) "Ceramics from Plymouth, 1635–1835: the Archaeological Evidence." In *Ceramics in America*, ed. Ian Quimby, pp. 15–40. Winterthur Conference Report. University of Virginia Press, Charlottesville.
——(1977) *In Small Things Forgotten: The Archaeology of Early American Life*. Anchor Books, New York.
——(1983) "Scientific Humanism and Humanistic Science: A Place for

228   ANNE YENTSCH

Paradigmatic Pluralism in Historical Archaeology." *Geoscience and Man* 23, 27–34.

——(1988) "Material Culture and Worldview in Colonial Anglo-America." In *The Recovery of Meaning*, eds Mark P. Leone and Parker Potter, pp. 219–35.

Detweiler, Susan G. (1982) *George Washington's Chinaware*. Harry N. Abrams, Inc., New York.

Douglas, Mary (1972) "Deciphering a Meal." *Daedalus* (Winter 1972) 61–81.

——(1986) *How Institutions Think*. Syracuse University Press, Syracuse, NY.

Elias, Norbert (1939) *The Civilizing Process: The History of Manners*. Basil Blackwell, Oxford.

Firth, Raymond (1975) *Symbols: Public and Private*. Cornell University Press, Ithaca.

Fox, Russell and K. G. Barton (1986) "Excavations at Oyster Street, Portsmouth, Hampshire, 1968–71." *Post-medieval Archaeology* 20, 31–256.

Fraser, Antonia (1985) *The Weaker Vessel*. Vintage, New York.

Glassie, Henry (1975) *Folk Housing in Middle Virginia*. University of Tennessee Press, Knoxville.

Goody, Jack (1982) *Cooking, Cuisine and Class*. Cambridge University Press, Cambridge.

Hamilton, Roberta (1978) *The Liberation of Women: A Study of Patriarchy and Capitalism*. Controversies in Sociology No. 6. George Allen & Unwin, London.

Hanawalt, Barbara A. (ed.) (1986) *Women and Work in Preindustrial Europe*. Indiana University Press, Bloomington.

Handsman, Russell (1984) "Merchant Capital and the Historical Archaeology of Gender, Motherhood, and Child Raising." Paper presented at the Council for Northeast Historical Archaeology Meetings, October 1984, State University of New York, Binghamton.

Henisch, Bridget Ann (1976) *Fast and Feast*. Pennsylvania State University Press, State Park, PA.

Howard, David S. (1974) *Chinese Armorial Porcelain*. Faber & Faber, London.

Levi-Strauss, C. (1958) *Anthropologie Structurale*. Paris (English translation, *Structural Anthropology*. Basic Books, Garden City, NY, 1963).

——(1965) "The Culinary Triangle." *Partisan Review* 33, 586–95.

——(1988) *The Jealous Potter* (trans. Benedicte Chorier). University of Chicago Press, Chicago.

Lewis, J. M. (1978) *Medieval Pottery and Metal-ware in Wales*. Amgueddfa Genedlaethol Cymru. National Museum of Wales, Cardiff.

Macfarlane, Alan (1988) "The Cradle of Capitalism: the Case of England." In *Europe and the Rise of Capitalism*, eds Jean Baechler, John A. Hall, and Michael Mann, pp. 185–204. Basil Blackwell, Oxford.

Mennell, Stephen (1985) *All Manners of Food*. Basil Blackwell, Oxford.

Mertes, Kate (1988) *The English Noble Household 1250–1600: Good Governance and Politic Rule*. Basil Blackwell, Oxford.

Neiman, Fraser (1978) "A Provisional Model of Culture Change in Westmorland County, Virginia." Paper presented at the Annual Meetings, Society for Historical Archaeology, San Antonio, Texas.

Nicholson, Linda J. (1986) *Gender and History: the Limits of Social Theory in the Age of the Family*. Columbia University, New York.

Norton, Mary Beth (1980) *Liberty's Daughters: The Revolutionary Experience of American Women, 1750–1800*. Little Brown & Company, Boston.

Ortner, Sherry B. (1972) "Is Female to Male as Nature is to Culture?" *Feminist Studies* 1, 5–31.

Ortner, Sherry B. and Harriet Whitehead (1982) *Sexual Meanings: The Cultural Construction of Gender and Sexuality*. Cambridge University Press, Cambridge.

Oswald, Adrian, R. J. C. Hildyard, and R. G. Hughes (1982) *English Brown Stoneware, 1670–1900*. Faber & Faber, London.

Outlaw, Alain and Amy Friedlander (1989) *The Compton Site circa 1651–1684, Calvert County, Maryland*, 18CV279, prepared by Cultural Resource Group, Louis Berger & Associates (East Orange, NJ, 1989) on file at the Jefferson Patterson Park and Museum, Calvert County, MD.

Patrick, Stephen (1990) *"Round the Social Bowl:" Elite Ceramics at the Calvert Site and Other Patterns of Consumer Consumption in the Chesapeake*. M.A. thesis, American Studies Program, College of William and Mary, Williamsburg, VA.

Rackham, Bernard (1948) *Medieval English Pottery*. Faber & Faber, London.

Reed, Michael (1983) *The Georgian Triumph 1700–1830*. Routledge and Kegan Paul, London.

Reiter, Rayna R. (1975) "Men and Women in the South of France: Public and Private Domains." In *Toward an Anthropology of Women*, ed. Rayna R. Reiter, pp. 252–82. New School of Social Research, New York.

Reitz, Elizabeth (1988) "Preliminary Analysis of Vertebrate Remains from the Calvert Site in Annapolis, Maryland and a Comparison with Vertebrate Remains from Sites in South Carolina, Georgia, and Jamaica." *Calvert Interim Report No. 6*. National Endowment for the Humanities Grant RO–21482–87. On file at Historic Annapolis, Inc., Annapolis, MD.

Rosaldo, Michelle Zimbalist (1974) "Women, Culture, and Society: A Theoretical Overview." In *Women, Culture, and Society*, eds. Michelle Z. Rosaldo and Louise Lamphere, pp. 17–42. Stanford University Press, Stanford.

——(1987) "Moral/Analytic Dilemmas Posed by the Intersection of Feminism and Social Science." In *Interpretive Social Science*, eds Paul Rabinow and William M. Sullivan, pp. 280–301 (revised edn). University of California Press, Berkeley.

Rye, O. S. (1976) "Keeping Your Temper Under Control: Materials and the Manufacture of Papuan Pottery." *Archaeology and Physical Anthropology in Oceania* 11, 106–37.

Sahlins, Marshall (1976) *Culture and Practical Reason*. Chicago University Press, Chicago.

St George, Robert B. (1982) "'Set Thine House in Order': The Domestication of the Yeomanry in Seventeenth-Century New England." In *New England Begins: The Seventeenth Century*, eds Jonathan L. Fairbanks and Robert F. Trent. Boston Museum of Fine Arts, Boston.

Schama, Simon (1987) *The Embarrassment of Riches: An Interpretation of Dutch Culture in the Golden Age*. Knopf, New York.

Schuyler, Robert L. (ed.) (1980) *Archaeological Perspectives on Ethnicity in America*. Baywood Press, New York.

Stansell, Christine (1987) *City of Women: Sex and Class in New York, 1789–1860*. University of Illinois Press, Urbana.

Thomas, Keith (1983) *Man and the Natural World*. Allen Lane, London.

Thrupp, Sylvia (1962) *The Merchant Class of Medieval London*. University of Michigan Press, Ann Arbor.

Ulrich, Laura T. (1982) *Good Wives: Image and Reality in the Lives of Women in Northern New England*, 1650–1750. Alfred Knopf, New York.

Upton, Dell (1988) "White and Black Landscapes in Eighteenth-Century Virginia." In *Material Life in America, 1600–1860*, ed. Robert St George, pp. 357–69. Northeastern University Press, Boston.

Wall, Diana D. (1987) *At Home in New York: Changing Family Life among the Propertied in the Late Eighteenth and Early Nineteenth Centuries*. Unpublished Ph.D. Dissertation, Department of Anthropology, New York University, New York.

Wilson, C. Anne (1974) *Food and Drink in Britain from the Stone Age to Recent Times*. Barnes & Noble, New York.

Yentsch, Anne E. (1990) "Minimum Vessel Lists as Evidence of Change in Folk and Courtly Traditions of Food Use." *Historical Archaeology* 24(3), 26–53.

——(1992) "Chesapeake Artifacts and Their Cultural Context: Pottery and the Food Domain." *Post-medieval Archaeology* 24 (forthcoming).

Yentsch, Anne E., Karen Bescherer, and Stephen Patrick (forthcoming) "The Calvert Ceramic Collection." *Calvert Interim Report No. 4* (Historic Annapolis Foundation, Annapolis, MD).

Yentsch, Ann and Larry W. McKee (1987) "Footprints of Buildings in Eighteenth-Century Annapolis, Maryland." *American Archeology* 6(1), 40–51.

11

Toward an Historical Archaeology of Materialistic Domestic Reform

Suzanne Spencer-Wood

Introduction and Statement of Problem

This essay developed in the context of historical archaeological research on similarities and differences between lifeways and consumer choices of historically dominant and subdominant socio-economic and ethnic groups (cf. Deagan 1983; Otto 1984; Schuyler 1980; Spencer-Wood 1987a). The framework of dominance and resistance has offered a new perspective in researching lifeways of minorities (cf. Rushing 1985; Rubertone 1985; Savulis 1985). In this framework, adhering to minority cultural patterns is viewed as an expression of resistance rather than as a failure to assimilate to the dominant culture. Although women are not a numeric minority, they have resisted sex discrimination and subordinate social, political, and economic status.

In the nineteenth century domestic reformers created a positive gender ideology that not only resisted male dominance, but empowered women to develop independent identities and to raise their status by creating female professions. The historical archaeology of domestic reform is an important addition to the growing amount of anthropological research on changes in gender roles, status, and the division of labor (Dahlberg 1981; Deetz 1978; Reiter 1975; Rosaldo and Lamphere 1974). Many studies have viewed changes in women's roles or status as responses to larger scale cultural processes, such as colonization (cf. Deetz 1960), economic development (cf. Leacock et al. 1986), or industrialization (Blewett 1984; Burns 1975:79; Mullings 1986).

Rather than viewing women as simply responding to such male-controlled processes, I have used a feminist perspective to understand how domestic reformers, both women and men, created large-scale changes in the construction of gender. In my approach women are not solely viewed as reacting to men's actions, or resisting male dominance

231

(Spencer-Wood 1989, 1990, 1991). Rather, attention focuses on how materialist domestic reformers created new gender ideology, identities, roles, relationships, and behaviors that were symbolized by and implemented with innovations in material culture, and spread by reform networks throughout the USA.

This essay synthesizes documentary, architectural, material culture, and archaeological data to develop a framework for historical archaeological research on materialistic domestic reform. These reform movements deserve study because they were instrumental in transforming American gender ideology and women's status from the nineteenth century into the twentieth century. Archaeological research is particularly appropriate in the study of materialistic domestic reform because these movements advocated material culture change as a primary mechanism for professionalizing aspects of housework both in the domestic and public spheres (Hayden 1981:1–5). Our understanding of the implementation and diffusion of domestic reform can be increased through historical archaeological research in nearly any American town or city. Historical archaeology may contribute to our understanding of relationships between the adoption of material culture innovations and their symbolic meanings in the ideological context of domestic reform. Although a relatively large number of new site types were generated by domestic reform, my Boston area survey indicates that few opportunities remain for archaeological research because new construction has destroyed most domestic reform sites (Spencer-Wood 1987b).

I shall offer information from initial stages of research, including historical background and archaeological survey. First, I define materialistic domestic reform and explain why I coined this term. Then major types of domestic reform are briefly described. Subsequent sections discuss: domestic reform's historical and archaeological significance; possible areas for historical archaeological research, to contribute to our understanding either of materialistic domestic reform, or of the archaeological record; and available and expected types of documentary, architectural, and archaeological data. Next I consider methods for identifying materialistic domestic reform sites: this is important because archaeologists may have excavated and analyzed sites without identifying their domestic reform use. General expectations are formulated about site formation processes, and the resulting relative frequency of artifacts expected at different types of materialistic domestic reform sites. Subsequent sections discuss types of sites, features and artifacts expected for each type of materialistic domestic reform movement. The domestic reform meanings of sites, features, and artifacts are discussed in their historical context. Expectations or hypotheses are developed about what historical archaeologists might learn from each type of site; these hypotheses require tests at a number of sites before any definite conclusions can be drawn.

Scope of Research

The term "domestic reform" is applied to a wide variety of social movements directed at improving the condition and status of women's lives and work. These reform movements are categorized as "domestic" because their purpose was to professionalize some aspect(s) of women's domestic work or skills. Domestic reformers resisted the male-dominated cultural categorization of women's work as inferior to men's work. Beyond resistance, they successfully empowered female dominance in a wide range of professional occupations. The adjective "materialistic" is used to refer to domestic reform movements that proposed innovations in material culture as a primary strategy for professionalizing aspects of housework. The names of some domestic reform movements reflect this strategy by referring to the domestic sphere or functionally specific household spaces, as in domestic science, home economics, the public kitchen, or day nursery movements. My term "materialistic domestic reform" is used rather than Smith's (1979) "domestic feminism," or Hayden's (1981) "material feminism," because most materialistic domestic reformers did not consider themselves feminists (Blair 1980; Rothman 1978; Strasser 1982:180–222).

Early histories of feminism focused on the suffrage movement, resulting in an overemphasis on its importance compared with domestic reform (Blair 1980:3; Gordon 1982; Zaretsky 1981). This emphasis on suffrage reflected a male-dominated world-view that assigned greater importance to women's political public sphere reforms than to their domestic reforms; the significance of domestic reform was overlooked because it seemed unrelated, or even opposed, to the suffrage movement. Recently feminist historians have realized that domestic reform was not only significant in achieving female suffrage, but was also important in its own right. Since the late 1970s a growing number of feminist historians have begun to analyze the significance of domestic reform movements less in terms of modern values, and more in terms of their own cultural milieu and how they changed it (cf. Berg 1978; Blair 1980; Bordin 1981; Clinton 1984; Cott 1977; Epstein 1981; Freedman 1981; Leach 1980; Hayden 1981; Rothman 1978; Strasser 1982; Wilson 1979).

Most domestic reformers were from the middle or upper class, and accepted the religiously sanctioned cultural ideals that limited women to the domestic realm. Yet, while adhering to the ideology of separate spheres, domestic reformers increased women's roles and status by blurring the boundary between the male and female domains. They worked within the normative cultural framework to indirectly undermine male dominance by expanding the domestic sphere, and female dominance within it. At the same time they raised the status of domestic work by applying to it scientific principles used in public sphere work. In contrast to the nineteenth-century suffrage movement, domestic reform was successful precisely because it did not directly attack male dominance by espousing absolute equality, or any radical transformation of women's roles. Instead domestic reformers used accepted beliefs about women's innately superior domestic abilities to expand women's roles both in the home and in the public realm. They successfully argued that their extensions of women's roles into the public domain were actually properly part of the domestic domain. By redefining woman's sphere, domestic reformers successfully decreased the scope of male dominance, and increased the number of public female professions. Domestic reformers created female dominance in an expanded domestic sphere, separate from, but equal to, male dominance in the public sphere. This form of equality may seem regressive by modern standards, but the revolutionary scope of domestic reform is evident from the fact that housework still has a lower status than work in the public domain (Clinton 1984:44, 183–7; Rothman 1978; Strasser 1982:195–8; Woloch 1984:285).

Domestic reformers sought control not only of the household, but also of domestic services in the community. They argued that just as women's natural abilities uniquely suited them for taking care of the family and home, so they also made women best suited to be caretakers of the wider family of the community, and its homes (Clinton 1984; Strasser 1982). In creating a continuum between the duties of women in the marital family and the duties of women as mothers of the community-as-family, domestic reformers created a powerful positive solution to the basic nineteenth-century social problem of "whether the existence of the marital family is compatible with that of the universal family which the term 'Community' signifies" (Smith 1979:238). The boundary was blurred between the private home and the public sphere by extending some aspects of domestic work, either literally or by analogy, into the public sphere.

Many domestic reformers focused on enlarging the number of professional occupations and public-sphere areas dominated by women, by arguing that women's innate domestic skills best suited them to perform a particular type of work. For example, women successfully argued for female dominance of grade school teaching as a logical extension of their naturally superior abilities as child rearers (Clinton 1984:44; Rothman 1978:56–60; Porterfield 1980:119–21). Similarly, women extended their role as nurses from the home into the public sphere, resulting in the female-dominated nursing profession (Donnelly 1986:100–1). In a more attenuated case women's sewing ability was used to successfully argue for female dominance in typing and typesetting (Baron 1987). In a second type of domestic reform, called "municipal housekeeping," women's domestic roles were extended from the individual family to analogous areas in the larger family of the community. Women lobbied male officials for municipal laws, water, sewers, parks, and tenement reform to ensure the adequate quality of food, space, air, water, and sewerage that women depended on to fulfill their roles as family caretakers (Beard 1915; Blair 1980:93; Melosi 1981:35, 117–33; Rothman 1978:124–7, 153–6; Woloch 1984:299). These types of domestic reform successfully opened new professional occupations and areas of influence to women. The importance of this cannot be discounted just because the continuation of male dominance in the culture as a whole led to the devaluation of women's work, regardless of the field involved.

The materialistic domestic reform movements discussed in this paper were selected for historical archaeological research for a number of reasons. First, innovation both in artifacts and in architectural features was their primary mechanism for professionalizing aspects of housework (Hayden 1976, 1981). Second, they professionalized easily recognizable aspects of housework, such as cooking, day care, laundry, cleaning, or sewing. In municipal housekeeping and in opening some new occupations, women had to influence men who held the power to change conditions. Many women's occupations were supervised by male overseers. In contrast, the materialistic domestic reform movements in this paper were initiated and controlled by women, and/or sympathetic men, for the benefit of women.

Materialistic domestic reform encompasses a large number of interrelated movements, ranging from those seeking female dominance in the home, to those seeking female dominance in housekeeping professions outside the home. The reformers argued that women's work should have the same status as men's skilled work in the public sphere. They applied public-sphere technology and methods to transform housework from a craft into a set of female-controlled scientific-domestic tasks and a set of female public professions (Giedion 1948; Hayden 1981:55–8; Strasser 1982:180–241). Outside the home materialistic domestic reformers professionalized aspects of housework through cooperatives, domestic service organizations, and educational institutions. Cooperative housework enterprises fulfilled the domestic reform goal of raising women's status by transforming housework from private unpaid domestic labor into remunerative skilled labor in the public sphere, equivalent to men's occupations. A variety of industrial scale cooperatives socialized aspects of housework, including bakeries, kitchens, laundries, and day care. Cooperative housekeeping facilities and equipment were used in utopian communities, working-class social settlements, homes for working women, middle-class dining clubs, and in popular urban apartment hotels for the wealthy. In many cases middle- and upper-class women designed professional housework enterprises, such as kindergartens, day nurseries, and public kitchens, to provide services to working women's families in order to alleviate women's double burden of work and housework. Domestic reformers founded schools and programs to train women as professional domestic science teachers, childcare providers, industrial scale cooks, laundresses, household managers and domestic servants.

While not all attempts were successful, materialistic domestic reform movements in aggregate did substantially expand women's opportunities for work in professional housekeeping occupations outside the home. The philanthropic or government-financed nature of most housekeeping service institutions kept them from possible exploitation by capitalists. These housekeeping institutions were run by women, provided employment to women, and served women and their families in cities and towns across the country (Hayden 1981; Rothman 1978).

Historical Context and Significance

Domestic reformers successfully changed their culture by building on the existing cultural milieu. They used mainstream philosophies to construct compelling arguments that made domestic reform widely popular among women and acceptable to men. Within the extant cultural situation domestic reformers created opportunities to improve the conditions and status of women's lives and work. The widely varying opportunities are reflected in a large diversity of domestic reform movements, from utopian communes to public kitchens, industrial schools, and the field of home economics. The different manifestations of domestic reform shared a number of popular beliefs and reform methods. Domestic reform organizations often shared ideas because they shared some members, linking them in an extensive reform network.

Domestic reform started in the early nineteenth century and proliferated into a large number of interrelated and influential movements by the end of the century. Domestic reform successfully created permanent large-scale cultural changes because of its widespread and long lasting popularity. It grew from initially small grassroots organizations in the East, into a nationwide network of organizations that cooperatively wielded influence through the great size and wealth of their collective membership. Through supportive networks with other reform movements, including suffrage, domestic reformers successfully extended the influence of their ideas even further. Domestic reform organizations changed American culture directly by modifying the beliefs and behaviors of many women, and indirectly by influencing men with the power to change women's social, economic, and legal status.

Philosophies and methodologies in domestic reform

Beneath their differences in form and substance, domestic reform movements were united by a number of shared beliefs. Most fundamentally, domestic reformers believed that every aspect of social life had a "domestic meaning" (Leach 1980:209). This belief redefined the "domestic sphere" as virtually unlimited, justifying the immense variety of women's domestic reform activities (Leach 1980:209). Domestic reform combined beliefs from philosophies of the enlightenment and utopian communitarian socialism Its success was possible in part because of its integration of a large number of both normative and reformist cultural beliefs. For example, domestic reformers championed the cult of domesticity that limited women to the domestic sphere, but combined it with enlightenment egalitarian beliefs, resulting in a philosophy of equality for women and men in their separate spheres. Domestic reformers used the nineteenth-century nostalgia for agrarian America to claim that women's domestic work in industrializing America had lost the equal status with men's work that it had enjoyed on farms (Peirce 1868). Enlightenment beliefs in rationally perfecting society were used to justify perfecting domestic work. Communitarian socialist beliefs justified perfecting domestic work through cooperative socialized labor and efficient scientific technologies (Hayden 1981).

Some domestic reform was justified by evangelical religious beliefs in the need to reform society for the second coming of Christ (Hill 1985; Mann 1954:87; McDowell 1982; Porterfield 1980:99–128, 155–88). Many domestic reformers concurred with the popular integration of science with religion as the "religion of science" (Leach 1980:136). In this view scientific laws of nature and principles of order were manifestations of the symmetry and harmony of God's creation (Turner 1985:181–3). Domestic reformers with this popular belief applied rational, scientific principles to aspects of domestic work, bringing them into harmony with God's natural order (Leach 1980:206–12).

A variety of domestic reform movements shared some basic methodologies for implementing the professionalization of aspects of housework, partly based on their shared beliefs. Domestic reformers used educational institutions, courses, and departments across the country to establish the professional nature of housekeeping occupations, from nursing to cooking and teaching. Education was a major means of changing women's housekeeping habits from the "irrational" craft level to the use of scientific methods and industrial equipment. The professional industrial status of women's domestic work was indicated by its rationalization and mechanization with material culture innovations. Cooperation was a widespread method accompanying the specialization and socialization of domestic work (Leach 1980:202–12).

The cultural milieu and opportunities for domestic reform

Domestic reformers used the rapidly changing conditions in nineteenth-century America to create opportunities for improving the conditions and status of women's lives. Many Protestant Anglo-Americans felt the social order was threatened by nineteenth-century industrialization, urbanization, and massive immigration. Poor working-class women and children were often exploited by capitalists, landlords, and abusive, often alcoholic, husbands. Because the United States as a new nation had adopted the English principle of couverture, in which married women and their children had virtually no legal rights, a husband could take all the wages and property from the family, leaving them penniless (Berg 1978:92, 103, 230; James 1981:6, 70; Pleck 1987:9, 63–88, 101–9). These conditions in slums bred crime, vice, and gangs that threatened the orderly lives of the middle and upper classes. Domestic reformers used the widely recognized need for social control of the poor to address the socially ignored needs of poor women and children for low-cost childcare, sanitary living conditions, and training for remunerative work, which they offered in domestic service jobs.

Domestic reform initially developed from religious beliefs and contexts that were retained in some organizations from the nineteenth into the twentieth centuries. Women's power and authority to reform society were derived from religious beliefs that women were innately pious and morally superior to men; therefore, when Protestant religions shifted from the elitist belief in predestination to a belief in universal salvation, they considered women best suited to save souls and reform society for Christ's second coming (Hill 1985; Welter 1966). To save others and themselves, as a result of their good deeds, women formed popular benevolent organizations working for temperance, social purity (a movement to save prostitutes), and prison reform (Berg 1978; Clinton 1984:172–83; Epstein 1981; James 1981:163–71; Wilson 1979:94). In domestic reform movements women used the skills they acquired in organizing and fund-raising for religiously sanctioned benevolent organizations. In religious missions in American cities women found that salvation could often be effected by eliminating the physical conditions of poverty and ignorance that led individuals into lives of vice and sin (Hill 1985; McDowell 1982). This argument justified some domestic reformers' municipal housekeeping, cooperative housekeeping, domestic services, and domestic education activities. Municipal house-keeping physically cleaned up slum living conditions, while educational organizations trained "unskilled" women for "decent" employment in housekeeping occupations. Domestic services for poor women, such as day nurseries, not only properly socialized and trained immigrant children, but also provided poor women with respectable employment, preventing families from falling into lives of beggary or crime. Domestic reformers used the power of their moral superiority to successfully lobby men to support legislation (e.g., child labor laws, pure food laws) protecting the family from exploitation by unscrupulous capitalists (Woloch 1984:299).

Domestic reform movements were widely popular and effective in professionalizing aspects of housework because they unified women in this task, despite their differences. For example, while many women believed that domestic reform could raise the status of women and their domestic work, some women participated in reform in order to increase the supply of adequately trained servants, or for social control of the growing immigrant working classes (Hayden 1981:319 n. 30, 320 n. 54; Ross 1976:34–7; Steinfels 1973:37–9; Strasser 1982:195–7). In the second half of the nineteenth century domestic reform movements became increasingly secular, following a general social trend (Turner 1985). In the Civil War women gained experience in fund-raising and cooperatively organizing to feed, clothe, and nurse the troops. These experiences were used in organizing a number of domestic reform movements, including cooperative housekeeping, domestic science education, nursing, and scientific nutrition (Hayden 1981:115–25; Woloch 1984:287).

The popularity, longevity, and success of domestic reform

The historical significance of domestic reform is indicated by its widespread popularity, evident in the large membership of organizations working for this goal. By the second half of the nineteenth century women had organized a "massive network of women's clubs" (Wilson 1979:95), that worked to improve the conditions of women's lives, often through some type of domestic reform. The total membership of women's clubs rapidly grew to over two million by the early twentieth century (Wilson 1979: 100–1). As increasing numbers of women worked for domestic reform across the USA, they created nationwide cultural changes (Woloch 1984:290).

The widespread success of domestic reform is indicated by national and international cooperative connections among domestic reform movements. For example, American kindergartens, day nurseries, public kitchens, social settlements, and housekeeping cooperatives in utopian communes and neighborhoods were inspired by the earlier development of similar movements in Europe (Beer 1942:27–8; Hayden 1981:33–8, 60–3, 159). Domestic reform organizations were usually interrelated by women who worked in more than one movement. An outstanding example is Ellen Swallow Richards, who wrote several scientific housekeeping manuals, and a domestic science textbook; founded the women's laboratory at MIT, the American public kitchen movement, and the home economics movement; worked for domestic science education; and sponsored a cooperative home for domestics (Hayden 1981:151–62, 171; Hunt 1912; James 1971). The large number of women working in a vast array of interrelated cooperative organizations indicates the mainstream nature of domestic reform, and the combined power of these reformers to influence the direction of cultural change (Woloch 1984:292–3, 299).

The effectiveness of domestic reform organizations is indicated by their propagation nationwide, and by their legacy of permanent cultural changes (Beard 1915; Berg 1978; Blair 1980; Clinton 1984:166–87; Hayden 1981:127; Wilson 1979). Many domestic reforms have become accepted aspects of American culture, including female-dominated domestic reform professions, women's schools, home economics departments and courses, kindergartens, and day care institutions found in communities across the country. Many domestic reform organizations, or their descendants, are still active today, providing a number of social services. A few examples are YWCAs, several United Way Agencies, the American Home Economics Association, a number of women's colleges; and in Boston: the Women's Educational and Industrial Union, Associated Day Care Services, United South End Settlements, the N. Bennet St Industrial School, and Rutland Corner House (Landy and Greenblatt 1965:14–21; Spencer-Wood 1987b).

The success of domestic reform's widespread influence

The success of domestic reform is indicated by its influence on other reform movements, through widespread networks. Domestic reformers established cooperative connections with other reformers at conferences promoting such interaction, including the Convention of the Friends of Universal Reform in Boston in 1840, the First Women's Rights Convention, Seneca Falls, 1848, the National Council of Women, the

International Council of Women (1888), and unions for national and international women's organizations. Domestic reform organizations were also often connected to other reform organizations by women who worked for more than one kind of reform. A famous case, Jane Addams, founder of Hull House, worked for suffrage, women's trade unions, labor legislation, and the Progressive party; and in 1915 became president of the International Congress of Women, and chairman of the Woman's Peace Party (Addams 1910; Blodgett 1971; Boorstin 1965:213; Clinton 1984:174; Foster 1971; Gilman 1972:353, 372, 379; Haraszti 1937; Hayden 1981:1–5, 7, 35–9, 67, 80, 102–3, 116–18, 157; Hawkins 1971; Keller 1971; Lefaucheux et al. 1966:7–13; Messerli 1971; Pearson 1971; Peirce 1868:515–19; Rossi 1974:323–5, 276; Scott 1971:277–8; Strasser 1982:196–8, 206–7, 219–27; Wilson 1979:97–8, 101).

The extensive influence of domestic reform is evident from its being in large part adopted and promoted by other reform movements, such as the Progressives (Wilson 1979:93). Domestic reform activities were also adopted by the large (over 200,000 members by the 1880s) nationwide temperance movement under the leadership of Frances Willard (1879–1898) (Clinton 1984:167, 175–7). Around the turn of the century the General Federation of Women's Clubs became officially committed to domestic reform, especially municipal housekeeping, implemented by its over one million members by 1910. Domestic reform was a basis for connections between a number of associations of women's organizations, including the General Federation of Women's Clubs, the Association of Collegiate Alumnae, the Women's Trade Union League, the National Civic Federation, the National Consumer's League and the National Education Association (Blair 1980:93, 101, 103–6; Wilson 1979:96–100; Woloch 1984:289–90).

Supportive relationships with domestic reformers gave suffragists increased influence and success in promoting culture change. Because suffrage was a smaller radical movement, it only succeeded by allying itself with the more popular domestic reform movements (Hill 1985:35; Kraditor 1971:vii, 51–2). The suffrage movement was not successful until they shifted from directly confronting male dominance to the domestic reform argument that voting women would improve the moral tenor of government and national politics. At the same time, it is evident that experiences of most domestic reformers led them to shift from an anti- to a pro-suffrage position, justified by the domestic reform philosophy that government needed women's innately superior moral influence. The successes of domestic reform in expanding women's roles from the private into the public sphere set the stage for successes by more confrontationally egalitarian public feminist movements in the twentieth century (Clinton 1984:183–7; Rothman 1978:127–32).

Archaeological Significance of Domestic Reform

Materialistic domestic reform deserves historical archaeological research for several interrelated reasons, not least its significant role in the transformation of women's status from the nineteenth into the twentieth centuries. Materialistic domestic reform is particularly appropriate for archaeological research because these movements advocated material culture innovation as the primary mechanism for raising the status of housekeeping occupations. In addition, my Boston area site survey indicates that opportunities to archaeologically research domestic reform are rapidly vanishing (Spencer-Wood 1987b).

Domestic reformers gave new meaning to technological and organizational innovations by using them both to implement and to symbolize the professionalization of housekeeping occupations in the domestic and public spheres. The reformers argued that the use of scientific, industrial scale, or specialized equipment and methods would lead to the treatment of aspects of housework as public professions, equal to men's professions. Material culture was used not only as technological improvements, but also to symbolize the equality of women and men by making their work similar in a number of ways. Housework was professionalized by segmenting it into specialized tasks that were rationally organized and mechanized for maximum efficiency in manufacturing the end products of domestic work, such as a meal, clean laundry, clothing, well-behaved children, or cleanliness, whether in the private home, or in a public institution. This meant that women's work and women were as rational as men and their work, which symbolically counteracted the negative cultural stereotype of women and their work as emotionally driven and irrationally organized. Just as "men's" work had been transformed from a craft level to a higher industrial status by the mechanization of manufacturing and agriculture, domestic reformers advocated mechanizing aspects of domestic work to give them the status of men's public industrial or professional occupations (Giedion 1948; Hayden 1981:55–8; Strasser 1982:180–241).

Materialistic domestic reformers were unusual because they made a conscious connection between changing material culture and changing the ideology of, and behaviors in, gender relationships. The reformers altered material culture and its spatial arrangements in order to create new behaviors related to the sexual division of labor. As in the case of status display, the type and arrangement of material culture was designed to elicit appropriate behavior. The view that material culture proactively causes behavior may be more productive for historical archaeologists than the more traditional, though equally valid, view that material culture reflects, and results from behavior.

The remainder of this section discusses two research areas. First, what can historical archaeologists contribute to our understanding of material-istic domestic reform? New insights into its historical significance and success may be gained through the conjunctive analysis of documents, oral histories, architecture, preserved material culture, and archaeological data. Second, what can historical archaeologists learn about the archaeological record of such cultural processes from the case of materialistic domestic reform? By contrasting documentary and archae-ological data, historical archaeologists may learn more about the biases in each.

The insights expected from historical archaeology may be formulated either as research questions or as hypotheses to be tested with archaeological data from site yards or dumps in communes, towns, or cities. The hypotheses are based on the kinds of data available from the documentary record and expected from the archaeological record. The hypotheses or expectations require tests at a number of sites before any definitive conclusions can be drawn about what archaeologists can learn by researching materialistic domestic reform.

Historical archaeology and our understanding of materialistic domestic reform

With site survey we can research how materialistic domestic reform was implemented by domesticating public space. My survey of 76 Boston sites ca.1865–1905 yielded insights into the way in which different types of domestic reform were implemented through spatial site distribution patterns designed to fulfill the purpose of each type of reform. For instance, kindergartens, day nurseries, and housekeeping cooperatives were located in the neighborhoods they served, whether working-class or middle-class. In contrast, sites for adult education in middle-class domestic science occupations were centrally located in downtown Boston for easy access by public transportation from a number of neighborhoods with potential students. Some types of domestic reform exhibited more than one pattern in domesticating public space. For instance, while the main New England Public Kitchen was centrally located and distributed school lunches throughout Boston, branches were located in the neighborhoods of the immigrant groups they served (Spencer-Wood 1987b). Site surveys in other cities and towns could increase our understanding of the importance of site location to the successful implementation of domestic reform.

Archaeological excavation may increase our understanding of the actual implementation of material culture changes advocated in domestic reform literature. Excavations may indicate if ordinary household utensils and/or specialized equipment were used in domestic reform at particular sites. This is important because reports of domestic reform organizations and institutions (except for some photographs) often do not have detailed descriptions of the equipment and artifacts that they actually used (cf. Cambridge Cooperative Housekeeping Society 1872:2; Massachusetts 1893:270–1; WEA 1872–82, 1873–1929; WEIU 1877–1930). Understanding how domestic reform was realized on the ground is important in understanding how change was successfully implemented by domestic reformers. For example, it can be hypothesized that the success of different domestic reform organizations was related to their degree of integration, both ideologically and materially, into the existing cultural fabric. Archaeological data could indicate the extent to which domestic reform material culture innovations were actually adopted at particular sites, and their path of diffusion among sites throughout America. The degree of implementation of prescribed material culture innovations could be related to degree of success, measured as the longevity of domestic reform activities at a particular site. Site dietary remains could also be compared with documented dietaries to determine any deviations from prescribed and reported diets. Comparison of documentary and archaeological data at well documented sites could shed light on the values of domestic reformers by indicating their extent of curation of materialistic domestic reform artifacts, compared with ordinary artifacts used at domestic reform sites. Comparison of the archaeological and documentary records may reveal some biases in each type of data.

Learning about the archaeological record of cultural processes

Compared with many other processes of culture change, materialistic domestic reform is relatively well documented. By researching this case archaeologists may learn more about the quality and quantity of archaeological data generated by such processes of culture change. Domestic reform ideology was expressed in prescriptive literature, in organizations, and in distinctive types of sites, features, and artifacts. Domestic reformers created grassroots organizations that grew and networked with each other, spreading ideological and material changes from the scale of individuals to the scales of households, groups, communities, regions, nations, and even internationally in Europe. The small- to large-scale direction of this process disproves the systems theory contention that large-scale structures and dynamics determine individual behavior (Binford 1983:221–3). In America domestic reform diffused predominantly among cities and towns first in the Northeast, then spreading to the West and South. In the second half of the nineteenth century the amount of female-dominated public space increased as domestic reform organizations, sites, features, and artifacts proliferated, domesticating the public landscape in urban areas across the United States. The diffusion pattern of many domestic reform sites expresses the pattern of women's networks as they were activated over time for domestic reform.

The question for archaeologists is: what material record is expected from this cultural process? Because it was initiated ideologically, few archaeological remains are expected of the incipient stages of the domestic reform cultural change process. Few distinctive features or artifacts are expected from the many sites where domestic reformers adapted standing structures to their purposes, and carefully curated their innovative artifacts: therefore, the few archaeological remains expected from the early stages of domestic reform have greater cultural significance than their numbers might seem to indicate. These archaeological data, even if few in number, are significant indicators of initial perturbations that aggregated over time to transform gender concepts and behaviors in a cultural system (Clarke 1978:23–148). The expected infrequency of early domestic reform sites, features, and artifacts means that a larger sample from early sites may be required to find archaeological evidence of incipient domestic reform, compared with its later stages.

As materialistic domestic reform endured, became more widespread, common and integrated into the cultural mainstream, its sites, features, and artifacts became more frequent, more widely distributed, and probably less carefully curated, resulting in more archaeological remains. If archaeological remains of these movements are usually found only after they become widespread, this would support the hypothesis of a temporal lag between the incipient stage of culture change and its archaeological remains. It is hypothesized that the documented diffusion paths of materialistic domestic reform would be incompletely expressed in the temporal distribution of its sites. Since the relationship between the spread of domestic reform ideology and the distribution of sites, features, and artifacts is documented to some extent, it forms an ideal case to test how the archaeological record is related to processes of cultural change in this case. By comparing documentary and archae-ological data, archaeologists can analyze how this process is expressed-in the archaeological record. It is possible that the absence of archae-ological data could be as important as its presence in learning about relationships between the archaeological record and processes of culture change.

Research Strategy

In order to research materialistic domestic reform sites, they must first be identified through documents or archaeological data. This section discusses methods and problems of using documents to identify such sites, the likelihood of finding domestic reform archaeological data at sites, the expected locations of archaeological remains, and the probable effects of site formation processes. Finally, I consider the probable effects of factors that create variation in archaeological potential among sites. These expected site differences in archaeological potential require tests at a number of sites to assess their probability of occurrence.

Identification of materialistic domestic reform sites

Due to a number of limitations, documentary data may not always permit archaeologists to identify materialistic domestic reform use(s) of a site. It is easiest to identify sites of well established property-owning organizations, which are often named on historic maps, starting in the second half of the nineteenth century. Looking up the names of mapped organizations in town histories and guidebooks often yields descriptions of their activities, permitting the identification of materialistic domestic reform functions of sites. Another, albeit more time consuming, method is to scan the separate list of social agencies found in many city and town business directories, again starting in the second half of the nineteenth century. Business directory addresses can be located on contemporary historic maps, and the mapped building footprint can be compared with any surviving building for information on site integrity and disturbance. Materialistic domestic reform institutions can be initially identified on the basis of the general type of social agency, such as industrial schools for girls, cooking or housekeeping schools, kindergartens, day nurseries, public kitchens, or cooperatives. However, the existence of a domestic reform function may not be identifiable from the name of the social agency at the site (e.g., the Door of Hope). Further identification of materialistic domestic reform activities and site addresses may be obtained from descriptions of social organizations in town histories, guidebooks, or in records of such organizations, if preserved in some town, school, or feminist archive (Spencer-Wood 1987b).

Starting with a site, it is difficult, and often impossible, to identify its rental or use for materialistic domestic reform activities. It is very time consuming to identify rentors from censuses, business directories, or town records, because they are not organized by address, requiring scanning of the entire list of residents' names. The shape and appearance of mapped and photographed buildings used for domestic reform may not be distinguishable from domestic buildings, or schools. Historic maps and deeds usually only name site owners, and possibly the occupation of the head of household; if a wife or daughter of a site owner or rentor used the site for domestic reform activities this will seldom, if ever, be recorded in the site documents normally used by archaeologists in reconstructing a site's history (Spencer-Wood 1984). In addition, sites rented for a short period or temporarily used for materialistic domestic reform activities are less likely to have archaeological remains of these activities than are the more easily identifiable sites owned and operated for a number of years by domestic reform organizations.

Materialistic domestic reform sites that cannot be identified from documents may be identifiable from archaeological remains of distinctive features and artifacts depicted in the wealth of domestic reform prescriptive literature. It is also possible that organizational records may include descriptions or photographs (more likely) of features or artifacts used in domestic reform activities. If domestic reform site information processes and the resulting archaeological deposits are not disturbed by subsequent site formation processes, distinctive features and artifacts may be recovered. The identification of domestic reform sites is often not obvious, because they may appear identical to domestic sites, both structurally and in many, if not most, of their artifacts. Some possible archaeological features, such as unusually large room divisions in a basement foundation, may result from cooperative housekeeping facilities. Domestic-type reform sites usually have back yards where archaeological deposits are expected (Spencer-Wood 1987b); primary deposition may occur through loss during activities in the yard, or through discard behaviours, such as the scatter of sheet refuse layers across a yard, or deposits of trash in trashpits, privypits, or outbuilding foundations.

Other materialistic domestic reform structures are institutional in size, and may be indistinguishable from other institutions. In basement foundations, industrial scale furnaces, chimneys, or footings for large-scale equipment may indicate cooperative housekeeping facilities in communes, hotels, tenements, or homes for working women; however, such industrial scale features could also be found at hospital and other institutional sites. Insitutional domestic reform sites may or may not have yards where primary deposition could take place, as described above. Municipal trash collection may have removed most archaeological remains from institutional sites in middle- and upper-class neighborhoods. Dumps for cities, towns, and communes are expected to include some materialistic domestic reform artifacts. However, many types of relevant artifacts may not be found archaeologically because they were carefully curated or were made of nondurable materials, such as wood, paper, and cloth, which are not usually preserved in archaeological contexts. Food remains, unless buried, would often have been eaten by animals such as dogs and rats.

Site formation processes and relative archaeological potential

Variety in human behavior creates variation in site formation processes and archaeological potential among different types of materialistic domestic reform sites. The possibility of finding relevant archaeological remains at any particular site results from the particular combination of behaviors at a site, in conjunction with preservation factors. Documentary and archaeological evidence indicates that some archaeological deposition is to be expected in most site yards. In many cases materialistic domestic reformers may have lost or discarded mostly ordinary artifacts in site yards, carefully curating material culture innovations of types depicted in prescriptive literature (cf.Wheelock College Archives). However, this hypothesis may only hold for the initial stage of materialistic domestic reform.

The class of site residents is expected to affect the amount and frequency of loss or discard of material in site yards. Middle- and upper-class sites often have a relatively low frequency of archaeological remains, because site residents usually conformed to cultural norms of landscaping and fairly complete trash removal. In contrast, municipal services, including trash removal, were often minimal to non-existent in poor neighborhoods, resulting in high archaeological potential for such site yards (Baldwin 1900:4–6, 19–20; Bangs et al. 1908:7–8, 20–1; Bangs et al. 1910:6–9; Blake 1959:209, 223, 237–8; Boston 1890:71–2; Bower et al. 1984:187–94, 212–14, 236; Bower et al. 1986; CAD 1851:v, 1852:6, 1864:18, 1879:326–7, 1891:258, 1985:15, 1897:260, 1914:168; Clarke 1879:4–5, 1885:11; Cox et al. 1981; De Cunzo 1987:278, 284, 286–8; 1983:379–81, 394; Dickens and Bowen 1980:46; Garrow 1982:1985–6; Henn 1985:206; Ingersoll 1971; Kleinberg 1976:59; LeeDecker et al. 1987:247; Melosi 1981:21–50, 134–9, 152–62; Nesson 1983:7; Porter 1889:27–45; RBPR 1919:71–3; Rothschild and Rockman 1982:4; Shephard 1987:173; Singer 1987:94–5; Spencer-Wood 1987b:9–10, 29; Strasser 1980:39–45; Woloch 1984:293). Class differences in municipal trash removal leads to the hypothesis that town and city dumps would contain more artifacts from materialistic domestic reform sites in middle- and upper-class neighborhoods, than from sites in poor neighborhoods. Data from urban dumps could indicate the spatial diffusion and relative density of wealthier types of materialistic domestic reform sites that had distinctive artifacts, such as cooked food delivery services.

The amount of archaeological deposition in a site yard is expected to vary with the age of its residents, with the greatest amount expected by children, the least by adults, and adolescents in between, all other factors being equal. Sites serving children, such as kindergartens and day nurseries, are expected to have the largest density of archaeological deposition, much of it from primary contexts of playing in yards. Sites serving adolescents, such as industrial schools for girls, are expected to have the second highest density of archaeological deposition, and site types used only by adults, such as adult domestic science schools, are expected to have the lowest density.

Greater density of archaeological deposition is expected at sites with the heaviest use, all other things being equal. The higher density of population in poor compared to middle- and upper-class neighborhoods leads to the hypothesis that sites in these areas may receive the greatest use and resulting archaeological deposition.

Despite the normal limitations of documentary and archaeological data, historical archaeological research could increase our understanding of materialistic domestic reform, and/or of the archaeological record of cultural processes, as previously discussed. To address either of these research areas archaeologists must first be able to identify relevant sites and recognize the meaning of their features and artifacts. The rest of this paper discusses distinctive types of features and artifacts that archaeologists can use to identify such sites. The meaning of features and artifacts is discussed in the particular context of materialistic domestic reform, so that they can be properly interpreted – this is important because ordinary domestic artifacts may have different meanings or functions in domestic reform than in the general cultural context in which they are usually interpreted. Arrangements of artifacts and features are discussed to provide the basis for interpretations of the domestic reform meanings of archaeological remains and contextual associations.

The rest of the chapter is divided into sections that describe different site types and hypothesize materialistic domestic reform site formation behaviors and relative archaeological potential. The sections progress from domestic reform in the home to extensions of the domestic sphere into the public sphere of the community, including cooperatives, domestic services, and domestic education. After discussing the meaning of sites, features, and artifacts in the context of materialistic domestic reform, the likelihood of finding archaeological remains, and the research problems that could be addressed, are discussed. The archaeological hypotheses for each site type, while reasonably formulated from documentary data, require testing at a number of sites before any definitive conclusion can be drawn about what historical archaeologists can learn from researching materialistic domestic reform.

Professionalizing Housework at Home

In the home the goal of materialistic domestic reform was to make women dominant in the domestic sphere, a radical change from the tradition of male dominance. The reformers argued that women's innately superior domestic abilities justified their control over domestic activities in the home. Scientific-industrial principles and technology were used to recreate housework as a female profession, and to argue that its status was equal to men's public sphere professions (Strasser 1982:188, 213; Woloch 1984:295–7).

Materialistic domestic reform was advocated in books and manuals advising homemakers. Starting in the nineteenth century, reform books provided systematically organized advice, replacing earlier disorganized collections of household hints. By recreating housekeeping as a profession, women could control household decisions through the use of specialized knowledge, facilities, and equipment (Handlin 1979:55–8). Materialistic domestic reformers promoted the efficient organization of household work processes through logical arrangements of furniture and equipment, sometimes modelled after steamship galley or hotel kitchen ideas (Beecher and Stowe 1869:32–4; Frederick 1923:394). As most nineteenth-century homes lost their earlier productive functions and became primarily places for consumption and reproduction, household recipes for the production of candles, soap, and other items declined, while advice on intelligent consumption, efficient housekeeping, and on raising children increased. Household needs for good food, water, air, and waste disposal connected family and community health, extending domestic sphere advice into areas of municipal housekeeping, including tenement reform, public hygiene, municipal water and sewerage, and regulation of food products and pollution (Beecher and Stowe 1869:433–52; Broadhurst 1918; Richards 1905, 1907, 1908, 1910).

The most widely popular ideas for materially reforming housework were in: (1) domestic science manuals by Catherine E. Beecher (1841) and by Beecher and her sister, Harriet Beecher Stowe (1869); (2) books in home economics by Ellen Swallow Richards (1901, 1904, 1905, 1907, 1908; and (3) Christine Frederick's household engineering manual (1923). The Beecher sisters' manuals combined a missionary religious world-view with a rational approach. They were the most popular books of their kind in the second half of the nineteenth century, and were the first manuals to apply scientific principles to professionalize housework (Handlin 1979:55). Richards, a sanitary chemist, was the first female student and professor at MIT (Hayden 1981:157). In the late nineteenth and early twentieth centuries she founded the home economics movement and wrote a number of advice books on household applications of scientific principles in nutrition and sanitation (Richards 1901, 1904, 1905, 1907, 1908). Richards promoted sanitary households through the use of material culture such as glass shelves and tables, which were used as antiseptic surfaces in hospitals (Richards 1905:72). In the early twentieth century Frederick applied Taylor's business principles to segment housework into specialized tasks, suggesting the most efficient method for accomplishing each task. She arranged laundry and kitchen equipment and furniture for efficient sequencing of tasks and advocated the use of all kinds of innovative electrical and mechanical appliances, fireless cookers, steam cookers, an icebox on a dumbwaiter that could be raised from the cellar for use in the kitchen, and a kitchen cabinet unit that combined a work table with pantry cupboards above and below (figure 11.1; figure 11.2; Frederick 1923:6–264; Strasser 1982:206–18).

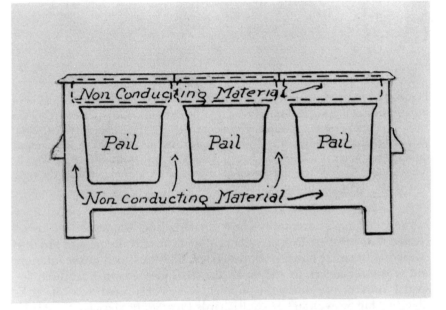

Figure 11.1 Frederick advocated using the fireless cooker. It cooks slowly by retaining heat in 3 covered pails packed in insulation in a box 1–2 feet wide by 3–4 feet long. Food first heated on a conventional stove was completely cooked by retained heat in a covered cylindrical handle-less pot that fit closely in one of the insulated pails. Soapstone disks could also be heated on a stove and used as the heat source for slow cooking by placing them under and on top of covered cylindrical pots in the insulated pails of the fireless cooker (Frederick 1923:130–2; Lynde 1916:108–9; Wellman 1928:249–52). The extent to which fireless cookers were used could be indicated by the frequency of parts, such as cylindrical handle-less pots and pails with lids, archaeologically recovered in household or town dumps

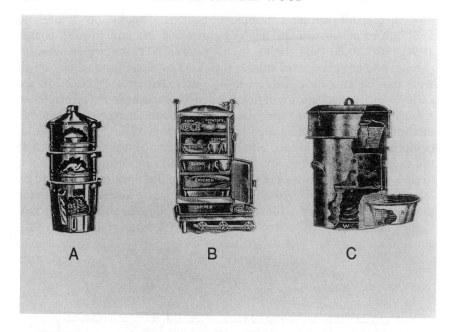

Figure 11.2 (A) 1902 steam cooker sold by S. W. Chamberlin Co., with food in metal dishes inside stacked metal pots ([advertisement] 1902). **(B)** and **(C)** Two later types of steam cookers recommended by Frederick (1923:132–3). Archaeologists could find metal parts of such steamers, including inner metal dishes with holes, outer metal containers, or doors from square cooker B. Remains of steam cookers in household or town dumps would indicate their use in households or communities respectively

These manuals exemplify how materialistic domestic reformers created rational spatial arrangements of innovative equipment in order to efficiently organize housework processes. They designed house interiors and work sequences to minimize the distance and time required for spatial movements among equipment used in related sets of tasks (Beecher and Stowe 1869:34–6; Richards 1905:86; Frederick 1923:22–3). The reformers promoted the application of the latest scientific technology to create efficient house designs and housekeeping machinery that would decrease the amount of work and time required by housework. The Beechers and Richards, as well as a number of other domestic reformers, also proposed dress reform to eliminate tight corsets and heavy petticoats that physically crippled women, making housework more difficult to perform (Beecher and Stowe 1869:158–66; Richards 1910, 1907:55; Russell 1892). Domestic reformers advocated women's autonomous control of the domestic sphere and of their persons.

Besides applying public sphere scientific, industrial, and business principles to professionalize housework, materialistic domestic reformers also expanded the domestic sphere into the public sphere. The Beechers designed efficient tenement layouts, and Richards and Frederick advocated efficient house designs for the working and middle classes (Beecher and Stowe 1869:433–47; Richards 1905:72, 86). Reformers also expanded the domestic sphere by arguing for the higher education of women in domestic science (Strasser 1982:202–23).

Historical archaeologists may be able to assess the degree of adoption of mechanization and efficient arrangements for household furnishings, equipment, and utensils. The popularity of domestic reform manuals increases the likelihood that their recommended material culture innovations would be implemented by some women who could afford them. In the late nineteenth and early twentieth centuries, it can be hypothesized that few archaeological remains may be found except in rural areas, because the wealthier urban households probably kept clean yards, and the poorer households could not afford the new material culture (Beecher 1841:291–4; Downing 1850; Fuller 1891; Wright 1980:10–11, 29). Over the twentieth century the cost of technological housekeeping innovations decreased, resulting in their diffusion into all but the poorest homes. Archaeological data from house yards in rural areas, or in neighborhoods without adequate municipal trash collection, may contribute to our understanding of how scientific housekeeping technology diffused from wealthier to moderate income homes (Strasser 1982; Woloch 1984:293). As these artifacts became increasingly common, archaeologists can expect to find a wider distribution of more remnants of recommended furniture, equipment, machines, or utensils in house yards and town dumps. Some materialistic domestic reform features might also be found in excavations of house foundations, such as the basement room layout and drain suggested by the Beechers (figure 11.3).

More information on the implementation of materialistic domestic reform may be gained from above-ground, rather than below-ground, archaeology. The Beecher sisters, Richards, and Frederick used their homes, as well as those of other interested housewives, to test innovative machinery, equipment, utensils and their best arrangement. Above-ground archaeology of structure walls might permit the reconstruction of room arrangements, while floor marks or built-in spaces in rooms can indicate the placement of equipment, such as stoves and refrigerators. Small utensils could be found in walls, just as they would be found in some house yards. The implementation of domestic reform ideals can also be researched in the houses of domestic reformers that are preserved and restored, as is the Harriet Beecher Stowe house in Hartford (Why 1975:10). Above- and below-ground archaeology at the house sites of materialistic

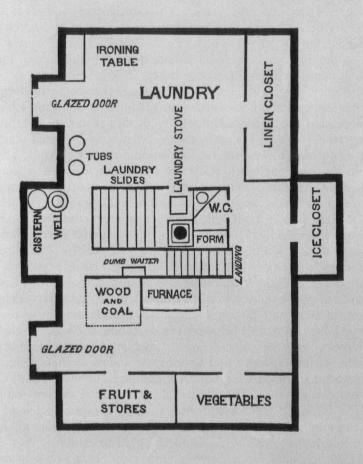

Figure 11.3 Beecher designed a basement laundry containing tubs efficiently arranged with pipes above to conduct cold water from a garret reservoir and hot water from the stove. Plugs in the bottom let water out to a drain in the floor. The laundry stove heated irons, while the laundry slides were drawn out for wet clothes and put in the linen closet to dry (Beecher and Stowe 1869:38–41). Archaeological remains, such as tub drains, could indicate the extent to which this type of design was implemented in middle and upper-class households

domestic reformers might permit some assessment of the extent to which they followed their own recommendations.

Cooperatives

Cooperatives resisted the cultural ideal of male-dominated individual households, where the same housework tasks were repeated by each woman in isolation. In housework cooperatives women from different families cooperated to rationally organize larger-scale production processes in the public sphere. Cooperatives drew on beliefs in the community as family, and in the scientific efficiency of collective labor, developed by communitarian socialists such as Fourier, Owen, Whitwell, and Brisbane. The idea of cooperatives spread from Europe to the United States, becoming most popular in the nineteenth century (Holloway 1966:101–59; Hayden 1981:7, 20, 35–9; Hayden 1976).

The professionalization of housework in the public sphere included both participant-cooperatives and commercial enterprises through which a number of households shared common cooking, laundry, or childcare facilities. While the religious and social purposes of cooperatives varied, they all implemented some form of socialized housekeeping, making it a profession similar to men's industrial scale work in the public sphere. Cooperative housekeeping enterprises included (1) utopian communities, (2) neighborhood housekeeping cooperatives, (3) cooperative tenements and apartment houses or hotels, and (4) working women's cooperative homes.

Cooperatives in utopian communities

Some of the most famous utopian communities that practiced domestic reform included 19 Shaker communities (founded 1774–1826), three Rappite Harmony Society towns (founded 1805–24), 15 Owenite communes (founded in the 1820s), 30 Fourierist Associations (1840s), the Oneida Perfectionists (1847–78), Brook Farm (1841–6), seven Amana Inspirationist communes (starting 1855), and Hutterites (Hayden 1981:35–8). Despite widely varying religious beliefs, most utopian communities had connections with other domestic reform movements philosophically, methodologically, and in personnel. Shared enlightenment beliefs led to the development of similar public cooperative housekeeping organizations, work processes, and types of material culture in communes and neighborhoods. Utopian communes usually included cooperative kitchens, laundries, infant schools, and kindergartens that served as models for the development of neighborhood cooperative enterprises in towns. In addition, many utopian communes served as gathering points and training grounds for reformers who often later worked in other domestic reform organizations. For example, Abby Morton Diaz taught at the Brook Farm infant school (1842–7), and subsequently became president of Boston's Women's Educational and Industrial Union (1881–92) (Bernardete 1971).

In the nineteenth century most communes subscribed to the philosophy of enlightenment egalitarianism. They considered all work equal, although traditional separation of sex roles continued and women usually performed cooperative domestic work. Communards believed that with efficient organization collective socialized labor could be more productive than the duplication of housework in individual homes. Utopian communities made housework equivalent to other types of public labor through mechanization and rationally organizing it on an industrial scale.

Following perfectionist beliefs, many communes increased the efficiency of socialized domestic work through labor divisions and specialization, standardized facilities for cooperative work, labor-saving innovations, and industrial scale equipment and furniture. At the Oneida Community, the latest heating, lighting, and sanitation devices were used to maximize members' health while decreasing domestic labor. Shaker domestic innovations for increased efficiency included a washing machine, the common clothespin, an apple peeler and corer, a pea sheller, a cheese press, a round oven, a double rolling pin, a removable window sash, the flat broom, and a conical stove for heating irons. The Oneida Perfectionists invented methods of fruit preservation, an improved washing machine, an improved mop wringer, an institutional potato peeler, and a "lazy susan" table to facilitate food service. A number of communes generated income by selling their labor-saving innovations, cooperative furniture, and toys to outsiders (Hayden 1976:23, 197–8, 200; Hayden 1981:39–49). In collective systems of cooking, eating, laundry, cleaning, and childcare, work was organized in large spaces with logical arrangements of industrial scale furniture and equipment and ordinary domestic utensils, often in larger numbers than would be used in a household (Anonymous 1873:13).

Historical archaeology has contributed, and could contribute further, to our understanding of cooperative communes. Although the sites of utopian communes are not as common as some other site types, several hundred were established in the United States between 1663 and 1918 (Hayden 1976:362–6). Excavations at Shaker communes have yielded some functionally specific artifacts and large foundation features indicating collective cooperation in cooking, weaving, and education in separate structures (figure 11.4). However, more artifacts were found in

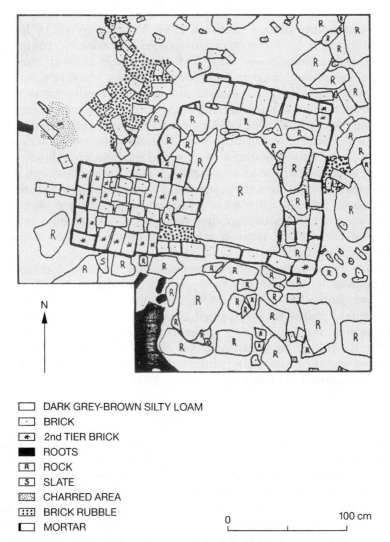

N

0   100 cm

Figure 11.4 Excavations in 1983 at the site of the North Family dwelling house at Hancock Shaker Village in Hancock, Massachusetts, revealed this large chimney foundation which probably supported a large brick hearth and oven similar to the one in Hancock's main Church Family dwelling. The fireplace in the North Family dwelling was used for large-scale communal cooking for the 28 to 40 church members living in this probably three-and-one-half storey dwelling. When it was built in 1821 the North Family dwelling measured 60 feet by 40 feet. As the membership of the North Family grew a northern wing measuring 24.5 feet by 28 feet was added in the 1830s or 1840s. The dwelling house was moved to the main Church Family settlement shortly after the North Family was dissolved in 1867 (Vaillancourt 1983:47, 57–9, 80, 83, 86–7)

large community dumps (Starbuck 1984; Vaillancourt 1983). In those communes that used basements for cooperative cooking, baking, and preserving, archaeologists may find foundations divided into large rooms; in addition, we may find footings for large chimneys, stoves, or communal housekeeping equipment, such as laundry presses. The distribution of cooking, eating, sewing and other domestic remains could indicate the extent to which domestic activities were centralized in a few large-scale cooperatives or distributed between cooperatives and private homes. The relative amounts of large versus small pots could indicate the degree of large-scale versus small-scale cooking. Such archaeological data could indicate how domestic cooperation was actually implemented, and whether it differed from what is documented for some communes. Excavation of communal trash dumps could yield information about the use and curation of labor-saving innovations from their degree of breakage, loss and discard.

From artifact analyses of non-commune domestic sites, archaeologists might be able to learn about the process and degree of diffusion of domestic (and other) innovations from communes into the larger society. Widespread diffusion is expected to result from the popularity of cooperation and labor-saving equipment. For example, archaeologists might be able to find out whether Shaker housework innovations diffused into the mainstream culture to the widespread extent that many of their products did (e.g., seeds, chairs, boxes).

Neighborhood cooperatives

Starting in the second half of the nineteenth century, neighborhood cooperatives included laundries, bakeries, dining clubs, and cooked food delivery services. Individual households in a neighborhood formed cooperatives in the public sphere that commercially performed certain household tasks on an industrial scale. These cooperatives run by women resisted male dominance both in the private home and in the public sphere. Despite some success, cooperatives never completely replaced housework in individual homes. The most successful types of neighborhood co-operatives were cooperative kitchens, dining clubs, and cooked food delivery services. At least 33 of these cooperatives operated for periods ranging from six months to 30 years, each serving between five and 20 families in towns across the USA between 1869 and the 1920s (Clinton 1984:193; Hayden 1981:66–89; 207–27).

It is possible that archaeological remains would be found in the yards or foundatons of cooperative sites that were occupied for a number of years. Such remains are most likely in site yards in rural areas, and in working-class or suburban neighborhoods with inadequate municipal trash collection. In contrast to domestic sites, sites of large-scale cooperative cooking institutions may yield industrial scale, or larger amounts, of cooking and food transporting equipment. Remains of specially insulated metal buckets for transporting food in stacked covered metal or glass cylindrical dishes may permit archaeologists to distinguish middle- and upper-class cooked food delivery sites from other industrial scale kitchen sites (figure 11.5; Hayden 1981:207–27, 345–55; Norton 1927:25–6; Schleier 1918). Faunal remains could indicate whether cooperative kitchens used unusually large cuts of meat, or cuts normally available in retail markets. Such data could yield information about the often undocumented diets offered by cooperative kitchens, and the extent of industrial versus household equipment use. In above- or below-ground archaeology large domestic structures with large rooms may distinguish middle- and upper-class dining clubs from working-class cooperative kitchens housed in ordinary domestic structures. Working-class cooperative kitchen site yards are expected to yield remains of inexpensive food and ordinary household equipment, in contrast to the remains of more expensive food and special equipment that would probably be found less frequently in the yards of dining clubs and cooked food delivery services in wealthier neighborhoods (figure 11.5; Anonymous 1918; Fox and Lendrum 1919). Dietary data from co-operatives could be compared with domestic reformers' ideal dietaries to assess the degree to which cooperatives followed these ideals (cf.Richards 1901, 1904; Rose 1916). Comparisons of cooperative and domestic site dietary remains could indicate whether and how cooperative diets varied from domestic diets.

Cooperative housekeeping in tenements and apartment hotels

Cooperative housekeeping facilities were sometimes constructed in working-class tenements, and were popular in apartment hotels for the urban middle and upper classes; both had common cooking, dining, laundry, and childcare facilities (Cushing 1982:74; Hayden 1981:156, 189–93, 229–61). Hotel servants freed women from performing housekeeping, and gave them time to organize social movements, such as domestic reform. However, in some apartment hotels cooperative cooking and dining was optional, with private dining rooms and kitchens in apartments, in addition to cooperative facilities (Hayden 1981:69–86; Handlin 1979:398–402).

More archaeological remains are expected in the yards of cooperative tenements than at the sites of cooperative apartment hotels. It is unlikely that much discard of industrial housekeeping equipment or expensive china would occur at the urban sites of upper-class apartment hotels,

Figure 11.5 Archaeologists might find remains indicating the extent to which specialized containers were used for the delivery of cooked food to wealthier homes, whether from food delivery services, cooperative kitchens, or dining clubs. Food transportation containers retained heat with insulation between an outer and an inner covered cylindrical metal bucket. In this pail were stocked a number of closely fitting cylindrical handle-less dishes of metal or glass. Liveried servants often made deliveries to middle and upper-class homes. In contrast, a working-class cooked food delivery service used children on foot to deliver food in fruit jars packed in newspaper in oatmeal cartons (anonymous 1918:97 Fox and Lendrum 1919; Hayden 1981:216–17, 222–3; Norton 1927:25–6; Schleier 1918:97)

except possibly in back alleys. The frequent use of hotel and tenement basements for cooperative housekeeping facilities may result in archaeologically distinct foundation features, such as large room divisions, large chimneys, and footings for industrial equipment (American Architect and Building News 1877:188; Hayden 1981:75–6, 199, 255–7). Archaeological deposition is likely in the yards of working-class tenements with cooperative facilities, due to lack of enforcement of clean-yard laws in working-class areas (Baldwin 1900; Henn 1985; Kleinberg 1976; Porter 1889; Rothschild and Rockman 1982; Woloch 1984:293). Archaeologists may find remains indicating the extent to which working-class cooperatives used household versus the industrial scale equipment prescribed in domestic reformers' cooperative tenement designs (cf. Hayden 1981:156). Archaeological food remains might indicate whether cooperative tenements had a higher quality diet than non-cooperative tenements. Further, the variation in cooperative tenement diets from materialistic domestic reform ideals might be assessed by comparing archaeological dietary remains with prescriptive literature (cf.Richards 1901, 1904; Rose 1916).

Cooperative Homes for Working Women

Homes with cooperative housekeeping were established by domestic reformers to support working women in resisting exploitation by slum landlords. By organizing cooperatively women could afford decent, pleasant housing and avoid the crowded unsanitary conditions in slum boarding houses. In addition, working women in cooperative homes supported each other to prevent those temporarily out of work or on strike from being put out on the street (Baldwin 1900; Eaves 1917:102; Hayden 1981:167–71; Porter 1889; Stein 1898).

Working women's homes can be divided into three types: (1) homes with cooperative housekeeping by and for the residents, (2) cooperative homes that also provided job training, work, and/or employment services, (3) social settlement houses, where working women (and/or men) reformers lived together to cooperate not only in housekeeping, but more importantly in providing social services to the community. Each of these types of cooperative homes is considered below in detail, including possible archaeological remains.

Cooperative working women's homes were the most successful widespread form of urban cooperative housekeeping, and are expected to have relatively high archaeological potential because they were located in poorer neighborhoods where clean-yard laws were often not enforced, and year-round refuse collection was often not implemented through the early decades of the twentieth century (Baldwin 1900; Hayden 1981:162,

169–70; Henn 1985; Kleinberg 1976; Porter 1889:27–9; Rothschild and Rockman 1982; Woloch 1984:293). In many cases typical domestic houses were used for such homes, making it difficult to identify these sites from the structure, or if rented, from documents (Spencer-Wood 1987b). In general, sites of cooperative women's homes may be archaeologically identifiable from the scarcity of distinctive male-oriented artifacts in site yards, and the subdivision of basement foundations into large rooms for cooperative housekeeping. Excavation of site yards may yield information about the seldom documented kinds of equipment and utensils of industrial or domestic types used in these homes. Archaeological food remains from site yards could yield information about diets at different types of homes for working women.

Working women's homes with cooperative housekeeping Homes with cooperative housekeeping by working women residents include two types: (1) homes organized by philanthropic groups for women temporarily out of work, and (2) homes shared and often organized by working women for mutual support. Examples of the latter ranged from the famous union-supporting Jane Club in Chicago (1891) and the Ladies' Garment Workers Union Unity House in New York (1919), to the common practice of working women co-renting an apartment or house and sharing housekeeping expenses (Hayden 1981:167–70).

Archaeological research may contribute information about the methods of cooperative housekeeping practiced at working women's homes. While many women's homes were located in typical domestic-type row houses, cooperative use of space often was evident in large common dining rooms, parlors, kitchens, and laundries (Hayden 1981:167–9). Large cooperative spaces may be identifiable through above- or below-ground archaeology, especially if remains of basement foundations are divided into large spaces with footings for a large chimney, industrial stove, or laundry equipment. Cooperative homes run by working women or philanthropic organizations probably used mostly ordinary domestic equipment, rather than more expensive industrial scale equipment. Archaeological testing in the back yards of cooperative homes could indicate whether or not residents used ordinary equipment and utensils. Archaeologists could also determine whether such homes used uniform sets or mixes of cheap and dear dishes and utensils. If old styles of dishes and other equipment were acquired second-hand and carefully curated, site deposits may appear older archaeologically than they actually were. Uniform dishes, glasses, and utensils might indicate a home with more restrictive regulation of its residents than homes without such uniformity.

Philanthropic women's homes with educational and employment services Some homes offered domestic employment managed by the home, which paid the residents for their production and sold their domestic goods to maintain the home. For example, the Temporary Home for Working Women in Boston employed women in sewing and laundry work for hospitals (Landy and Greenblatt 1965:14–15). Of homes offering domestic education YWCAs were the most widespread and numerous; these were first organized in London in 1855, modelling after YMCAs. The first American YWCA was organized in Boston in 1866, and they soon increased in number, spreading to 225 cities by 1891 (Clinton 1984:170; Wilson 1979:99). YWCAs offered a wide variety of services, including domestic education and employment services. Besides cooperative dining rooms, kitchens, parlors, and laundries, YWCAs had lecture halls, reading rooms, gymnasiums, class rooms, and cafés or club rooms (Hayden 1981:199; King 1885:205; Wilson 1979:99; Stein 1898).

In the yards of institutions providing domestic education or employment archaeologists may find more housekeeping equipment and utensils than at sites of homes using cooperative housekeeping only for living needs of the house residents. In the yards of such homes archaeologists can expect to find small-scale housework tools, such as sewing needles, pins, buttons, and hooks, or kitchen utensils from cooking classes. The relative frequency of some domestic reform activities might be indicated by the frequency of archaeological remains of small artifacts associated with different activities. In addition, archaeology at the sites of institutions providing domestic education or employment might find the large foundations divided into a number of large work and class rooms. In the yards of YWCAs archaeologists might also find remnants of industrial scale equipment, used to train women for professional domestic jobs, such as in commercial laundries. Archaeologists could also find remnants of YWCA-imprinted white tableware, and possibly even its silverware (less likely). It is hypothesized that only working women's homes such as the YWCA, because of its large number of homes nationwide, could afford to have tableware and silverware made with its own insignia.

Comparative analysis of diets at women's homes Archaeologists may also find dietary remains in the yards of cooperative homes for working women. Such remains could be compared with documentary records of diets offered at homes. Differences between the archaeological and documentary records of such diets could be explained in some cases by bias in the archaeological record, and in other cases could increase our information about the range of variation in diets and nutrition offered to working women in cooperative homes. A 1917 study reports the diets supplied in 20 women's homes, ranging from charitable to cooperative. These records could be compared with the ideal and experimental diets suggested in nutrition books by domestic reformers (Eaves 1917:101–25; Richards 1901:37–51; Rose 1916:82–96). Archaeological data might corroborate part of the documented diet for working women's homes, or it might indicate some deviations in the actual diet from that reported for a particular site.

Social settlement houses At social settlement houses, such as Hull House in Chicago, college-educated women and/or men cooperated both in housekeeping and in providing social services to the community. The number of American settlement houses grew from six in 1891 to over 400 by 1910 (Clinton 1984:178; Wilson 1979:100). Social settlement workers held professional jobs outside the settlement, and shared equally in the costs of cooperative housekeeping, including cooks, laundresses, and domestics. They also cooperated on the social work projects of the settlement, as volunteers after work hours. Hull House social projects included (1) evening classes in cooking, sewing, music, literature, trade-union organizing; (2) social clubs; (3) a day nursery and kindergarten for working mothers, established in 1891 by Jane Addams and Jenny Dow; (4) a public kitchen; (5) successful lobbying for legislation to improve the health and safety of industrial working conditions, to limit child labor, and to recognize trade unions; and (6) agitation for public parks (Addams 1910; Clinton 1984:181; Rothman 1978:112–19).

At settlement house sites above- and below-ground archaeology could find foundations and footings for the same types of cooperative housekeeping facilities and equipment expected in many working women's cooperative homes. In addition, foundations might be found of social work spaces which were often even larger, in order to serve the surrounding community. While Hull House was unusual in having a public kitchen, the large community day nursery, class and club rooms could be expected in many other settlement houses (Davis 1967; Woods 1898). Excavations of site yards may yield remains of industrial scale cooking and laundry equipment in combination with expensive tableware. Additional specialized equipment was used at some settlements in classes such as cooking, sewing, and gymnasium, in day nurseries, and public kitchens. In the yards of settlement houses archaeologists might find remnants of a mix of ordinary tableware, or uniform tableware in some cases, bunsen burners and utensils from cooking classes or a public kitchen, sewing needles, pins, and possibly toys from a day nursery (Hayden 1981:164–73).

Domestic Reform and Community Services

Materialistic domestic reformers founded a number of institutions that provided domestic services to working-class communities and families. Three types of domestic service institutions are discussed below: (1) day care and infant education, including day nurseries, kindergartens, and kitchen gardens, (2) industrial schools for girls, and (3) public kitchens. Such institutions provided domestic services, such as childcare and cooked food, that working women often could not provide to their families. In addition, these institutions provided socially meaningful domestic professions outside the home for non-working wealthier women, and assisted in socializing immigrant children, women, and families into American cultural values and normative behaviors. Some of these institutions also provided working women with job training in domestic services. Some institutions combined more than one domestic service; for example, social settlement houses offered professional housekeeping services and education in the public sphere, such as industrial school for girls, day nurseries, kindergartens, and public kitchens. The following discussion pertains to settlement houses, as well as to other institutions offering one or more of the above services (Ross 1976:34–47).

Day care and infant education

The meaning of the terms "kitchen garden," "kindergarten," and "day nursery" have changed and merged over time. The first two types of childcare services were designed to be educational. The kitchen garden, designed by American domestic reformer Emily Huntington in 1875, provided domestic education and skills to poor or black primary-grade children after school, using miniature domestic equipment (Hayden 1981:125–8). The kindergarten encouraged harmonious creative self-development of children's mental and physical capacities, through orderly educational play that combined mental and manual training. Specially designed toys were used to symbolically communicate to children beliefs as well as scientific facts. The kindergarten was invented by Friedrich Froebel (1782–1852), a German, and the first German-American kindergarten was established by Froebel's student Mrs Carl Schurz in Watertown, Wisconsin, in 1855, followed by the first American English kindergarten, founded by Elizabeth Peabody at 15 Pinckney Street, Boston, in 1860 (Snyder 1972:9–12, 19–21, 41). Kindergartens proliferated rapidly across the USA, from only ten before 1870, to about 5,000 by 1900 (Bain 1964:13; IKU 1897; Ross 1976;

Snyder 1972). Kindergartens were usually limited to wealthier white children. Day nurseries, inspired by French creches (day nurseries), initially were childcare facilities emphasizing physical and custodial care. While the earliest American day nursery was established in 1854 in New York City, day nurseries proliferated from the 1870s, when they became popular charities. Over time many day nurseries came to include kindergarten classes, kitchen garden classes, and/or domestic education classes for older children after school and mothers in the evening (Steinfels 1973:34–9, 42–55; Beer 1942:33–41, 48–51, 144–51).

Around the turn of the century Maria Montessori, building on Froebel's principles, developed equipment to manually train children's perceptions and cognition. Many kindergartens and nursery schools rejected Montessori's emphasis on individual freedom in learning processes, because it contrasted with the more rigid routines Froebel designed for the use of his gifts. Some feared that permitting individual liberty, even in Montessori's specially prepared environment, would not allow children to learn "the concept of collective responsibility" that was considered important to proper socialization (Deasey 1978:81–6). Just before World War I, American kindergartens began to adopt some Montessori methods and equipment (Steinfels 1973:58).

Because the types of equipment and toys used at day care sites were usually inadequately documented, archaeological data may shed light on the actual material culture and activities for children at day care sites, in contrast to the ideals in prescriptive literature (Douai 1872; Massachusetts 1893:271; Peabody and Mann 1877). The most interesting question is the extent to which materialistic domestic reformers implemented their plans to provide children and women with domestic or manual education. Archaeologists are relatively likely to find remains in the yards of day care facilities because (1) it is likely that children would lose or discard toys and equipment in these yards, and (2) they were often located in working-class neighborhoods. At all day care sites archaeologists may find remnants of childcare, such as diaper pins, tins of talcum powder, small combs, toothbrushes, and shoes (if preserved). Day nursery sites that provided only physical care may yield few toys. Miniature domestic equipment, such as irons, washboards and basins, pots, pans, and dishes found in yards would indicate that kitchen garden classes were held at the site to train children in domestic tasks. At such sites ordinary domestic equipment would indicate some deviation from prescribed kitchen garden training (cf.Henry and Williams 1985:45). Remains of specialized Froebelian or Montessori toys would indicate the use of these particular educational systems, at least to some extent.

The degree of deviation by different kindergartens (and day nurseries with kindergartens) from the use of Froebel's or Montessori's teachings and materials might be indicated by the relative quantities of non-Froebel or non-Montessori toys found at these sites. While Froebel's ideal kindergarten materials are well documented, archaeologists may be able to gain information about the often undocumented extent of integration of these ideal materials with ordinary toys or kitchen garden equipment. The degree of integration may be related to the class and ethnicity of the neighborhood the kindergarten served. From the quality and relative quantities of types of toys in site yards, archaeologists might be able to assess to what extent childcare institutions were segregated into kindergartens for the wealthy whites and kitchen gardens and day nurseries for the poor (Steinfels 1973:47). As the meaning of the term "kindergarten" broadened to include all sorts of infant education, archaeologists may find increasing numbers of non-Froebelian toys, including miniature domestic equipment, as training in household industries came to be included with other forms of manual training (Hoxie 1904). Historical archaeologists can expect to contribute to our understanding of the actual practice of day care offered by materialistic domestic reformers.

In order to unify spiritual and physical development with the "divine nature of work," Froebel designed a sequence of unified material "gifts," boxes of wooden building blocks, wooden slats, and tools and supplies for drawing, sewing, weaving, and modelling (Bowen 1893:179–81, 191–3). Of these materials, only the non-perishable ones are likely to be found archaeologically, including metal rings, modelling clay, modelling wax in a tin box, cut lengths of straight wire for model building, paper weaving and paper pricking needles, glasses for paint and metal parts of paint brushes, slates, slate pencils, pencil leads, shells, seeds, and metal fasteners for wooden slats and hanging wooden objects (figure 11.6; Peabody and Mann 1877). While some of these items could be found at any type of childcare site, finding a number of them together in a yard would indicate the use of Froebelian toys and instruction at a site. While the children's use of Froebel's educational equipment was supposed to be highly structured, some documentation of their actual use indicates a high probability of loss through disorganization and outdoor play (Henry and Williams 1985:cover; Standing 1957:242).

Archaeologists may gain information about the use of Montessori methods and equipment in kindergartens, if excavations in site yards recover remains of Montessori equipment, such as the iron geometrical form cutouts, small metal bells, metal knobs from wooden cylinders, brass beads, zippers, hooks, and buttons (Montessori 1914:22, 30, 44–8, 60; Standing 1957:211, 242–3; Smith 1912:52, 70). The domestic artifacts are distinctive, although they could be found at sites of institutions not using Montessori methods. Montessori school yard deposits are expected

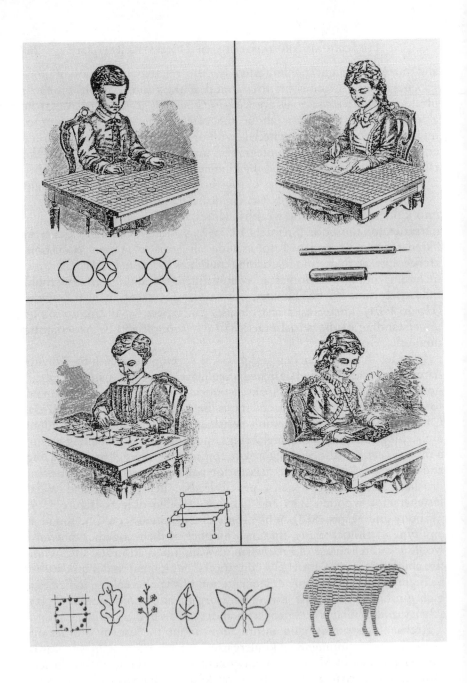

Figure 11.6 Advertisements for Froebel kindergarten gifts with durable parts that archaeologists might recover. These include metal rings (top left), wire model parts (below left), pricking needles (top right), weaving needles (below right), shells and seeds (bottom). Children's clay products could also be found by archaeologists. The relative numbers of Froebelian and other toys would indicate the degree of adherence to Froebel lessons (Peabody and Mann 1877: [publisher's ads 1884] 14, 16–18, 21, 26, 36–7; Palmer 1916:130–1, 136–7, 146–7)

to be clearly archaeologically distinguishable from other infant schools by the absence of non-Montessori equipment and toys, although their presence could indicate less orthodox implementation of Montessori methods than is expected from the prescriptive literature. Archaeologists may also be able to contribute to our understanding of the kinds of kindergarten methods and equipment integrated into public schools, initiated in Boston in 1888 by Lucy Wheelock (Bain 1964:10–11).

Industrial schools for girls

Industrial schools had a long history of providing manual training in trades, especially for paupers. In the nineteenth century industrial schools for girls often provided training for domestic service. In the second half of the century they were influenced by the kitchen garden and domestic science movements, resulting in manual training in household industries (Bowen 1893:181–2).

Industrial schools had separate segregated programs for boys and girls, even if both were housed in one building. As a result, above-ground archaeology of a segregated school is expected to find two sets of stairs to two physically separated parts of the building, often on each floor. In the case of a destroyed building archaeologists might find the basement separated into two sections, each with its own staircase, since the basement was also used for classrooms in some cases (Woodward 1887:346–54).

Since industrial schools were usually located in working-class neighborhoods, some discard may be expected by girls using the school yard. Excavation of school yards might yield remains of miniature domestic equipment if the school had kitchen garden classes. Domestic science classes for older girls might result in loss or discard in the school yard of small tools used in domestic tasks, such as sewing needles, pins, or hooks, or remains of ordinary dishes or bunsen burners used in cooking classes (Arnold 1917:23; Hayden 1981:124–31; Massachusetts 1893:270–1). Since industrial schools usually trained working-class girls to be domestics, any remains of industrial cooking or laundry equipment would indicate an unusual level of training for public sphere professional domestic jobs. Archaeological remains might also yield information about the equipment used when domestic training classes were adopted by public schools, such as the sewing classes in Boston's schools, initiated in 1865 by Mary Heminway (Hayden 1981:126).

Public kitchens

In 1890 Ellen Swallow Richards and Mary Hinman Abel, an expert in nutrition who had studied philanthropic kitchens in Europe, initiated the

American public kitchen movement. Boston's public kitchens reflected Richards's concern for pure unadulterated nutritious food, clean air, and water. Richards advocated that these basic elements of public health be attained through what she called "Euthenics: the science of the controllable environment" (Richards 1910). In Richards' public kitchens the new principles of scientific nutrition were applied in professional industrial scale cooking cooperatives, in order to provide adequate nutrition to the poor and working classes. Working women often lacked the time and energy, and sometimes the kitchens, to cook for their families in their crowded tenements. In public kitchens middle- and upper-class women developed the professions of nutritionists, dietitians, and cooks. Richards and Abel publicized their idea at the 1893 World's Columbian Exposition, with an ideal cooperative public kitchen that operated at the fair, called the Rumford Kitchen. Its nutrition-education lunchroom menu included baked beans, brown bread, rolls, apple sauce, milk, cocoa, tea, and coffee.

The function(s) of Boston's New England Public Kitchen changed over time. Sanitary scientific methods of food preparation were visible to promote cleanliness among the working-class patrons, and to pressure restaurants to disclose their kitchens to the public and either eliminate unsanitary practices or close. The kitchen's free distribution of hot and cold water, both difficult to obtain in tenements, attracted immigrants. Experimentation resulted in a number of dishes that could be consistently supplied. They were nutritious, relatively inexpensive in materials and labor, and could be easily kept without losing flavor. The foods included evaporated milk, beef broth, beef stew, pressed beef, vegetable, tomato and pea soups, corn mush, oatmeal mush, boiled hominy, cracked wheat, fish chowder, Indian pudding, rice pudding, and oatmeal cakes (Hunt 1912:219). Although the evaporated milk and beef broth were popular, the Yankee menu offered by the kitchen was rejected by most immigrants. Despite attempts to offer ethnic foods, by 1893 the kitchen's major business became lunches for 500 students and 300 working girls (Richards 1893:356–60). In 1894 the Boston School Committee negotiated with the New England Kitchen to provide lunches for all public schools, taking this job from janitors because of their lack of knowledge of scientific nutrition. The kitchen came under the management of the Women's Educational and Industrial Union (WEIU) and by 1912 served about 5,000 students per day (Hunt 1912:226–7). Public kitchens following the Boston model were established in New York, Chicago, Philadelphia, and Olneyville, Rhode Island (Hunt 1912:220–1; Levenstein 1988:51–2).

Relatively few archaeological remains are expected in the yards of public kitchens because of their emphasis on sanitation. The foods served by the New England Public Kitchen would leave few archaeological remains other than vegetable seeds, some fishbones, and bones from cheap cuts of beef. If food remains were found in public kitchen yards, they could be compared with (1) documented New England Public Kitchen lunches served to women students for a week in 1893, (2) documented lunches served to women students in homes in Boston in 1917, and (3) published ideal dietaries (Eaves 1917:112; Richards 1899:93–4, 1904, 1901). This research might reveal deviations in actual diets from those documented, as well as biases in the archaeological record. Few remains are expected of public kitchen equipment because it was probably carefully curated. However, some loss of small items, such as parts of bunsen burners, scales, scientific glassware, measures, or food transportation containers, could occur from use by inexperienced students from MIT, the Boston Cooking School, and the WEIU School of Housekeeping. The plain dishes used in public kitchens probably suffered some breakage by students and immigrant patrons. Depending on the quality of municipal trash removal, more remains of public kitchen equipment might be found in the city dump than in the yards of public kitchens. With the exception of Atkinson's Aladdin Oven (figure 11.7), most public kitchen equipment could not be distinguished in city dumps from equipment used in scientific laboratories, domestic kitchens, commercial kitchens, or cooked food delivery services (Atkinson 1896:52–6, 218–21; Kinne and Cooley 1917:43). The incomplete documentation of equipment used in public kitchens gives added significance to the few historic photographs of the arrangement of furnishings and artifacts in public kitchen interiors (cf.Hunt 1912:218–19; Richards 1899). The preservation of photographs and drawings of equipment used in these kitchens may be the only recoverable material culture permitting us to understand the inadequately documented methods of scientific nutrition used in them.

Higher Education in Domestic Science and Home Economics

Starting in the early nineteenth century, domestic reformers successfully argued that women's motherly role in training children required secondary education for women. In the second half of the nineteenth century some specialized schools developed to train teachers in specific areas of childhood education, such as kindergartens. Froebel's explicit concern with nurturing religious morality, in conjunction with the study of humanity and nature, was particularly conducive to women becoming kindergarten teachers, with their supposedly natural abilities as moral nurturers of children (Peabody 1886:157–71). Kindergarten training

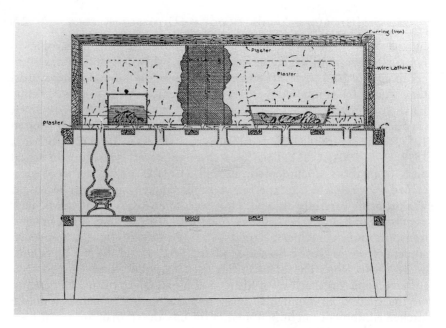

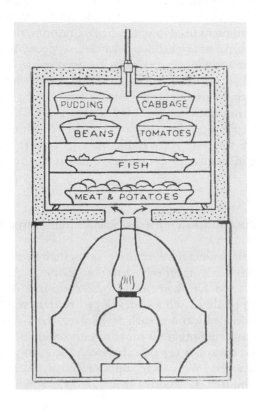

schools, and departments in normal schools, colleges, and universities, increased rapidly in the late nineteenth century, to at least 180 by 1900, including the Garland and Wheelock schools in Boston (Bain 1964:13). Although Froebelian toys were probably lost or discarded by children at kindergarten sites, it is less likely that they would be found in the yards of adult kindergarten teacher training schools, unless the school included a kindergarten.

Domestic reformers also successfully argued that women needed to be taught the new principles and methods of domestic science at schools providing training for the domestic professions, just as schools provided men with training for their professions. Female public high schools, and private secondary schools for women, such as Catherine Beecher's Hartford Academy (1823), and the Troy Seminary (1821), were followed by the development of women's colleges, such as Mount Holyoke (founded as a seminary in 1836), Wellesley, Smith (1875) and Radcliffe (1894) Colleges (Bunting 1985:128–33; Converse 1939:17; Hawkins 1971; Knowles 1985; Solomon 1985:14–21, 47). Many early academies, normal schools, and colleges admitted young women of high school age. Domestic reformers established private cooking and housekeeping schools in organizations such as YWCAs, WEIUs and the famous Woman's Education Association's Boston Cooking School. Domestic science courses and departments in women's schools were replaced with home economics departments after this field developed around the turn of the century (Cannon 1927; Leake 1918:80; Loring 1929; Mark 1945; Shapiro 1986:69; Spencer-Wood 1987b:20–1; Strasser 1982:207–12; WEA 1872–82:June 1879; WEIU 1905). Home economics, nursing, and

Figure 11.7 Two versions of the slow cooking Aladdin Oven, invented by Edward Atkinson in the late 1880s. Heat from one or more lamps was retained in an insulated box of wood, in which dishes of food were placed to cook for a number of hours, often overnight. The Aladdin Oven took about 5 hours to cook meat, reaching a maximum temperature of about 350° a few hours after the door was opened to put dishes in the oven (Levenstein 1988:48). Atkinson used a wood box lined with tin on a metal topped table. He advocated the use of earthenware jars and dishes for cooking, except for metal roasting pans for broiling or sauteing. Atkinson designed the five lamp Aladdin Oven, top, for the kitchen of Alabama's Tuskegee Normal and Industrial Institute. The cook was pleased with this oven. It was insulated with a coat of plaster, attached to the inside of the wood box with wire lathing nailed to iron furring rods. The food vessels sat on iron grates on the top of the galvanized iron table on which the oven was built (Atkinson 1896:52–6, 218–22). Below, in a 1917 illustration of an Aladdin Oven, the dishes are stacked vertically on metal shelves in a wood box lined with sheet iron. The heat source could be a rose-type bunsen burner that used only a small amount of gas, instead of a lamp (Kinne and Cooley 1917:43)

social work departments increased the demand for female professors, widening this employment opportunity for women (Solomon 1985:11–61).

Domestic reformers overcame male exclusivity in many institutions of higher education, and gradually gained entry for women to many state colleges and universities. The reformers succeeded by arguing that higher education was needed by female teachers, nurses, social workers, dietitians, and nutritionists. However, schools and courses were often segregated by class and race, with poor women being taught to be domestics, while wealthier women were trained for public sphere housekeeping occupations (Crawford 1904:263; Hayden 1981:172; Shapiro 1986:68–9).

Archaeology may be able to contribute to our knowledge of equipment used in domestic education schools and classes, since it is seldom adequately documented (cf.Leake 1918; Massachusetts 1893:270–1; WEA 1872–82; WEIU 1877–1930). While few archaeological remains are expected on landscaped college campuses, rural colleges could have their own dumps for college trash. Sloppy trash collection could result in some archaeological deposition in the yards of domestic science classroom or laboratory sites in urban areas, such as the MIT women's laboratory, or Boston's numerous cooking and housekeeping schools. Researchers at Richards's MIT women's laboratory used standard scientific methods and equipment to analyze the quality of household foods, air, and water (Richards and Woodman 1909). College textbooks used scientific experiments and equipment to teach principles of chemistry or physics used in both household and industrial scale housekeeping (Dodd 1914; Lynde 1916). Middle- and upper-class schools and courses in cooking and domestic science used a combination of scientific and household equipment to train women both for homemaking and for professional jobs in institutions such as hospitals or public kitchens (Kinne and Cooley 1917; Riddle 1906). In back yards of domestic science laboratories remains of broken scientific glassware and domestic pottery might be found, and possibly small metal parts of bunsen burners, scales, weights, measures, fireless cookers, or other domestic science equipment. Excavations in the yards of domestic science schools in working-class neighborhoods would probably yield more ordinary household equipment and little, if any, scientific equipment. From the relative amounts of scientific and domestic equipment, archaeologists might be able to assess whether a school's domestic science courses emphasized science or domestic skills. It might be possible to relate such differences to the class of students attending a school or classroom (Arnold 1917:23; Hayden 1981:172; Leake 1918:176–7; Massachusetts 1893:Plates LXII, LXIV; Rothman 1978: 166–74; White 1919:xvi–xvii).

Conclusion

In this paper a framework has been developed to encourage further historical archaeological research on materialistic domestic reform sites. My survey of Boston area sites demonstrated a research model for domestic reform and found that these sites are being rapidly destroyed (Spencer-Wood 1987b). Historical archaeology could research how domestic reform movements used material culture innovations to symbolize and implement professional housework occupations in the home and in the public sphere.

On the basis of documentary and archaeological information, hypotheses were made concerning the potential of different site types for archaeological research on materialistic domestic reform. Site yards with the hypothesized highest archaeological potential include tenements with cooperative housekeeping, cooperative homes for working women, working-class neighborhood housework cooperatives, day nurseries, kitchen gardens, and kindergartens. Site yards with hypothesized medium–low archaeological potential include industrial schools for girls, housework cooperatives in communes, and public kitchens. Site yards with the hypothesized lowest archaeological potential include middle- and upper-class neighborhood housework cooperatives, cooperative apartment hotels, and institutions for higher education in domestic science, home economics, cooking, sewing, housekeeping, or infant education.

It is important to archaeologically research domestic reform because it was instrumental in transforming gender ideology, identities, roles, relationships, and women's status over the nineteenth century and into the twentieth century. By developing their own positive domestic reform ideology women empowered each other to overcome the male-dominated ideology limiting women to the home. Domestic reformers used accepted beliefs in women's innately superior domestic talents as a source of power in expanding women's roles into "domestic" areas of the public sphere. They also used public sphere technology to transform domestic tasks into a variety of female professions, arguing for equal status with men's professions. Domestic reformers redefined the domestic sphere so that it increasingly overlapped the public sphere, empowering women's increasing employment outside the home. Over the nineteenth century domestic reform diffused from the Northeast to the West and South, domesticating public space by increasing the number of female-dominated public places in town and city landscapes across America. Domestic reform has left a strong legacy of women's organizations and occupations that are essential aspects of modern life.

Large-scale cultural changes were created by reformers who spread their new ideology from the small scales of individuals, households, groups, and communities, to large-scale regions, nations, and even across national boundaries. Disproving the widely accepted theory that large-scale structures and dynamics determine individual behavior, the domestic reform process started with small-scale changes that were reproduced, accumulating until the construction of gender changed throughout the cultural system.

REFERENCES

Addams, Jane (1910) *Twenty Years at Hull-House* (1981 reprint). The new American Library, Inc., New York.
[Advertisement] (1902) Buy the Celebrated Chamberlin Steam Cooker. *The Boston Cooking School Magazine of Culinary Science and Domestic Economics* VII(2), xxxii.
American Architect and Building News (1877) "Hotel Kempton, Berkeley Street, Boston, Massachusetts, Messrs. Cummings and Sears" *American Architecture and Building News* 2, 188.
Anonymous (1873) "The Shakers." *Frank Leslie's Illustrated Newspaper* (Sept. 13), 13–14.
Anonymous (1918) "How Are We Going to Live the New and Different Ways that are Coming? One Kitchen fire for 200 People." *Ladies Home Journal* (Sept.), 97.
Arnold, Sarah L. (1917) *The Story of the Sargent Industrial School at Beacon, New York, 1891–1916*. Merrymount Press, Boston.
Atkinson, Edward (1896) *The Science of Nutrition. Treatise on the Science of Nutrition*. Damrell and Upham, Boston.
Bain, Winnifred D. (1964) *Leadership in Childhood Education, Images and Realities: A History of Wheelock College 1888/89–1963/64*. Wheelock College Bureau of Publications, Boston.
Baldwin, Spencer F. (1900) *The Housing Problem: A Study of Tenement Reform in Cities*. Civic Department of the Twentieth Century Club, Boston.
Bangs, Francis R., Arthur M. Huddell, Frank L. Young, and William Jackson (1908) *The Report of the Special Commission to Investigate Questions affecting the Collection and Disposition of Garbage and Offal in the City of Boston*. Boston Municipal Printing Office, Boston.
Bangs, Francis R., X. H. Goodnough, A. M. Huddell, W. T. Sedgwick, F. L. Young, and G. C. Emerson (1910) *Report of the Second Special Commission Appointed by His Honor George A. Hibbard, Mayor of Boston, to Investigate the subject of the Collection and Disposal of Refuse in the City of Boston*. City of Boston Printing Dept, Boston.
Baron, Ava (1987) "Masculinity and the Woman Question: The Transformation of Gender and Work in the Printing Industry, 1850–1920." Paper presented at the Berkshire Conference on the History of Women, Wellesley College, June 19–21.

Beard, Mary R. (1915) *Woman's Work in Municipalities*. D. Appleton & Co., New York.

Beecher, Catherine (1841) *A Treatise on Domestic Economy*. Marsh, Capen, Lyon and Webb, New York; reprint edn Schocken Books, New York, 1977.

Beecher, Catherine E. and Harriet Beecher Stowe (1869) *The American Woman's Home, or Principles of Domestic Science*. J. B. Ford & Co, New York; reprint edn with Introduction by Joseph Van Why, Stowe-Day Foundation, Harford, 1985.

Beer, Ethel S. (1942) *The Day Nursery*. War Edn. E. P. Dutton & Co., New York.

Berg, Barbara J. (1978) *The Remembered Gate: Origins of American Feminism. The Woman and the City 1800–1860*. Oxford University Press, Oxford.

Bernadete, Jane J. (1971) "Abby Morton Diaz." In *Notable American Women 1607–1950*, eds Edward T. James et al., Vol. I, 471–3. Belknap Press of Harvard University Press, Cambridge, MA.

Binford, Lewis R. (1983) *Working at Archaeology*. Academic Press, New York.

Blair, Karen J. (1980) *The Clubwoman as Feminist: True Womanhood Redefined, 1868–1914*. Holmes and Meier, New York.

Blake, John B. (1959) *Public Health in the Town of Boston, 1630–1822*. Harvard University Press, Cambridge, MA.

Blewett, Mary H. (1984) "The Sexual Division of Labor and the Artisan Tradition as Resistance to Early Industrial Capitalism: The Case of New England Shoemaking, 1780–1860." Paper presented at the Sixth Berkshire Conference of Women Historians, June 1–3, Northhampton, Massachusetts.

Blodgett, Geoffrey (1971) "Pauline Agassiz Shaw." In *Notable American Women 1607–1950*, eds Edward T. James et al., Vol. III, 279–80. Belknap Press of Harvard University Press, Cambridge, MA.

Boorstin, Daniel J. (1965) *The Americans: The National Experience*. Random House/Vintage Books, New York.

Bordin, Ruth (1981) *Woman and Temperance: The Quest for Power and Liberty, 1873–1900*. Temple University Press, Philadelphia.

Boston, City of (1890) *City of Boston Manual of the Statutes and Ordinances relating to the Public Health and the Rules and Regulations governing the Health Department*. Rockwell and Churchill, Boston.

Bowen, H. C. (1893) *Froebel and Education by Self-Activity*. Charles Scribner's Sons, New York.

Bower, Beth A., Sheila Charles, John Cheney, and Woodard Openo (1986) *The "Stone Jail" Site, Roxbury, Massachusetts: Report on the Phase III Excavation*. Unpublished report for the Massachusetts Bay Transportation Authority, Boston.

Bower, Beth A., Constance Crosby, and Byron Rushing (1984) *A Report on the Phase II Archaeological Subsurface Testing of the Southwest Corridor Project Area, Roxbury, Massachusetts*. Unpublished report for the Massachusetts Bay Transportation Authority, Boston.

Broadhurst, Jean (1918) *Home and Community Hygiene*. J. B. Lippincott Co., Philadelphia.

Bunting, Bainbridge (ed. and completed by Margaret H. Floyd) (1985) *Harvard:*

An Architectural History. Belknap Press of Harvard University Press, Cambridge, MA.

Burns, Scott (1975) *The Household Economy: Its Shape, Origins and Future.* Beacon Press, Boston.

CAD (Cambridge Annual Documents) (1851) *1851 City of Cambridge Mayor's Address at the Organization of City Government and the Annual Reports of the Committees on Finance, Overseers of the Poor, and the School Committee.* John Ford, Cambridge, MA.

——(1852) *1852 City of Cambridge Mayor's Address at the Organization of City Government and the Annual Reports Made to the City Council.* John Ford and Co., Chronicle Press, Cambridge, MA.

——(1864) "Corporations." In *1863 City of Cambridge Mayor's Address at the Organization of City Government and the Annual Reports Made to the City Council.* Dakin and Metcalf, Cambridge, MA.

——(1879) "An Ordinance in Relation to Health." In *1878 City of Cambridge Mayor's Address at the Organization of City Government and the Annual Reports Made to the City Council.* Franklin Press: Rand, Avery & Co., Boston.

——(1891) "Report of the Superintendent of Streets." In *1890 City of Cambridge Mayor's Address at the Organization of City Government and Annual Reports Made to the City Council.* Harvard Printing Co., Cambridge, MA.

——(1895) "Report of the Superintendent of Streets." In *1894 City of Cambridge Mayor's Address at the Organization of City Government and Annual Reports Made to the City Council.* Cashman, O'Connor and Co., Printers, Boston.

——(1897) "Report of the Superintendent of Streets." In *1896 City of Cambridge Mayor's Address at the Organization of City Government and Annual Reports Made to the City Council.* Press of Lombard and Caustic, Cambridge, MA.

——(1914) "Revised Ordinances of 1892, City of Cambridge, as amended, 1899." In *1913 City of Cambridge Mayor's Address at the Organization of City Government and Annual Reports Made to the City Council.* E. L. Grimes Co., Boston.

Cambridge Cooperative Housekeeping Society (1872) *Report of the Cambridge Cooperative Housekeeping Society.* Press of John Wilson and Son, Cambridge, MA.

Cannon, Cornelia James (1927) *The History of the Women's Educational and Industrial Union: A Civic Laboratory, 1877–1927.* Thomas Todd Co., Boston

Clarke, David L. (1978) *Analytical Archaeology.* Columbia University Press, New York.

Clarke, Eliot C. (1879) "City Scavengering in Boston." Paper read at the 7th annual meeting of the American Public Health Association, Nashville, Tennessee, Nov. 17, 1879.

——(1885) *Main Drainage Works of the City of Boston.* Rockwell and Churchill, Boston.

Clinton, Catherine (1984) *The Other Civil War: American Women in the Nineteenth Century.* Hill and Wang, New York.

Converse, Florence (1939) *Wellesley College: A Chronicle of the Years 1875–1938*. Harvard University Press, Cambridge, MA.

Cott, Nancy F.(1977) *The Bonds of Womanhood: "Woman's Sphere" in New England, 1780–1835*. Yale University Press, New Haven, CT.

Cox, Stephen, Ronald Lettieri, Seven Pendery and James Vaughan (1981) "Historical and Archaeological Assessment and Data Recovery Program for Deer Street Site, Portsmouth, N.H." Ms. on file at Strawbery Banke, Inc., Portsmouth, NH.

Crawford, Mary C. (1904) *The College Girl of America*. L. C. Page & Co., Boston.

Cushing, George M., Jr with Ross Urquhart (1982) *Great Buildings of Boston: A Photographic Guide*. Dover, New York.

Dahlberg, Frances (ed.) (1981) *Woman the Gatherer*. Yale University Press, New Haven, CT.

Davis, Allen F.(1967) *Spearheads for Reform: The Social Settlements and the Progressive Movement, 1890–1914*. Oxford University Press, Fair Lawn, NJ.

Deagan, Kathleen (1983) *Spanish St. Augustine: The Archaeology of A Colonial Creole Community*. Academic Press, New York.

Deasey, Denison, (1978) *Education under Six*. St Martin's Press, New York.

De Cunzo, Lu Ann (1983) *Economics and Ethnicity: An Archaeological Perspective on Nineteenth Century Paterson, New Jersey*. Unpublished Ph.D. dissertation, University of Pennsylvania.

——(1987) Adapting to Factory and City: Illustrations from the Industrialization and Urbanization of Paterson, New Jersey, In *Consumer Choice in Historical Archaeology*, edited by Suzanne M. Spencer-Wood. Pp. 261–95. Plenum Press, New York.

Deetz, James D. F. (1960) *An Archaeological Approach to Kinship Change in Eighteenth-Century Arikara Culture*. Unpublished Ph.D. dissertation, Harvard University, Cambridge, MA.

——(1978) "Archaeological Investigations at La Purisima Mission." In *Historical Archaeology: A Guide to Substantive and Theoretical Contributions*, ed. R. L. Schuyler, pp. 160–90. Baywood Publishing Co., Farmingdale, New York.

Dickens, Roy S., Jr and William R. Bowen (1980) "Problems and Promises in Urban Historical Archaeology: The MARTA Project." *Historical Archaeology* 14, 42–57.

Dodd, Margaret E. (1914) *Chemistry of the Household*. American School of Home Economics, Chicago.

Donnelly, Mabel Collins (1986) *The American Victorian Woman: The Myth and the Reality*. Greenwood Press, New York.

Douai, Adolf (1872) *The Kindergarten. A Manual for the Introduction of Froebel's System of Primary Education into Public Schools*. E. Steiger, New York.

Downing, Andrew J. (1850) *The Architecture of Country Houses*. D. Appleton & Co., New York: reprint edn Dover, New York, 1969.

Eaves, Lucile (1917) *The Food of Working Women in Boston. An Investigation by the Dept. of Research of the Women's Educational and Industrial Union*,

Boston, in cooperation with the State Dept. of Health. Wright and Potter, Boston.

Epstein, Barbara L. (1981) *The Politics of Domesticity: Women, Evangelism and Temperance in Nineteenth Century America.* Wesleyan University Press, Middletown, CT.

Foster, Charles H. (1971) "Elizabeth Palmer Peabody." In *Notable American Women 1607–1950,* eds Edward T. James et al., Vol. III, pp 31–4. Belknap Press of Harvard University Press, Cambridge, MA.

Fox, Myrtle Perrigo and Ethel Lendrum (1919) "Starting a Community Kitchen. Just How it Can be Done With Little Outlay." *Ladies' Home Journal,* June, 111.

Frederick, Christine (1923) *Household Engineering: Scientific Management in the Home* (5th edn). American School of Home Economics, Chicago.

Freedman, Estelle B. (1981) *Their Sister's Keepers: Women's Prison Reform in America, 1830–1930.* University of Michigan Press, Ann Arbor

Fuller, Albert W. (1891) *The National Builder's Album of Beautiful Homes, Villas, Residences, and Cottages.* National Builder Publishing Co., Chicago.

Garrow, Patrick H. (ed.) (1982) "Archaeological Investigations on the Washington, D.C. Civic Center Site." Report on file with the Historic Preservation Office, Department of Housing and Community Development, Government of the District of Columbia.

Giedion, Siegfried (1948) *Mechanization Takes Command* (reprinted 1975). W. W. Norton & Co., New York.

Gilman, Charlotte Perkins (1972) "The Living of Charlotte Perkins Gilman." Excerpts in *The Oven Birds: American Women on Womanhood 1820–1920,* ed. Gail Parker, pp. 353–87. Doubleday & Co., Inc./Anchor Books, New York.

Gordon, Lynn D. (1982) "History Book Review." *Signs* 7(4), 891–3.

Handlin, David P. (1979) *The American Home: Architecture and Society, 1815–1915.* Little Brown and Co., Boston.

Haraszti, Zoltan (1937) *The Idyll of Brook Farm, As Revealed by Unpublished Letters in the Boston Public Library.* Trustees of the Public Library, Boston.

Hawkins, Hugh (1971) "Elizabeth Cabot Cary Agassiz." In *Notable American Women, 1607–1950,* ed. Edward T. James et al., Vol.I, pp. 22–4. Belknap Press of Harvard University Press, Cambridge, MA.

Hayden, Dolores (1976) *Seven American Utopias: The Architecture of Communitarian Socialism, 1790–1975.* MIT Press, Cambridge, MA.

——(1981) *The Grand Domestic Revolution: A History of Feminist Designs for American Homes, Neighborhoods, and Cities.* MIT Press, Cambridge, MA.

Henn, Roselle E. (1985) "Reconstructiong the Urban Foodchain: Advances and Problems in Interpreting Faunal Remains Recovered from Household Deposits." *American Archeology* 5(3), 202–9.

Henry, Sarah and Mary A. Williams (1985) *North Bennet Street School: A Short History 1885–1985,* ed. Laura Stanton. Chadis Printing, Boston.

Hill, Patricia R. (1985) *The World Their Household: The American Woman's Foreign Mission Movement and Cultural Transformation, 1870–1920.* University of Michigan Press, Ann Arbor.

Holloway, Mark (1966) *Heavens on Earth: Utopian Communities in America 1680–1880*. Dover Publications, New York.

Hoxie, Jane L. (1904) *Hand Work for Kindergartens and Primary Schools*. Milton Bradley Co., Springfield, MA.

Hunt, Caroline L. (1912) *The Life of Ellen H. Richards*. Whitcomb and Barrows, Boston.

Ingersoll, Daniel W. (1971) *Settlement Archaeology at Puddle Dock*. Unpublished Ph.D. Dissertation, Harvard University, Cambridge, MA.

IKU (International Kindergarten Union) (1897) Report of the Second Annual Meeting of the IKU, St Louis, April 20–22.

James, Janet Wilson (1971) "Ellen Henrietta Swallow Richards." In *Notable American Women 1607–1950*, eds. Edward T. James et al., Vol. III, pp. 143–6. Belknap Press of Harvard University Press, Cambridge, MA.

——(1981) *Changing Ideas About Women in the United States, 1776–1825*. Garland Publishing, New York.

Keller, Phyllis (1971) "Mary Porter Tileston Hemenway." In *Notable American Women 1607–1950*, eds Edward T. James et al., Vol.II, pp. 179–81. Belknap Press of Harvard University Press, Cambridge, MA.

King, Moses (1885) *King's Handbok of Boston, 1885*. Moses King, Cambridge, MA.

Kinne, Helen and Anna M. Cooley (1917) *Foods and Household Management: A Textbook of the Household Arts*. Macmillan, New York.

Kleinberg, Susan J. (1976) "Technology and Women's Work: The Lives of Working Class Women in Pittsburgh, 1870–1900." *Labor History* 17, 67–73.

Knowles, Jane S. (1985) "A Roof of One's Own: Radcliffe's Fay House." *Radcliffe Quarterly* 71(3), 19–21.

Kraditor, Aileen S. (1971) *The Ideas of the Woman Suffrage Movement 1890–1920*. Doubleday and Co., Inc/Anchor Books, Garden City, NY.

Landy, David and Milton Greenblatt (1965) *Halfway House: A Sociocultural and Clinical Study of Rutland Corner House, a Transitional Aftercare Residence for Female Psychiatric Patients*. US Dept. of Health Education and Welfare, Washington, D.C.

Leach, William (1980) *True Love and Perfect Union: The Feminist Reform of Sex and Society*. Basic Books, New York.

Leacock, Eleanor, Helen I. Safa, et al. (eds) (1986) *Women's Work: Development and the Division of Labor by Gender*. Bergin and Garvey, S. Handley, MA.

Leake, Albert H. (1918) *The Vocational Education of Girls and Women*. Macmillan, New York.

LeeDecker, Charles H., Terry H. Klein, Cheryl A. Holt, and Amy Friedlander (1987) "Nineteenth Century Households and Consumer Behavior in Wilmington, Delaware." In *Consumer Choice in Historical Archaeology*, ed. Suzanne M. Spencer-Wood, pp. 233–59. Plenum Publishing Co., New York.

Lefaucheux, Maire-Helene, et al. (1966) *Women in a Changing World: The Dynamic Story of the International Council of Women since 1888*. Routledge and Kegan Paul, London.

Levenstein, Harvey (1988) *Revolution at the Table: The Transformation of the American Diet*. Oxford University Press, New York.

Loring, Katherine P. (1929) "A Review of the Fifty Seven Years' Work." In the *Fifty Seventh and Final Annual Report of the Woman's Education Association for the Year Ending January 17, 1929*. WEA, Boston.

Lynde, Carleton J. (1916) *Physics of the Household*. Macmillan, New York.

McDowell, John P. (1982) *The Social Gospel in the South: The Woman's Home Mission Movement in the Methodist Episcopal Church, South, 1886–1939*. Louisiana State University Press, Baton Rouge.

Mann, Arthur (1954) *Yankee Reformers in the Urban Age*. The Belknap Press of Harvard University Press, Cambridge, MA.

Mark, Kenneth L. (1945) *Delayed by Fire. Being the Early History of Simmons College*. Privately printed, Concord, NH.

Massachusetts, State of (1893) *Report of the Commission Appointed to Investigate the Existing Systems of Manual Training and Manual Education*. Wright & Potter Printing Co., Boston.

Melosi, Martin V. (1981) *Garbage in the Cities: Refuse, Reform and the Environment 1880–1980*. Texas A&M University Press, College Station.

Messerli, Jonathan (1971) "Mary Tyler Peabody Mann." In *Notable American Women 1607–1950*, eds Edward T. James et al., Vol.II, 448–89. Belknap Press of Harvard University Press, Cambridge, MA.

Montessori, Maria (1914) *Dr. Montessori's Own Handbook* (1964 reprint). Robert Bentley Inc., Cambridge, MA.

Mullings, Leith (1986) "Uneven Development: Class, Race and Gender in the United States Before 1900." In *Women's Work: Development and the Division of Labor by Gender*, eds Eleanor Leacock, Helen I. Safa, et al. Bergin and Garvey, S. Hadley, MA.

Nesson, Fern L. (1983) *Great Waters: A History of Boston's Water Supply*. University Press of New England, Hanover, NH.

Norton, Alice P. (1927) *Cooked Food Supply Experiments in America*. Institute for the Coordination of Women's Interests, Smith College, Northampton, MA.

Otto, John S. (1984) *Cannon's Point Plantation, 1794–1860: Living Conditions and Status Patterns in the Old South*. Academic Press, New York.

Palmer, Luella A. (1916) *Play Life in the First Eight Years*. Ginn & Co. Boston.

Peabody, Elizabeth P. (1886) *Lectures in the Training Schools for Kindergartners*. D. C. Heath & Co., Boston.

Peabody, Elizabeth P. and Mary Mann (1877) *Guide to the Kindergarten and Intermediate Class; and Moral Culture of Infancy*. E. Steiger, New York.

Pearson, Norman H. (1971) "Sophia Amelia Peabody Hawthorne." In *Notable American Women 1607–1950*, eds Edward T. James et al., Vol.II, pp. 162–3. Belknap Press of Harvard University Press, Cambridge, MA.

Peirce, Melusina Fay (1868) "Co-operative Housekeeping." *The Atlantic Monthly* XXII, 513–697.

Pleck, Elizabeth H. (1987) *Domestic Tyranny: The Making of Social Policy Against Family Violence from Colonial Times to the Present*. Oxford University Press, New York.

Porter, Dwight (1889) *Report upon A Sanitary Inspection of Certain Tenement-House Districts of Boston*. Rockwell and Churchill Press, Boston.

Porterfield, Amanda (1980) *Feminine Spirituality in America*. Temple University Press, Philadelphia.
RBPR (Rochester Bureau of Public Research) (1919) *Report on the Problem of Refuse Collection in the City of Rochester, N.Y.*, submitted to the Mayor and Commissioner of Public Works. City of Rochester.
Reiter, Rayna R. (ed.) (1975) *Toward an Anthropology of Women*. Monthly Review Press, New York.
Richards, Ellen H. (1893) "Scientific Cooking – Studies in the New England Kitchen. *The Forum* XV, 355–61.
——(1899) (ed.) *Plain Words about Food. The Rumford Kitchen Leaflets 1899*. The Home Science Publishing Co., Boston.
——(1901) *The Cost of Food: A Study in Dietaries*. John Wiley & Sons, New York.
——(1904) *First Lessons in Food and Diet*. Whitcomb & Barrows, Boston.
——(1905) *The Cost of Shelter*. John Wiley & Sons, New York.
——(1907) *Sanitation in Daily Life*. Whitcomb & Barrows, Boston.
——(1908) *The Cost of Cleanness*. John Wiley & Sons, New York.
——(1910) *Euthenics: The Science of Controllable Environment*. Whitcomb & Barrows, Boston.
Richards, Ellen H. and Alpheus G. Woodman (1909) *Air, Water and Food from a Sanitary Standpoint*. John Wiley & Sons, New York.
Riddle, Mary M. (1906) "A Modern Hospital Kitchen." *The Boston Cooking-School Magazine* XI(2), 61–6.
Rosaldo, M. Z. and L. Lamphere (1974) *Woman, Culture and Society*. Stanford University Press, Stanford.
Rose, Mary S. (1916) *Feeding the Family*. Macmillan, New York.
Ross, Elizabeth D. (1976) *The Kindergarten Crusade: The Establishment of Pre-School Education in the United States*. Ohio University Press, Athens.
Rossi, Alice S. (ed.) (1974) *The Feminist Papers*. Bantam Books, New York.
Rothman, Sheila M. (1978) *Woman's Proper Place: A History of Changing Ideals and Practices, 1870 to the Present*. Basic Books, New York.
Rothschild, Nan A. and Diana di Zerega Rockman (1982) "Method in Urban Archaeology: The Stadt Huys Block." In *Archaeology of Urban America: The Search for Pattern and Process*, ed. Roy S. Dickens, Jr, pp. 3–18. Academic Press, New York.
Rubertone, Patricia E. (1985) "Strategies of Resistance: Historical Indian–European Contact in Southern New England." Paper presented at the 18th Annual Meeting of the Society for Historical Archaeology, Boston, Jan. 9–13.
Rushing, Byron (1985) "Integration and Separation in Boston's Nineteenth-Century Black Community." Paper presented at the 18th Annual Meeting of the Society for Historical Archaeology, Boston, Jan. 9–13.
Russell, Frances, E. (1892) "A Brief Survey of the American Dress Reform Movements of the Past, with Views of Representative Women." *The Arena* Vol.VI, No.XXXIII, 325–39.
Savulis, Ellen R. (1985) "Alternative Communities in Nineteenth Century New England." Paper presented at the 18th Annual Meeting of the Society for Historical Archaeology, Boston, Jan. 9–13.

Schleier, Matilda (1918) "As Montclair Delivers its Dinner." *Ladies' Home Journal* (Sept. 1918), 97.

Schuyler, Robert L. (ed.) (1980) *Archaeological Perspectives on Ethnicity in America: Afro-American and Asian American Culture History.* Baywood Publishing Co., Farmingdale, New York.

Scott, Ann F. (ed.) (1971) *The American Woman: Who Was She?* Prentice-Hall, Englewood Cliffs, NJ.

——(1971) "Jane Addams." In *Notable America Women 1607–1950,* eds Edward T. James et al., Vol.I, 16–22. Belknap Press of Harvard University Press, Cambridge, MA.

Shapiro, Laura (1986) *Perfection Salad: Women and Cooking at the Turn of the Century.* Farrar, Straus and Giroux, New York.

Shephard, Steven J. (1987) "Status Variation in Antebellum Alexandria: An Archaeological Study of Ceramic Tableware." In *Consumer Choice in Historical Archaeology,* ed. Suzanne M. Spencer-Wood, pp. 163–98. Plenum Press, New York.

Singer, David A. (1987) "Threshold of Affordability: Assessing Fish Remains for Socioeconomics." In *Consumer Choice in Historical Archaeology,* ed. Suzanne M. Spencer-Wood, pp. 85–99. Plenum Press, New York.

Smith, Daniel S. (1979) "Family Limitation, Sexual Control, and Domestic Feminism in Victorian America." In *A Heritage of Her Own,* eds Nancy F. Cott and Elizabeth H. Pleck, pp. 222–45. Simon and Schuster, New York.

Smith, Theodate L. (1912) *The Montessori System in Theory and Practice.* Harper & Bros, New York.

Snyder, Agnes (1972) *Dauntless Women in Childhood Education 1856–1931.* Association for Childhood Eduction International, Washington, D.C.

Solomon, Barbara M. (1985) *In the Company of Educated Women: A History of Women and Higher Education in America.* Yale University Press, New Haven, CT.

Spencer-Wood, Suzanne M. (1984) "Status, Occupation, and Ceramic Indices: A Nineteenth-Century Comparative Analysis." *Man in the Northeast* 28, 87–110.

——(1987a) *Consumer Choice in Historical Archaeology.* Plenum Press,New York.

——(1987b) "A Survey of Domestic Reform Movement Sites in Boston and Cambridge, ca.1865–1905." *Historical Archaeology* 21(2), 7–36.

——(1989) "Toward a Historical Archaeology of the Construction of Gender." Paper presented in the session "Gender in Historical Archaeology," at the Chacmool Conference, "The Archaeology of Gender," Nov. 11.

——(1990) "A Feminist Approach for Future Archaeological Theory and Gender Research." Paper presented at the SIU Visiting Scholar's Conference, "The Future of the Past: American Archaeology in A.D.2001," May 5.

——(1991) "Feminist Empiricism: A More Holistic Theoretical Approach." Paper presented in a mini-Plenary session at the Annual Meetings of the Society for Historical Archaeology, Richmond, Virginia, Jan. 9–13.

Standing, E. M. (1957) *Maria Montessori: Her Life and Work.* Academy Library Guild, Fresno.

Starbuck, David R. (1984) "The Shaker Concept of Household." *Man in the Northeast* 28, 73–86.

Stein, Robert (1898) "Girls' Cooperative Boarding Homes." *The Arena* (March 1898), 397–417.

Steinfels, Margaret O'Brien (1973) *Who's Minding the Children?* Simon and Schuster, New York.

Strasser, Susan (1980) "An Enlarged Human Existence?" In *Technology and Household Labor*, ed. S. F. Berk, pp. 29–51. Sage Publications, Beverly Hills.

——(1982) *Never Done: A History of American Housework.* Pantheon Books, New York.

Turner, James (1985) *Without God, Without Creed. The Origins of Unbelief in America* Johns Hopkins University Press, Baltimore.

Vaillancourt, Dana R. (1983) "Archaeological Excavations at the North Family Dwelling House Site, Hancock Shaker Village, Town of Hancock, Berkshire County, Massachusetts." M.S. Project, Rensselaer Polytechnic Institute, Troy, NY.

WEA (Woman's Education Association) (1872–1882) Boston Woman's Education Association Industrial Committee Minutes of Meetings. Ms in The Colonel Miriam E. Perry Goll Archives, Simmons College, Boston.

——(1873–1929) Records. Schlesinger Library, Radcliffe University, Cambridge, MA.

WEIU (Women's Educational and Industrial Union) (1877–1930) Records. Schlesinger Library, Radcliffe University, Cambridge, MA.

——(1905) *A Report of Progress Made in the Year 1905, Being the 25th Anniversary of the Incorporation of the Women's Educational and Industrial Union.* Merrymount Press, Boston.

Wellman, Mabel T. (1928) *Food: Its Planning and Preparation. A Junior Course in Food Study with a Recipe Book for Use at Home and at School.* J. B. Lippincott Co., Philadelphia.

Welter, Barbara (1966) "The Cult of True Womanhood: 1820–1860." *American Quarterly* 18, 151–74.

Wheelock College Archives: Collection of Froebel Gifts and Montessori Equipment. Boston.

White, Eva W. (1919) *The Gary Public Schools: Household Arts.* General Education Board, New York.

Why, Joseph Van (1975) "Introduction." In *The American Woman's Home*, by Catherine E. Beecher and Harriet Beecher Stowe (1869), reprint edn Stowe-Day Foundation, Hartford.

Wilson, Margaret Gibbons (1979) *The American Woman in Transition: The Urban Influence, 1870–1920.* Greenwood Press, Inc., Westport, CT.

Woloch, Nancy (1984) *Women and the American Experience.* Alfred A. Knopf, New York.

Woods, Robert A. (ed.) (1898) *The City Wilderness: A Settlement Study by Residents and Associates of the South End House.* Houghton Mifflin & Co., New York; reprint edn Garrett Press, New York, 1970.

Woodward, C. M. (1887) *The Manual Training School, comprising a full* statement of its Aims, Methods and Results, with figured drawings of Shop Exercises in Woods and Metals. D. C. Heath & Co., Boston.

Wright, Gwendolyn (1980) Moralism and the Model Home: Domestic Architecture and Cultural Conflict in Chicago 1873–1913. University of Chicago Press, Chicago.

Zaretsky, Eli (1981) Book Review. Signs 7(1), 230–3.

Index

Massachusetts Bay Colony, 56, 81
Massachusetts Institute of Technology, 240,
250, 271, 274
material culture, 10, 14–20, 30–1, 55–6, 61,
107–8, 150–3, 175, 195, 232, 242, 245, 251–5,
260, 266–8, 272–3; as text and symbol,
153–6, 165–7, 193; see also bottles,
ceramics, Colono ware, gravestones, pipes
Material Culture, 175
mausoleum, 113, 114
Maverick, S., 57
Maya, 14, 15
Medicine Lodge Treaty of 1867, 65
Medieval period see Great Britian, Medieval
Mendelssohn, K., 9
mental templates, 2
Mercer, C., 167
Mesoamerica, 15, 162
metal detectors, 70
Methodists, 128
middle-range theory, 178
Middletown, 107
Middletown, RI, 85
Miles, Indian Agent, 66
Millennium, the, 129
Miller, D., 6
Miller, G. L., 152
millet, 33
Millwood Plantation, SC, 49–50
missions, Spanish, 32
Mississippi: Delta, 41, 44; Monroe County,
46; Rankin County, 46
Montalban, R., 74
Montana, 64, 65, 76
Montessori, M., 266–9
monumental architecture, 4, 9, 15, 116–19
Moody, D. I., 130
Moore, T., 59
mortuary analysis, 4, 14
Moulsham Street deposit, 209, 210
Mount Holyoke, College, 273
Mrozowski, S. A., 17–18, 161, 171, 177
mulattoes, 59, 61

Narragansett Indians, 56, 162
Nash, G., 59
National Civic Federation, 241
National Consumer's League, 241
National Council of Women, 240
National Education Association, 241
Native Americans, 16, 17, 28, 154, 161–2,

179, 192; as slaves, 28, 56, 57–8, 59, 60, 61;
stereotypes of, 76; see also Catawba Indians;
Cheyenne; Colono Ware; Narragansett
Indians; Pequad Indians; Yamasse Indians
Nebraska, 64–8; sand hills, 67
neolithic, 14
New Archaeology, 175, 176
New England, 17, 18, 200, 204, 207, 221;
commercial cities, 81–7; factories, 15,
87–90; free African-Americans in, 59–62;
industrial cities, 87–96; slavery in, 56–60,
61, 179; urban society, 80
New England Public Kitchen, 243, 270–1
New Jersey, 204
New York: City, 109, 171, 270; upstate, 18;
see also Broome County, New York
Newport, RI, 18, 80, 81–2, 85–6, 96; class
divisions, 86; map, 84
Nigeria, 38
Nöel Hume, I., 175
North Bennet St Industrial School, 240
North Platte River, 66
North Providence, RI, 85
Nowak, L., 48

O'Brien, P., 178
Oklahoma, 65, 66, 67, 74
Oklahoma City, OK, 66
okra, 35
Olmec, 15
Olneyville, RI, 270
Oneida Perfectionists, 255, 256
oral history, 30–1, 35, 36, 43–4, 45, 46, 49, 64,
65, 109, 110, 123; as resistence, 74–7
Orser, C., 16, 161
Otto, J. S., 32, 36
Owenite Communes, 255

Paca, W., 14, 156–7
panopticon, 8–9, 15
Papua pottery, 213
Pasbehay Tenement, 214
Passing the Time in Ballymenone, 150, 163–4
Paynter, R., 151
Peabody, E., 265
Pearson, P., 4, 14
peasants, 3–4, 11, 15
Peña, E. S., 177
Peña, J. T., 177
Pennsylvania, 109
Pequad Indians, 56

Peter, H., 58
Philadelphia, PA, 270
photographs, use of in analysis, 49, 70, 119, 247
Pine Ridge Indian Reservation, SD, 67, 68
pipes, smoking, 18, 166, 167–8, 174, 175
Piscattaway, MD, 220
Pitcher, B. L., 15
plantations, 28–9, 35, 36, 40, 49–50, 55; agricultural ladder, 42; cotton, 41–5, 49–50; layout, 49–50; postbellum labor systems, 41–7; rice, 28–9; values of, 44, West Indian, 59
Plat Book of Broome County 1908, 141
Porcupine, 68
Port Crane, NY, 142
Port Royal, VA, 220
positivism, 151–2, 161, 175–6
post-positivist archaeology, 151, 175
Potter, P., 159–61, 178
pottery *see* ceramics; Colono Ware
Powder River, 65–6, 67
power, social *see* social power
privies, 82, 94
Providence, RI, 18, 80, 82, 85
Providence Island, West Indies, 56
public kitchens, 269–71

race relations, 16–17, 28–31, 36–7; gender, 31–2; miscegenation, 59; racism, 55, 61; *see also* African-Americans; slaves and slavery
Radcliff College, 273
Randolph, governor, 58
Randolph, M., 35
Ranger, T., 2
Raper, A. F., 47
Rappite Harmony Society, 255
realization crisis in capitalism, 102, 105–6
Red Cloud, 67; agency, 67
Reiter, R. R., 205
Religious Emblems, 132
religious revivals, 128–30; businessmen's revival, 129
rent relationships; cash renter, 42, 46–7; share renting, 42, 46–7; standing rent arrangement, 42, 43, 46–7
reproduction: biological, 6; of the material world; 7 social, 16
resistence, 1, 4, 9, 10–13, 40, 45–7, 50–1, 113–14, 123, 233, 255; archaeology as a tool of, 64, 77; geography of, 15; heterogeneity

of, 12–13; of incongruity, 29; material aspects, 14–20, 31–2, 51; unconscious, 28–9; verbal, 45, 64–5, 74–7
revolts, 40
revolution, 12, 13, 15, 102, 121–2; Bolshevik 105
Rhode Island System, 87
rice, 33, 35
Richards, E. S., 240, 250–3, 269–70, 274
Rising Sun, T., 68, 72, 74
Rochberg-Halton, E., 154
Rochester, NY, 126, 130, 143
Rome, NY, 126
Root, D., 14
Rosaldo, M. Z., 204
Rosenzweig, R., 179
Rowland, G., 74
Rowland, W., 68
Rubertone, P., 161–2, 179
Rumford Kitchen, 270
Rutland Corner House, 240
Rye, O. S., 213

Sahlins, M., 215, 219
St George, R. B., 179, 201
Sankey, I., 130
Schmidt, P. R., 161
Schrire, C., 164
Schurz, C., 265
Schuyler, R. L., 195
Scott, J. C., 12, 158
Second Great Awakening, 18, 126–31, 141, 143–6; symbolism of, 127, 131–6, 137, 138, 142
settlement houses, 264
sexual pleasure, 6, 11, 201
Shakers, 16, 255–7, 258
Shanks, M., 14
Sharecroppers' Union, 51
sharecropping, 41–5, 46–7
Shaw, N., 43
shoe manufacturing, 114–15, 116, 123
Sierra Leone, 38
Silverblatt, I., 7
Simms, W. G., 35
sinners, 128
site formation processes, 248–9
slaves and slavery, 4, 11, 16–17, 48, 129, 154, 158, 178, 179, 197, 207, 221; African languages among, 57; in Boston, 56–60; breeding, 57; ceramics *see* Colono Ware;